War and the Media

War and the Media

Reportage and Propaganda, 1900-2003

Edited by MARK CONNELLY & DAVID WELCH

I.B. TAURIS

LONDON · NEW YORK

Published in 2005 by I.B. Tauris and Co Ltd

6 Salem Road, London W2 4BU

175 Fifth Avenue, New York NY 10010

www.ibtauris.com

In the United States of America and in Canada distributed by St Martins Press, 175 Fifth Avenue, New York 10010

International Library of War Studies 3

ISBN: 1 86064 959 9

EAN: 978 1 86064 959 2

A full CIP record for this book is available from the British Library

A full CIP record for this book is available from the Library of Congress

Library of Congress catalog card: available

Printed and bound in Great Britain by TJ International Ltd, Padstow, Cornwall from camera-ready copy edited and supplied by the editors

CONTENTS

Illustrations

Introduction
'WINNING HEARTS AND MINDS': THE CHANGING CONTEXT OF REPORTAGE AND PROPAGANDA, 1900-2003
David Welch

This volume developed out of an international conference sponsored by the Centre for the Study of Propaganda held at The University of Kent in September 2001. It was the first major international conference on the impact of the media on war. The conference coincided with the conflict in Macedonia, which has been largely overshadowed now in the light of events of 11 September 2001. The contributors represent not only a distinguished collection of internationally acclaimed specialists but, more importantly, the pick of the outstanding young scholars in this field.[1]

Enormous social and technological changes have radically changed our lives over the past 150 years. The aim of this volume is to discover not only how the means of transmitting news and propaganda has changed, but more significantly how these developments have altered the relationships between politicians, the military and the media in the shaping of policies that may lead to conflict. The Gulf War in 2003, for example, produced a number of technological shifts in the reporting of war, particularly the decision to 'embed' reporters and television journalists as actual members of the invasion forces, allowing on the one hand a direct immediacy never before possible, and on the other hand introducing a new intensity of information overload. The multitude of news channels beaming constant images attracted two different types of criticism. Some critics suggested the twenty-four hours news channels were little more than purveyors of 'war porn' for the manner in which they broadcast relentless images shown without context or explanation. Others, such as the British Foreign Secretary Jack Straw, fear that too much reality could have serious effects on morale. 'Had the public been able to see live coverage from the First World War trenches... for how long could the governments of Asquith and Lloyd George have maintained the war effort? Imagine the carnage of the Somme on Sky and BBC News 24.' Straw claimed that twenty-four hour news changed the reality of warfare and compressed timescales. The Foreign Secretary wondered whether it would have been possible to have evacuated 300,000 troops from Dunkirk under the scrutiny of twenty-four hour rolling news.[2]

The complex relationship between propaganda and censorship and the effect of the media on the formation of public opinion together with journalistic ethics and motives are also probed. The perception of war increasingly affects its cost, duration and outcomes. It is not by chance that the title of the book is called 'the management of perception'. Modern warfare entails 'winning hearts and minds' and weapons of mass persuasion become the prime source of its attainment.

The volume begins with Jacqueline Beaumont's account of the press coverage of the South African War (otherwise known as the Second Boer War) and the stultifying effects of poorly organized censorship on the reporting of the sieges of Mafeking, Kimberley and Ladysmith. The fraught relationship between the military and the media – and specifically war correspondents reporting action from the ground – is the major theme that recurs throughout this book. During the Boer War, correspondents wore military style uniform but the culture clash between the British Army and the press was never completely bridged. Whereas previous British colonial wars had been covered by a handful of reporters, the South African War involved at its height approximately 200 journalists. This led to the improvisation of new forms of accreditation and censorship that laid the foundations for much greater control of the press (and the media) in twentieth century wars. There was no book of rules for the guidance of censorship until 1901 and few rules to help the inexperienced war correspondent. In the absence of accurate news, the reporting of the Boer War provided a rich market for rumour and half truths.

The advent of total war in the twentieth century led to the use of the media for political purposes. In 'total war', which required civilians to participate in the war effort, morale came to be recognised as a significant military factor, and propaganda began to emerge as the principal instrument of control over public opinion and an essential weapon in the national arsenal. In both World War I and World War II the democracies and totalitarian regimes imposed constraints on the flow of information and used the media for their own ends. David Welch sets out the attempts by the German government to mobilize the means of communications for official propaganda purposes during the Great War. Inevitably censorship came to be seen as an important weapon in controlling the flow of information.

During much of the twentieth century, governments and military leadership could generally rely on the journalists and news agencies to cooperate in supporting nationalistic and patriotic causes. The media willingly collaborated in disseminating propaganda justifying war aims, sustaining the morale of the home and fighting fronts and demonising the enemy. Such collaboration inevitably resulted in a form of war reporting that was less concerned with accuracy than with propaganda.

However even after the outbreak of war in 1914, British military authorities viewed propaganda with caution and scepticism. The clash of cultures between the GHQ staff officers and professional journalists is taken up in 'the missing Western Front'. Stephen Badsey re-examines the events of 1918 and how the British government not only directed the war, but also manipulated the war's portrayal to its own people and to others. According to Badsey, one of our finest military historians, the British played a leading role in defeating the last great German attack on the Western Front (the so-called *Kaisersschlacht* – the spring offensive of 1918) yet both the political and military authorities pursued policies that led to the propaganda neglect of the Western Front. Crewe House failed to project an image of a British Army that was superior to its enemies. What should have been a propaganda coup celebrating a great British military victory remained not so much forgotten as never properly told.

Propaganda during the First World War was not confined to government or military agencies disseminating 'official' news and information. Governments could rely on private individuals or commercial agencies to support the war effort. The British press for example, mainly of its own volition, acted as a propaganda weapon to sustain the war effort and to maintain the patriotic fervour. In the early months of the war notions of 'good' and 'evil' featured in both official and unofficial propaganda and all the belligerents mobilised sacred images on behalf of their cause. Samantha Johnson looks at the role of *Everyman*, the British journal edited by Charles Saroléa in Edinburgh and published in London. Saroléa, a committed Europeanist, believed that Germany had ceased to become a 'good' European state and was largely responsible for causing the war. Accordingly, a concerted propaganda campaign was launched by the journal to convince opinion leaders that Britain, France and Russia had a moral responsibility to safeguard Europe from the spiritual and military tyranny of Prussian Germany.

The First World War gave the cinema its great opportunity and as cinema audiences continued to increase governments gradually began to appreciate the possibilities of the cinema for influencing morale and public opinion. Roger Smither (curator of film at the Imperial War Museum) provides a case study of German film propaganda towards the end of the war. In 1917, the Germans produced a film about the U-boat war called *Der magische Gürtel* (The Enchanted Circle), to justify and glorify unrestricted submarine warfare. The film not only records a new form of warfare but also demonstrates the existence of an 'Ace' phenomenon (built around the U-boat captains) which was as great as that which surrounded the 'Red Baron' and other 'Knights of the Air'. Above all there is the issue of the use made (by all sides) of the theme of the submarine in the propaganda war. *Der magische Gürtel* was produced for morale boosting purposes on the home front but also to provide evidence for neutral audiences of both the efficacy and (in a post-Lusitania world) the humanity of the U-Boat weapon. Smither argues that while the propaganda succeeded in the former role, it had a considerably more mixed reception in the latter.[3]

Between 1914 and 1918 the wholesale use of propaganda as an organized weapon of modern warfare transformed it into something more sinister – something to be ashamed of.[4] Propaganda was now widely viewed as a pejorative term associated with lies and falsehood. One of the most significant lesson to be learned from the experience of World War I was that public opinion could no longer be ignored as a determining factor in the formulation of government policies. The British government, for example, regarded propaganda as politically dangerous and even morally unacceptable in peacetime. It was, as one official wrote in the 1920s, 'a good word gone wrong – debauched by the late Lord Northcliffe.' Thus whereas the democracies disbanded rather shamefacedly their wartime propaganda machines, the totalitarian and fascist regimes drew

xii   War and the Media

different lessons from the wartime experience, having had few qualms about establishing 'propaganda ministries' for disseminating ideological propaganda both at home and abroad.

During the inter-war period, radio and film emerged as genuinely mass media – reaching listeners in their homes and viewers in their places of entertainment and relaxation. The two media possessed a natural connection – both were relatively new forms for transmitting propaganda and both assumed primary importance during the Second World War because of their effectiveness as a means of conveying information and their popular appeal. It was, therefore, not unusual to find the two linked and, often, used together. Not surprisingly each medium became an integral part of propaganda when war broke out in 1939. In a fascinating study, Jo Fox reveals how Britain and Nazi Germany mobilized these media in unison to enhance their respective propaganda campaigns for total war.

Jeffrey Richards pursues the importance of the cinema in World War II by analyzing the films produced by the extraordinary British documentary film-maker, Humphrey Jennings. Jennings' films provide a short-hand for British national identity; a combination of reportage, historical reconstruction, propaganda and personal poetic image. The film critic, Dilys Powell memorably referred to them as: 'the imaginative interpretation of everyday life'.[5] Richards argues that Jennings' films represent the lived experience of a nation at war. Humphrey Jennings represents the voice of the individual, the poet as propagandist – divorced from the official propaganda campaigns launched and coordinated by the Ministry of Information. Ilaria Favretto and Oliviero Bergamini on the other hand chart the efforts of British and American propaganda agencies (notably the Psychological Warfare Executive [PWE] and the Office of Strategic Services [OSS]) to achieve a greater understanding of the new Italian war theatre confronting the Allies as a result of the landings in Sicily. During the last year of the war (from D Day to VE Day) half of the British population listened nightly to a news programme 'War Report'. (The programme also features in Jennings' masterpiece *Diary for Timothy*, 1945). Siân Nicholas traces one of the most vivid and eclectic war coverage operations of any of the belligerents. According to Nicholas 'War Report' represented a revolution in aims and internal administrative of the BBC and consolidated a new kind of war reportage, mixing news and eye-witness 'actuality'.

If the two world wars had demonstrated the power of propaganda, the post-1945 period witnessed the widespread utilization of the lesson drawn from the wartime experience within the overall context of the Cold War and the 'communications revolution'. Tony Shaw examines the similarities and differences between the approaches to the Cold War taken by the American and British film industries. The two industries showed signs of being at odds with one another, economically, stylistically and ideologically. This contrasts with the more homogeneous approach to the Cold War taken by Eastern bloc filmmakers. Shaw also shows how television's challenge to the cinema led to a new phase in the Cold War from the early 1960s onwards, one in which visual propaganda achieved even great immediacy and intimacy.

The Cold War was the struggle between the USA and the USSR for ideological supremacy and a psychological war for the minds of the non-aligned world. The chief agent for the United States was the United States Information Agency (USIA), known overseas as the United States Information Service (USIS). In 1953 USIA coordinated a massive propaganda operation to include such diverse activities as the Voice of America, the embassy press and cultural programmes and overseas film, television and the printed page. During John F. Kennedy's presidency USIA expanded its activities especially under the leadership of the former CBS-journalist Edward Murrow. In the aftermath of Kennedy's assassination and the death of Murrow, President Johnson appointed Carl T. Rowan to oversee a new USIA propaganda initiative. Nicholas Cull's critical analysis of Rowan's tenure underlines the structural problems within the US information machine, particularly the perennial difficulty of combining the political need to manipulate information with the ethical emphasis on accurate news demanded by Voice of America. Cull also shows how an individual like Rowan could sway the operations of such a large bureaucracy. However Rowan's eagerness to boost USIA's profile in South Vietnam had profound implications as USIA's role in Vietnam escalated in tandem with America's military activity.

By the summer of 1965 the ramifications of America's military and propaganda campaign in Vietnam is taken up by David Culbert in his analysis of American television coverage of the Vietnam War. Vietnam remains (for Americans, at least) a fertile ground for 'contested historical memory'. For example, it is now widely accepted that television's impact was overrated and that the 'living-room' war is remembered fiction. However, the execution by Colonel Nguyen Ngoc Laon, head of the South Vietnamese police, of a Vietcong terrorist on 1 February 1968 remains an indelible and haunting image of the Vietnam War. Culbert argues that the photograph and footage of the Loan execution acted as a genuine catalyst for change and legitimized the moral arguments of the anti-war movement. The confluence of this extraordinary image, which appeared to represent the practice of justice by the government of South Vietnam – together with the uncertainty of American foreign policy following the Tet Offensive – makes the Loan photograph and television newsfilm a significant element in America's move from hawk to dove in early 1968. Christine Whittaker provides a brief overview of how the Tet Offensive was covered on British television.

In contrast to the Vietnam War, the South Atlantic campaign was *not* a television war. Instead, radio reporters such as Brian Hanrahan and Robert Fox became household names. According to Robert Harris this conflict was 'the worst reported war since the Crimea' in the nineteenth century.[6] British Prime Minister Margaret Thatcher was determined that her government would not 'lose' the Falklands on TV in the same way that the Americans had (allegedly) lost Vietnam on US television. Indeed, for some years after the successful South Atlantic campaign, political and military leaders embroiled in subsequent conflicts approvingly referred to the Falklands War as an example of 'good practice'.[7] Thatcher was not alone in misinterpreting the so-called lessons of what has been termed the 'Vietnam syndrome'. At a time of Cold War tensions and intercontinental missile technology, it was striking to see a territorial conflict unfold through a medium that was thought to have reached its pinnacle in World War II. Klaus Dodds' analysis of the Falkland conflict raises questions about the importance of public opinion and morale and acceptable levels of state censorship and news management in times of war. In the aftermath of the conflict, the House of Commons Defence Committee concluded that there had been a greater level of censorship than could be reasonably justified under the guise of 'operational security'.

The wave of adverse media criticism in the wake of the Falklands brought into sharp focus the relationship between the state and journalists in times of war. Although the manner in which the news has reached its audiences has changed over the last 100 years the role of the war correspondent remains an enduring factor that links the past with the present. A popular image of the war correspondent in the public imagination is of a gallant, heroic figure bringing us impartial reports from conflict zones around the world. The fact that these journalists cover war itself gives them a romantic edge over other correspondents as although 'under a cloak of military splendour and the prospect of glory, war is cruel, bloody and destructive. Its reporting, however, makes brilliant news; it offers excitement, anxiety and horror and sometimes exultation or despair'.[8] The public's perception is given added glamour by the fact that such well-known personalities as Winston Churchill, Ernest Hemingway and Ian Fleming were war correspondents.

The image of the war correspondent as the noble warrior of truth risking his (or her) life in unpleasant war zones is, of course, an oversimplification. Evelyn Waugh's *Scoop*, first published in 1938, and loosely based on the author's own experience in covering the Abyssinian War of 1935, largely demythologised this inflated image. In Waugh's fictional account, the hapless William Boot, a nature correspondent for the newspaper *The Beast*, becomes a reluctant war correspondent covering the crisis in 'Ishmaelia' as a result of mistaken identity. The reader is introduced to the widely-used journalistic language of 'cablese' which derived from the need to save wordage, and therefore money, in sending telegrams, and, in the desperate, unprepared circumstances he finds himself in, Boot is taken under the wing of Corker, a correspondent for Universal News, the 'hottest' news agency in Britain. Waugh contrasts the newspaper and the agency correspondent, but basically presents the profession as one that routinely misleads the domestic press and public with made-up stories.

Wars offer unique opportunities for reporters to impose themselves on a news story (witness John Simpson's 'liberation' of Kabul). To Waugh's cynical view of the war correspondent has been added contemporary criticism of 'the narcissism of war reporting'. Mark Pedelty, who carried out an anthropological study of the correspondents working in El Salvador in 1991, noted that journalists themselves helped to foster such popular impressions of their work through boldly publishing their autobiographies with title such as 'War Reporter', 'Means of Escape', 'From the House of War' and 'Trial by Fire', and emphasising the more dangerous aspects of their work.[9] There can be little doubt that in recent conflicts, war correspondents have acted not simply as conduits of information, but as personalities in their own right. It has become *de rigueur* for correspondents to publish their memoirs of war. After the conflict we now anticipate the publicity fanfare of a war correspondent hawking his or her story around the media. The 'celebration of the correspondent', whereby the messenger becomes as important – if not more important – than the message has, according to some critics, led to a 'dumbing-down' of reporting news from war zones Moreover, due to the demands of 24 hours continuous news broadcasts, some analysts, including defence journalist, Robert Fox, suggest that current war journalism produces less detailed and analytical information than in the past. Fox argues that the demands of the contemporary media have led to bland analysis and greater visual gimmicks and less interest in the wider context. Nik Gowing was making a similar point when he coined the phrase the 'tyranny of time'.[10]

The evolution of the personality cult of the war correspondent has coincided (no coincidence?) with the increasingly complex and emerging military doctrinal thinking especially in the area of 'Information Operations' (IO) – an umbrella term for military communications in the Information Age. IO represents, for the military at least, a flexible set of guidelines that sets out the importance of good military-media relation particularly with a view to influencing adversaries. The military's engagement with the media in this respect is open to charges of manipulation, dissimulation and propaganda. Critics of IO, and its close relative 'Media Operations', claim that it is simply the military's attempts to stage manage the public's perceptions of war. Phil Taylor's chapter on 'the Fourth Arm and the Fourth Estate' unscrambles the murky world of psycho-operations (or PSYOPS – not to be confused with psychological warfare) and argues that historically policies of official secrecy serve to create an information vacuum that is filled by all sorts of speculation and misinformation.

Partly as a result of America's defeat in Vietnam, military psychological warfare entered a period of decline and discredit in the United States. President Reagan was responsible for revitalising US PSYOPS in the 1980s. At a strategic level this involved flooding the Soviet bloc with western propaganda – especially after the arrival of satellite TV and new communication technologies such as video-cassette and fax machines, and mobile phones. Following Iraq's invasion of Kuwait in August 1990 President Bush was persuaded to incorporate PSYOPS as an integral part of Operations Desert Storm. Taylor claims that PSYOPS came of age with the surrender of 69,000 Iraqi troops that had been bombarded with PSYOPS leaflets – a case of persuasion in association with force.[11]

The changing nature of international crises, from inter-state to intra-state, saw a series of military interventions on the part of the US led international community which placed emphasis on troops being able to communicate with local populations rather than to fight battles with them. In such a new non-combat environment the importance of information is both strategic and tactical. After the 1991 Gulf War a series of conflicts in Bosnia, Serbia, Rwanda, Kosovo and East Timor which all saw PSYOPS deployed in support of military operations. Since September 11, there has been a discernible shift back on to people, in what the Pentagon term 'Perception Management' - the latest in a long line of euphemisms devised by western democracies to avoid admitting that they are in the business of propaganda. Taylor argues that the rise of professional military communicators created a situation whereby the media have become part of the problem, not the solution. These issues are taken up in the final two chapters in the book.

In the second half of the twentieth century, rapidly spreading digital technology has given television correspondents unimagined new capabilities both for news gathering and input – and this clearly has profound implications for war reporting. However as Godfrey Hodgson has pointed out, although this should be a golden age for news, the audience is drifting away.[12] Hodgson's contention is that people no longer find news as compelling as they did when it was a matter of life and death for us all. For the past decade, we have been living after the end of what Eric Hobsbawm called 'the short twentieth century'. That period has been marked by a grand narrative of world wars and their consequences. One familiar explanation is that there is less interest in news because of 'the end of the Cold War'. The other explanation according to Hodgson is that while the volume of dramatic and horrifying news has not dried up, the perspective of the readers and viewers who constitute the market for news has been changing. This is particularly true in the USA, Britain and Western Europe, which have traditionally supplied the main markets for the international news system.

According to Hodgson and his theory of the 'grand narrative', readers and viewers in developed countries understand that, when people say that 'Europe is at war' because NATO planes are bombing Bosnia or Kosovo, that is not true in the sense in which Europe experienced 'total war' in 1914-18 or 1939-45. Then civilian populations became an intrinsic part of the war effort, every bit as important as the fighting front. However in recent conflicts since the collapse of the Berlin Wall and the end of the Cold War, the populations of Western Europe and the Unites States have not considered themselves at risk. 'From 1914-1991, international news was frightening. It could kill you. Now, rightly or wrongly, people are not afraid that a war (as opposed to terrorist attacks) is going to affect them'.[13] Western audiences are therefore drawn to reading about or watching international conflicts not by a sense of personal engagement, but idle curiosity. War becomes a 'spectator sport' with 'zero casualties'.[14]

Since Vietnam there has been a desire to create a Third World battlefield where maximum weaponry and minimal US (and European) casualties would guarantee public support. The Kosovo conflict illustrated the changing nature of wars involving the United States and its allies (as opposed to regional conflicts). Put simply, American and British troops were not engaged in Yugoslavia in the traditional sense of war against 'Johnny Serb'. As the British television news presenter and former war correspondent, John Snow, pointed out at the time: 'The only British representatives on this field of battle are not tanks, but laptops in Belgrade hotels'.[15] Initially at least Kosovo proved a difficult war for the media. Partisan or patriotic coverage proved difficult when the only military to be seen 'in theatre' were the enemy – or more specifically enemy buildings being 'degraded' by a 'tomahawk' fired by invisible military operatives from some unknown destination.

The issue of extensive image management and the military's growing concern with 'information control' is addressed in the chapter 'Missing in Authenticity? Media in the Digital Age'. Susan Carruthers discusses how western militaries, led by the US and eager to forestall 'another Vietnam', have refined their strategies for *virtualising* the representation of war. Moreover, technology is changing the nature of war. Picking up where the Gulf War left off, the 1999 Kosovo campaign saw extensive efforts on the part of NATO spin-doctors to convince its citizens that they were witnessing a new concept of 'humane warfare' in which no one (on our side) gets hurt. James Der Derian has talked about the 'reality and virtuality of war' and Michael Ignatieff has asserted that; 'war without death—to our side—is war that ceases to be fully real to us: virtual war'.[16] For the citizens of NATO, war in Kosovo was a 'virtual' conflict whereby they were mobilized not as combatants but as spectators. The notion of a 'virtual war' – whereby television audiences voyeuristically 'graze' upon television coverage – resembles a TV war or a computer game, and not reality. Civilian publics may be engaged by the spectacle and the symbolism of war but, according to Carruthers, participation is minimal and distant. A 'death-free' war becomes a spectator sport – with commercial breaks!

The Kosovo war also anticipated changes that are to come and confirmed new developments in the 1990s. In the campaign to 'liberate' Kosovo both sides in the conflict understood the importance of manipulating real-time news to their own advantage. This was also the first war in which the Internet featured as a significant part of the information and propaganda campaign. It has been said that the internet was to Kosovo what television was to the Korean war.

The internet was employed not only as a propaganda tool but it was also used for humanitarian purposes.[17]

Having declared war on Serbia (or more accurately, on Slobodan Milosevic – 'a new Hitler'), NATO sought to justify its war aims by stressing the humanitarian aspect of its aerial bombing campaign and the accuracy of its weapons. Jamie Shea, the NATO spokesman, insisted 'Our cause is just'. NATO briefings during the Kosovo conflict were primarily platforms to disseminate sound-bites and NATO propaganda. Milosevic, also revealed that he was capable of using the media for propaganda purposes. By allowing the BBC and CNN to continue to broadcast from Belgrade he hoped to fragment Western opinion with nightly stories of 'innocent' civilians killed by NATO air strikes. As the most effective propaganda is that which can be verified, NATO was placed on the defensive in the propaganda war by having to confirm the accuracy of Serbian claims. Although NATO's military strategy was ultimately vindicated, the ongoing Balkans wars of the 1990s reinforces the centrality of propaganda to war. The propaganda war in the Kosovo conflict, and particularly the use made of the Internet by all sides, including non-government actors, highlights the forces of change between the pre-Cold War era and the current globalized information environment.

Angus Taverner's 'Learning the Lessons of the Twentieth Century' provides a penetrating military perspective on military-media relations over the past twenty years. This essay covers not only the impact of technological change, but also the changing nature of the media itself from a military perspective. Taverner (who refers to these changes as 'revolutionary') claims that the British military, including the Ministry of Defence, has heeded criticism levelled in the wake of the Falklands ('an unsatisfactory benchmark') so that a more balanced understanding has emerged. Not only has technology freed the media from the physical constraints under which correspondents used to labour, but there is now a recognition that the media is going to be present in large numbers and have therefore to be factored into the military plans. By the time the British-led ground force crossed the Macedonian border into Kosovo in 1999 it is estimated that 3574 correspondents were registered by NATO. In such circumstances the military concede that they will almost certainly have more contact with cameramen than with the enemy.[18] This explains why the military needs to work with the media. Taverner concludes that the military now understand that its dealings with the media must be founded on respect and recognition of the role that they carry out.

This rather cosy view is challenged by Philip Knightley (among others) in the revised edition of The First Casualty. Knightley argues that Kosovo marked the final victory of the 'minders' over the media. He concludes that: ' the age of the war correspondent is clearly over. Whether they wish to continue as propagandists and myth makers, subservient to those who wage the war, is a decision they will have to take themselves.'[19] In the final chapter of the volume Mark Laity takes up the issues raised in Taverner's essay and challenged by Knightley and others. Laity – a poacher turned gamekeeper – believes that new mobile technology has given journalists unparalleled independent access to the frontline free of 'minders'.[20] Moreover, when war becomes a spectator sport the media become the decisive theatre of war, which in turn transforms journalists from mediators into protagonists.[21] Laity suggests that far from being the stooges of NATO, the media and journalists have failed to face the challenge and responsibilities of the new power that has been thrust upon them.

It is certainly true that changes in the nature of conflict have also affected both the ability to cover and the style of reporting war. The First and Second World Wars presented a fight for national survival not evident in late twentieth century conflict involving American and Western Europeans forces. The post-1945 Cold War era, whereby a bipolar ideological conflict defined the nature of 'hostilities', has also passed with the collapse of the Soviet Union. Even during the relatively short span between the Gulf War and the Kosovo conflict (what distinguishes a 'war' from a 'conflict'?) it is evident that different military, political and ideological incentives for entering and justifying hostilities have formed. Furthermore, once conflict has begun its nature is also susceptible to change. The Gulf War required a decisive ground offensive, while Kosovo was fought from the air. Moreover, the Kosovo operations were fought under NATO command unlike the Gulf War which was largely led by the United States. Gulf War II in 2003 was a unilateral invasion by 'Coalition Forces' (a euphemism for American and British forces) who claimed international legality under UN Resolution 1441, but in prosecuting the war, sidelined both the Security Council and NATO.[22]

Asymmetric warfare is surely going to be the dominant form of conflict in the modern age, simply because of the lack of enemies capable of contemplating a conventional war against the West. So in the face of conventional firepower, the weaker state, or organization, uses different weaponry. Thus according to Laity, asymmetric warfare could be terrorism, guerrilla warfare or information warfare. Laity claims that terrorism is itself 'a particularly nasty form of information warfare'. The events of 11 September 2001, have, certainly in the short term, shifted perception, particularly in the United States. For the first time since Pearl Harbor Americans feel threatened on their own soil. Laity claims that for Osama bin Laden the actual death toll was incidental to his real purpose of terrorising the billions who had a grandstand view. Some commentators such as Philip Bobbitt have argued that the real significance of September 11 was that it represented more than an act of terrorism. After all, there had been many terrorist attacks before, particularly in Europe. According to Bobbitt, we are entering a new phase in which small numbers of people, operating without overt state sponsorship, will be able to exploit the vulnerability of contemporary 'open' societies. Terrorist groups such as Al-Qaeda represent a new and profoundly dangerous type of organization, a 'virtual state', borderless but global in scope.[23] If this is the case, then more than ever before, modern military campaigns are likely to become struggles of information in the battle for the high ground of public opinion. In such a struggle the management of perception – the battle for 'hearts and minds' – will continue to be about words and pictures and not just about bombs and aeroplanes.

NOTES

1. One casualty of the Macedonian crisis was Mark Laity who was scheduled to deliver the key-note address. The organisers of the conference happily acknowledge the generosity of Nik Gowing for stepping into the breach and providing such a thought-provoking address that kicked off the conference in such style. Gowing's provocative paper set the agenda and provided a stimulating touchstone for subsequent presentations. The essays in this volume are largely taken from the proceedings. Mark Laity, Angus Taverner and Siân Nicholas who were unable to attend agreed to write-up their papers.

The editors would also like to thank Professor Colin Seymour Ure, Dr Piers Robinson, Christine Whittaker and Ronnie McCourt for their contributions to the conference.

2. *Observer*, 30 March 2003; *Observer*, 6 April 2003. See responses to these allegations from Nick Pollard (Head of Sky News), Richard Sambrook (BBC Director of News) and Chris Cramer (President of CNN International Networks), *Media Guardian*, 31 March 2003, p. 7. On 'war porn' see *Guardian (G2)*, 26 March 2003. For a perceptive journalistic analysis of media coverage of Gulf War II see, Peter Preston, 'Here is the news: Too much heat…too little light', *Observer*, 30 March 2003.

3. See, M. Sanders and P. Taylor, *Propaganda During the First World War 1914-1918* (London Macmillan, 1982); G. S. Messinger, *British Propaganda and the State in the First World* War, (Manchester, 1992); Martin J. Farrar, *News From the Front: War Correspondents on the Western Front 1914*-1918, (Sutton, 1998); Nicholas Reeves, *Official British Film Propaganda During the First World* War, (London, 1986); Jane Carmichael, *First World War Photographers*, (London, 1989); Roger Smither (ed.), *Imperial War Museum Film Catalogue Volume 1: The First World War Archive*, (London: Flicks Books, 1994; David Welch, *Germany, Propaganda and Total War 1914-1918*, (London, 2000); Mark Cornwall, *The Undermining of Austria-Hungary: The Battle for Hearts and Minds*, (London, 2000); John F. Williams, *ANZACs, The Media and the Great War*, (Sydney, 1999).

4. The film also provides a fascinating example of how the same images can be used for counter-propaganda purposes. In the immediate post-war years, the British, the Americans and the French all produced their own propagandistic versions of the German footage. See, R. Smither (ed) *First World War U-Boat* (London, Imperial War Museum, 2000). This is the excellent booklet that accompanies the video of *Der magische Gürtel*.

5. Dilys Powell, *Films Since 1939*, (London, 1947), p. 40.

6. See the analysis in R. Harris, *Gotcha! The Media, the Government and the Falklands Crisis* (London, 1983).

7. According to Angus Taverner this is no longer the case and is now viewed within the Ministry of Defence as an 'unsatisfactory benchmark'. See Taverner, 'Learning the lessons of the Twentieth Century: The Evolution in British Military Attitude to the Media on Operations and in War'.

8. Quoted in M. Hudson and J. Stanier, *War and the Media. A Random Searchlight* (London, 1997), pp. xi-xii.

9. M. Pedelty, *War Stories: The Culture of Foreign Correspondent* (London, 1991) pp. 29-30.

10. Cf. Robert Fox, BBC Radio 4, 20 May 2002; Nik Gowing, 'Real Time Television Coverage of Armed Conflicts and Diplomatic Crises: Does it Pressure Or Distort Foreign Policy Decisions?' (John F. Kennedy School, Harvard University, 1994).

11. Revealingly Gulf War II continued where the 1991 Gulf War left off. US and GB 'Coalition' forces intensified the use of psychological operations, known as psy-ops. The US military has a long tradition of radio psy-ops that can be traced back to the Vietnam War. Similar broadcasts were used in the campaign in Afghanistan to persuade citizens to reveal Taliban and Al-Qaeda factions. In Gulf War II, the US in particular engaged in a comprehensive airwaves campaign to soften its enemy and soothe its population at home. Spearheading the electronic propaganda campaign were converted C-130 US

cargo planes transmitting a mixture of Arabic and Western music and spoken announcements to the troops and citizens of Iraq, urging them not to fight and how to surrender. The planes were the Coalition's weapons of mass persuasion. The radio transmissions were backed up by an intense leaflet-dropping campaign. Over 17 million leaflets were dispersed in the first week of the war, offering detailed information on how to signal surrender to advancing coalition troops. Warnings printed on the leaflets include: 'Attacking coalition aircraft invites your destruction. Do not risk your life and the lives of your comrades. Leave now and go home. Watch your children learn, grow and prosper'. (Examples of psy-ops leaflets during Gulf War II can be downloaded Central Command's website; cent.com.)

12. According to Hodgson, in the USA the combined audience of the big three networks (CBS, NBC, and ABC) has fallen from over 90 to under 60 per cent of the audience. Moreover since the economic crisis for television in the 1990s, the networks have been closing most or almost all of their overseas bureaux. In Britain the number of television news outlets has increased by 800 per cent in the last ten years but in the same period the aggregate audience for news has fallen by 20 per cent. See, G. Hodgson, 'The End of the Grand Narrative and the Death of News', *Historical Journal of Film, Radio and Television*, Vol. 20, No. 1, (2000), pp. 23-31.

13. Ibid, p. 27.

14. If Hodgson is right and the perspectives of western audiences have changed, there can be no doubt that war still attracts large audiences, for whatever reasons. On Wednesday 24 March 1999, the start of the NATO bombing of Yugoslavia, the combined audience for the main scheduled bulletins from ITN and BBC1 was more than 27 million. See Richard Tait, 'The Future of International News on Television' *Historical Journal of Film, Radio and Television*, vol. 20, No. 1 (2000), p. 51. Tait is the former Editor-in-Chief of ITN and both Hodgson and Tait's articles formed part of a special *Historical Journal of Film, Radio and Television* issue devoted to 'News into the Next Century'.

15. John Snow, *The Guardian*, 26 April 1999, pp. 4-5.

16. Michael Ignatieff, *Virtual War: Kosovo and Beyond* (London, 2000); James Der Derian, *Virtuous War: Mapping the Military-Industrial-Media-Entertainment Network* (Boulder: Westview Press, 2001)

17. The importance of the internet was employed not only as a propaganda tool, but it was also used for humanitarian purposes. For example, to find relatives separated or killed in the war and the establishment of 'web-witnesses' whereby individuals tell their own stories and experiences of the conflict.

18. This is precisely the point made by Ronnie McCourt (Ministry of Defence) in his paper to the conference.

19. P. Knightley, *The First Casualty: The War Correspondent as Hero and Myth-Maker from the Crimea to Kosovo* (London, 2000), p. 562. See also, P. Knightley, 'Fighting Dirty', *The Guardian*, 20 March 2000, pp. 2-3.

20. This interpretation is at odds with the experience of war correspondents such as Robert Fisk and David Beresford who have criticised the 'buddy-buddy' relationship engineered by the coveted 'pool' positions during the Gulf War in 1991. Fisk argues that having 'embedded' reporters into military units they could be more easily managed and censored; 'Eleven years ago, they turned up at Dhahran in Saudi Arabia, already kitted out with helmets, gas capes, chocolate rations and eyes that narrowed when they looked into

the sun, just like General Montgomery'. Fisk, 'War Journalists Should not be Cosying Up to the Military', *The Independent*, 21 January 2003, p. 9. Cf. Beresford, 'Writes, and Wrongs, of War', *The Observer*, 26 January 2003, p. 6

21. Cf., Ignatieff, *Virtual War*, pp. 191-93.

22. For a brief analysis of propaganda employed in Gulf War II see, D. Culbert, N. Cull and D. Welch (eds), *Propaganda and Mass Persuasion. A Historical Encyclopaedia, 1500 to the Present* (ABC-Clio, 2003), pp. 159-162.

23. P. Bobbitt, *The Shield of Achilles. War and Peace and the Course of History* (London, 2002).

Chapter One
THE BRITISH PRESS DURING THE SOUTH AFRICAN WAR: THE SIEGES OF MAFEKING, KIMBERLEY AND LADYSMITH
Jacqueline Beaumont

The sieges of Kimberley, Ladysmith and Mafeking are central to the first stage of the South African war. They determined the actions of British forces to a degree which was not initially expected. Nobody thought that Ladysmith would be besieged; few imagined that Kimberley would be. Their relief, achievable before Christmas, was assumed almost immediately by the Press to signify the end of the war. The failure of this goal, followed by growing evidence of the inadequacies of British preparations for the war, both material and mental, let loose in the Press an almost universal chorus of criticism, some levelled against the military authorities, some against the Government. The sieges were followed with intense interest by the Press, any scrap of information being seized upon and, as the stock of the relieving forces fell, so admiration for the courage and endurance of the besieged, both military and, especially, civilian, was dwelt upon by military commentators and leader writers. A myth of British endurance in appalling circumstances in which the very best characteristics, typical of the British at bay, were demonstrated, was born. It counterbalanced the feelings of humiliation at the defeats suffered by Gatacre, Methuen and Buller during Black Week, in mid December 1899. The fate of the three towns was watched with eager attention by the newspaper reading public too. Commenting on Mafeking Lady Stanley wrote, "The excitement and the gloom passes anything one has ever seen or known before. One does feel proud of being English, for we have come out splendidly."[1] "Today has been a real cheer with news of Cronje's capitulation, though the terrible fighting round Ladysmith and the awful list of officers killed and wounded and men is a most heartrending one," wrote Agnes Jekyll, wife of John Morley's political secretary, on the day that news of Paardeberg reached London.

"One thinks and talks of nothing else but war and when the newspaper carts flew along this morning wearing Union Jacks people dashed out and stood clapping their hands in Oxford St - a very unusual sight"[2] These sentiments were fuelled by telegrams and letters from correspondents in the three towns. The constraints under which these were composed were considerable and affected what was published during the course of the sieges. This in turn had its effect on public perceptions of the sieges.

Coverage of the three sieges was uneven. This was in part due to an unequal distribution of correspondents. London editors knew that when an attack came it would be concentrated on northern Natal. So the majority of the war correspondents who left England early in September ended up there.[3] They included some of the best-known names of the day. Bennett Burleigh, the veteran correspondent of the *Daily Telegraph*, was one of the few who managed to escape just before the siege set in. George Steevens of the *Daily Mail*, died there, and H. H. S. Pearse, another veteran, represented the *Daily News*. There was also a clutch of journalists, not as well known or as experienced as war correspondents, but good all-round professionals, some with literary talent. These included Henry Nevinson of the *Daily Chronicle*, already an established author and a powerful political voice while H W Massingham edited the paper; indeed, he was one of the few war correspondents who was a "pro-Boer" and he had been writing leaders for his paper criticizing Chamberlain's policy almost up to the day he prepared to sail for South Africa.[4] Like Nevinson, William Maxwell of the *Standard* had only recently started his career as a war correspondent. Nevinson had two campaigns behind him, Maxwell had one, the final lap of the campaign culminating in the battle of Omdurman in the Sudan the previous year. But he was a highly successful journalist of some twenty years standing and his letters from Ladysmith were polished and literary in character.[5] Ernest Smith of the *Morning Leader*, another experienced journalist, admitted that Elands Laagte was his first battle.[6] Ladysmith also attracted artists and photo-journalists. George Lynch, the moving spirit behind the correspondents' newspaper, the *Ladysmith Lyre*, wrote a handful of reports for the *Morning Herald* and sent many excellent photographs to the *Illustrated London News* before marching out of Ladysmith to join the Boers; he was subsequently accused by military intelligence of being unacceptably pro-Boer and forfeited his war medal.[7] Melton Prior, another veteran, representing the *Illustrated London News*, and W. T. Maud, working for the *Graphic*, provided drawings of incidents accompanied by a narrative of events which for many readers of the special editions of these two illustrated papers which appeared in the spring of 1900 after the siege had been raised probably provided the definitive account of the siege. There were many others, some representing both London and South African papers. Some papers had two correspondents in Ladysmith, one from London and a second, recruited locally.[8] All together there were probably more than twenty correspondents in the town.

Ladysmith had the cream of the correspondents; neither Kimberley nor Mafeking could compete in numbers, or in the quality and experience of correspondents. At Mafeking, even before war broke out, a siege was expected. It was known that Baden-Powell had been sent out to South Africa in July with a small group of officers to arrange some kind of diversion in the Northern Cape. By September he had dug himself in at Mafeking. As a result several war correspondents made their way there and by the time war broke out there were at least nine newspaper men in this little town. Of these only Reuters correspondent, Vere Stent, sent from Kimberley before the end of August, had covered a campaign before. Of the others all but one, David Baillie of the *Morning Post*, who had recently retired from the Army, had journalistic experience, but none were experienced war correspondents and only one, Angus Hamilton of *The Times*, went on to make a career as a war correspondent and editor. Little is known about the others. Two of the correspondents were on the staff of South African newspapers but also acted for London papers with whom their local newspapers were associated. The *Daily Mail* had a close link with the *Cape Times*: its correspondent in Mafeking, Hellawell, in peace time a sports correspondent in Cape Town, had originally come to Mafeking as a volunteer. The *Daily Chronicle* had for correspondent N. G. Parslow, a young journalist, originally from England, who was on the staff of the *South African News* in Cape Town.[9] The *Daily Mail* also received despatches from H. G. Whales, editor of the *Mafeking Mail*, and from Lady Sarah Wilson, the wife of Baden-Powell's staff officer.

By contrast, there were very few correspondents in Kimberley, despite the fact that it was the largest, most prosperous and most populous of the three siege towns. In England a siege was not anticipated and, as a result, few national newspapers had coverage. Reuters, which had an unrivalled network of correspondents in South Africa had as correspondent E.W.C. Luard, an ex-Etonian. Nothing is known of his journalistic credentials. Only three London newspapers were represented. The *Daily Telegraph* asked George Green, editor of the *Diamond Fields Advertiser* to act for it hours before the town was cut off and the *Daily News* had reports from a member of the *Advertiser*'s staff, Herbert Oliver, whose father was a journalist in London, more than likely with the *Daily News*. The *Daily Mail* also had a correspondent, probably Green. Julia Maguire, wife of Rhodes's friend and business associate Rochfort Maguire, wrote a couple of articles for *The Times* after the siege had been lifted. She was one of the few women correspondents during the war and, like the *Daily Mail*'s Lady Sarah Wilson in Mafeking, was appointed primarily to give the "womens' point of view" in a siege in which civilians played a central role.[10] All other accounts of the siege of Kimberley were written by civilians in the town and few appeared in London newspapers; indeed few appeared outside South Africa. Today the accounts written by "A man of the Potteries" and by H Clement Notcutt, Headmaster of the Boys Public School in Kimberley, both published in Kimberley in 1900 are rare collectors' items. Only the Kimberley doctor, Oliver Ashe, had widespread readership throughout the Empire at the time.[11]

Coverage of Ladysmith was greater than that of the other two sieges because it was generally agreed by editors and military experts at home that Ladysmith was the most important of the three towns. Most of the British troops in South Africa, hastily sent from India, were stationed there and the correspondents were expected to send home details of how Sir George White held off the enemy until further troops had arrived from England. And in the first few weeks there was plenty of military movement and several engagements to recount. Once the siege started in early November there was much discussion by military experts as to the best way to relieve the town. For it was inconceivable that so many British soldiers could be left to their fate. So from the start of the war Ladysmith – ironically dubbed "the Aldershot of South Africa" by correspondents – and the relief of the forces trapped there were seen as crucial. Until Lord Roberts started his campaign coverage of events in Natal took pride of place in news reports. Newspapers with no correspondent there borrowed the work of others. Evening papers in particular relied heavily on the news agencies, Reuters, the Central News Agency and Dalziel, all of whom had correspondents in Ladysmith and elsewhere in Natal, but they also borrowed accounts from any other paper which offered anything interesting. When it came to covering Mafeking and Kimberley editors, pressed for space, seem to have made a choice. If they had a correspondent in one or other town, they did him and his siege full justice; if not they used Reuters and often left it at that. The *Pall Mall Gazette*, the first paper to send a correspondent out to South Africa early in the summer of 1899, had Emerson Neilly in Mafeking and therefore covered that siege fully, not only printing Neilly's despatches, but also many other articles about Mafeking and about Baden-Powell. By contrast, the *Daily Telegraph* printed whatever telegrams and letters were sent by George Green and followed the siege with interest, while publishing only news agency reports from Mafeking. The balance changed as time passed and first Kimberley, then Ladysmith were relieved in February 1900. Attention was thereafter focussed on Mafeking by all newspapers.

There were reasons other than military importance for focussing attention on one or other of the sieges. The *Daily Mail* was the only newspaper with correspondents in all three siege towns Like all other newspapers, it concentrated on Ladysmith. But it chose to focus on Mafeking and, in particular, on Baden-Powell; indeed, the first article on personalities of the war was devoted to Baden-Powell, even before Buller and White were written up. Since its launch in 1896 this newspaper had always concentrated on personalities and the picturesque. Such stories, invariably illustrated, appeared on page seven which was normally reserved for family reading, including items on fashion, cookery and other feminine topics together with a portion of a novel. It was here that articles, accompanied by pictures and sketches from South Africa, appeared during the war. During the course of the sieges the *Daily Mail* devoted one article to Sir George White describing his military career in India and suggesting that, while brave in the conventional way that soldiers were supposed to be, he was not particularly good at strategic planning.[12] There was also one devoted to Kekewich, which appeared a week before the siege of Kimberley ended. This too paints a portrait of an agreeable, conventional officer, no more.[13] But Baden-Powell was the regular subject of special articles and from the start he is made out to be far more versatile and interesting than either of the other two commanders, while sharing the essential qualities of bravery and effectiveness. On October 12 he is described as:

> an excellent officer, a good sportsman, an inimitable entertainer, and a bit of a literary swell to boot. He went through the two Matabele wars, and gained experience, honour and no wounds. In some way he seems to bear a charmed life, because he is a reckless sort of fellow, and fears no amount of danger. He also has a quite remarkable gift of locality. That is to say, he is able by some extraordinary instinct to find his way about a totally unexplored country, and always to turn up just where he wished-or thereabouts. The natives think he is "uncanny". [14]

Alfred Harmsworth seems to have decided at an early stage that, while Natal was strategically important and therefore required full news coverage, for human interest Baden-Powell and Mafeking were more interesting to his readers than Kimberley – and would sell more newspapers.

If the marketing of one paper was a determining factor in the level of coverage and comment, the politics of another was equally important. Kimberley hardly merits a mention in the *Morning Leader* beyond the necessary news coverage provided by the news agencies, Reuters in the town and Dalziel from the Boer laager. The paper had no correspondent there but that was not why its coverage was so slight. The *Morning Leader* and its sister evening paper, the *Star*, were both steadfastly hostile towards Cecil Rhodes and De Beers. Months before war broke out they adopted the argument that South African capitalists, of whom Rhodes was the most hated example, were responsible for bad feeling and a build-up of tension in the Transvaal. The *Star* published letters from Francis Statham, a long-standing friend of the Transvaal Government, in support of President Kruger. The first of these, published as early as January 1899, contained a version of the theory of a conspiracy of international capitalism in South Africa later popularised more widely by J A Hobson.[15] In May both papers condemned the involvement of the British South Africa Company in the spectacle at Olympia, "Savage South Africa", as a typical example of capitalist exploitation of blacks. When the siege was raised not a word was said in editorials beyond the recital of the bare facts of relief and when, two weeks later, Ladysmith was relieved the *Morning Leader* editorial made it plain that it rejoiced ". . . not because any great commercial asset has been saved for the British flag, not because diamond mines or gold fields are intact, . . " a clear reference to the supposed role of South African capitalists.[16]

But the level of coverage of each siege depended primarily on information coming out of the three towns. In all three cases one of the first actions of the Boers was to destroy the railway lines and to cut the telegraph which ran alongside them. In the early weeks of the sieges the flow of information was therefore dependent on the bravery and resourcefulness of runners, mainly blacks, and despatch riders, who could evade the Boers and get telegrams through to the nearest working telegraph station and letters through to the nearest functioning post office. Their success depended on their knowledge of the country and their ability to take cover if necessary, the vigilance of the Boers and the co-operation of the military authorities in the siege towns. Acquiring a runner was not always easy. In Mafeking the runner service was organized by Sol Plaatje for both military and civilians. It worked quite well, especially once it had been realized that the southern route via Kimberley to De Aar was too dangerous and therefore was generally avoided after the first couple of weeks. A good proportion of telegrams found their way by runner north to working telegraph stations at Mochudi or Malagapye, where they were transmitted to Beira and then sent by boat and train to Lourenço Marques. If successful the entire trip took a couple of weeks. Letters, if they got through at all, and many did not, took up to three months. There does not seem to have been conflict between the correspondents and the military over sending messages. Vere Stent of Reuters did a deal with Baden-Powell by which he was allowed to send all his telegrams free of charge by the runners engaged by the military who took the northern route on condition that he sent copies of military despatches with his duplicate telegrams by the southern route to Kimberley, a service for which Reuters had to pay.[17] At Kimberley the military allowed the handful of correspondents to use their runners and despatch riders. Cecil Rhodes also had his own runners and riders and seldom bothered to tell the military when he was sending or receiving despatches. A correspondent who wanted to send despatches which might be unacceptable to the censor, had an alternative to the military resources though there is no evidence that it was used. [18] Once the Boers had cut telegraphic communication to north and south on October 14 telegrams from Kimberley generally went by despatch rider to Orange River. Initially telegrams were quite frequent and took between four and seven days to reach London newspaper pages, but they became less frequent as November proceeded, and the journey took longer. After the battle of Magersfontein on December 11 1899, telegrams became even sparser and it was evidently more difficult for runners and despatch riders to get through the Boer cordon. From the end of January 1900 most telegrams came via heliograph from Modder River, Methuen's main base, which cut down the transmission time but also cut the length and content. Longer letters were not sent at all until after the siege was over. In Ladysmith the Army had its own exclusive runners and despatch riders and would not allow the correspondents to send despatches with them. Correspondents had to make their own arrangements and this was often difficult. It could take days to find a man who was prepared to make the journey and the price rose as dangers increased. Often the runner was either captured or returned, too frightened to proceed or having failed to evade the Boers, who took his despatches and, if he was lucky, gave him nothing more than a good beating before sending him back. Correspondents who saw their runners returning, were naturally frustrated and annoyed but there was nothing they could do about it; they just had to hope for the best. Many seem to have sent out multiple copies by different runners, whom they sometimes shared.

Communication difficulties ensured that accurate news from the siege towns was often a matter of luck. Often telegrams took at least a week to reach London; sometimes they never came at all, or were in the wrong order, or had portions missing. Breakdowns of the telegraph line, which were frequent, were as much to blame as runners not getting through. So too were the actions of censors who sometimes hung on to telegrams, waiting for approval from above, or overburdened by other tasks. Moberly Bell of *The Times* complained that Reuters was regularly getting its telegrams through more quickly than anybody else, and blamed the censor for giving Reuters unwarrantable priority treatment.[19] Indeed the Army often was to blame for the haphazard way in which news was treated, particularly in Natal. Many Army officers regarded the Press as a nuisance and could be hostile and unhelpful. Early in the siege Henry Nevinson reported that while searching for a runner:

> ...I lost two hours through the conscientiousness of the 5th Lancers who arrested me and sent me from pillar to post just as if I was seeking information at the War Office. At last they took me - the Colonel himself, three privates with rifles and a mounted orderly with a lance – took me to the General Staff itself. And there the absurdity ended. But seriously what is the good of having the very highest and most authoritative passes possible – one from the War Office and one from the head of the Intelligence Department here – if any conscientious colonel can refuse to acknowledge them and rag a correspondent about amid the derision of Kaffirs and coolies, and of Dutchmen who are known perfectly well to send every scrap of intelligence to their friends outside? I lost two hours; probably I had lost my chance of getting a runner through. I had complied with the regulations in every possible respect my pass was in my hand; and what was the good of it?"[20]

Correspondents had to get to know and make friends with individual army officers, who would then ease the way for them, keeping them up to date with events and tipping them off when there was to be an action so they could be there if it were permitted. But there were always problems. In Ladysmith Sir George White had tried to arrange for women, children and non-combatants to travel south once a siege looked inevitable. Joubert had refused, but he had allowed a neutral camp to be set up at Intombi, a few miles outside the town. Joubert imposed rules governing the neutrality of the camp which were stringently observed by the camp commandant, anxious not to infringe them and bring the Boers down on him. When black runners, leaving Ladysmith with letters and telegrams, stopped at the camp on their way through the Boer lines, he decided that it would be a breach of rules governing the neutrality of the camp to allow them to proceed. So everything sent after 2 November was impounded and the runners had to stay in the camp. More than a fortnight later the sacks full of messages were returned to Ladysmith. The result was a complete lack of news from Ladysmith throughout November which continued well into December, a fact ruefully mentioned by many of the correspondents in their letters and diaries. By then runners and the occasional pigeon had been supplemented by heliographic contact with Buller's forces and correspondents were allowed to use this form of communication. This helped to speed up the receipt of information in London, but they were restricted to a maximum of thirty words per message, the tone had to be bright and optimistic and certain information was removed.

Censorship was a major impediment to the free flow and accuracy of news. In Ladysmith the brief heliographed telegrams very often gave almost no information and would end with the words "all well". The few original telegrams which survive show that the Army did not want anything about the health of the town or the inefficient management of the camp at Intombi to be released. Henry Nevinson, for instance, telegraphing to his newspaper on December 14, included a sentence about the increase of enteric in the town and the sickness of Steevens of the *Daily Mail*, which was cut. Similarly a whole passage was blue pencilled in his telegram of December 28 which gave details of an enquiry into the state of Intombi camp. Hutton of Reuters and James of *The Times* had similar experiences and many of the correspondents complained about it.[21] The censor, Edward Altham, became a focus for resentment, generally disliked by the Press and young officers alike. Correspondents complained of his excessive pruning of their copy; army officers complained about his inadequate intelligence.[22] In Mafeking the censor, Hanbury-Tracy, seems to have had good relations with the correspondents in general, though they complained about his excessive use of the blue pencil and his failure to return rejected copy. Neilly of the *Pall Mall Gazette*, objected at an early stage of the siege to the kinds of information which were banned. Writing to his editor, Sir Douglas Straight, on November 16 he complained:

> We are being disgracefully treated here as correspondents. Young Hamilton's wires are frequently torn up by the censor and I was refused permission to report certain atrocities perpetrated by the enemy such as firing on our red cross flag, and advancing troops and a gun to fight under cover of their own ambulance wagon. And a few days ago I prepared a cable for you showing the slight damage we had providentially sustained and it was refused because the people at home might fancy that the siege was a farce.[23]

Neilly decided that he would send no more telegrams, leaving that part of the job to Reuters, and would confine himself to writing "human interest" letters. In fact, he had little choice, for his letter so enraged the staff that he had his license revoked and had to make humble apology in order to be allowed to send anything at all. Moreover, the other correspondents in Mafeking supported the Staff, signing a statement of support for the action taken against Neilly by Lord Edward Cecil.[24] Thereafter Neilly sent no telegrams, but his letters were allowed through and many appeared in the *Pall Mall Gazette*. The decision to concentrate on human interest letters was adopted by several of the correspondents. In Mafeking and Kimberley where the fate of many civilians was at stake this was an obvious decision, but it happened in Ladysmith too, partly because of the censorship, partly because after the early battles before the siege set in, there was not a great deal to write about if one only reported military manoeuvres unless a correspondent fancied himself as an expert on military technicalities.

Officers in charge were concerned to maintain morale and avoid providing information for the enemy. In all three towns they did so by restricting information as far as possible, particularly bad news, and insisting on a bright, positive approach. In their view there was good reason for doing so. In Ladysmith the news of Colenso caused widespread despondency among the troops, a fact which was hidden from readers at home until much later. Telegrams from Ladysmith all stressed how little effect this news had had and how well prepared the town was to face a prolonged investment. Unfortunately none of the original telegrams have survived, but the terseness of what was allowed through suggests some pruning by the censor. On Christmas day the Royal Artillery held a service. Lieutenant Douglas Gill reported in his diary that the parson, a civilian, preached:

> a dreadfully gloomy sermon contrasting the black side of our present Xmas with the bright picture of former ones & drew such touching pictures of homes, empty chairs etc that half the men were in tears. This is just what we are trying to avoid. . .[25]

It was not until the end of January that a glimpse of what Christmas day had really been like reached the select breakfast tables of readers of the *Morning Leader*. Ernest Smith was the only correspondent to dwell on the fact that Christmas day had a sombre and uncomfortable aspect, prefacing and interleaving his description of the church service in the English church with the words of a hymn of peace sung at that service

> O God of love, O King of Peace,
> Make wars throughout the world to cease;
> The wrath of sinful men restrain,
> Give peace, O God, give peace again.

Smith was careful and skilful. He never once says that the men were demoralized; the censor would never have passed that. He concentrates on the bombardment and the heat, leaving it to the imagination of his readers to follow through the implications. It is the tone of the piece that suggests demoralization, a tone tempered also by his knowledge that he was writing for one of the few anti-war newspapers in England with a large non-conformist readership. Other correspondents who wrote about Christmas chose to be much more light hearted, in line with army requirements; they mentioned that the Boers fired a plum pudding into Ladysmith and concentrated on the party that evening organized by the Imperial Light Horse for the 200 children still in the town. That Smith got away with his piece at all is perhaps a sign of the often-mentioned inconsistency of the censor's office, or of the censor's lack of imagination. But with skill and care it was possible to include forbidden information. Lionel James complained about the cutting of his criticism of a weak link in the fortification of Wagon Hill, which had made the carnage much worse in the one major battle at Ladysmith on January 6th. The censor admitted that this was so but would not allow it to be said and James accepted this, albeit reluctantly. His mistake was in drawing attention too openly to the error. Smith smuggled in the same information without comment as part of the narrative, and got away with it. [26] John Stuart of the *Morning Post* wrote openly and at length on the subject, and on many other areas open to criticism in the conduct of the siege. All was duly published appeared in his newspaper, but none of his copy was sent to London until after the siege had been lifted.

In Kimberley the details about the terrible defeat at Magersfontein started to arrive a week later. Only the privileged few, officers who had access to the Kimberley Club and Headquarters, were allowed to see the full text. The following afternoon Howard Pim, a volunteer officer, in peace time a chartered accountant, who had already seen the full version, went to the office of the *Diamond Fields Advertiser* to view newspapers smuggled in for Cecil Rhodes and left there for the general public to see. He found that the censor had suppressed all accounts of the events of Black Week, on the orders of the garrison commander, Colonel Kekewich, who had himself seen the newspapers two days earlier. Kekewich claimed to be motivated by the knowledge that there were so many spies and enemy sympathizers in the town that any news would at once go to the enemy outside. But the Boers would hardly have needed their spies in Kimberley to give them this information, which was trumpeted in their own press. It is much more likely that his motives were the protection of the Army's reputation and the maintenance of morale in the town. Kekewich was undoubtedly conscious of the blow to British – and Army – prestige of the defeats. He was also concerned that the inhabitants of Kimberley should not be demoralized or, even worse, become mutinous. He was probably right as to the civilian view of Army management. Writing to his wife in his letter diary after having seen the full text in newspapers at the officers' mess, Pim exclaimed:

> . . . where are the army's brains? Gatacre loses 600 men in a way that a child should have foreseen and we are gradually arriving at the scandalous truth of the action near Spytfontein & approximately at the losses sustained there. . . . The disgrace of it all, the scandalous inefficiency of the men on whom we have showered honours without stint is dreadful. The loss of prestige too which is the pass to come we shall so suffer for. The best fighting material in the world chucked away. However we recover our losses many years must elapse before we regain our lost prestige, & thousands of lives will be wasted in the attempt.[27]

Kekewich's attitude towards the Press was both authoritarian and fearful. He credited it with enormous power and influence. He knew that the surrounding Boers received copies of the *Diamond Fields Advertiser* from their many friends in the town, so he deliberately inserted false information to mislead the Boers as to his intentions. He also published ordinances and instructions in the newspaper for the information and guidance of the townspeople. To that extent the Press was useful to him. But he failed entirely to take into account that the Editor might see himself as the voice of Kimberley's civilian population and he underestimated the power in Kimberley of Cecil Rhodes, to whose company, De Beers, the paper belonged. George Green, the youthful editor of the local newspaper, is largely silent about his professional experiences during the siege in his autobiography, but we know that on two occasions he wrote leaders in the *Diamond Fields Advertiser* on the orders of the paper's owner, Cecil Rhodes.In both cases the leaders treated subjects of great importance, not just to Rhodes personally, but to the entire community, and in both cases his action infuriated Kekewich. The first related to Buller's plan to evacuate all civilians, other than a few judged to be necessary for the defence of the town, once Kimberley had been relieved. Kekewich was informed of the bare facts early in December in a telegram from the High Commissioner He gave Rhodes a copy of the telegram. To his dismay, Rhodes told the directors of De Beers what was in the wind and the directors drafted a private memorandum to Kekewich expressing their concern at the Army's plan. Thee days later, a despatch came from Methuen announcing that:

> not a civilian or native is to remain in Kimberley unless he satisfies you and myself his services are essential for the protection of Kimberley or for some other good reason stop. The slightest evasion of this order will not only cause delay, but it will render the offender liable to be expelled from Kimberley and he will have to find his own way and food.[28]

The Mayor and Town Council did not like this and demanded that their views be forwarded to the High Commissioner, to which Kekewich agreed. They continued to express an opposition, which Kekewich attributed to Rhodes, who, following the news, was in an "impossible mood." Kekewich resented what he saw as Rhodes' betrayal of a confidence and felt that Rhodes was trying to place the needs of his company above the needs of the military situation. He accused Rhodes, in selfishly putting his business interests above the national interest, of behaviour which was little short of treason. He was angry when on 15 December a leader appeared in the *Diamond Fields Advertiser* notifying the whole town of the Army's plans, at that stage still known only to Rhodes, the De Beers directors, the Mayor and Town Council. But he contented himself with giving Green a dressing down for ignoring censorship. In fact, by the time the leader was published the plan was already a dead letter, following the defeats of Black Week and the removal of Buller from supreme command.; nothing further is heard of it. Kekewich must have considered that the newspaper was too useful to him to risk its closure by punishing Green. The second incident occurred a few days before the town was relieved. Again a leader was written giving details of the parlous state to which the townspeople had been reduced by four months of siege. Again it was inspired by Rhodes, who had been agitating for a speedy relief ever since he knew that Lord Roberts had started to move. This time Kekewich felt that he had to take a stand, but he hesitated to do so. The leader was, in his view, treasonous, for it gave away vital information to the enemy. On the other hand, if he arrested Green on a charge of treason, he was afraid that the garrison, largely civilian and many of them employees of De Beers in peace time, might mutiny and upset the plans of the Commander-in-Chief. So he held back until Kimberley had been relieved and then demanded that Green be arrested. The result was disastrous for him. Sir John French was totally unsympathetic. A transcript of their conversation was later sent to Rhodes which makes it clear that French considered that Kekewich had failed in his duty by his inability to work with Rhodes amicably. That night French left Kimberley without having settled the matter with Kekewich and the following morning, when he went to his office, Kekewich discovered that he had been replaced in command of the garrison on French's orders.[29] As Kekewich later wrote of Rhodes "I was very unlucky in being associated with one who in my opinion had such a poor conception of his duty to his country. My experience of him was that nothing was too mean or too underhand for him to do in his own interests." The presence of Rhodes in Kimberley during the siege undoubtedly exacerbated relations between civilians and military there and the local press was inevitably drawn into the row on the side of the boss. In Mafeking Baden-Powell also used the local newspaper for purposes of propaganda and information. Its editor did not like being subject to censorship and control either, and said so in the introduction to his souvenir edition of the *Mafeking Mail.* But he had to put up with it: there was no Rhodes to tell him different.[30]

In the absence of accurate news gathered on the spot, there was a rich market for rumour and half-truth, some of which inevitably made its way into London newspapers. During the weeks when no news at all was coming out of Ladysmith in November and early December 1899, correspondents with Buller's force had to take over the job. There was little they could do except travel on the armored train as far towards Ladysmith as it dared to go and report hearing sounds of bombardment. This was supplemented by news from an occasional escapee from Ladysmith or a runner who had managed to evade the Boer cordon and bring despatches through from General White. But there was not much that could be told for, even if there was a story, the censorship imposed by Colonel Jones at Chieveley was stringent. A few runners, acting for correspondents in Ladysmith, or for Natal newspapers managed to get through to Pietermaritzburg or to Buller's force during this period. They sometimes brought with them stories of brilliant victories involving massive Boer losses, which had later to be revised. Within the three towns civilians and army alike fretted at the lack of news from outside. Many were convinced that the "authorities" knew more and were deliberately keeping quiet. The thirst for news, any news, was universal and inhabitants of each siege town particularly wanted news of when they were to be relieved and what was happening in the other two. In place of fact rumours abounded. Siege town inhabitants did not know and would probably not have believed that senior officers were often as much in the dark as they were themselves; neither Buller nor Methuen were much given to communicating information. But, as Kekewich complained, ". . . for months I have done my best to supply daily all intelligence information that I considered might be useful, but I have never been furnished with an intelligence report, or with any information except on one occasion when I notified that unless I was supplied with some details as to the military situation I should not be able to answer to the question as to the garrison considered necessary to leave in this place.[31] The war correspondents sometimes found that civilians expected them to have the latest information simply because they were news men. Neilly came to dread the cross questioning to which he was subjected in Mafeking:

When a more than usually important lie is circulated, puzzled citizens crowd around the equally puzzled special correspondent to know if he has heard anything on the subject from the Staff. They believe that the unfortunate newspaper man is a kind of wizard who knows everything, past, present, and to come.[32]

The effects of poor communications, Boer interventions and censorship were that news both from and to the three towns came sporadically and much pruned, days and weeks after the events had taken place, and sometimes out of sequence. In Natal this happened even before the siege set in; several correspondents found that their accounts of the battle of Elandslaagte were mangled. The censor was blamed and Bennett Burleigh soon peppered his despatches to the *Daily Telegraph* with vigorous complaints. Editorial staff and military correspondents at home tried to explain events as best they could, but all agreed that one could not know what was happening in the three towns until they had been relieved. Even when fuller news did come through in the form of letters and diaries from the correspondents, there were often gaps in the narrative, or they came in the wrong sequence. In many instances the greater part of a correspondent's copy arrived after the siege had been raised and was often published in no particular date order. There was a flood of letters from Ladysmith in late March and early April relating to events as far back as November. Some correspondents seem to have given up trying to send out their copy at all. The *Daily Telegraph* received no news from the town except indirectly through Bennett Burleigh and its correspondent in Pietermaritzburg, both of them dependent on news from runners and the occasional successful escapee from the town. Burleigh left in Ladysmith a local reporter, R. J. McHugh, who had covered the situation in northern Natal before his arrival. McHugh's copy was sent off after the siege was raised and was published in the newspaper between March 28 and April 3. [33] There was a lesser trickle of letters from Kimberley by mid March covering the whole of the siege. Only letters from Mafeking came through in significant quantity before the siege was raised, but the last six weeks of the siege were given little coverage, being overtaken by the relief. Once Mafeking had been relieved the Press concentrated on accounts of the relief, before dropping the whole subject as events moved on towards the march on Pretoria. Those correspondents who subsequently published their despatches as books did so partly because of public interest and partly because their newspapers had published only a fraction of what they wrote. This was usually because the Boers had captured and retained despatches, but not always. A good proportion of Hamilton's despatches from Mafeking were not published either by *The Times* or by *Black & White*, his other employer. Most of these probably never got through, but of those that did many were significantly different in the book because passages which had been censored were replaced; but for this it would not have been so obvious that in Mafeking the Barolong were armed by the British and fighting with them from the start.[34] By contrast Pearse of the *Daily News* had his copy severely cut by his paper. Very little of it had got through the Boer lines during the siege. Some letters have survived among the papers of Reuters' correspondent with the Boer army at Ladysmith, James De Villiers Roos, who used them and other correspondents' despatches as a source of intelligence for the military authorities in Pretoria and then handed them out to soldiers in the camp as souvenirs.[35] The editor of the *Daily News*, confronted with a massive bundle of papers at the end of March, almost as month after the siege had been raised, picked out a few picturesque anecdotes culminating in Pearse's account of Christmas Day to make two short articles for the newspaper. Everything else was ignored, so Pearse had no option but to find a publisher. As for Kimberley, the big story there, the running row between Rhodes and Kekewich, was deliberately suppressed by the Government. Kekewich sent an account to *The Times* which was not published, probably because of the intervention of St John Broderick, soon to replace Lord Lansdowne at the War Office, on the orders of Arthur Balfour.[36]

Some of the difficulties encountered by journalists in the siege towns were also found by others accompanying the relieving forces and were to recur throughout the war. The Army's attitude towards war correspondents was not in general helpful. Although the correspondents wore military style clothing, they were civilians and there was a culture clash between Army and Press which some never bridged. Many senior officers shared the aristocratic disdain for the Press still expressed by some prominent public figures and were suspicious of journalists. The war did much to improve matters as Army and Press got to know each other on an unprecedented scale. Some life long friendships were made in the unpromising surroundings of a siege town, to be cemented annually for decades at the Ladysmith dinner held in London. Some of the difficulties, particularly the delays and disorder in sending off despatches were due quite simply to unfamiliarity among officers with the practicalities of dealing with Press matters. In the many small wars of the late Victorian period there was only one censor and a handful of Press men. In South Africa, there were dozens of censors, scattered over a vast country, often not knowing quite what they should do or even who to ask for advice. There was no book of rules for the guidance of censors until 1901 and very few to help the inexperienced correspondent. But most correspondents accepted, albeit with a grumble, the need for care and secrecy over operational matters. As John Stuart, speaking for most of the correspondents in Ladysmith, remarked "I fully recognize the need of a Press Censorship, especially in such a siege as this." He just wished it was better organized and more helpful.[37]

NOTES

1. Bodleian Library: Lady Milner Papers VM52 13.2.1900 Constance Stanley Countess of Derby to Violet Cecil. Lord Edward Cecil was in Mafeking with Baden-Powell.
2. Bodleian Library: Lady Milner Papers VM 682/15 27.2.1900 Agnes Jekyll to Violet Cecil
3. There is little evidence as to how newspapers planned their strategy in the early stages. *The Times* sent out its chief war correspondent, Lionel James, early in September with instructions to join Sir George White in Natal and take orders from its Johannesburg correspondent, W F Monypenny, who was initially put in charge of all *Times* correspondents in the field. (News International Archive Moberly Bell Letter Books Letter to Lionel James 27.9.1899. Bennett Burleigh of the *Daily Telegraph* and Henry Nevinson of the *Daily Chronicle* visited the Transvaal first and travelled to the Boer camp at Sandspruit, but they were not permitted to stay and were in Ladysmith by October 5. (Bodleian Library: Ms Eng Misc e 610/6 Henry Nevinson Diaries entries for October 3-6 1899)

4. Bodleian Library Ms Eng misc e 610/6 Nevinson left for South Africa on September 9 having completed his last leader on September 6.

5. Rhodes House Library, Lionel James Papers. James to his wife 1 August 1898 Atbara Camp ". . . A lot more correspondents arrived yesterday . . . Maxwell of the Standard, the last named is an awful creature making his maiden debut as a war correspondent" James later revised his opinion of Maxwell and during the siege they messed together.

6. *Morning Leader* 18 November 1899 Letter written 23 October ". . .The brilliant feat of arms accomplished at Elandslaagte on Saturday by Gen French and our troops was the first real battle I had ever seen."

7. There are several accounts of Lynch's defection, eg W Hutton Ladysmith journal National Army Museum 82392-6-1-13 entry for Monday December 4. In his autobiography Lynch claimed that he was only trying to make his way to the British lines on the Tugela and was caught by the Boers. The British military authorities, however, did not believe this. Lynch was sent to Pretoria where he continued to send telegrams, apparently stopped by the censor at Aden, as none were published. The censor recommended that he lose his license "for sending press messages which are very pro-Boer" (PRO/WO108/306 Telegram from Aden 3 January 1900 to the War Office.) Lynch's name appears on the list of correspondents recommended for a medal but has been struck off.(PRO WO 100/371)

8. The *Daily Mail* had two correspondents, Steevens and Reid. The latter also represented the Natal Witness. He covered events in Ladysmith before Steevens arrived and sent occasional telegrams to the Daily Mail after Steevens died. Similarly, the Standard had Maxwell but also used Mitchell who had been on the staff of the Johannesburg Star before the war. Mitchell covered events in Northern Natal for the Standard until Maxwell arrived and continued to send occasional telegrams when Maxwell was too unwell to get about. He died of enteric fever in January 1900.

9. J Beaumont 'Reporting the Siege' in Iain R Smith (ed), *The Siege of Mafeking* 2 vols (Brenthurst Press, 2001), vol 2 ch 3 for the Mafeking correspondents.

10. For Luard; University of Witwatersrand William Cullen Library A1566 Mafeking Siege records,(Papers of Vere Stent while in Mafeking) Letter from Vere Stent to E W C Luard dated Mafeking February 20, 1900. Luard appears in the Eton Register but nothing is said about his being a journalist. According to J Howard Pim, a volunteer officer during the siege "Luard has behaved in a very sickening way over the shelling which undeniably was very unpleasant. Be this as it may he need not have cleared out of Kimberley and lived in some place beyond Beaconsfield for the last week. He has also sent some ludicrous telegrams with sheer funk in every word. He is unfit to be allowed outside, a bounder but plays the part of the tame cat to perfection." (University of the Witwatersrand Wiliam Cullen Library A881/Ca 3 Letters of J H Pim to his wife) In his autobiography, *An Editor Looks Back*, Green mentions his connection with the *Daily Telegraph* and also that he had worked for Reuters. The lists of accredited corespondents which survive among the papers of De Villiers Roos in Pretoria (National Archive Pretoria A739/4) show him as a correspondent for the *Daily Mail* on October 14. The *Daily News* published letters and telegrams from Oliver anonymously, but in one

instance mentions that their correspondent was called Herbert Oliver and was the son of a London journalist. *Daily News,* 19 March 1900.

11. E Oliver Ashe, *Besieged by the Boers* (London, 1900) was one of two accounts widely available. There was also a colonial edition. The account by T Phelan, *The Siege of Kimberley,* was not published until 1913. George Green sent portions of his wife's siege diary for publication in the *Daily Telegraph* after the siege was raised

12. *Daily Mail,* 22 September 1899 article by Ian McAllen "He no doubt knows the game of war by heart, but he is better at playing than planning it."

13. *Daily Mail,* 8 February 1900. Article by Major Arthur Griffiths. The article is not devoted exclusively to Kekewich and is one of the few devoted to him that appeared in the press at all.

14. For other examples of the treatment of Baden-Powell see too J Beaumont Art. Cit. op.cit. above

15. *The Star,* 2 January 1899. Letter written 31 December 1898 in the wake of the Edgar case, which gave rise to meetings of protest in Johannesburg, described by the Star as "the new Rhodesian agitation at Johannesburg."

16. *Morning Leader,* 2 March 1900

17. Wits William Cullen Library A1566 Vere Stent to H A Gwynne no date but probably early February 1900: "Runners, too, are of course a source of great expense, and I have been sending south, to Kimberley, duplicates of my despatches, which the Government sent north. There are a number of correspondents here and the Government were forced to curtail the length of our messages, and I was only able to obtain special privileges for the Agency by undertaking to send runners south at my own expense, carrying the Government despatches, in return for their despatch of my rather voluminous correspondence north.

18. *Morning Leader,* 30 April 1900. Letter from Ernest Smith in Kimberley: "Kimberley was well served in the matter of runners, the Pressmen locked up there being so few that they were allowed to use the military official runners to get their news through the Boer lines."

19. *News International Archive:* Moberley Bell Letter Book Bell to Leo Amery 27.10 1899 ". . . Reuter still manages to get telegrams generally before any paper, always before us (so far as wires from the field are concerned.) It seems to me that the Press Censor may favour them on the ground that they supply <u>all</u> the papers but this is not at all in accordance with our views and we maintain that telegrams should be sent forward in precisely the order that they are forwarded from the front or reach the Censor. That this is not so is evident from the list sent you in my last and I beg that you will use all practicable measures to get this done.

20. News International Archive: Moberley Bell Letter Book: Bell to Leo Amery 27.10 1899 ". . . Reuters still manages to get telegrams generally before any paper, always before us (so far as wires from the field are concerned.) It seems to me that the Press Censor may favour them on the ground that they supply <u>all</u> the papers but this is not at all in accordance with our views and we maintain that telegrams should be sent forward in precisely the order that they are forwarded from the front or reach the Censor. That this is not so is evident from the list sent you in my last and I beg that you will use all practicable measures to get this done.

21. National Army Museum Walker Archives 7611 - 87 December 14 by heliograph "heavy firing heard yesterday near Colenso our two howitzers keep down fire boer six inch gun west town all well but enteric increases Steevens has it slightly. Nevinson (then signature of Altham) In the paper of December 18 this appeared as follows:-Heavy firing was heard yesterday morning near Colenso. Our two howitzers are keeping down the fire of the Boer 6-inch gun west of the town. All is well here *Daily Chronicle*, Monday January 1 1900. December 28 (By heliograph via Weenen, December 30, 10.10am) This morning our two naval 4.7 guns fired seven shots in rapid succession at the Boer 6-in gun on the side of Mount Bulwan. It has not fired a shot since. Yesterday the bombardment was very heavy and at night there was a scare in the Boer lines, and a violent outburst of rifle firing. The two wounded officers of the Devons are doing well. National Army Museum 7611 - 87 Walker Archives Dec 28 our two naval four point seven guns fired seven rapid shots at six inch gun on Bulwan five this morning it has not fired since (then a passage struck out - official enquiry into complaints into mismanagement Intombi) bombardment very heavy yesterday scare at night in Boer lines violent rifle fire Devon wounded officers doing well (the top part of this has been removed all that can be seen is . . ambulance." For Hutton and James see, J Beaumont 'The British Press and Censorship During the South African War 1899-1902', *South African Historical Journal*, vol 41, pp. 271-2.

22. UNISA Archive S968.04881 Diary of Douglas Howard Gill Lieut 21st Batt R.F.A On October 13 there was a chance of an engagement with the Boers, but nothing happened. "We heard afterwards from outposts of BMR that the Boers were there, about 7 miles further on, taking up a position. The BMR officers had been watching them all day, but our Intelligence Officer (Major Altham) would not believe them. If we had attacked them in this favourable position at the beginning of the campaign, it would doubtless have had a material effect." Frank Rhodes Boer war Diary National Army Museum 718-26-1, 2 February 1900; "Altham as head of the Intelligence was an unfortunate appointment, he has rubbed so many people up the wrong way."

23. Hanbury Tracy papers owned by Mr R.W. Nicholson. Letter to Sir Douglas Straight November 16 1899, transcribed from shorthand by the censor. It was never sent to London as it accompanied an uncensored report which Neilly tried to sneak out of Mafeking along with a letter addressed to his wife. Subsequently the objections made by the censor were withdrawn, but by then the Boers had reinforced their guns with Long Tom guns, so the bombardment was no longer farcical.

24. Hanbury Tracy papers include a copy of a letter of support signed by the other correspondents and a letter of apology from Neilly.

25. Douglas Gill Diary, UNISA Archive S968.04881 p.105

26. *Morning Leader*, 23 January 1900, for the Christmas day service. Smith also wrote about the party in a letter which left Ladysmith on January 10 and was finally published on February 27. His account of Wagon Hill, dated January 10 was published on February 26. He draws attention to inadequate fortifications in the flow of the narrative eg The Boers managed to take fortifications at the southern end of the hill in a surprise attack and use them for cover but at the other end "they clambered to the top of the hill with

equal stealth, but as we had next to no earth works there they were unable to obtain such advantageous shelter." For James see J Beaumont art. Cit. loc. Cit.

27. University of the Witwatersrand Wiliam Cullen Library A881/Ca 3 Letter from J Howard Pim to his wife 19 December 1899; Queens Lancashire Regiment Museum Preston Diaries of Lieutenant Colonel Kekewich entry for 17 December 1899: "I have thought fit to publish only a portion of what is in the papers. It is difficult to realize the difficulties we are under as to spies, and enemy's sympathizers in our midst. It is impossible here to arrange anything in connection with an attack without its being at once communicated to the enemy outside. I feel certain that the different columns have found, and will continue to find, all their intended movements are notified to the enemy".

28. The Queens Lancashire Regiment Museum Diaries of Lt Col Kekewich, Accession No 650.002, entry for 11 December 1899.

29. This account is based upon material in a document Kekewich prepared after the war for the War Office in which he made a formal complaint against Rhodes. It seems to have been given at some stage to his Chief of Staff in Kimberley, Major O'Meara, who used it when he wrote his book *Kekewich in Kimberley*, published in 1926. O'Meara's papers, including the document, are now in University of the Witwatersrand William Cullen Library Ms A64 . Rhodes House Ms Africa s 228 for the transcript of the conversation with French.

30. *Mafeking Mail,* preface to the souvenir edition; "The scruples of the Press Censor frequently came in between preparation and publication." The Editor, G.N. Whales, implies that this was every bit as great an impediment to publication as paper shortages and bombardment.

31. Kekewich, Diaries, ref. cit, entry for 18 December 1899.

32. *Pall Mall Gazette,* 18 April 1899. Article written ca 11 February 1899. When a more than usually important lie is circulated, puzzled citizens crowd around the equally puzzled special correspondent to know if he has heard anything on the subject from the Staff. They believe that the unfortunate newspaper man is a kind of wizard who knows everything, past, present, and to come.

33. McHugh succumbed to enteric in December which may explain his lack of enterprise. By mid December most native runners had become too scared for their safety to send messages for the correspondents – see Nevinson telegrams dated December 21and 22, *Daily Chronicle,* December 30 1899.

34. J Beaumont Reporting the siege in op cit above pp.337-8.

35. Pretoria Archive A 739/4 for original despatches from Pearse to the *Daily News* dated November 9, November 14 and December 11 written on flimsy sheets from a manifold book. None show evidence of having been censored.

36. British Library: Add 49773 Balfour to Chamberlain 10 April 1900. Balfour believed that Rhodes has been maligned by Kekewich and should be cleared, but privately since Kekewich made his accusations privately and "I do not want the amount of dirty linen which after this war must inevitably be washed in public to be unnecessarily increased." Bodleian Library: Lady Milner Papers VM35 29.3.1900 St John Brodrick to Violet Cecil "I hope I stopped the publishing of the Rhodes-Kekewich squabble by very drastic use

of Arthur's name and the harm it would do. Let there be a spice of heroism about the defence of Kimberley . . ."

37. John Stuart, *Pictures of War* (London, 1901), pp.213-5.

Chapter Two
MOBILIZING THE MASSES: THE ORGANIZATION OF GERMAN PROPAGANDA DURING WORLD WAR ONE
David Welch

The First World War made greater demands on the material and human resources of the nations involved than any previous conflict. It was no longer sufficient simply to organise industry or to mobilise manpower in order to carry a modern state through a long war. Of course it would prove to be a war of intense industrial competition and scientific innovation; the manufacture of arms and munitions became critically important. But equally important was the need to engage the will and support of whole nations. For the first time belligerent governments were required to mobilise entire civilian populations into 'fighting communities'. Consequently all governments were faced with the urgent task of justifying their entry into the war to their own people. In Germany the necessity for the Imperial government to generate popular support in the first phase of the war was largely superfluous. The immediate emotional impact of the announcement of war led to a sense of unity and togetherness on the part of the German people, which invariably manifested itself in an hysterical hatred of the 'outsider' or enemy.

   The German government on the outbreak of war at once surrendered to the local army commanders extensive political powers over civil administration. General mobilisation was accompanied by the proclamation of the Prussian Law of Siege which gave sole responsibility for 'public safety' to the Deputy Commanding Generals in each of the twenty-four army corps districts.

   The vagueness of this law not only allowed the army to wrestle responsibility and power from the Reichstag but significantly it marked the beginning of military interference in all aspects of internal affairs for the duration of the war. The growing political power of the German military extended far beyond the Prussian War Ministry which they, and not civilians, controlled. At the same time, a Bavarian State-of-War Law transformed authority to local Deputy Commanding Generals, subject to the supervision of the War Ministry in Munich. The elitist background and anachronistic values of the German officer corps and their belief in the primacy of 'militarism' over political considerations meant that they were largely ill-prepared and ill-suited for taking control of internal affairs. As all matters concerning the war effort were considered to be within their domain, the military also assumed responsibility for manipulating public opinion by means of propaganda and censorship. From the beginning their overriding fear was that the soldiers' morale could be undermined by the home front. Wartime measures that affected the civilian population were invariably taken with the troop's welfare uppermost in mind. The army leadership's contempt for politics and for civilian bureaucrats together with their suspicion of the masses whom they perceived as a threat, resulted in a crucial failure to understand or trust the home front and led inevitably to a widening polarisation of views about the nature of the war and how it should be conducted. This was somewhat ironic, for in many ways the army saw themselves as *the* integrating force in German society. Indeed, in their desire for stability they were even prepared to support, for example, trade union demands for political and economic reforms. In return they wished to conduct the war removed from all criticism and would not tolerate any form of parliamentary control. As such they were not prepared to allow politicians or political parties to participate in the decision-making process. Even Chancellor Bethmann Hollweg was removed from office when his differences with the High Command became irreconcilable. It is in this context that we see the major failure of the Kaiser - his inability and unwillingness to use the monarchy to provide the necessary unifying force between conflicting interest groups. I have argued elsewhere that the eventual collapse of Germany was due less to the authorities' failure to disseminate nationalist propaganda (as right-wing apologists would later claim) than to the inability of the military command and the monarchy to reinforce this propaganda by acknowledging the importance of public opinion in forging an effective link between leadership and people. It was not simply a question of the military cliques' reluctance to establish the machinery for manipulating public opinion, rather they failed to take the trouble to understand the psychology of the German people. Indeed, their own reactionary attitudes and fears prevented them from recognising propaganda's *real* potential as an integrating force to be used positively. However, this would emerge later. In 1914 the public's ignorance concerning the Law of Siege and the extent to which the army (a 'collection of tyrannies') had now become the arbiter of the nation's civil and domestic life had yet to be fully recognised.[1]

The Organisation of Official Propaganda

The first impression that emerges from the study of propaganda in the Great War is one of generally un-coordinated improvisation. By the end of the conflict, however, propaganda would, for the first time, be elevated to the position of a branch of government. It is ironic (in the light of later criticisms) that of all the belligerents, Germany had been the only power to pay serious attention to propaganda before 1914. For some years and with considerable thoroughness, Imperial Germany had been attempting to influence popular and official opinion in foreign countries. Therefore when war broke out in August

1914 it had a distinct initial advantage over the propaganda of the allied governments. Germany had been developing a semi-official propaganda network through her embassies, legations, consular offices and branches of German banks and shipping companies - all of whom acted as agents for the dissemination of literature favourable to the Fatherland.

After the proclamation of hostilities and the unprovoked invasion of Belgium, German propaganda was immediately directed towards putting out in neutral countries the German version of the causes of the war, and the hostile intentions of her enemies. One of the first propaganda agencies set up to influence neutral opinion was the so-called Erzberger Office, named after its director Matthias Erzberger a leading figure of the Zentrum Party (Catholic Centre Party). It was set up under the auspices of the Navy Ministry and worked in close collaboration with the Foreign Office.[2] Erzberger's first task was to co-ordinate the work of foreign propaganda, for after the outbreak of war, official and semi-official propaganda agencies had proliferated. In October 1914, there were some 27 such agencies. Erzberger was instrumental in establishing a central co-ordinating body, the Central Office for the Foreign Service (*Zentralstelle für Auslandsdienst*), attached to the Foreign Office and under the direction of the former ambassador to Tokyo, Baron von Mumm. Its main function seems to have been to analyse the general war situation and to issue propaganda directives and distribute its own literature, but it was never totally successful in reducing the chaos.

The Wolff Telegraph Bureau, which was subsidised by the German Government, also attempted to feed a steady stream of pro-German news into international channels. However, its effectiveness was limited by the fact that under a pre-war agreement with Reuters and Havas, Wolff was responsible only for Germany, her colonies, Austria-Hungary, and Scandinavia. At the very outset of hostilities, one of the first major acts taken by Great Britain to undermine the German propaganda effort was to cut the undersea cables between Germany and America (the Emden-New York cable line). Thus, all news from Germany, with the exception of wireless reports, had to proceed via London, the cable centre of the world. The result was that Germany's wireless transmitter at Nauen became her sole means of telegraphic communication with the world outside Europe. To offset this catastrophe, Germany made great strides in wireless telegraphy during the war. A special agency, the überseedienst Transozean GmbH, was set up to disseminate a wide variety of propaganda and to protect the Reich's interests abroad. The Nauen station, the most powerful transmitting station in the world, reaching as far afield as Persia and Mexico, gradually developed into an efficient and skilful distributor of propaganda. It turned out war news 24 hours a day, and while it was not always blatantly pro-German, it constantly emphasised German victories and the superiority of German culture and the German way of life.[3]

From the first, Transozean utilised its large pecuniary resources by either acquiring control of neutral newspapers or launching new ones. Most notable was *Germania* covering South America and in association with Ostasiatische Lloyd, it founded 'The War' and a Chinese edition of *Deutsche Zeitung*. The *Continental Korrespondenz* was published in English, Spanish and Portuguese and was designed to furnish the neutral press with ready made copy. Numerous polyglot periodicals and leaflets were also distributed.[4] Furthermore a huge propaganda campaign was launched in the United States of America spearheaded by the *Staats-Zeitung* in New York.[5]

The semi-official *Presse-Abteilung zur Beeinflussung der Neutralen* was responsible for the 'War Chronicle' in German, English, French, Spanish, and Dutch, and *Die Toekomat* published in Holland in Dutch. This organisation was also responsible for a propagandistic comic paper printed in Spain (La guasa international). The *Hamburger Fremdenblatt* with its 'Welt im Bild' published in twelve languages and the *Hamburger Nachrichten* with Spanish and Portuguese editions were the first German newspapers to recognise the importance of propaganda directed at neutral countries. But despite all attempts to supervise their work in neutral, allied, and enemy countries, German propaganda remained generally uncoordinated and heavy-handed. The chief themes of foreign propaganda were: to give an exaggerated impression of the military successes achieved by Germany in the war; to influence neutral opinion; to show the dissension's that existed between the Entente powers due to their divergent war aims; and to encourage nationalist and revolutionary movements within the British and Russian empires. These campaigns were used in an attempt to control neutral opinion, and the object seems to have been to impress, even at the risk of intimidating, rather than to persuade. Because the Supreme Command remained wedded to an expansionist programme, this made it difficult to appeal to groups like the Poles, Finns, and the revolutionary Russians. Nevertheless, it was undoubtedly concerned to win over neutrals and proclaim their support for self-determination of national groups, freedom of the seas, etc. It is not the purpose of this work to gauge the success or otherwise of German propaganda abroad. By emphasising common interests and the certainty of a German victory, evidence suggests that Germany was able to control opinion and encourage her allies in Austro-Hungary, Bulgaria and Turkey. However despite elaborate explanations justifying her military actions, German propaganda failed (with one or two notable exceptions) to prevent the majority of neutral opinion from remaining sharply anti-German, as it had been since the invasion of Belgium.[6]

Clearly in the initial stages of the war, Germany was more conscious of the need to influence neutral countries than her enemies. After the violation of Belgian sovereignty, neutral opinion quickly crystallised against Germany. Therefore unlike Britain and France, German propaganda was immediately thrown on the defensive and subsequently there was a greater need to explain her war aims and to justify her position. The manner in which the war started also forced the Government and the military authorities to take energetic measures to control public opinion at home. The initial measures taken reveal again that Germany was ahead in this respect, although partly as a result of the *Burgfrieden* (literally 'fortress truce', but in practice, a 'political truce' or 'spirit of 1914'), it tended to concentrate on establishing propaganda agencies for abroad. Nevertheless, during the first year of the war, numerous bodies were set up and guidelines laid down in order to mobilise opinion within Germany. Despite the self-congratulatory nature of British propagandists and the criticisms of German nationalists after the War, Germany was better prepared and more willing to manipulate and manage news and opinions than her enemies.

The military offensive that Germany had undertaken (and the hostile reaction which greeted it) had persuaded it that morale at home mattered a great deal and that total warfare could not be confined to the military sphere. Even Lord Northcliffe, who was later to become British Director of Propaganda to Enemy Countries, acknowledged that Germany had taken the initiative in stimulating the interest of the public in the war. As early as November 1914 he wrote in a letter to Asquith: 'I find that whereas there is in Germany immense enthusiasm for the war, there exists in many parts of this country apathy, ignorance, or ridiculous optimism'.[7] Northcliffe contrasted the position in Germany and in Britain. In Germany a xenophobia was being whipped up by the work of photographers, artists, war correspondents, posters, and the new medium of the cinema, whereas the British people were offered 'nothing but casualty lists'.[8] Such propaganda was also being reinforced by the actual military successes of the German armies in the first year of the war, which suggested a rapid victory.

The major concern of the German Government was to maintain the *Burgfrieden* by uniting the 'fighting people' at home behind their troops fighting abroad, in support of the objectives for which it had gone to war. From the beginning then, policy makers were significantly influenced in their political decisions by considerations of propaganda and public opinion. It was felt absolutely crucial to link the domestic 'political truce' with the notion of a defensive war. In many ways the propaganda of World War I was pre-eminently a propaganda of war aims. This was particularly the case in Germany after the invasion of Belgium and the early military successes. However the mobilisation of the masses was looked upon essentially as a negative task. The military groups tended initially to resent the claims of the new weapon of propaganda as a slur on their own abilities. Their instinctive reaction was to restrict or forbid discussion of war aims by means of censorship and coercion.[9] Nevertheless in order to build on the foundations of the *Burgfrieden* it was also necessary to stress the positive aspects of Germany's new found unity. This meant concentrating on certain themes that reinforced the official view that Germany was waging a war of self-defence against the aggressive encircling Entente. The main topics stressed in home propaganda were: the superiority of German military organisation and the certainty of a swift victory; the need for fortitude (*Durchhalten*) and unity; and the historic mission of German culture in the face of the image and ways of the enemy. Not surprisingly, the desire for national expansion which was associated with influential Pan-German groups, was played down in the first year of the war. To disseminate these themes the military authorities called upon the resources of the individual media. The way they were employed and the degree of control and censorship exercised, depended largely on how important they were considered for the programmes of 'patriotic instruction'.

However, we need first to return to the origins of the war to discover the true explanation for Germany's relative preparedness. Because Germany was immediately forced onto the defensive, she was required to explain her war aims not only to neutrals but also to the German people. Although the announcement of war was greeted with considerable enthusiasm, there were still deep divisions and anxieties within German society despite the spontaneous demonstrations of patriotism. The *Burgfrieden* did not symbolise the end of these divisions, rather it was an act of faith on the part of the nation and represented reserved support of a just war and a swift victory.

The German authorities' attempts to construct a propaganda machinery to explain war aims and maintain morale reveals their concern and their recognition of the need for an enduring consensus. Contingency plans for co-ordinating such measures had already been formulated in July 1914 when the Prussian War Ministry issued instructions that were to be carried out in the event of war. Their overriding fear was that the demands of war might exacerbate internal divisions in different parts of the country, especially among national

minorities seeking substantial gains. Accordingly they confirmed that the Military
Commanders would be given full powers under the Prussian Law of the State of
Siege in 1851 to take whatever measures they felt necessary in their respective
districts.[10] Chancellor Bethmann Hollweg immediately attempted to persuade
Erich von Falkenhayn, the Prussian War Minister, that such a declaration could
have 'disastrous consequences for the solidarity and strength of patriotic feeling,
and that any possible military advantages would not compensate for the harm
that could be caused in the area of politics or ideals'.[11] The military retorted that
as plans for mobilisation had already been based on the declaration of the State of
Siege, then it was too late to change them now. Although this was intended to
facilitate the co-ordination of the war effort, in practice it led to individual
military commanders arbitrarily suspending different sections of the constitution.
Eventually in December 1916, the War Minister was given the title of 'Supreme
Military Commander' (*Obermilitärbefehlshaber*) and with it the power to co-ordinate
the measures taken by the Military Commanders but not to issue orders to them.
Only in the last days of the Reich would the War Minister be given the authority
to issue such orders.

In order to appreciate the complex manner in which the German
Empire was administered, it is imperative to have some understanding of the role
of the Prussian War Ministry in defining social and economic policies. But having
said that, the most important and certainly the largest formation within the
General Headquarters (*Grosse Hauptquartier* - GHQ) was the High Command
(*Oberste Heeresleitung*, or OHL). The General Headquarters was so immense that it
needed 11 railway trains to transport it from one theatre of war to another. The
Kaiser as 'Supreme Warlord' was formally its head, although under the provisions
of the Imperial Constitution, the Chief of the Prussian General Staff was
responsible for giving operational orders for the entire German army, and as such
was given the new title of Chief of the General Staff of the Field Army. The
important task of providing a link between the OHL and the Government in
Berlin was undertaken by representatives of the Chancellor and the Foreign
Office who were allocated staff and a department within the OHL.[12] The OHL
was divided into various divisions. Section I was the largest division and was
responsible for operational planning, and played little part in political matters.
Section II, under the ambitious leadership of General Bauer, would eventually
assume an important role in the militarisation and control of the German
economy under the Auxiliary Labour Law (see chapter 4). However it was Section
IIIb, the News Section (*Nachrichtungabteilung*), that was responsible for the military
management of all questions dealing with censorship, public opinion, and
propaganda. The head of Section IIIb for the entire war was the rather
mysterious figure of Major (later Lieutenant Colonel) Walter Nicolai.

Section IIIb had been set up in 1870/1 when it developed out of
Section B of the Third (French) Section of the General Headquarters. It was at
first charged to gather news of the enemy, but not to print it. Up until 1904
Section IIIb consisted mainly of a few officers responsible for protecting the
French news gathering service. It was expanded to include Russia after the Russo-
Japanese War of 1905. The navy possessed their own news gathering service
dealing specifically with the movements of the English fleet. Indeed, this division
was maintained even during the First World War, although the army High
Command recognised its drawbacks. At the outbreak of war, Section IIIb was
responsible for the collection of intelligence reports from abroad and for counter-

espionage at home. However as the war progressed, and the strains within German society became more acute, Section IIIb increasingly concerned itself with political and economic analyses. Eventually it developed into one of the most important sections within the OHL, dealing mainly with censorship and establishing guidelines for propaganda.

Given the antiquated organisational structure of the German army, it is perhaps surprising to discover that Section IIIb responded to the demands of war with considerable efficiency (though with little imagination or flexibility). It attempted to solve the problem of co-ordinating propaganda through the *Zivilversorgungsschein* – penetrating civil society with military values. Such reactionary ideas were bound, in a society undergoing profound structural changes, to cause further polarizations of opinions. And they did. However in 1914, the nation was held together by a rare agreement that existed within the OHL on the objectives to be pursued regarding the civilian population. Quite simply these objectives were: 1) to maintain the *Burgfrieden*, and 2) to prevent criticism of Germany's war aims, which in practice meant suppressing the radical left.

The most pressing concern in August 1914 was to prevent the fragile 'political truce' from collapsing. As the organisational structure for the co-ordination and dissemination of propaganda had yet to be established, the OHL was more concerned with establishing general principles and guidelines. Thus on 13 August, the Chiefs of the General Staff of the Field Army issued a proclamation to the various government ministries and the General Commanders stressing the importance of safeguarding the *Burgfrieden* at all costs. Signed by Moltke's First Quartermaster General, Hermann von Stein (later to become Minister for War), the document emphasised that the 'favourable attitude of the parties and the press towards the war is of great importance to the OHL', and warned that any attempts to undermine this unity would be 'energetically suppressed'.[13]

Censorship and the Press

The outbreak of war saw the establishment of censorship in all the belligerent countries. Most nations considered it vital from the point of view of national security to control the means of communication. And of all the means available none was more highly regarded (or suspected depending on one's political allegiances) than the press. It was invariably argued that a rigid censorship was necessary to prevent the enemy from securing valuable information. In Germany, the justification for tight censorship was the upholding of the *Burgfrieden* and a fear that newspapers might publish sensitive military information. There was little in this fear, for the only wire service in Germany was the 'official' Wolff Telegraph Bureau (WTB) established in 1871 with a government guarantee that it would deal exclusively with all official news. In return, Wolff agreed that all 'sensitive material' would first be cleared with the Foreign Office. Thus when war broke out, WTB became the German newspapers' sole source of official war news.[14]

The most striking features of the German press on the eve of the war were its decentralisation, its commercialism and its size. Although a product of nineteenth century liberalism, the popular press, far from being a source of conflict, must be viewed as a force for stability and integration within German society. A tradition of government management of news had been established under Bismarck and Wilhelm II. Between 1878 and 1890, for example, over 155 journals and 1,200 other publications had been banned under anti-socialist legislation. The press was not regarded as an independent check on government in the political process, or even as the conscience of the political parties. It was used instead as an instrument of sectionalist propaganda to champion specific causes. Generally it encouraged acceptance of the social system and frequently propagated nationalist and even imperialist ideals. By remaining sectarian in its appeal and outlook and by avoiding contentious issues, the press served as an agent of the *status quo*.

The proliferation of German newspapers in the last decades of the nineteenth century was due to a number of factors associated with Germany's industrial revolution. The unification of Germany was followed by the consolidation of the political parties, growing urbanisation, universal education, and an expanding economy. In 1866 there were approximately 1,500 newspapers, of which 300 were dailies. By 1900, this figure had increased to 3,500 and by 1914 the number of newspapers had risen above 4,000, with a total circulation of between 5,000 and 6,000 million copies.[15] Great Britain by comparison possessed only 2,400 newspapers; and while Germany could boast of almost 2,000 dailies, France had fewer than 500.[16]

Another important feature of the German press during this period was the discovery that newspapers could be profitable commercial enterprises. Therefore along with the 'quality' press, the end of the nineteenth century saw the growth of what later became the mass circulation press. Based on the example of the 'penny press' in Britain, the German *Generalanzeiger*, as this new type of paper was called, flourished largely in the form of provincial and local papers catering for the tastes of the mass reading public. By keeping subscription rates low through extensive advertising and by successfully giving the public what they wanted, the *Generalanzeiger* proliferated, making up nearly half of the newspapers established between 1871 and 1914.[17] The formula was invariably the same; it offered human interest stories, entertainment and news, and often provided extra inducements by way of insurance policies at discount rates. These papers professed a non-political editorial policy though in practice many eventually drifted into specific political allegiances. The *Berliner Lokalanzeiger*, for example which was founded in 1883 by August Scherl, claimed political neutrality but was blatantly conservative in outlook. In 1898 Leopold Ullstein set up the *Berliner Morgenpost* styled on the *Generalanzeiger* but with firm political opinions. The ensuing circulation battle between Scherl and Ullstein resulted in the incorporation of more enlightened editorial comment. By February 1914 the *Morgenpost* had a circulation of 400,000, compared with the 250,000 of the *Lokalanzeiger*.

While the *Generalanzeiger* were becoming politically conscious and more commercialised, the prestigious papers such as the *Frankfurter Zeitung* (founded in 1856 by Leopold Sonnemann) and the *Berliner Tageblatt* (set up in 1871 by Rudolf Mosse), were gaining international reputations for their quality and liberal outlook. Of the overtly political press, the *Norddeutsche Allgemeine Zeitung* (1862), although nominally independent, eventually became an official government daily mouthpiece. By 1894 the Social Democratic Party, despite anti-socialist legislation resulting in fines and imprisonments, could claim 75 newspapers. The central organ of the party was *Vorwärts*, a successful daily which set the example for socialist newspapers throughout Europe. It was particularly admired in Britain, where the socialist press had been slower to get off the ground.[18]

Conservative elites in Germany possessed a deeply entrenched hostility towards commercialisation. By the turn of the century a large portion of the newspaper market was concentrated in the hands of three publishers, Ullstein, Scherl, and Mosse. The consolidation of commercial interests with the advent of the mass circulation press, led to the growth of publishing houses, newspaper chains and advertising agencies. For many conservatives the publishing world of Mosse and the Ullsteins with their liberal notions of gradual political reform, represented the corrupting influence of big-business, and Jewish big-business at that. Traditionally the German press had an educational role which in practice meant that a newspaper was not simply expected to inform but to instruct as well. It was feared that commercial considerations and gimmicks might result in declining standards. Even the *Generalanzeiger* had a seriousness that would have been inconceivable in a Northcliffe or Hearst paper. Nevertheless, the lingering contempt among sections of the ruling elite for the growing commercialism of the German press and their distrust of the motives of the press barons, provides one of the explanations for the immediate imposition of press censorship in August 1914.

Even though most German newspapers supported the *Burgfrieden* and the national cause once the war had started, neither the government nor the military had much confidence in them. The public's thirst for news about the war caused the circulation figures to soar and many papers doubled their daily printings. The government immediately imposed direct controls on the press, creating what one journalist referred to as 'a state of siege on truth'.[19] In addition to controlling news at source, the government also relied on a plethora of regulations issued nationally by the General Staff and regionally by local military commanders. Military policy towards the press, or 'news management', was again the responsibility of Major Nicolai's Section III B of the OHL. The Law of the State of Siege had specifically suspended 'the right to express opinion freely by word, print or picture', only in areas directly endangered by the fighting. However this was quickly applied to the whole country. The military in particular were more or less united in believing that journalists would be unable to distinguish between sensitive and harmless information. They therefore wanted laws passed forbidding the publication of military information, thereby removing their own actions from public criticism. On the same day as the announcement of the State of Siege, Chancellor Bethmann Hollweg issued instructions to the press containing 26 comprehensive prohibitions intended to prevent information that had not been passed by the military censor from being printed.[20]

A day later on 1 August in a secret memorandum sent to every publisher in the Reich, the military authorities outlined with typical thoroughness the guiding principles for the reporting of military information should war break out.[21] The press, they said, must first of all be conscious of their 'heavy responsibility and the consequences of their reports'. The welfare of the Fatherland demanded strict discretion in all matters concerning the High Command. For this reason the press would 'give thanks to the war leadership' for providing guidelines to 'protect the Fatherland'. Tact and insight was required but the Press Bureau of the General Staff would assist the legitimate demands of the nation for news by issuing reports 'as often as possible' to the Military Commanders to pass on to the publishers in their respective districts. Even the act of censorship itself was to be suppressed. Instead the newspapers should 'patriotically educate' the nation of the need for secrecy and remind it of its duty. However they warned ominously: 'By refraining unselfishly from publishing military reports it will spare the military and naval authorities the necessity of taking legal action, the strictest enforcement of which in cases of violation of this prohibition is demanded in the interests of the state.' As far as the press was concerned 'tact and insight' were of little value in such a military straightjacket. Any possibility of a constructive press policy had been destroyed even before the announcement of war. Ironic then that on 2 August the Chief of the General Staff von Moltke remarked that a close relationship between the war leadership and the press was essential as the press 'was an indispensable means of waging war'.[22] A few days later on 10 August a special Press Service was set up under the control of Section IIIb in order to establish clearly defined areas of responsibility between different ministries and to facilitate as efficiently as possible the management of military information.[23] Since the 3 August representatives of the press had been briefed daily by an officer from Section IIIb in the Reichstag. These briefings were to continue and the Foreign Office expanded its section issuing reports (*Referate*) on the domestic and foreign political and economic situation. At these briefings the press were informed of the plans of the General Staff and a principle was quickly established that: 'we will not always be able to reveal everything, but what we will say will be true'.

The effect of these measures was not lost on the press, and the socialist press in particular. *Vorwärts* published a muted editorial protest on 1 August: 'The orders issued by the military authorities force restrictions upon us and threaten the existence of our paper... We take for granted that the members of our Party, because of their training and their loyalty to their convictions, will understand the restraint forced upon us and will remain faithful to us in these trying days'.[24] The military, on the other hand, were concerned that newspapers were still printing military news. On 8 August in a statement issued through the Wolff Telegraph Bureau (WTB) to all publishers, General von Kessel, the Chief Commander in the Marken (the military district which included Berlin), reminded the press, 'for the last time... the printing of news regarding military affairs is prohibited... unless the censorship has made an exception'. Editors were warned in no uncertain terms that 'from now on measures of force will be resorted to against the transgressors. Public warnings have not been lacking'. Emphasising the government's determination to apply coercive measures to recalcitrant editors, the same communiqué announced that the *Tägliche Rundschau für Schlesien und Posen* had been suppressed for publishing military news 'in spite of repeated general warnings'.[25]

The following day *Vorwärts* informed its readers that the paper 'was limited in its freedom of action. It is extremely difficult for the editors of a socialist labour paper to combine the duty of protecting the interests of the labouring class with the task of conforming with the regulations of the military authorities'.[26] Clearly *Vorwärts* felt that support for the German war effort did not preclude it from discussing social and economic conditions at home. Towards the end of the month the military censor actually asked the paper to write more enthusiastically about the war, and a few days later, the War Minister von Falkenhayn, rescinded a ban imposed on revolutionary and Social-Democratic literature dating back to 1894, providing 'it was published after 31 August 1914... and did nothing to endanger the spirit of loyalty in the army'.[27] By the middle of

September the fragility of the *Burgfrieden* was already beginning to show as news of military victories became less frequent. Writing in his diary on 11 September, Reichstag Deputy Hans Peter Hanssen noted the quickly changing mood of Berliners:

> Spirits are not so jubilant... reports from the battlefield are not so stimulating... The High Command has already pampered the morale of those at home. At least one victory a day is demanded. When that fails, general apathy is evident. Street life is approaching normal. The war spirit is passing into the background because of the desire for amusement. One sees many women dressed in black and many unemployed. A poor, undernourished, suffering family, consisting of the father and four daughters, was standing on the Potsdamer Platz, selling homemade wooden swords. The swords were painted green, and written on them in large red letters were these words: "Each shot - a Russian." Brutality is on the increase.'[28]

Worried that increasing indiscretions by the socialist press might inflame such a situation, von Kessel issued an order on 27 September suppressing *Vorwärts*. After pleas from Hugo Haase and Richard Fischer, both Reichstag Deputies and members of the editorial board, the order was lifted three days later with the stipulation that any reference to 'class hatred and class struggle' was to be avoided in future.[29] Even the bourgeois press did not escape the wrath of the censor. On 1 December 1914 the Finance Committee of the Reichstag met to appropriate five billion marks for the continuance of the war. Bethmann Hollweg opened the session by emphasising the brilliant feats performed by the German troops but stressing the need to save in case the war lasted longer than expected: 'We must tighten up our belts in time if we are going to hold out.' (*Durchhalten*) Reporting on the speech the oldest and stylistically most conservative newspaper, the *Vossische Zeitung*, stated that the Chancellor had urged the German people to 'tighten up the hunger-belt before it is too late'. The Government immediately ordered the suppression of the paper and the Finance Committee issued a statement condemning the account as false, pointing out the difference between a 'girth' and a 'hunger-belt'.[30]

The enormous discretionary powers vested in the Deputy Commanding Generals inevitably led to complaints from the press of unevenhandedness. The position was further complicated by the fact that certain army corps districts interpreted the Law on the State of Siege in different ways. The VIII Army Corps in the Cologne and Koblenz area, for example, whilst retaining control over the censorship of newspapers in their large urban connurbations, delegated such powers to the Landrat in the remaining areas of the administrative district.[31] Such discretionary powers placed the press in an invidious position as they were never completely sure how their military overlords would respond to their reports. As early as 28 August the Secretary of State, Gottlieb von Jagow, in a telegram to the Foreign Office, conceded that some military censors were being over-zealous and inconsistent and called for the two sides to reach some form of agreement.[32] Bethmann Hollweg even hinted that the powers of the Deputy Commanding Generals might have to be brought more into line with the wishes of the Imperial Chancellor.[33] The government on the one hand considered that newspapers needed to be contained, yet they had no wish to alienate the press or in any way disturb the *Burgfrieden*. As a result of an official complaint made by the German

Publishers' Association (*Verein Deutscher Zeitungsverleger*) that some military censors were actually suppressing news that had been officially cleared, the General Staff were forced to admit that there was indeed a lack of uniformity in the handling of press censorship.[34] In October Section IIIb informed the Imperial Naval Office that the 'unfortunate tone taken by the military censors and their eagerness to employ "sharp" measures against newspapers was resulting in general bad feeling. It even went so far as to claim that the authorities' lacked sufficient knowledge of the newspaper world and that a concerted approach to censorship was required. The General Staff supported the idea first put forward by the German Publishers' Association of a Supreme Censorship Office (*Oberzensurstelle*) to coordinate this work, although for different reasons.[35] The publishers' hoped it would act as a court of appeal and undermine the power of their provincial military overlords. The OHL saw it as a way of increasing their own position over the Deputy Commanding Generals and a means of providing much needed guidance and coordination. The organisational structure was agreed in December and the *Oberzensurstelle* began operating in earnest in February 1915.[36]

However before the Supreme Censorship Office could begin functioning a crisis arose in November which required the direct intervention of the Chancellor. For some time the military authorities had been concerned that press criticism was undermining morale and that a new clamp down was needed. This led to some absurd decisions being implemented. For example in early November a North Schleswig paper was suppressed for 'scarcely mentioning the birthday of the Empress' and for giving the impression that the University of Copenhagen 'is a local university'. Banning the paper for a week the Deputy Commander commented: '...one can see that the whole race is painfully and deplorably lacking in patriotism'.[37] Two days later on 9 November the Commanding Generals received new instructions from the War Ministry on tougher new measures to be taken against newspapers or individuals criticising the government.[38] When the press got hold of this document, which was leaked to MP's, a storm of protests erupted over what was feared to be the enthusiastic enforcement of preventive censorship making public criticism virtually impossible. On 30 November Bethmann Hollweg was forced to hold a press conference in the Reichstag to explain the government's position and to defuse the situation. His statement was read out by von Mumm. The Chancellor, it said, recognised the constraints now imposed upon the press but assured them that no plans were being made to introduce preventive censorship for all news and reports. Articles dealing with political matters would not be first vetted by the Foreign Office. The 'instructions' issued by the OHL on the command of the Kaiser were 'merely guidelines'. However the Chancellor hoped that as the press were a party to the *Burgfrieden* they would abide by these guidelines which had been instigated '*by the imperative need for the Reich to be united against enemy countries*'. Once peace negotiations had been entered into then 'the voices of public opinion will and must be once more fully heard'.[39] The proclamation concluded by saying that the Chancellor's statement was not intended to precipitate further discussion on the subject.

This fooled no-one. In early December Reichstag Deputies renewed their attack on censorship and called for the repeal of the Exceptional Laws. Adolf Gröber of the Centre Party opened the debate by quoting the words of the Kaiser: 'I recognise no parties'. Referring to the position of the Jesuits, Gröber pointed out that the Government gratefully accepts their services as army chaplains, in civil capacities, and in the service of the Imperial Navy, but refuses to abolish the Jesuit Law, 'which places members of the order outside the protection of the law and the courts'. The next speaker, Dr. Andeas Blunck of the Liberal Party, claimed that had the Government been in touch with public opinion they would have recognised the call to abolish these hated laws. This was followed by two bitter attacks on censorship by the SDP leader, Hugo Haase and the Liberal Dr. Müller-Meiningen, both of whom condemned the encroachments of the censorship. Concern in the Reichstag was that there had been no political checks on the Commanding Generals, although here politicians had to be careful that their complaints were not construed as an attack on the principle of military security. Replying for the Government, Dr. Clemens Delbrück, Prussian Minister of the Interior, claimed that it had in fact avoided enforcing the Exceptional Laws, but conceded that censors had often made mistakes. Adding that this 'was unfortunate since all the party papers seem to be patriotic', but warning that 'censorship could not be avoided'.[40] It was during the course of his speech that Delbrück made the significant but fateful announcement that 'the magnitude of the times, the unity of the people, and the enormous sacrifices which the preservation of this unity requires, must lead to a new orientation (*Neuorientierung*) of our domestic policy'.[41] The failure of the Imperial Government to carry out these promised reforms was destined to play a crucial role in its eventual downfall. On 10 December Section IIIb called to the attention of the Deputy Commanding Generals the mistakes that had been made and the role of censorship in the war effort. They pointed out that the people had a right to share in the excitement of the war for it was never envisaged that all news and observations about the war should be suppressed. 'Censorship should only seek to prevent exaggeration, distortion, and lack of judgement... which could either arouse false hopes at home or provide encouragement to the enemy...'[42] 1914, then, drew to a close with the questions of political reforms, war aims, and censorship, very much in the air.

One of the first tasks facing the newly created Supreme Censorship Office (*Oberzensurstelle*) was to clarify the legal position of the press and the enforcement of pre-censorship (*Präventivzensur*). Immediately on publication, publishers of all material subject to press inspection had, since the beginning of the war, to present a copy to the local police authorities who had been delegated these independent powers by the Military Commanders. This led to so many complaints that by February 1915 the Prussian Minister of the Interior von Loebbel was forced to advise the police that 'preventive censorship should generally be applied only to military articles'.[43] Nevertheless, in reply to a query from the XVII Army Corps, the *Oberzensurstelle* confirmed in a letter of 12 February 1915 that under the Law of Siege, freedom of the press was suspended for the duration of the war and therefore it was legally possible to apply pre-censorship to both military *and* domestic news.[44] Nothing was more guaranteed to incur the hostility of the press than the demand that all 'unofficial' news must first be submitted to the censors before publication. However two weeks later von Moltke wrote to the Military Commanders in an attempt to defuse the situation and to widen the discussion on relations between the military authorities and the press. He pointed out that bearing in mind the recent criticisms of press censorship in the Reichstag, simply banning guilty newspapers was not the only solution. He suggested instead that it might be wiser to scale down the disciplinary measures and rely more on warnings and 'enlightened' education. To support his argument he made four points: 1) banning a newspaper affects the innocent readership as much as the guilty editorial board, and attracts considerable undesirable publicity abroad; 2) infringements of the censorship regulations are not normally the result of malice; 3) banning a paper does not rectify the damage already done; and 4) a stronger call to the responsibility and feelings of honour of the press will probably bring about the desired response better than repressive measures. Moltke believed that the press for their part would see this as an act of faith and would seek to repay the renunciation of repressive measures with more editorial consideration for the position of the military.[45] To some extent Moltke found support from the Kaiser who in August issued a Cabinet order to the War Ministry that the handling of press censorship needed improving. The King believed this could only be achieved through greater centralisation and called upon the War Ministry and the OHL to extend the *Oberzensurstelle*.[46] Accordingly in September extensive plans were drawn up to establish the War Press Office (*Kriegspresseamt* - KPA).

The War Press Office (Kriegspresseamt)

As a result of the enlargement of the *Oberzensurstelle*, ordered by the Kaiser, the *Kriegspresseamt* (KPA) was established in Berlin in October 1915 under the direct control of the OHL and Major Nicolai's Section IIIb. Its first head was Major Erhard Deutelmoser (who would be dismissed by Hindenburg and Ludendorff in 1916 when they were appointed to lead the OHL). The plans setting out its responsibilities were extraordinarily detailed but three major tasks stand out:[47]

1. To facilitate co-operation between the OHL and the civilian authorities with regard to the press;
2. To provide as much controlled information as possible to the various authorities and to the press;
3. To establish and supervise the uniform application of the censorship.

The KPA was divided into the Information Office (Major Hosse), the Supreme Censorship Office (von Olberg), and the Office for Foreign Affairs (von Herwarth), each with clearly defined responsibilities but with the overriding aim of providing a centralised source of information, propaganda, and censorship, both for home and abroad. As the contradictions within German society became more and more acute under the stress of war, the KPA came to play an increasingly important role countering internal unrest.

It was hoped that the Information Office in particular would establish a well oiled chain of command ranging down from the OHL, via the civilian and military authorities to the press. It had the crucial task of disseminating propaganda and manipulating public opinion according to the intentions of the High Command. In order to facilitate this function the Information Office was organised into three sections:

Section Ia: to observe the German press and report on it.
Section Ib: the answering of questions and the releasing of news to officials and to the press.
Section Ic: the administration of the archives and the library. These were to be built 'as quickly as possible' so as to guarantee a 'swift and

constructive approach not only to the contemporary situation but to all
the important military, political, and economic questions'.

Section Ia consisted of six Referate (reporting bodies) dealing with
German political parties, a Referate for Austro-Hungary, and an editorial office.
The Referate were expected to prepare short extracts from the papers, magazines,
leaflets, books, etc given to them to work on. The editorial office would then
compile these into concise reports. Furthermore a daily survey of the morning
and evening papers would be undertaken and at the end of the week a more
comprehensive weekly survey (Wochenübersicht) produced. They were also
expected to brief the OHL about forthcoming events of interest and the current
state of civilian morale. Many of these reports were passed on to Section Ib to be
released to the press.

Section Ib received information, reports, and directives from every
available source. The foreign office of the KPA sent news from abroad; the
Supreme Censorship Office issued directives of new measures taken, reports of
Reichstag sittings were received in full, and journalists were encouraged to file
individual reports. The news material collected was then fed back to the OHL
and to other offices designated by them. It was used in particular to brief the
censorship authorities on the military and political situation in the hope that such
information would help them to arrive at balanced judgements.

Finally, Section Ib provided a carefully controlled forum in which the
press could pose questions to the military and the KPA would issue public or
confidential statements depending on the situation. In order to supply the press
with as much military information as they required, the KPA published three
periodicals: *Deutsche Kriegsnachrichten*, *Nachrichten der Auslandspresse*, and *Deutsche
Kriegswochenschau*. For expediency the daily army reports (*Heeresberichte*) were given
at 11 a.m. for the evening papers. By October 1916 the KPA decided to add an
evening update to this briefing and a summary of both reports was sent over the
WTB wire.[48] In an effort to satisfy a public clamouring for more news, regular
'press discussions' (*Pressebesprechungen*) between a committee of journalists (headed
by Georg Bernhard, editor of the influential *Vossiche Zeitung* and director of the
Ullstein publishing house) and officials from all the ministries (chaired by Major
Schweitzer), were held in the Reichstag two or three times weekly. Such
'discussions' were nominally independent of the KPA, although they were of
course closely studied by Section Ia. The new system functioned quite efficiently
from the military point of view and one can detect, at least until 1917, a growing
sense of purpose articulated through increasing co-ordination. This was to change
in 1917.

The re-organisation of the *Oberzensurstelle* into the KPA was undertaken
so that censorship could be administered 'with justice and uniformity'. However,
according to the plans setting out the new organisation, this 'justice' had to be
tempered by the imperative needs to 1) maintain the *Burgfrieden* and public faith in
the Government and High Command; and 2) avoid providing the enemy with
useful military, political or economic information. Under its re-organisation, the
Supreme Censorship Office was to consist of five specialist departments
covering; the General Staff, War Ministry, the Imperial Navy, the Colonial Office,
and domestic policy. Its functions were to establish general directives, to
encourage widespread acceptance of its policies, and to arbitrate in disputes
where mistakes had been made. However only the head of the KPA (not the

chief of the *Oberzensurstelle*) could approve major changes to existing censorship regulations.[49]

The High Command expected that the establishment of the KPA together with the centralisation of censorship, would greatly help to improve relations between the press and the censor. It did not, and was bitterly attacked by both press and parliament as yet one more effort by the military authorities to monopolise the channels of opinion reaching the public through the press. Nevertheless in November 1915 the KPA met representatives of the *Reichsverband der deutschen Presse* and the *Verein Deutscher Zeitungsverleger* in a further attempt to construct an 'efficient and positive censorship programme in a spirit of co-operation'. They praised and thanked the press for 'their honourable contribution to the war effort', but complained that confidential information was still finding its way into enemy newspapers. Deutelmoser, the head of the KPA, was particularly concerned that the press should avoid using 'semi-official' headlines and reporting war bulletins in a sensational manner. In order to assist the press wade through the plethora of censorship regulations more quickly, the *Oberzensurstelle* optimistically provided a reference catalogue with a card index of all censorship measures currently in force. In a rather obvious attempt to stress their sincerity the KPA also re-affirmed that the *Oberzensurstelle* would willingly investigate all complaints made against local censorship offices.[50] The press for their part was not convinced.

Nevertheless, 15 months after the outbreak of war the basis for a centrally guided and controlled press and for the coordination of propaganda in general had been set up. The creation of the War Press Office had not only given the OHL direct control over censorship, but it had strengthened its position at the expense of the War Ministry. Licking its wounds, the War Ministry struggled to retain its independence by accepting a restrained role setting up committee meetings, dealing with strikes and monitoring the movements of the political parties, especially the minority radical groups. Although it is difficult to gauge the success of the War Press Office, it did provide a much needed centralised source of news and censorship, and if anything, appeared to deal more effectively with internal dissent than did its counterparts in Britain and France - at least until the final year of the war. As the war progressed and public opinion began to polarise over Germany's war aims, the KPA played an increasingly important role as vehicle for maintaining the *status quo*. Through the KPA, information was controlled at source by preventive censorship, nationally by means of directives sanctioned by the OHL and regionally by the Deputy Commanding Generals. The prestige of the OHL normally guaranteed that local military commanders would follow its guidelines. Suppression ranged across military reverses, war aims, food shortages, peace demonstrations, strikes, casualty lists and notices of deaths, and military and industrial technology. Indeed, any information likely to demoralise the troops or the home front was censored. It has been suggested that the all-embracing nature of military censorship led the German press to lose touch with public opinion.[51] To some extent this was true; as one newspaper tended to offer the same censored news as another, its credibility in the eyes of the reading public gradually began to be eroded. Moreover the censorship regulations were so deliberately complex and time-consuming that editors simply complied by dutifully printing only official news distributed through the Wolff Telegraph Bureau.

However uniform the news, the 'state of siege on truth', was not as constricted as is often supposed. Germans could read accounts in the neutral press which were published in Germany, and most surprising of all, German newspapers were allowed to print enemy army reports, provided they were published in full. Criticisms levelled against the Government in the Reichstag were also carried by the papers. The debate about Germany's war aims, for example, provided, as we shall see in the next chapter, a striking example of the ability of the press to accurately reflect the divisions that existed in Germany. Such a debate, with its bitter attack on censorship, would have been inconceivable in Britain or France. Moreover, censorship was not severe enough to prevent numerous indiscretions by the German socialist and even bourgeois press. One explanation for this is that while Moltke was Chief of the General Staff and Deutelmoser head of the KPA, both showed considerable restraint in the face of growing press and parliamentary criticism of political interference by the military. Even Nicolai as chief of Section IIIb was prepared to play a relatively low keyed role in political matters. This was to change with the appointment of Hindenburg and Ludendorff to the OHL in August 1916. Both were populist figures conscious of the need to manipulate public opinion and determined to use the mystical prestige of the OHL in pursuit of their own political ambitions and the further militarisation of German society. Deutelmoser was removed as head of the KPA for being too sympathetic to Chancellor Bethmann Hollweg, and replaced by the more compliant Major Stotten. Once Deutelmoser was out of the way, Ludendorff could pursue his personal campaign for an even more rigorous suppression of the press and a demand for a Ministry of Propaganda to co-ordinate a massive propaganda exercise of patriotic 'enlightenment'. But more of this later. By the beginning of 1916, the main channels of Imperial propaganda organised by the OHL looked as shown in Figure 1.

War and Imperial Film Propaganda, 1914-16

By the end of the nineteenth century, the major advances made by the economy had created in Germany a mass urban population that enjoyed increasing leisure time with the necessary disposable income to demand more and more amusement and diversion.[52] Such demand, as we have seen, led directly to the growth of the popular press. It also resulted in arguably the first true mass entertainment medium, the popular cinema. By the outbreak of the War in 1914, the cinema had become *the* entertainment medium of the masses. It is therefore surprising to discover that the German authorities were rather slow to systematically manipulate the medium for their propaganda purposes. It would take the war and the need to sustain civilian morale to persuade the governing elite in imperial Germany of its importance and subsequently to bring about a fundamental shift in official policy towards the cinema. By 1918, military opinion had swung to such an extent that many experts (including General Ludendorff) were clearly exaggerating the cinema's importance as an instrument of psychological warfare.

The First World War gave the German cinema its great opportunity and as cinema audiences continued to increase the government gradually began to appreciate the possibilities of the cinema for influencing morale and public opinion. However, on the eve of war few believed that film was a suitable medium for the dissemination of propaganda.[53] By the outbreak of war in August 1914, cinemas in Germany were more tightly regulated than any other European country and every major city could boast of a central state film censor's office. Such measures would greatly facilitate the mobilization of the medium for propaganda purposes during the ensuing conflict.

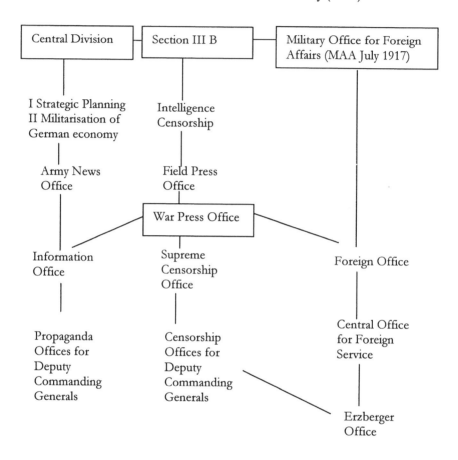

Chief of General Staff of the Field Army (OHL)

Fig. 1: The Organisation of Official Propaganda, 1914-16

Initially the military authorities feared that the movies could disrupt the established social order and immediately sought to impose even more restrictions. Accordingly on 11 August 1914, cinemas and music halls were warned that unless their programmes reflected the 'seriousness of the time' and the 'patriotic mood of the nation', then films would be confiscated and entertainment premises closed.[54] On the other hand, General von Kessel, the Chief Commander in the Marks, reminded theatre and cinema proprietors that it was simply counter-productive to exaggerate the certainty of a German victory by means of cheap and boastful pronouncements from the stage.[55] Towards the end of 1914 concern for the moral welfare of cinema and theatre audiences led the Berlin censor, for example, to ban a number of films and plays on the grounds that they were liable to 'inflict spiritual and moral damage'.[56] Humorous films in particular were viewed by the authorities as frivolous indulgences that could be tolerated only within certain limits and only provided 'the Fatherland, the military, and the uniform were not ridiculed'.[57] This prompted one member of the German Committee of Stage Associates to complain that the censor was taking humour too seriously! The writer, Dr. Hans Günther, argued that in grave times, laughter was a 'wholesome, liberating experience that should not be construed as being disrespectful to the state'.[58] Nevertheless, the Prussian War Minister went so far as to blame superficial foreign films that had been imported into the country for poisoning 'the nation's healthy instincts', and suggested that the German film industry should, instead, produce 'serious' films that reflected the true feelings of the Fatherland.[59] A group of cinema owners had already issued an *Aufruf zur nationalen Selbsthilfe*, calling upon their colleagues not to exhibit foreign films, and in September 1914, the police authorities began confiscating foreign films.[60]

The government responded first by imposing a ban on the importation of all new foreign films, and in January 1915, a decree by the War Ministry issued through the local military commanders informed the cinema industry that in future only films likely to 'uphold morale and promote patriotism for the Fatherland' would be passed by the censor. All so-called 'trash' films (including the detective genre that had proved so popular with pre-war audiences) that were not in keeping with 'the gravity of the present times' were to be banned, and failure to comply with these measures would lead to cinema closures.[61] This represented the first official evaluation of commercial films from both a political and artistic viewpoint. The response of the cinema industry was to produce a series of melodramatic *kitsch* films known as the 'field-grey' genre, as the action invariably centred on the heroism of German soldiers. Included in this genre were films with titles such as: *How Max Won the Iron Cross; On the Field of Honour; Miss Field Grey; I Know No Parties;* and *Christmas Bells.* Freed from the burden of foreign competition and encouraged by the government to produce indigenous works, the film industry began to attract directors and actors from the legitimate theatre. Such collaboration resulted in rare films like *Der Golem* (1915) and *Homunculus* (1916) which foreshadowed the fantastic themes and sets to be found in the expressionist films of the Weimar period.

The awakened nationalism of 1914 turned not only against foreign films but against foreign culture in general. The pressure of patriotic opinion resulted in the elimination of foreign elements from most forms of entertainment. The historic mission of German high culture formed one of the government's main propaganda platforms. Foreign *Unkultur* was portrayed as the antithesis of German civilization and its cultural achievements. Posters and postcards in particular, proclaimed the superiority of German culture and were skilfully exploited to channel patriotic emotions such as courage or hatred. Postcards showed the first foreign prisoners of war being escorted in German cities, while others printed slogans such as: *Jeder Tritt ein Britt* ('for every step, a Brit'); *Jeder Stoss ein Franzos* ('for every blow, a Frenchy'); *Jeder Schuss ein Russ* ('for every shot, a Russki'). From the very outset of the war, Germany seized upon the poster as one of the most powerful and speedy means of influencing popular opinion. [62] Posters were used in numerous campaigns ranging from requests for war loans, recruiting, information about food and fuel substitutes, calls for greater industrial effort, and a series entitled 'Wir Barbaren!' (We Barbarians!) which compared favourably the cultural achievements of Germany to those of Britain and France. A more light-hearted example of this national self-consciousness can be gauged from the outcry that greeted a circular by the Syndicat de la Parfumerie Français that was printed in the German press which claimed that Eau de Cologne was really a French invention. One journalist even demanded that all French scent and soaps on sale in Germany should be immediately destroyed and citizens encouraged to use only German toilet products![63]

Despite its new found ideological chauvinism, the cinema continued to attract criticism and hostility from sections of the established order. Discussions on what was regarded as the low moral level of the cinema figured prominently in Reichstag debates. In March 1915, for example, Deputy Marx of the Centre Party stressed the importance of the cinema as a means of maintaining wartime solidarity. However while he welcomed the 'cleansing' of foreign elements from the industry he warned that frivolity and permissiveness were already creeping back into commercial films and urged the government to become even more vigilant. Replying for the government, Loebell, the Minister of Interior, assured the House that the government had no intention of relaxing the stringent controls over the cinema industry and expressed the hope that the exigencies of war might bring about a lasting improvement in public morality.[64] Towards the end of 1915, as the *Burgfrieden* began to break down, fears were expressed in the Reichstag that popular films were exacerbating class tensions by portraying the social behaviour of the upper classes in a negative and misleading manner. One deputy warned that stereotyped images of the 'idle rich' could well lead to resentment and envy among the lower classes.[65] In a later sitting, von Mumm argued that such films 'were no friend of the German art' and served only to 'debase our people'.[66]

However the major concern both inside and outside the Reichstag was that with fathers being conscripted and more and more mothers contributing to the war effort, children would spend increasing time in cinemas watching escapist trivia without parental control. As early as March 1915 therefore, police authorities issued instructions that cinemas would be closely watched to make sure that banned films were not shown to children.[67] Furthermore, singing and declamatory shows were forbidden during matinee performances when children might be present, and in the evenings, cinema theatres were not allowed to remain open after 11 p.m.[68] These measures were prompted by the dramatic rise in juvenile crime during the first year of the war. Figures taken from Stuttgart, for example, for the period 1914-15, revealed a 100 per cent increase in crimes carried out by juveniles, mostly consisting of theft and damage to property. In Bremen, the Senate immediately banned juveniles under 18 years of age from visiting public houses, coffee houses, or confectionary establishments (*Konditoreien*) after 8 pm, nor were they allowed to attend music halls or even vocal and declamatory recitals which 'are devoid of a higher scientific or artistic interest'.[69]

After numerous complaints from religious leaders and other civic groups and working on the premise that the 'youth of today are easily excited by the sensationalist and criminal action they see in films', the local military authorities launched in July 1916 a two-pronged attack on the commercial cinema industry. First of all they considerably tightened-up their supervision of films regarded as suitable for children. Secondly, they attacked the excesses of commercialism and in particular the ubiquitously provocative film posters that many conservatives believed were even more lurid than the films themselves and which, it was claimed, unscrupulously manipulated children. In what formed part of a wider clamp-down on commercial exploitation, the authorities now imposed stringent restrictions on the size of film posters, where they could be displayed, and what could and could not be advertised.[70] Such measures were generally welcomed in official circles. In the Reichstag, Dr. Stresemann (National Liberal Party) announced that specialist committees had been formed to establish guidelines for the distribution of literature and films designed for children.[71] However there were parliamentarians who argued that the claims made against the commercial cinema were largely unsubstantiated. Gustav Noske of the SDP, for example, persuasively argued that the authorities should concentrate on the positive aspects offered by film. To do this, he suggested, the government needed to apply a fairer system of censorship similar to the one governing the legitimate theatre. Noske criticised the *Kriegspresseamt* for failing to control the prejudices of local military commanders and called for a more enlightened and uniform policy of censorship.[72]

Such a reversal of policy was in fact only a year away. Despite the hostility and all the restrictions imposed, the war had revealed the immense power of film as a means of influencing public opinion and providing relaxation. Eventually the government was forced to recognise that the commercial cinema would not be suppressed but could be used to bolster morale. Thus towards the end of 1916, the War Ministry began secretly commissioning a number of private companies to produce propaganda feature films for home consumption. In January 1917 the High Command not only introduced censorship of films for export in an attempt to control the image of Germany abroad, but it also set up its own organization, the Photographic and Film Office (Bufa) whose role was to co-ordinate the wartime activities of the German film industry. Throughout 1917 General Ludendorff had been stressing the importance of film as a propaganda medium and calling for the industry to be centralised. As a result of Ludendorff's 'suggestions', a new umbrella organization financed jointly by the state and private industry was founded on 18 December 1917 and became known as *Universum-Film-Aktiengesellschaft* (Ufa). Although Ufa was the realization of a centralized and carefully coordinated German film industry, it was, in fact, established too late to make a major contribution to the war effort.[73]

At the beginning of the war, the government was largely poorly equipped and ill-prepared to conduct a propaganda campaign through the medium of film. The early wartime controls of the film industry and the harsh censorship of films reflected the hostility of the ruling elites towards the cinema. Although during the course of the war the middle class began to take the cinema more seriously, it remained what it had been before, the opiate of the working masses.[74] Nevertheless, by the end of the war the cinema had emerged not simply as a means of mass entertainment, but as a widely accepted art form, anchored in German culture and with its respectability firmly enhanced. The combination of exciting, escapist, feature films together with the first crude newsreels depicting German military successes proved irresistible - for a number of reasons. During the exhilaration of the first months of the war the public's demand for glimpses of total war was insatiable. However once the German advance had been halted, audiences looked increasingly to the cinema for shelter and warmth and to the films for entertainment. Between 1914 and 1917 the number of German cinemas increased by 27 per cent, from 2,446 to 3,130.[75] The First World War also placed the German film industry on a firm financial footing. In 1914, film production in German was dominated by France and Denmark, and only 15 per cent of all feature films exhibited in Germany were of German origin.[76] The war forced the German market to produce its own films and consequently German film companies increased fivefold from 25 in 1914 to 130 in 1918 and the number of distributors doubled.[77] Initially the OHL largely failed to recognise the public's increasing interest in film. Gradually, however, the need to sustain civilian morale and to effectively disseminate German war aims (both at home and in neutral countries), forced the military to turn to film propaganda as the most important means, together with the press, of mobilising opinion. On 4 July 1917, in a celebrated letter to the War Ministry, Ludendorff underlined the importance of film as a propaganda medium for such purposes:

> The war has shown the overwhelming power of the image and the film as a medium for education and influence... For the rest of the war the film will continue to play an immensely significant role as a medium of political and military influence. It is therefore essential to ensure, if the war is to be brought to a successful conclusion, that film be used to its maximum effect wherever possible.[78]

The First World War brought about momentous changes in all aspects of German life, and none more so than in the breaking down of authoritarian attitudes towards the urban masses and a grudging recognition of their importance to the war effort. During the Second Reich, as in all the belligerent states, the governing elite was forced to recognize that victory demanded not only military and economic preparedness, but equally importantly, the mobilization and participation of the entire civilian population. In order to sustain the *Burgfrieden* and public support for Germany's war aims, the Imperial Government - more specifically, the military cliques - sought to organize and direct nationalist passions by means of a systematic manipulation of the mass-media. Generally this took the form of a bludgeoning censorship supported in some cases by crude coercion. In the second half of the war, in response to the alarming deterioration of the population's morale, the Government set up a national network of observation stations in an attempt to monitor public opinion. Government action and directives were to be reported but not critically debated. Moreover the extent and arbitrary nature of censorship only exacerbated tensions and led, in many cases, to a re-examination of loyalties to traditional institutions and values. The film industry, for example, responded to repressive censorship and the hostility of the legitimate theatre and survived the war to become *the* popular entertainment medium of the first half of the twentieth century. Similarly, the degree of censorship actually forced the press to re-examine their editorial and news content. Gradually, as circulation figures began to soar, the press came to realize the *political* importance of newspapers. The public's insatiable thirst for news spelt the death of the old amusement only papers. The impact of war on German society, therefore, produced positive as well as negative consequences. As the early crude form of censorship gave way to more constructive and organized propaganda, national unity could not be indefinitely maintained by propaganda alone. The ultimate failure, however, of the German war effort can be found not in inept propaganda but in the Imperial government's blind contempt for the suffering of its own people and their aspirations. The paradox of German propaganda during the First World War was that the government had constructed the means to read the mood of the people, but failed to act upon what it read. But that is another story.

NOTES

1. These are the ideas that I set out in *Germany, Propaganda & Total War 1914-1918. The Sins of Omission* (London, 2000).

2. Further information about Erzberger's role can be found in K. Epstein, *Matthias Erzberger: And the Dilemma of German Democracy* (Princeton, 1959), pp. 103-5. See also Erzberger's brief account in 'Die Mobilmachung' in *Der Deutsche Krieg*, vol. 5, (Stuttgart, 1914).

3. Despite the great strides that Germany made in wireless telegraphy during the war, the effectiveness of the Nauen station was constantly undermined by Marconi operators in Britain who were able to monitor its messages. The revelation of the decoded Zimmermann telegram, for example, which revealed Germany's clumsy attempts to establish a German-Mexican alliance against the United States, played a considerable part in inducing Congress to accept the idea of war with Germany.

4. Much of this information comes from a fascinating intelligence report of German propaganda up to 1917, unearthed by the British War Office in 1939 and sent to the Foreign Office for possible comparison with Nazi propaganda. Public Records Office (PRO), INF 1/715, 11 May 1939. I am grateful to Philip Taylor for drawing my attention to this source.

5. Different aspects of German propaganda directed at American public opinion can be found in the following: H.C. Peterson, *Propaganda for War: The Campaign against American Neutrality, 1914-17* (University of Oklahoma, 1939); A.R. Buchanan, 'European Propaganda and American Public Opinion, 1914-17', unpublished PhD thesis, (Stanford University, 1935). See also the series of pamphlets issued by the Committee on Public Information (Washington), including: 'Conquest and Kultur of the Germans in their own words', W. Notestein and E. Stoll (eds.), No. 5, January 1918; and 'German Plots and Intrigues', E.E. Sperry (ed.), No. 10, July 1918.

6. Very little work has been published on this subject. In 1916 the German Foreign Ministry conducted a report into its own propaganda in neutral countries and appeared quite satisfied with its performance. Foreign Office Library, GFM/HO 58169-58172, dated 1916. At the time of writing these photostat German Foreign Ministry documents were in the process of being returned to the PRO. Certainly during 1915 the British War Ministry was complaining bitterly to the Foreign Office about the failure of British propaganda to match Germany's success in neutral countries. CF. PRO/FO 371/ Vol. 2579/188244, War Office to Foreign Office December 1915. Comprehensive documentation of German propaganda abroad can be found in Bundesarchiv Militärarchiv Freiburg (hereafter MAF), RM5 (Admiralstab der Marine), Bd I, 3769-3782, 3809-11.

7. Quoted in H.Y. Fyfe, Northcliffe, *An Intimate Biography* (London, 1930), p. 205.

8. Ibid., p. 174ff.

9. Cf Letter from the Acting General Command of the 8th Army Corps to the Ministry of Interior, re: How to deal with Social Democrats, 19 August 1914:

Deist, *Militär und Innenpolitik* (2 vols., Düsseldorf, 1970), vol. 1, pp. 194-96. While the military did not expect immediate problems with 'clever' SPD Deputies the letter made it clear that should social democrats transgress the Burgfrieden then 'severe measures' would be taken against them. For a general discussion of the notion that the Great War was pre-eminently a propaganda of war aims see, H. Lasswell, *Propaganda Techniques in the World War* (New Haven, 1927).

10. The full text of the law of 27 July 1914, is reproduced in full in W. Deist, *Militär und Innenpolitik*, I, pp. 188-192.

11. J. Schellenberg, 'Die Herausbildung der Militärdiktatur in den ersten Jahren des Krieges', in *Politik in Krieg 1914-18* (Berlin, 1964), p. 33. For a perceptive analysis of Falkenhayn see, H. Afflerbach, *Falkenhayn Politisches Denken und Handeln im Kaiserreich* (Munich, 1994).

12. A succinct summary of the organization of the High Command can be found in Martin Kitchen's greatly underrated book; *The Silent Dictatorship* (London, 1976), pp. 45-63.

13. Proclamation from Chief of General Staff to War Ministries and the Deputy Commanding Generals re; Safeguarding the Burgfrieden, 13 August 1914; Deist, *Militär und Innenpolitik*, vol. 1, pp. 193-94. For a fascinating analysis of the importance of the Burgfrieden and the myth of 'spirit of 1914' see, J. Verhey, *The Spirit of 1914. Militarism, Myth and Mobilization in Germany* (Cambridge, 2000).

14. Wolff's main global rival was Reuters whose chief executive at the time was Baron Herbert Reuters. Baron Herbert had spent his whole life in England and regarded Reuters as safely 'British'. Nevertheless, he bore a German name after its founder, Julius Reuter. Once the arrangement between WTB and the German Government became known in Britain, questions were asked whether Reuters had also been subverted by German influence. In fact, according to Donald Read, in his official history of the Reuters organization, Reuters placed its reputation as well as its network at the service of the British Government. 'At Reuters', wrote one Department of Information (DOI) official revealingly on 11 July 1917, 'the work done is that of an independent news agency of an objective character, with propaganda secretly infused... it is essential that independence should be preserved'. Read, *The Power of News. The History of Reuters* (Oxford, 1992, 2nd edition, 1998), pp. 127-28. The German Government remained convinced that Reuters was a propaganda agency for the British and depicted the organization in its propaganda as 'the Lying Toad' ('Die Lügenkröte') seated on telegraph wires spewing-out its propaganda. For a somewhat protracted narrative on the organization of the German press during wartime see K. Koszyk, *Deutsche Presspolitik im Ersten Weltkrieg* (Düsseldorf, 1968). For a brief and rather superficial comparative analysis see A.G. Marquis, 'Word as Weapons: Propaganda in Britain and Germany During the First World War', *Journal of Contemporary History*, vol. 13 (1978), pp. 467-98.

15. A concise account of the role of the press in the nineteenth century Germany can be found in M. Eksteins, *The Limits of Reason. The German Democratic Press and the Collapse of Weimar Democracy* (Oxford, 1975), pp. 13-27. For a more detailed analysis see K. Koszyk, *Deutsche Presse im 19. Jahrhundert* (Berlin, 1966).

16. Eksteins, *The Limits of Reason*, p. 13; Koszyk, *Deutsche Presse*, pp. 307f.

17. Koszyk, *Deutsche Presse*, pp. 267ff.

18. See A. Hall, Scandal, *Sensation and Social Democracy. The SPD Press and Wilhelmine Germany, 1890-1914* (Cambridge, 1977). Vorwärts daily circulation increased from 56,000 in 1902 to 165,000 in 1912. This increase reflected the growth of the SPD. See, V. Schulze, 'Vowärts', in H.D. Fischer (ed.), *Deutsche Zetungen*, pp. 331-342.

19. From a censored article by Arthur Bernstein of the *Berliner Morgenpost*; see Eksteins, *The Limits of Reason*, p. 29. Circulation figures for the press can be found in O. Groth, *Die Zeitung* (4 vols., Mannheim, Berlin, Leipzig, 1928-30), I. pp. 251-3.

20. The full text of the Chancellor's proclamation is printed in Koszyk, *Deutsche Presspolitik*, pp. 22-3. For a detailed discussion of press censorship during the war see H.D. Fischer (ed.), *Pressekonzentration und Zensurpraxis im Ersten Weltkrieg* (Berlin, 1973). See also, W. Deist, 'Zensur und Propaganda in Deutschland während des Ersten Weltkreiges,' in Deist, *Militär, Staat und Gesellschaft: Studien zur preussisch-deutschen Militärgeschichte* (Munich, 1991), pp. 153-64.

21. MAF, RM5, Bd. 1, 2413, Instructions from military authorities to the press, 1.8.1914. The original 26 prohibitions slapped on the press by Bethmann-Hollweg were now added to by the military.

22. W. Nicolai, *Nachrichtendienst, Presse und Volksstimmung im Weltkrieg* (Berlin, 1920), p. See also Nicolai, The German Secret Service (London, 1924). Nicolai is an illusive figure, although he was probably the most important single individual associated with the dissemination of German propaganda. The surviving papers show that he was not a great innovator but a conscientious and devoted administrator. Cf. Ludendorff's comments, *My War Memories, 1914-18* (2 vols., London, 1919), I, p. 17. Wherever possible I have used the English translation of Ludendorff's memoirs penned in exile. However when the English edition fails to provide a sufficiently precise translation or an exact 'flavour' of Ludendorff's thoughts I have cited the German edition; *Urkunden der Obersten Heeresleitung über ihre Tätigkeit 1916-1918* (Berlin, 1920).

23. MAF, RM3 (Akten des Reichsmarineamtes), Bd. 4, 10294, 10.8.1914.

24. *Vorwärts*, 1 August 1914.

25. Lutz, *Fall of the German Empire*, I, p. 169.

26. *Vorwärts*, 9 August 1914; also Lutz, *Fall of the German Empire*, pp. 169-70.

27. Hanssen, *Diary of a Dying Empire*, p. 51, in conversation with Rudolf Hilferding (one time editor in chief of *Vorwärts*); *Vorwärts*, 2 September 1914; Lutz, *Fall of the German Empire*, p. 20.

28. Hanssen, *Diary of a Dying Empire*, p. 64.

29. Quoted in Lutz, *Fall of the German Empire*, II, p. 12.

30. This episode can be found in Hanssen, *Diary of a Dying Empire*, pp. 83-4.

31. Order of the Deputy General Command of VIII Army Corps to the civil and military authorities, 28.11.1914, Deist, *Militär und Innenpolitik*, pp. 83-85. It has been decided on 1 September that the police authorities should not exercise such powers. See letter from Bavarian War Ministry to military commanders in Deist, p. 71.

32. MAF, RM3, Bd. 4, 10294, telegram from Secretary of State von Jagow to the Foreign Office, 28 August 1914.
33. Telegram from the Imperial Chancellor to the Foreign Office regarding the guiding principles for the handling of censorship over the question of war aims, quoted in Deist, p. 40.
34. MAF, RM3, Bd. 4, 10294, Deputy General Staff to Bavarian War Ministry, 1 September 1914. A former German journalist catalogued six different censorship and 15 other bureaus through which a single news item might theoretically travel. See, K. Mühsam, *Wie Wir Belogen Wurden* (Berlin, 1920), p. 130.
35. MAF, RM3, Bd. 4, 10294, Deputy General Staff to Imperial Naval Office re: setting up a Supreme Censorship Office, 3 October 1914.
36. The meeting setting up the Supreme Censorship Office took place on 3 December 1914. For a discussion of its development see Nicolai, *Nachrichtendienst*, p. 73ff.
37. The events leading up to this incident are described in Hanssen, *Diary of a Dying Empire*, pp. 79-80.
38. MAF, RM3, Bd. 4, 10294, Prussian War Ministry to Military Commanders, 9 November 1914.
39. MAF, RM3, Bd. 4, 10294, minutes of press conference held in the Reichstag, 3 November 1914.
40. The Secretary of State (Staats Sekretär) was the head of an administrative department in the Imperial Government. He was appointed by and responsible to the Chancellor. Verhandlung des Reichstags, 3 December 1914, p. 20; see also Hanssen, *Diary of a Dying Empire*, pp. 86-88. The Reichstag renewed their attack on the Exceptional Laws on 10 March 1915, but again with little success.
41. Verhandlung des Reichstags, 3 December 1914, p. 20; see also Hanssen, *Diary of a Dying Empire*, pp. 86-88. The Reichstag renewed their attack on the Exceptional Laws on 10 March 1915, but again with little success.
42. Deputy General Staff to Military Commanders, 10 December 1914, quoted in Deist, pp. 87-8.
43. MAF, RM3, Bd. 4, 10294, Prussian Minister of Interior to Oberpräsident, 9 February 1915.
44. MAF, RM3, Bd. 4, 10305, Supreme Censorship Office to censorship office of Acting General Command of XVII Army Corps, 12 March 1915.
45. MAF, RM3, Bd. 4, 10305, Chief of Acting General Staff to Military Commanders, 26 March 1915.
46. MAF, RM3, Bd. 4, 10296, Cabinet Order of Wilhelm II to Prussian War Ministry, 4 August 1915.
47. MAF, RM3, Bd. 4, 10317, Acting General Staff's plans for the organization of the War Press Office, September 1915.
48. This remained a constant source of complaint. As early as February 1915 the German Publisher's Association unsuccessfully asked the General Staff to distribute war communiqués directly rather than through the WTB, Koszyk, *Deutsche Presspolitik*, p. 29. For a detailed outlined of the new format of the Deutsche Kriegsnachricten see, MAF, RM5, Bd. 2, 3722, 8 September 1916.

49. See note 47. The document contains a separate section dealing with the responsibilities of the Supreme Censorship Office. See also folder on press censorship for the period 15 September 1914 to 25 December 1915, Militärarchiv, Stuttgart (hereafter MAS), M77/1 (Stellvertretendes Generalkommando XIII), Bü 60.

50. MAF, RM3, Bd. 4, 10317, War Press Office to representatives of the press, 6 November 1915. For an analysis of the War Press Office see, M. Creutz, *Die Pressepolitik der kaiserlichen Regierung während des Ersten Weltkriegs* (Frankfurt am Main, 1996).

51. This argument is central to Koszyk's work, *Deutsche Presspolitik*; cf. also Eksteins, *The Limits of Reason*, pp. 28-9; Marquis, 'Words as Weapons', p. 476.

52. For different estimates see the following works: F. Zglinicki, *Der Weg des Films* (Frankfurt, 1956); O. Kalbus, *Vom Werden deutscher Filmkunst*, vol. 1 (2 vols., Altona, 1935); C. Moreck, *Sittengeschichte des Kino* (Dresden, 1926); J. Toeplitz, *Geschichte des Films*, vol. 1, 1895-1928 (Munich, 1975); H. Knietzsch, *Film, gestern und heute: Gedanken und Daten zu sieben Jahrzehnten Geschichte der Filmkunst*, 3rd ed. (Leipzig, 1972).

53. This is not intended to be a comprehensive account of the relationship between the cinema and the state in nineteenth century Germany. See, Gary D. Stark's excellent 'Cinema, Society, and the State: Policing the Film Industry in Imperial Germany', in G.D. Stark and B.K. Lackner (eds.), *Essays on Culture and Society in Modern Germany* (Texas A & M University Press, 1982), pp. 123-66. More recently, Stark, 'All Quiet on the Home Front: Popular Entertainments, Censorship and Civilian Morale in Germany, 1914-1918,' in F. Coetzee and M. Shevin-Coetzee (eds.), *Authority, Identity and the Social History of the Great War* (Providence and Oxford, 1995), pp. 57-80. See also, D. Welch, 'Cinema and Society in Imperial Germany 1905-1918', *German History*, vol. 8, no. 1, February 1990, pp. 28-45. Figures for cinema audiences can be found in H. v. Boehmer and H. Reitz, *Der Film in Wirtschaft und Recht (Berlin, 1933), p. 5. Cf. also O. Kalbus, Vom Werden*, I, p. 17. The Navy League were the exception in that they had been exploiting the possibilities offered by film before 1914. See W. Deist, *Flottenpolitik und Flottenpropaganda. Das Nachrichtenbureau des Reichsmarineamtes 1897-1914* (Stuttgart, 1976).

54. StA.P, Rep. 30 Berlin C, Th. 134, Berlin police memorandum, 11 August 1914.

55. StA.P, Rep. 30 Berlin C, Th. 134, Kessel to Police-Präsidium, Theatre-Censor, 20 October 1914.

56. StA.P, Rep. 30 Berlin C, Th. 134, undated newspaper clipping quoting Dr. Günther in the *Berliner Morgenpost*.

57. StA.P, Rep. 30 Berlin C, Th. 134, Berlin Police report to Minister of Interior, 27 September 1914.

58. See note 57.

59. StA.P, Rep. 30 Berlin C, Th. 134, Prussian War Minister to Local Military Commanders, 15 December 1914.

60. Zglinicki, Weg des Films, p. 388.

61. StA.P, Rep. 30 Berlin C, Th. 134, Merkblatt für Kinematographentheater, 13 January 1915.

62. See M. Hardie and A. Sabin, *War Posters issued by Belligerent and neutral nations 1914-19* (London, 1920); M. Rickards, *Posters of the First World War (London,*

1969); J. Darracott and B. Loftus, First World War Posters (HMSO/IWM, 1972); J. Darracott, *The First World War in Posters* (New York, 1974); P. Paret, B. Irwin Lewis, P. Paret, *Persuasive Images. Posters of War and Revolution* (Princeton, NJ, 1992).

63. IWM, Weekly Report on German and Austrian Papers, Foreign Office, 15 May 1915 - 1 January 1916, quoting Kölnische Zeitung, 18 May 1915. For a more detailed account see chapter 3, pp. 88-92.

64. StA.P, Rep. 30 Berlin C, Th. 134, copy of Reichstag sitting, No. 103, of 2 March 1915.

65. Quoted in Zglinicki, *Weg des Films*, p. 367.

66. Verhandlung des Reichstags, 20 May 1916, p. 1157.

67. StA.P, Rep. 30 Berlin E, Th. 135, 8 March 1915.

68. StA.P, Rep. 30 Berlin E, Th. 135, singing was forbidden on 18 May 1915 and instructions to close cinemas at 11 pm was issued on 10 May 1915. At the very end of 1916 all cinemas and theatres and other places of entertainment were ordered to close at 10 pm (issued on 31 December 1916). Two months later, cinema owners had to leave an interval of 1½ hours between two showings (issued on 21 February 1917).

69. Bremer Bürger-Zeitung, 11 May 1916. The article (which is partly taken from the Schwäbischer Merkur of 3 May) also printed a table of the break down of convictions for the age group 12 to 18 years of age. The Bremen assembly subsequently banned the sale of alcohol to juveniles for home consumption on risk of a 150M fine or even imprisonment.

70. Cf Berlin police instructions for 11, 13 July 1916 and 23 July December 1916, StA.P, Rep. 30 Berlin E, Th. 135.

71. Verhandlung des Reichstags, 30 May 1916, p. 1309

72. Ibid., p. 1296.

73. See D. Welch, 'A Medium for the Masses: Ufa and Imperial German film propaganda during the First World War', *Historical Journal of Film, Radio and Television*, vol. 6, No. 1, (1986), pp. 85-91.

74. Writing after the war on 'Vodka, the Church and the Cinema', Trotsky argued that the cinema was the most powerful means of collective education for the working class: 'it amuses, educates, strikes the imagination by images, and liberates you from the need of crossing the Church door. The cinema is a great competitor not only of the public-house, but of the Church. Here is an instrument which we must secure at all costs!'. L. Trotsky, *The Problems of Life* (London, 1924), pp. 34-43.

75. Zglinicki, *Der Weg des Films*, p. 328.

76. Boehmer & Reitz, *Der Film in Wirtschaft und Recht* (Berlin, 1933), p. 5; Kalbus, *Vom Werden deutscher Filmkunst*, vol. 1, p. 17.

77. Traub, Die Ufa, p. 19; Boehmer & Reitz, *Der Film in Wirtschaft*, p. 6.

78. The full text of Ludendorff's celebrated letter can be found in Traub, *Die Ufa*, pp. 138-9; Zglinicki, *Der Weg des Films*, pp. 394-5; Barkhausen, *Filmpropaganda*, pp. 259-61. The role of film propaganda during the final two years of the war see, Welch, *Germany, Propaganda & Total War*, pp. 211-18.

Chapter Three
'THE MISSING WESTERN FRONT': BRITISH POLITICS, STRATEGY, AND PROPAGANDA IN 1918
Stephen Badsey

In the last two decades, pioneering research work has been done by historians into British politics and grand strategy in the First World War that has greatly improved wider understanding of this complex issue.[1] Equally substantial work has been done by historians on the role of propaganda and the press in the war, especially from the British side.[2] Some studies of British politics and grand strategy mention the propaganda institutions in the events of 1918, and most make some use of press reporting and editorials as sources of evidence. But the media and their role has remained largely an addition to the narrative of events, rather than an intrinsic factor. The present contribution represents, in part, a synthesis of the work on both strategy and propaganda, with the purpose of demonstrating how the actions of the 'high politics' of British grand strategy must be integrated with the 'low culture' of the role of propaganda and the media, in order to understand events of 1918 more fully.

This research may also throw some illumination onto an important historical debate regarding both the First World War and the modern popular perception of its nature. On one side of this debate is historical investigation into the cultural meaning and symbolism of the Western Front, which is for most English-speaking people the most significant single aspect of the war. This investigation into cultural meaning has become a well-established field of history with its own distinctive view of the First World War as a uniquely terrible event, including the meaning given to its ending in 1918.[3] On the other side of the debate is the substantial change in historical understanding about the conduct of battle on the Western Front brought about in recent years through the extensive use of primary sources by military historians, particularly focussing on the British

Army. The work of these revisionist military historians has challenged the modern popular view of the war as either uniquely terrible or incompetently conducted. For these revisionists, who stress the introduction of new technologies and tactics and a 'learning curve' in British war fighting methods, 1918 is also a year of great importance, including the argument that by the end of the war the British Army on the Western Front was the decisive instrument of the Allied victory.[4] This revisionist position has conflicted with that of more traditional British military historians (or those seeking to preserve or revive the traditional position); with the historical tradition in Germany of the inherent superiority of the German Army even in defeat; and also with historians in the United States and Canada whose writings are very much derived from a German tradition, or who prefer to emphasise the role of the French Army and the American Expeditionary Force (AEF) in 1918. The resulting difference in perspectives has been called the 'Two Western Fronts' debate: the Western Front of British military history and the Western Front of wider popular cultural understanding.[5]

The British revisionist position has gained wider acceptance among historians as it has accumulated more evidence, some of it drawn from the work on the culture of the war and from wider history.[6] It is now generally accepted that the highly critical perspective of a British cultural and social elite (including the more famous of the 'trench poets') during and after the war was not necessarily shared by the majority of participants. The next stage has been to link the findings of cultural history with those of battlefield history to produce a more complete picture of the war. How has it happened that the British Army's victory on the Western Front in 1918, one of the greatest and most important in British history, has somehow been forgotten in popular culture? Investigation has focussed in particular upon the period of 'disillusionment' in the 1930s, and the period of social revolution in the 1960s. This represents an issue of considerable size and importance on a critical event in 20th Century history.

Recent findings on the press and propaganda, taken together with those on British grand strategy, now make it possible to re-examine the events of 1918 and how the British government not only directed the war, but also directed the war's portrayal to its own people and others. In the German *Kaiserschlacht* spring offensive of 1918 the British (including forces of the Dominions of the British Empire) played the leading role in defeating the last great German attack on the Western Front. In the 'Hundred Days,' from the Battle of Amiens on 8 August to the Armistice on 11 November, the British Army took more German prisoners than the other Allied armies on the Western Front combined, it dominated its enemy in the critical area of artillery tactics, and it broke the formidable Hindenburg Line.[7] However much it may have been influenced by other events in subsequent decades, the British undervaluing of these achievements on the Western Front in 1918 has its origins in British propaganda policy of the year itself. The British government under Prime Minister David Lloyd George, its propaganda institutions, the British press, and Field Marshal Sir Douglas Haig's own General Headquarters (GHQ) in France, all pursued policies in 1918 that led to a propaganda neglect of the Western Front. While the British people welcomed the Armistice with enthusiasm and relief, they were not particularly aware of these British military victories. Also, at the end of the war, just as the British were in the process of disbanding their propaganda apparatus, the German Army contrived one of the most successful propaganda coups of the war, the foisting of the _Dolchstosslegende_ ('stab in the back' myth) upon the German people, that also downplayed the British military triumph on the Western Front, leading swiftly to an outright German denial that their soldiers had ever been defeated at all.

The end of 1917 represented a low point for the British in the First World War, with the loss of Russia to revolution, mutinies in the French Army, and their own failure in the Third Battle of Ypres. By this time, Lloyd George genuinely believed (with what accuracy it is still hard to judge) that he was facing a military faction led by Haig and by General Sir William 'Wully' Robertson as Chief of the Imperial General Staff (CIGS) that represented a serious challenge to democracy in Britain, and that was orchestrating a press campaign against his government. The situation as regards manpower had changed utterly from that of 1916 when the Army, and specifically Haig's GHQ in France, had asserted and expected absolute priority on a virtually limitless supply of men.[8] From November 1917 onwards the new Ministry of National Service under Sir Aukland Geddes placed Army recruiting under civilian control as one part of a diminishing manpower pool. A direct result of this was the enforced reorganisation and reduction of British divisions from twelve to nine infantry battalions during winter 1917-1918, although Dominion divisions remained at the higher strength. In December 1917, Haig regarded only the Canadians and Australians among his reserve divisions as fit for front line duty.

Over winter 1917-1918, Lloyd George both constructed a coherent British grand strategy for the future, and attempted to convince his War Cabinet colleagues, his Allies, and the British people of its merits. The reason for fighting on the Western Front at all was the familiar one of preserving Britain's security against a continental aggressor; but this was a defensive objective, if a critical one. Lloyd George, in a speech in Paris on 12 November 1917, had described the German line as 'an impenetrable barrier'. After the failure of the Third Battle of Ypres (Passchendaele) in July-November and the repulse of the initial success at Cambrai by the German counter-attack in November-December, the War Cabinet could be forgiven for concluding that there was no breakthrough for _either_ side on the Western Front in 1918. Indeed, the War Cabinet at first expected the Germans to stand on the defensive in the West in 1918, and to exploit their success in the East. Since the manpower reserves for a major British offensive were no longer available, British troops on the Western Front should also go onto the defensive for a year or more, until the American arrival in force in 1919. In the interval, further British, Dominion, and Indian troops could be transferred to the campaign against Ottoman Turkey and to other projects in the East. The purpose of this was a double one: to win propaganda victories such as General Sir Edmund Allenby's spectacular capture of Jerusalem on 9 December 1917, as a way of boosting Home Front morale; but also to stake out positive British gains in the East, to offset both the German success against Russia and also the possibility of a negotiated peace in the West.[9]

On 5 January 1918, at Caxton Hall in London, Lloyd George gave his first major policy speech on British war aims to a gathering of trade unionists. Coming only three days before President Woodrow Wilson's 'Fourteen Points' speech, this was clearly aimed at influencing the United States, while references to self-determination for the peoples of Austria-Hungary signalled the government's new strategy of concentration on the East. But the speech was aimed also at healing political rifts on the Home Front. Later in the month, new food regulations placed rationing in Britain on a more equitable basis, and the Ministry for National Service was given extended powers for 'combing out' manpower, with the Army placed last in the new priorities. Next month the new (and it was hoped also more equitable) Military Service Act passed into law, together with the Representation of the People Act, extending the franchise to all men over 21 years old, and all women over 30 years old. All this contrasts strongly with the food riots and strikes which took place in Germany in January and February, as the German Home Front began to show signs of collapse.

In the absence of opinion polls and much more than anecdotal or indirect evidence, there is almost no way for historians to asses with accuracy the impact of these measures on British domestic morale and opinion. But most of the evidence available for attitudes on the Home Front, including the incidence and severity of strikes, suggests that public opinion rallied both to the government policy initiatives, and also in the face of the threatened German victory. It has been well argued that from the viewpoint of the British government and its propaganda, 'the Germans were in many ways the perfect enemy' since 'their conduct throughout the war seemed almost designed to offend British liberal sensibilities and to galvanize public opinion in support of the war effort'.[10] Although it cannot be proved, it is highly likely that the single greatest factor in unifying the British Home Front behind the war effort was the punitive nature of the Peace of Brest-Litovsk, announced on 3 March only days before the German offensive in the West. This evidence of what a 'German peace' would mean was a gift to British propagandists, and one more example of strategic mistiming on Germany's part during the war.

Given Lloyd George's strategy of opportunism in the East, of minimising and isolating Haig and the Western Front, and of maintaining the morale of the Home Front through a difficult year, it was logical that he should bring into his government the leading British newsmen. With a General Election constitutionally inevitable in 1918, regardless of whether the war had ended, it was also well understood at the time that Lloyd George, who had no majority support in any political party, needed the support of the London newspapers and their owners to survive in office.[11] Faced with the problem of identifying and directing public opinion in a new era of mass politics, British politicians of the First World War placed disproportionate faith in the press, and awarded its owners and editors considerable respect. Since 1916, Lloyd George had progressively involved several press magnates and important editors with his government, including Sir George Riddell, Sir Robert Donald, Lord Beaverbrook and Lord Rothermere. Beaverbrook described the resulting Whitehall infighting as a conflict between self-made 'new men' like himself and the patricians of the Foreign Office, including his own particular Foreign Office *bête noire* Lord Robert Cecil.[12]

In addition to owning the *Daily Express* and other newspapers, Beaverbrook had established in 1915 the Canadian War Records Office in London, and held *de facto* control over Canadian propaganda for the Western Front, with the rank of colonel in the Canadian militia. He was also chairman of the War Office Cinema Committee, created in November 1916 as the fruit of his personal association with the Permanent Secretary at the War Office, Sir Reginald Brade.[13] This committee had extended its authority by the end of 1917 to control all British filming of the fighting fronts and in Britain itself, including all Dominion filming, (to the annoyance of Dr Charles Bean, the official Australian war correspondent, whose claim to an *ex officio* place on the committee for an Australian representative was rejected). On 10 February 1918, Beaverbrook became Minister of Information, and also Chancellor of the Duchy of Lancaster, giving him a seat in the Cabinet. It is a measure of the importance that Lloyd George placed on propaganda in sustaining the Home Front throughout 1918 that he took such a political risk. The prominent Conservative Austen Chamberlain's reaction was that Beaverbrook's appointment 'can scarcely be described as a popular one. It adds to the prevalent feeling of irritation and soreness'.[14] Beaverbrook was himself warned by his friend Andrew Bonar Law that senior Conservative politicians and powerbrokers were prepared to tolerate in office either Beaverbrook himself or Lord Northcliffe, the owner of *The Times* and the *Daily Mail* and self-styled 'Ogre of Fleet Street', but not both. Nevertheless, Beaverbrook undertook to bring Northcliffe into the government with him.[15]

The Ministry of Information (MoI) was largely the work of Colonel John Buchan, head of the Department of Information (DoI) since its creation in January 1917, and was itself created by amalgamating Buchan's DoI with the War Office Cinema Committee in early March. Beaverbrook owed his new position to some extent to Buchan's lobbying on behalf of the importance of propaganda, although Buchan would have entertained the idea of Northcliffe as minister if necessary. The new MoI shared its powers with the National War Aims Committee, created in August 1917 partly again through Buchan's work, and also chaired by Lloyd George; with the Official Press Bureau which since 1914 had been responsible for daily Press censorship; and with MI7, the Directorate of Special Intelligence at the War Office.

Absent in the United States heading the British War Mission until November 1917, Northcliffe had been a strong supporter of the Army and of Haig against the government, as had his newspapers.[16] But after some preliminary negotiations with Lloyd George on his return to London, Northcliffe's transfer of allegiance began on 7 December 1917, when on his visit to GHQ Haig showed boredom and indifference over Northcliffe's account of his achievements in the United States. The public effect of this switch was visible in the Northcliffe press's attack on the British handling of the German counterattack at Cambrai that month. On 18 February, co-incidentally the same day that Robertson departed as CIGS, Northcliffe took up a government post (although he maintained that unlike Beaverbrook he did not become a *member* of the government) as Director of the Department of Propaganda in Enemy Countries, with its headquarters at Crewe House in London. The London Headquarters of the British War Mission continued in existence, and in August all Northcliffe's responsibilities, including Crewe House, were placed in the Mission's name. Although the British War Mission was strictly separate from the MoI, the relationship between Northcliffe and Beaverbrook was very close in a professional sense. On 21 February, Robert Donald, the Editor of the *Daily Chronicle*, became Director of the Department of Propaganda in Neutral Countries. The links between these various organisations were informal and personal as much as institutional, and their ability to dictate propaganda themes was in practice sometimes limited. The London press in particular was sufficiently powerful to be left as effectively self-regulating. Some sections, notably the *Morning Post* under H.A. Gwynne and the *Spectator* under John St. Loe Strachey, remained openly very critical both of the government and of Lloyd George personally. In consequence, the abilities of Beaverbrook, Northcliffe and Donald to influence the press in their private capacities was an important part of their public and governmental power, as well as the target of acrimonious complaint from Lloyd George's critics.

This new British propaganda apparatus, and the new and close relationship between the Lloyd George government and what some called the 'Beavercliffe' press, was put to the test with the *Kaiserschlacht*, starting with Operation 'Michael' on 21 March. The British government reaction to the crisis caused by the initial success of 'Michael', and the reaction of British government propaganda, was an integral part of the much larger Allied crisis, deftly handled at the Doullens Conference on 26 March at which Marshal Ferdinand Foch was appointed Generalissimo of the Allied forces. From the German perspective they had achieved a major victory, and indeed on 23 March First Quartermaster General Erich Ludendorff advised Kaiser Wilhelm II that the war had been won. The French perspective was that they had rescued the British from defeat and established their dominance over the Allied coalition, a dominance that was to last to the end of the war despite the weakness of the French Army. But no British perspective on their own achievements was forthcoming from the MoI, which failed to respond both to criticisms of British strategy and to French claims of widespread British cowardice and desertion. According to Major the Honourable Neville Lytton, the staff officer responsible for the French and Allied press at GHQ, there was already in March 'beginning to be quite a serious anti-British feeling in France. "Les Anglais f[outent] le camp" was on every one's lips'.[17] British propaganda continued to fail to respond to the situation as the German attacks continued. 'In every city, town, village and hamlet in France the story is told of how the soldiers of the British 5th Army ran away,' one eyewitness reported to the British government in June, 'Times out of number I have been asked how it happened, not if it were true'.[18] The Foreign Office complained that its representatives had needed to go to MI7 at the War Office to obtain briefings on the British government's position in the face of these accusations.

In his memoirs in 1956, Beaverbrook offered a very plausible explanation for the MoI's failure: that because of Foreign Office and War Office hostility to British propaganda the MoI was created from a blank slate in early March, only a few days before the German offensive. 'There was no blueprint to work on,' he wrote, 'No experience to guide the new department. There was no office, no staff. There was nothing but a decision of the War Cabinet decreeing that such a Ministry should be created and that I should be Minister'.[19] Beaverbrook's claim went substantially unchallenged at the time of publication, largely because little contemporary evidence existed on British wartime propaganda, as he well knew. As an investigation in 1938 concluded, the MoI's papers had been destroyed or had mysteriously vanished soon after December 1918 (some of them into Beaverbrook's own private collections).[20] It was not until after Beaverbrook's death in 1964 that historians were able to piece together the story, and expose his statement as a barefaced lie. Beaverbrook also seems to have left his biographer with the impression that the MoI had no part in propaganda aimed at the Home Front, which was also quite untrue, although overall management of Home Front propaganda was in the hands of the National War Aims Committee, not the MoI.[21]

The institutions of British propaganda were all in place in March 1918, but the failure of the MoI, rather than happening in isolation, reflected the shock within Whitehall as a whole at the impact of the German offensive; a very public piece of evidence on Whitehall attitudes that has not been given its full weight in the wider political history of 1918. The lack of any British propaganda plan shows clearly how complete a surprise the German attack had been in Whitehall. The substantial German gains did indeed look like a British defeat, especially to politicians who had come to expect the worst of their own generals; and in his speech to the House of Commons on 9 April, defending himself over the events of the 'Michael' offensive, Lloyd George himself appeared to give credence to the view that British troops had fled in large numbers. Also, the focus of both official Whitehall and the London press was entirely away from the Western Front at this time: on 21 March the War Cabinet's chief topic for discussion was a possible Japanese intervention in Siberia, while the Western Front hardly featured at all.[22] In a reflection of this, on 23 March a leading article in the influential weekly *The Sphere* headlined not the German advances on the Western Front, but 'The German Move Towards the Western Asiatic Lands,' of the central Caucasus.

A further reason for the MoI failure to deal effectively with the news and propaganda implications of the German spring offensive was that Beaverbrook and Northcliffe were preoccupied both with securing their immediate positions and with their wider political ambitions. Throughout the year, both men were also plagued by persistent ill-health. By late 1917 it was an open secret that Lloyd George planned to replace Lord Derby as Secretary of State for War. In fact he decided in January on Lord Milner, who succeeded to the post on 18 April. But there were other candidates at the time, including both Beaverbrook and Northcliffe, whose appointment Haig considered would be 'fatal to the Army and the Empire'.[23] Northcliffe rejected the new Air Ministry in December 1917; Beaverbrook claimed to have declined control of the Ministry of Munitions, and his own candidacy for the War Office in February was real enough for the story to reach Austen Chamberlain, whose reaction was 'I do not think that Lloyd George yet desires to commit political suicide'.[24] Between February and August, repeated threats by both Beaverbrook and Northcliffe to resign alternated with strident demands from both men to Lloyd George that they should be protected from parliamentary calls for their dismissal. Donald actually carried out his threat of resignation in May, following this up by appointing Sir Frederick Maurice, author of the notorious 'Maurice Letter' attacking Lloyd George, as military correspondent of the *Daily Chronicle*. After repeated criticisms of Lloyd George in the *Daily Chronicle*, including by Maurice, the paper was bought in October by a syndicate of Lloyd George's backers headed by Sir Henry Dalziel and by Riddell, and Donald resigned as editor.

The assessment of domestic political profit and loss for Lloyd George in creating the new MoI under Beaverbrook and the independent departments under Northcliffe and Donald was therefore not at all straightforward. The support of Northcliffe and Beaverbrook certainly helped Lloyd George with the dismissal of Robertson, and later to survive the Maurice Letter crisis. It is also probable that the output of propaganda aimed at the Home Front did achieve something of what its purveyors hoped, in strengthening the morale of the British people. But what was achieved may have depended more on the ability of the various sub-departments to function without clear leadership from the top, which was generally not forthcoming. As for Northcliffe's Crewe House, it is doubtful if any of its propaganda contributed very much to the defeat of the German spring offensive. Its main contribution was probably no more than assistance with the production of propaganda leaflets aimed at German troops on the Western Front.

Lloyd George's political strategy of limiting Haig's power to challenge his own position, in step with his intention to downgrade the importance of the Western Front, was marked by the creation of the Allied Supreme War Council and the Air Ministry in November 1917, Robertson's replacement by General Sir Henry Wilson as CIGS in February, and the creation of the independent RAF in April. An important part of this was the enforced replacement of General Sir Launcelot Kiggell as Haig's Chief Staff Officer, and Brigadier-General John Charteris as his Chief of Intelligence (although Charteris remained at GHQ until August, attached to Transportation). Faced with these replacements, GHQ took the opportunity to restructure itself, in order both to better cope with the impending German offensive and to resist further incursions by Whitehall. This restructuring was again to play a significant part in the reporting of the events of 1918. Charteris' replacement, Brigadier General Edgar Cox, arrived at GHQ on 24 January, whereupon General Sir Herbert Lawrence, who had temporarily held the post, moved to replace Kiggell. Cox was fresh from heading MI3 at the War Office, the Intelligence section responsible for studying the structure and organisation of the German Army, and was the principal author of the main Intelligence handbook on the subject.[25] Haig's strategy for defence against the forthcoming German offensive depended very heavily on Cox's skill in determining the fighting quality of the various German divisions, and with his arrival GHQ ring-fenced Intelligence in order to concentrate on this role. Cox's only known involvement with the press was the decision to leak in advance the fact that GHQ knew the date of the German offensive to be 21 March, in the hope of disturbing German preparations.[26]

On 14 March, GHQ created a new Directorate of Staff Duties under Major General Guy Dawnay, as a *portmanteau* for a number of GHQ functions now regarded as peripheral to Intelligence. One of these was the GHQ Press Section, transferred from Intelligence and renamed the Censorship and Publicity Section, which consequently suffered from the double neglect of losing an influential patron in Charteris, and the more mundane fact that Dawnay himself took little interest in it.[27] It was widely agreed, both in London and in GHQ itself, that the number of official reporters, cine-cameramen and photographers in the new Censorship and Publicity Section was utterly inadequate to their task. But the political and administrative problems of creating even the very limited press structure that existed at GHQ had proved so great over three years that by 1918 even the major newspaper proprietors were more than content to leave well alone. There were usually about six British correspondents based at GHQ, together with a number of visiting reporters from other Allies, two or three official cameramen and the same number of photographers, to cover an Army of more than sixty divisions across the entire British sector of the Western Front. The Canadians and Australians, and even the New Zealanders, were distinctly better off, with their own propaganda and publicity organisations and their own cameramen.[28] The fact that the reporters were allowed to mention specific nationalities such as the Australians but not to identify British units also led to Dominion troops receiving more than their fair share of British publicity.

This neglect of the press and propaganda was entirely in keeping with Haig's own personal command style. He had learned to trust a handful of the senior reporters at GHQ, but he engaged with the press only indirectly and with difficulty. The press was tolerated at GHQ, but only just; indeed, a group of staff officers, including Lieutenant Colonel James Edmonds (later the British official historian) regarded it as amusing to pass false information to the reporters as a test of their credulity, something of which Edmonds boasted after the war to Charles Bean.[29]

Part of Cox's concern to be rid of responsibility for the press at GHQ was a dislike of having to deal directly with Northcliffe and Beaverbrook. Both men took the position that their respective organisations should control all aspects of propaganda, and they began to demand their own appointees within GHQ for that purpose.[30] The result was an institutional war to rival that going on in Whitehall, in which staff officers at GHQ used every device to block such appointments. Beaverbrook resorted to granting some of his men Canadian commissions, and temporarily paying their salaries from his own substantial private fortune. There was also an inevitable clash of cultures between the GHQ staff officers and these professional journalists: Harry Bartholomew, an experienced picture editor sent out to GHQ to oversee photographs, wrote to his superior in London in January that 'I would rather sweep a crossing than work with the crowd here;' Major Arthur Lee, one of the officers responsible for dealing with the press at GHQ, in turn complained that 'the war correspondents were always prepared to find fault with anything and everything'.[31] Not until 16 August was the official establishment for the Censorship and Publicity Section agreed. It took Crewe House until September to get complete control of propaganda leaflets from MI7, and even then Major Lee confidently pronounced these to be not 'worth wasting balloons on', despite his own confessed inability to read either German or French.[32] The MoI's attempts to increase even by a handful the number of photographers and cameramen continued to be blocked well into October, on one occasion by the argument that the GHQ officers mess did not have enough waiters to serve them all. 'Do think that I am depressed', Bartholomew wrote to London over this fiasco, 'I only wish the war would end, or a bomb drop on this establishment'.[33]

In covering the fighting on the Western Front in 1918, the correspondents and cameramen, British and Allied, faced the same problems as the troops themselves. The change in tactics and methods that had made breakthough and a restoration of mobility on the Western Front possible in 1918, itself a product of the 'learning curve' for all sides, produced wide, deep, confused and often infiltrated combat zones in which it was difficult to discover what had happened, and where the opposing forces actually were. Northcliffe was scathing about his own *Daily Mail* for publishing photographs entitled 'Street Snapshots At Maidenhead' on 23 March, as 'an absolute waste of space on the second day [*sic*] of the greatest battle in the world'.[34] Two days later GHQ introduced a ban on all visitors to the British Army on the Western Front, which was not eased until the middle of June. The daily difficulties of travelling out to a main battlefield perhaps fifty miles across, and then back to GHQ at Montreuil, led the reporters increasingly to fall back on GHQ briefings, while the photographers suffered similar problems. 'Out of 124 photographs received here of the offensive,' an MoI official in London wrote to his subordinate at GHQ on 11 April, 'there is only one with any sign at all of actual warfare, and that is a distant shell burst'.[35] Haig's famous 'Backs to the Wall' order in April 1918, read out as a press release at his GHQ at Montreuil by his private secretary Major Philip Sassoon, was aimed as much at Home Front consumption as at the troops; and perhaps also, as one historian has suggested, at the history books in case of outright defeat.[36]

British losses as a result of the German spring offensive also led by late March to the second Military Service Act, extending military service to men up to 50 years old, and sending 18 year old boys and convalescents to the Western Front. The political impossibility of enforcing this act's extension of conscription to Ireland led rapidly to the recognition at GHQ of the critical importance to the continued fighting effectiveness of the British Army of the strong Canadian Corps and two Australian Corps, together with the New Zealand Division. From Whitehall the perspective was slightly different, but the need for the Dominions to maintain their forces at full strength became an increasingly important part of the Lloyd George strategy of lasting out 1918. In turn, this increased importance of Dominion troops became a main theme in British official propaganda. The assembly of Dominion leaders in London in June for the meetings of the Imperial War Cabinet consequently took on a new and much greater significance.

During summer 1918, British newspapers largely continued to reflect the main government propaganda themes of holding out on the Home Front, the importance of the Dominion and Imperial effort, the build-up of American troops, and opportunities in the East. As a populist, Beaverbrook also prided himself on a deliberate change of emphasis in propaganda directed at the Home Front from the written to the visual media, which became probably the most important aspect of Home Front propaganda in 1918. For official Whitehall it was still the London quality press that mattered, but the mass of the people gained their information from the picture-spreads of the tabloids such as the *Daily Mail* and the *Daily Mirror*, together with the provincial press, and most importantly newsreel film. The most visible sign of this policy (in more ways than one) was the change to official film propaganda. In 1918 a large minority of the British people attended the cinema as their principal source of entertainment and information. From the propagandists' viewpoint they were not quite the ideal audience, as they included a majority of women and a significant number of younger people and children, but they represented by far the largest single working-class audience in the country.[37] The War Office Cinema Committee's twice-weekly newsreel, *The War Office Official Topical Budget*, which competed directly with commercial newsreels, reached an audience of about three million for each issue, about three times the circulation of Northcliffe's *Daily Mail.* According to his biographer, Beaverbrook claimed that, 'The Topical Budget shown in every picture palace was the decisive factor in maintaining the moral [*morale*] of the people during the black days of the early summer of 1918'.[38] If it cannot be supported, this claim at least conveys the importance attached to visual propaganda by the government at the time.

In February the newsreel underwent a name change to *The Pictorial News (Official).* This co-incided with Beaverbrook becoming Minister of Information, and marked his successful conclusion of a six-month battle to wrest complete control of the newsreel, including its content and style, away from its original commercial owners. Filming on the Western Front had, since its inception in late 1915, been dogged by considerable technical and administrative problems, including the impossibility of filming actual combat and the delays in the military censorship process. Some months *before* the change in government strategic thinking which devalued the importance of the Western Front, but fitting perfectly within it, Beaverbrook and his propagandists had decided for entirely practical and commercial reasons to emphasise the unusual and picturesque in their newsreel, including particularly film of Palestine and Mesopotamia. The newsreel's name change co-incided with the dedication of an entire issue to the newly-arrived film of Allenby's entry into Jerusalem. By a synergy rather than a coincidence, the film of this 'Christmas present to the British nation,' released on 23 February 1918, became the visible symbol of the new government strategy and propaganda policy.[39]

Other than the changes to the newsreel, the solution adopted by the film and photograph propagandists under Beaverbrook to the problem of obtaining good, authentic and topical images on the fighting fronts was, very much in keeping with the response of the print journalists to their own problems, largely to cease to try. Although filming of the fighting fronts continued, the MoI began in 1918 to emphasise instead cartoons and short fictional films with far better production values. There was also a move away from a fact-based approach to overt hate-propaganda of a distinctly crude sort. One notorious short fictional film, *The Leopard's Spots* (often known as *Once A Hun, Always A Hun*) made by Hepworth for the MoI, drew criticism from Parliament in August, not so much for its portrayal of German soldiers as swaggering, drunken baby molesters, but for its proclamation that Britain would not buy German goods after the war.[40] A large part of the hostility felt within the Foreign Office in particular towards Beaverbrook and Northcliffe was the manner in which they openly intruded in political and strategic issues, going far beyond their notional roles as propagandists and publicists. But Beaverbrook saw no discrepancy in the MoI dictating post-war trade policy, or indeed wartime foreign policy, arguing that 'we have a diplomacy of our own to conduct, a popular diplomacy'.[41] Again, the impact of such rabble-rousing material on the British people cannot be assessed in any definite sense. What can be said is that the government itself believed firmly in the power of such images, and that British Home Front enthusiasm for the war finished in the last months of 1918 on a high point not seen since its beginning.[42]

The contribution of Crewe House to the image of the British performance on the Western Front in 1918 appears to have been negligible, although promoting British successes in enemy countries certainly fell within its remit. A frequent complaint from Crewe House was that propaganda must follow government policy, and that no policy towards either Germany or Austria-Hungary was forthcoming. Northcliffe used this as an excuse to generate his own policy, with propaganda towards Austria-Hungary going far beyond government policy on promises of self-determination. Claims for the importance of its role were made in 1920 with the publication of *Secrets of Crewe House* by Sir Campbell Stewart, one of Northcliffe's subordinates. In Germany in particular, Northcliffe enjoyed quasi-demonic status in 1918 as the 'Father of All Lies' and master propagandist.[43] Colonel E. M. House, President Wilson's personal envoy, wrote to Northcliffe in July quoting United States' diplomatic cable dispatches from neutral countries close to Germany, passing on a German fear of 'the propaganda which Lord Northcliffe is directing against us. The English are doing more to defeat us in this way than the armies in the field'.[44] But historical research has modified the view that Northcliffe and Crewe House played the dominating role in Allied propaganda against the Central Powers, or that this had a major effect on the German Home Front collapse. Certainly, Crewe House plans for a propaganda offensive against Germany existed, but Northcliffe's political and bureaucratic struggles, together with his own continual illness, meant that it was not until August-September that Crewe House became effective as a propaganda organisation, and by that time the Central Powers were already collapsing, starting with Bulgaria. In keeping with government policy, and on the advice chiefly of Henry Wickham Steed, the main focus of Crewe House's efforts was not Germany but Austria-Hungary, where the role played by Italian propaganda both before Crewe Houses's involvement and through to the end of the war was probably more important.[45]

Well into summer 1918, both the British government and its propaganda apparatus continued to show the same indifference to the Western Front, and particularly to the role of the British Army. Leopold Amery, Assistant Secretary to the War Cabinet and a lifelong Imperialist, wrote to Lloyd George in early June in a way intended to delight him that, 'When this little "side show" in the West is over, whether the line gets stabilised or disappears altogether, we shall have to take the war for the mastery of Asia in hand seriously'.[46] Political attacks on both Lloyd George and on Beaverbrook and Northcliffe diminished significantly by the end of June, and it would be logical to associate this with a recognition in political London of the British success on the Western Front, but the evidence does not support this interpretation. Only a few days before the Battle of Amiens, the War Cabinet discussed halving Haig's Army to 35 divisions or less, in order to conduct the war better elsewhere. Haig's reputation in Whitehall was in fact no higher in summer than in spring, and this was reflected in the press coverage, with its concentration on the East, on the increasing importance of the Americans and on the global nature of the war. In July the weekly *The Sphere*'s front covers featured the arrival of A. F. Kerensky in London, King George V's silver wedding, the King of the Belgians, and the Second Battle of the Marne. The *Illustrated London News* for the same month featured on its front covers the King's silver wedding, American soldiers, French soldiers, and Czech troops on the Western Front. Haig appeared on the front cover of the *Illustrated London News* just once in 1918, on 31 August in reference to the Battle of Amiens, while its Armistice edition featured on its front cover a picture of Marshal Foch.

All this provided the context for the remarkable under-reporting of the Battle of Amiens and the Hundred Days' advance by the BEF. A new concern with security meant that, in marked contrast to the Battle of the Somme in 1916, the press were not told of the forthcoming offensive, and the doyen of the GHQ press corps, Philip Gibbs, was actually at home in Britain resting from illness when the battle began.[47] The remaining reporters and cameramen were occupied covering one of King George V's periodic visits to the Western Front, which began on 5 August. These Royal visits received great publicity in the belief that they boosted morale on the Home Front as much as in France. In the next few months of the Hundred Days, the strain on the reporters at GHQ trying to cover the advance was easily as great as that on any of the divisional staffs. 'Three of my colleagues at one time could scarcely endure to enter a motor-car except under compulsion', wrote William Beach Thomas of the *Daily Mail*, 'so worn were their nerves'.[48] It is not surprising that most of the correspondents reported the last great British victories and the Armistice in a subdued manner, the re-invigorated Philip Gibbs being an exception. Moreover, and again entirely in keeping with government policy, during summer and early autumn 1918 the resources of Beaverbrook's MoI were principally directed not to promoting Haig's forces but to publicising the role of the American troops who were at last making an impact on the Western Front. British propaganda resources were also directed not only at the Dominion leaders present for the Imperial War Cabinet, but also at their own accompanying pressmen from the Dominions. On 21 July, Haig himself was asked by London to make the time to meet a party of 26 Canadian newspaper owners at his headquarters chateau at Montreuil, and a further party of Dominion journalists on 7 September.[49] Beaverbrook ruled it more important that the GHQ cameramen and photographers should cover this latter excursion than that they should be out filming the front. Nor was he above diverting British cameramen and photographers to cover the Canadian Corps, at a time when their numbers had dropped to only one or two to record the battles of the entire British Army on the Western Front.

A last chance to boost the public image of Haig's Army came in October, as both the possible end of the war and the British General Election loomed. On 3 October, just before the *Daily Chronicle* was bought by Lloyd George's friends, it carried an article by Sir Frederick Maurice pointing out that 'the British successes on the Western Front since 8th August are much the greatest in scale ever won by the British Army or a British general,' but that the War Cabinet, which had sent official congratulations to General John J. Pershing and also to Allenby, had failed to do so to Haig.[50] Beaverbrook resigned as Minister of Information on 21 October, from ill-health due to swollen neck-glands, but also as it had also become apparent to him that his ambition for the MoI to become a permanent peacetime organ of government stood no chance of becoming a reality, and that he would not be offered a government post of real power. Just before his own resignation, Beaverbrook wrote to Northcliffe with the suggestion that he should take over as Minister of Information.[51] The MoI itself officially ceased to exist on the stroke of midnight on 31 December 1918, despite Beaverbrook's suggestion in October that it should be kept in existence at least until the signing of the peace treaties, in order to promote the British perspective.[52]

For Northcliffe the situation was rather different; from August onwards, he had been negotiating for, at least, a Cabinet seat in the next government, and a permanent and influential role for his British War Mission in any peace settlement. Beaverbrook put Northcliffe's ambition much higher, as 'a Lloyd George-Northcliffe administration,' and on 3 October Northcliffe wrote to Riddell that he and his newspapers would not support a future Lloyd George government unless he knew 'definitely and in writing, and can conscientiously approve, the personal constitution of the Government', a suggestion that Lloyd George naturally rejected.[53] This break between Northcliffe and Lloyd George became Haig's opportunity to win back Northcliffe's favour. Correspondence between Northcliffe and Major Sassoon resumed in September after a gap of several months, with a letter in which Northcliffe deplored the fact that Haig's name was hardly mentioned when the war was discussed in Britain.[54] Northcliffe continued to write to Haig through Sassoon, stressing the need for better publicity for Haig and his victories. Haig himself was usually absent from Montreuil at this stage of the war, preoccupied with directing his Armies from various temporary headquarters, or from his headquarters train. The first mention of the press in his diary for some time came on 12 October, when he recorded that he had received at his temporary headquarters in Arras 'six journalists from South Wales, who the propaganda department [sic] specially wanted me to see'. But on 17 October the Editor of the *Times*, Geoffrey Dawson, came out to Haig's headquarters, now based temporarily at Bertincourt, calling his attention to what Haig described as 'the very small support given by the English press to the British Army. Papers seem to vie with each other in cracking up the French, and running down British military methods and Generals!'.[55] Dawson's behaviour reflected Northcliffe's change of allegiance away from Lloyd George only a few days earlier. The final break between the two men came on 3 November, when Lloyd George refused Northcliffe's demand for a seat at the Peace Conference. On 12 November Northcliffe resigned from the British War Mission, which was disbanded.

This change of heart and policy by Northcliffe only just before the Armistice was too late to change the propaganda themes and Home Front impressions of the year. Haig himself from August to October had alternated between a belief that the war could be won in 1918 and a belief that the Germans might yet stabilise their line. In fact the conclusion that the German Army had lost the war on the Western Front came much earlier to the German Great General Staff, after the defeat at Amiens on 8 August, Ludendorff's famous 'black day of the German Army'. The General Staff's response to the prospect of defeat was to work to ameliorate its effect on the German Army, rather than on Germany or its people, by the creation of the *Dolchstosslegende*. As recent historical investigation has shown, for the senior officers of the General Staff this myth was an essential part of the mechanism of ending the war, by deflecting responsibility and criticism for Germany's defeat away from themselves and the German Army, and onto their political enemies.[56] As Hindenburg himself put it, with complete falsehood, 'Like Siegfried, stricken down by the treacherous spear of savage Hagen, our weary front collapsed'.[57] The belief that Crewe House had contrived the collapse of the German Home Front in 1918 was subsequently promoted in the 1920s by one of the strangest alliances of convenience in history: a mixture of British and European pacifists, boastful British journalists, League of Nations supporters, American isolationists, and German proto-Nazis. But by then any official British government institutions that might have challenged the German claim to be undefeated on the Western Front had been disbanded, and their real work forgotten.

The achievement of the British Army on the Western Front in 1918 was undervalued at the time through the cumulative effect of several apparently unrelated decisions. Reduced in importance at the year's start by Lloyd George's grand strategy, Haig's GHQ reduced still further its own interest in publicity and propaganda. Beaverbrooke's insistence on the shift to visual propaganda also played a part in reducing the impact on the public of a new and more technological style of fighting battles that was, by its very nature, neither as simple nor as accessible to reporters or cameramen as the methods of 1916, and not as picturesque as scenes of camels and ancient ruins in Palestine. Largely through the distractions caused Northcliffe's vast political ambitions, Crewe House also failed to project an image of a British Army superior to its enemies. Taken altogether, the British Army's colossal victory on the Western Front in 1918 was a story that was not so much forgotten as just never properly told.

NOTES

1. Most notably David French, *British Strategy and War Aims 1914-1916*, (London: Allen & Unwin, 1986), and *The Strategy of the Lloyd George Coalition*

1916-1918, (Oxford: Clarendon Press, 1995); David R. Woodward, *Lloyd George and the Generals*, (Newark: University of Delaware Press, 1983); Brock Millman, *Pessimism and British War Policy 1916-1918*, (London: Frank Cass, 2001).

2. Much has been done since the pioneering M. L. Sanders and Philip M. Taylor, *British Propaganda During the First World War 1914-1918* (London: Macmillan, 1982), which still remains the best starting place for this subject. Evidence cited in this paper is taken, in particular, from Gary S. Messinger, *British Propaganda and the State in the First World* War, (Manchester: Manchester University Press, 1992); Martin J. Farrar, *News From the Front: War Correspondents on the Western Front 1914*-1918, (Thrupp: Sutton, 1998); Nicholas Reeves, *Official British Film Propaganda During the First World* War, (London: Croom Helm, 1986); Jane Carmichael, *First World War Photographers*, (London: Routledge, 1989); Roger Smither (ed.*), Imperial War Museum Film Catalogue Volume 1: The First World War Archive*, (London: Flicks Books, 1994); Nicholas Hiley, 'Making War: The British News Media and Government Control 1914-1916,' PhD Thesis, Open University, 1984. Important studies of the media and propaganda in other countries during the war include David Welch, *Germany, Propaganda and Total War 1914-1918*, (London: Athlone, 2000); Mark Cornwall, *The Undermining of Austria-Hungary: The Battle for Hearts and Minds*, (London: Macmillan, 2000); John F. Williams, *ANZACs, The Media and the Great War*, (Sydney: University of New South Wales Press, 1999).

3. Paul Fussell, *The Great War and Modern Memory*, (Oxford: Oxford University Press, 1975); Modris Eksteins, *Rites of Spring: The Great War and the Birth of the Modern Age*, (London: Bantam, 1989); Samuel Hynes, *A War Imagined: The First World War and English Culture*, (London: Bodley Head, 1990); Jay Winter, *Sites of Memory, Sites of Mourning*, (Cambridge: Cambridge University Press, 1995); Joanna Bourke, *Dismembering the Male: Men's Bodies, Britain and the Great War*, (London: Reaktion, 1996); George Robb, *British Culture and the First World War*, (London: Palgrave, 2002).

4. Gary Sheffield, *Forgotten Victory: The First World War – Myths and Realities*, (London: Headline, 2001); Paddy Griffith, *Battle Tactics of the Western Front: The British Army's Art of Attack 1916-18*, (New Haven: Yale University Press, 1994); Robin Prior and Trevor Wilson, *Command on the Western Front*, (Oxford: Blackwell, 1992); Peter Simkins, 'Somme Reprise: Reflections on the Fighting for Albert and Bapaume, August 1918,' in Brian Bond et al, *Look To Your Front: Studies in the First World War*, (Staplehurst: Spellmount, 1999); Jonathan B. A. Bailey, 'The First World War and the birth of modern warfare,' in Macgregor Knox and Williamson Murray (eds.), *The Dynamics of Military Revolution 1300-2050*, (Cambridge: Cambridge University Press, 2001), pp. 132-153.

5. The various arguments are well covered in Brian Bond, *The Unquiet Western Front: Britain's Role in Literature and History*, (Cambridge: Cambridge University Press, 2002). See also Brian Bond (ed.), *The First World War and British Military History*, (Oxford: Clarendon Press, 1991); Stephen Badsey, '*Blackadder Goes Forth* and the "Two Western Fronts" Debate,' in Graham Roberts and Philip M. Taylor (eds), *The Historian, Television and Television History*, (Luton: University of Luton Press, 2001), pp. 113-126; Dan Todman, 'The Reception

of *The Great War* in the 1960s,' *Historical Journal of Film, Radio and Television*, Volume 22, Number 1, March 2002, pp. 29-36.

6.   Ian F.W. Beckett, *The Great War 1914-1918*, (London: Longman, 2001), especially pp. 158-179, 428-461; Michael Howard, *The First World War*, (Oxford: Oxford University Press, 2002), especially pp. 120-130; Hugh Cecil and Peter H. Liddle (eds.), *Facing Armageddon: The First World War Experienced*, (London: Leo Cooper, 1996).

7.   J.P. Harris with Niall Barr, *Amiens to the Armistice*, (London: Brassey's, 1998); John Terraine, *To Win a War: 1918 the Year of Victory*, (London: Sedgwick & Jackson, 1978).

8.   For manpower issues the author has relied particularly on Keith Grieves, *The Politics of Manpower 1914-1918*, (Manchester: Manchester University Press, 1988). See also R. J. Q. Adams and Philip P. Poirier, *The Conscription Controversy in Great Britain 1900-1918*, (London: Macmillan, 1987), pp. 205-244.

9.   This summary is based in particular on French, *The Strategy of the Lloyd George Coalition*, pp. 193-212.

10. John Bourne, *Britain and the Great War 1914-1918*, (London: Edward Arnold, 1989), p. 210; see also the discussion of British propaganda and the press in the same work pp. 202-209.

11. J. Lee Thompson, *Politicians, The Press and Propaganda: Lord Northcliffe and the Great War 1914-1919*, (Kent OH: Kent State University Press, 1999), pp. 175-6.

12. See in particular Philip M. Taylor, *British Propaganda in the Twentieth Century: Selling Democracy*, (Edinburgh: Edinburgh University Press, 1999), pp. 5-34.

13. See S. D. Badsey, '*Battle of the Somme*: British War Propaganda,' *Historical Journal of Film, Radio and Television*, Volume 2, Number 2, 1984, pp. 99-116.

14. Robert C. Self (ed.), *The Austen Chamberlain Diary Letters* (Cambridge: Royal Historical Society, 1995), p. 71.

15. For Beaverbrook's becoming minister see A. J. P. Taylor, *Beaverbrook*, (London: Penguin edition, 1974) pp. 188-194 *et seq*. Northcliffe's involvement with Lloyd George and the war effort in 1918 is extensively discussed in Thompson, *Politicians, The Press and Propaganda*, pp. 170-218.

16. For Northcliffe's involvement in propaganda in 1918 and his relationship with Haig and GHQ see Reginald Pound and Geoffrey Harmsworth, *Northcliffe*, (London: Cassell, 1959), pp. 598 *et seq*. See also Stephen Badsey, 'Haig and the Press,' in Brian Bond and Nigel Cave (eds.), *Haig: A Reappraisal 70 Years On*, (London: Leo Cooper, 1999), pp. 176-195.

17. Neville Lytton, *The Press and the General Staff*, (London: Collins, 1920), p. 152.

18. See file INF 4/6 'Confidential report on the need and form of British propaganda in France,' National Archives of Great Britain, Public Record Office, Kew [PRO].

19. Lord Beaverbrook, *Men and Power*, (London: Collins, 1956), p. 267

20. INF 4/1A and CAB 24/5 'Liquidation of the Ministry of Information' 20 December 1918, PRO. Some Ministry of Information documents exist in the Beaverbrook Papers in the House of Lords Record Office, and others have been found in Canadian collections (I am grateful to Roger Smither for this last information).

21. Taylor, *Beaverbrook*, p. 198.

22. Woodward, *Lloyd George and the Generals*, pp. 282-6.
23. Robert Blake (ed), *The Private Papers of Douglas Haig 1914-1919*, (London: Eyre & Spottiswoode, 1952), p. 287. Passages from the Haig diaries not found in this edited version are given as 'Haig Papers'. The original diary is part of the Haig Papers held at the National Library of Scotland, Edinburgh. A Photostat copy is held as file WO 256 1-37 PRO.
24. Robert C. Self (ed.), *The Austen Chamberlain Diary Letters* (Cambridge: Royal Historical Society, 1995), p. 71. See also [George Riddell], *Lord Riddell's War Diary 1914-1918*, (London: Ivor Nicholson and Watson, 1933), p. 310.
25. David Nash (ed), *German Army Handbook April 1918* (Reprinted London: Arms and Armour, 1977); for Cox's career see Frank Davies and Graham Maddocks, *Bloody Red Tabs*, (London: Leo Cooper, 1995), p. 56.
26. Lytton, *The Press and the General Staff*, p. 146.
27. Ibid, pp. 141-2.
28. Farrar, *News From the Front*, pp. 189-224; Reeves, *Official British Film Propaganda During the Great* War, pp. 77-88; Carmichael, *World War One Photographers*, pp. 46-75; Peter Robertson, 'Canadian Photojournalism during the First World War,' *History of Photography*, Volume 2, Number 1, January 1978; Leonard Bickel, *In Search of Frank Hurley*, (Melbourne: Macmillan, 1980), pp. 55-72.
29. Letter from Edmonds to Bean 16 October 1928, File of Correspondence with J.E. Edmonds 1927-1939, Papers of Charles Bean, Australian War Memorial, Canberra; see also the critical comments of Major (later Lieutenant Colonel) A.N. Lee in his own papers, 'The World War I Diary of Lt. Col. Arthur Neale Lee,' Reference 66/121/1 Department of Documents, Imperial War Museum, London [IWM], hereafter 'Lee Diary'.
30. Lytton, *The Press and the General Staff*, p. 140; Lee Diary, page 172, IWM.
31. Bartholomew to Holt, 14 January 1918, Bartholomew File, Papers of the Ministry of Information Photographic Department [MoI (Photo)] held by the Department of Photographs, IWM; Lee Diary, page 137, IWM
32. Lee Diary, pages 180-1, IWM.
33. Letter Bartholomew to Roon, 22 October 1918, Bartholomew File, MoI (Photo) Papers, IWM.
34. Pound and Harmsworth, *Northcliffe*, p. 628
35. Holt to Clough, 11 April 1918, File 'The Ministry of Information 1918,' Papers of the War Office Cinema Committee and Ministry of Information [MoI (Film) Papers] held by the Film and Video Archive, IWM.
36. Millman, *Pessimism and British War Policy*, p. 251; although Millman is wrong to think that all those in France who received this order were dismissive about it.
37. Nicholas Reeves, 'Film Propaganda and its Audience: The Example of Britain's Official Films during the First World War,' *Journal of Contemporary History*, Volume 18, 1983, pp. 463-494; Nicholas Hiley, 'The British Cinema Auditorium,' in Karel Dibberts and Bert Hogenkamp (eds.), *Film and the First World War*, (Amsterdam: Amsterdam University Press, 1995), pp. 160-170.
38. Taylor, *Beaverbrook*, p. 197 (Taylor attributes this quotation to Beaverbrook, but leaves it unreferenced); see also Luke McKernan, *Topical Budget: The Great British News Film*, (London: BFI, 1992).

39. Luke McKernan, '"The Supreme Moment of the War": *General Allenby's Entry Into Jerusalem,'* *Historical Journal of Film, Radio and Television*, Volume 13, Number 2, 1993, pp. 169-180; Matthew Hughes, *Allenby and British Strategy in the Middle East 1917-1919*, (London: Frank Cass, 1999).

40. Messinger, *British Propaganda and the State in the First World War*, pp. 137-8; Brock Millman, *Managing Domestic Dissent in First World War Britain*, (London: Frank Cass, 2000), p. 240-5, Smither, *Imperial War Museum Film Catalogue Volume 1*, p. 449.

41. Taylor, *Beaverbrook*, p. 203.

42. Nicholas Reeves, 'The Power of Film Propaganda – Myth or Reality?' *Historical Journal of Film, Radio and Television*, Volume 13, Number 2, 1993, pp. 181-202.

43. Welch, *Germany, Propaganda and Total War*, pp. 229-232; General Erich Ludendorff, *The Concise Ludendorff Memoirs 1914-1918*, (London: Hutchinson, n.d.), pp. 171-175; Sir Stewart Campbell, *Secrets of Crewe House: The Story of a Famous Campaign*, (London: Hodder and Stoughton, 1920); [Anon], *The History of The Times Volume IV: The 150th Anniversary and Beyond 1912-1948, Part 1, Chapters 1-XII 1912-1920*, (London: Times Publishing, 1952), pp. 350-366; Messinger, *British Propaganda and the State in the First World War*, pp. 154-5, 169-83; Pound and Harmsworth, *Northcliffe*, p. 671.

44. Pound and Harmsworth, *Northcliffe*, p. 656.

45. Cornwall, *The Undermining of Austria-Hungary*, passim; Taylor, *British Propaganda in the Twentieth Century*, pp. 49-62; Messinger, *British Propaganda and the State in the First World War*, pp. 162-183.

46. Quoted in Woodward, *Lloyd George and the Generals*, p. 315.

47. Philip Gibbs, *The Pageant of the Years*, (London: William Heinemann, 1946), p. 225.

48. Quoted in Farrar, *News From the Front*, p. 207.

49. Haig Diary, 21 July 1918 and 7 September 1918, Haig Papers.

50. *Daily Chronicle*, 3 October 1918.

51. The reply, declining the offer, is a letter from Northcliffe to Beaverbrook, 13 October 1918, Beaverbrook Papers, House of Lords Record Office.

52. Memorandum from Beaverbrook to the War Cabinet, 16 October 1918, File 'Memorandum to War Cabinet on the Setting Up of the Imperial News Wireless Service,' Beaverbrook Papers, House of Lords Record Office.

53. Beaverbrook, *Men and Power*, p. 88; Pound and Harmsworth, *Northcliffe*, p. 666; *Lord Riddell's War Diary*, p. 366; Beaverbrook, *Men and Power*, p. 88.

54. Thompson, *Politicians, The Press and Propaganda*, p. 209.

55. Haig Diary, 12 October 1918, Haig Papers; Blake, *The Private Papers of Sir Douglas Haig 1914-1919*, p. 332.

56. Welch, *Germany, Propaganda and Total War*, p. 253; Holger H. Herwig, *The First World War: Germany and Austria-Hungary 1914-1918*, (London: Arnold, 1997), pp. 425-6; Laurence V. Moyer, *Victory Must Be Ours: Germany in the Great War 1914-1918*, (London: Leo Cooper, 1995), pp. 276-83; Robert B. Asprey, *The German High Command at War: Hindenburg and Ludendorff Conduct World War I*, (New York: William Morrow, 1991), pp. 479-80.

57. Marshal [Paul] von Hindenburg, *Out of My Life*, (London: Cassell, 1920), pp. 436-440.

Chapter Four
HOLY WAR IN EUROPE: CHARLES SAROLÉA, *EVERYMAN* AND THE FIRST WORLD WAR, 1914-1917
Samantha T. Johnson

In the early months of the First World War, the role of 'good' and 'evil' featured in the propaganda of both sides, and, as one historian has indicated, 'mobilized sacred images and words on behalf of the cause'.[1] During these initial stages, the national churches of the protagonists promoted the war as a holy mission, and the apparent righteousness of the war was promoted by politicians and priests alike.[2] As the war dragged on, however, the role of religion in propaganda decreased considerably. Where, after all, was God to be found in the desolation of No Man's Land? But there were, in Britain, pockets of intellectuals who continued to place great emphasis on the part played by religious and moral justice in the war. Indeed, these individuals viewed the conflict as a holy war. It was being fought not by the Entente against the Dual Alliance, but by the Protestant and Catholic Churches. The pan-European disaster of 1914-1918 was regarded as the final battle in a war that had begun with the religious Reformation in the sixteenth century.

Such a view of the Great War and its place in history was a frequent subject of discussion in *Everyman*, a British weekly journal edited in Edinburgh and published in London. It was founded in 1912 by the publisher J.M. Dent and Dr Charles Saroléa, head of the department of French at the University of Edinburgh. Saroléa was editor and frequent contributor to *Everyman*, although as proprietor Dent felt a need to interfere regularly in matters of content. Fundamentally of populist leanings, it tackled a wide variety of topics, including literature, political affairs, history, education and the role of the church. It featured articles by some well-known contemporary commentators, including Hilaire Belloc, G.K. and Cecil Chesterton, George Bernard Shaw, the leading pacifist Norman Angell and the Polar explorer Ernest Shackleton. There were also contributions from European figures, most notably the leader of the Belgian socialist party, Émile Vandervelde, Russian exile George Raffalovitch, German military historian Hans Delbrück, and the French playwright Henri Mazel.[3]

From the outset *Everyman* owed much of its early success and character to Charles Saroléa (1870-1953).[4] The considerable weekly endeavour of getting the journal from the editing process into the nation's newsagents was testament to his boundless energy and commitment. A Belgian by birth, he had arrived in Edinburgh in 1894 to take up his post at the University, and was to spend the rest of his life there, taking citizenship in 1912. His academic duties were never sufficient to engage his restless and industrious spirit, and amongst his many other roles he was Belgian consul in Edinburgh (1908-1953) and literary advisor to a number of publishers.[5] He occupied his free time with three hobbies: travel, learning languages and book collecting. Before 1914, Saroléa had visited most European states and claimed knowledge of around eighteen languages.[6] Given the outlook of its editor, it was hardly surprising that *Everyman* was every bit as cosmopolitan as Saroléa.

Everyman regularly contained a host of articles by European commentators on European themes, all of which resulted from Saroléa's personal connections and outlook. He was frequently at pains to stress that *Everyman* had an international perspective, and the advantages of European co-operation were emphasised. In 1912, Saroléa wrote: 'In order to be good Englishmen and good Germans, we must, first of all, be good Europeans'.[7] The war would, of course, challenge such a standpoint, and even before 1914 it was apparent that Saroléa did not, as he claimed, view every state from an equal or temperate perspective. But from its birth *Everyman* attempted to broadly analyse European matters and would continue to do so during the war.

When it came to domestic issues, *Everyman* stood to the right of contemporary politics, or more accurately right-radical. Once again this was due to Saroléa's influence, and many of his grievances featured as regular themes and threads. In particular, he took exception to democracy, party politics, capitalism and socialism. He held a disparaging view of the working classes, believing their psychology was like that of children, and did not approve of universal suffrage.[8] Such notions were markedly similar to those of G.K. Chesterton and Hilaire Belloc, or the 'Chesterbelloc' as their collective ideas were christened by George Bernard Shaw. Saroléa had been introduced to these two popular figures in 1911, and their world-views shared distinct elements. Central to the outlook of all three was the role of religion, and to some degree all were 'militant Catholics'.[9] The important of religion was accompanied by an admiration for France and all-things French. This respect for France was inspired partly by its social structure and, in particular, its supposedly conservative peasantry which, all three believed, acted as a bulwark against greatly-feared proletarian revolution.[10] Another source of stability and continuity in France was the Catholic Church. Indeed, Rome was viewed as the repository and sentinel of European civilisation. The inevitable corollary to such beliefs was a rejection of Protestantism and the Protestant Church. Imperial Germany was, therefore, the very antithesis of politically and spiritually stable France, and regarded as the 'barbarous destroyer of Europe's democratic tradition and the repository of all evil'.[11] Clearly, although Saroléa comprehensively assessed and discussed European matters in *Everyman*, not all states were appraised equally. In 1912, Saroléa fully expected a pan-European conflict to occur in the near future and only Catholic France, he believed, could save civilisation from the evils of Prussianised Protestant Germany.[12] Britain, it was believed, could assist in this mission, but its role as a moral champion was a mute point.[13]

For Saroléa, and to some extent the Chesterbelloc, Tsarist Russia also occupied an important place in his affections. Although not a Catholic state, Saroléa believed that the purest form of Christianity in the world could be found amongst Russia's millions of peasants. Such a view emphasised the important role Saroléa ascribed to peasants, who, in Russia, apparently practised a form of Christianity that was not adulterated by external influences. Neither was religion closely aligned to the state, in contrast to the church in Imperial Germany.[14]

On the eve of the First World War, Saroléa's religious, political and social affiliation had been clearly defined in *Everyman*. Although a committed Europeanist, he believed that some states were planning to undermine the continent's stability. In this respect, the guiltiest state in Saroléa's mind was Germany. He believed that the Kaiserreich had long ceased to behave as a 'good' European state. It was the moral responsibility of Britain, France and Russia to safeguard Europe from the spiritual and military tyranny of Prussianised Germany. If forced to take up the sword in defence of Europe's freedom, any battle in which Britain participated would be wholly justifiable and righteous.

The Opening Salvoes: Saroléa and Germany

At the outbreak of hostilities in August 1914, Saroléa found himself in a particularly advantageous position. Only months before, in May 1914, he had become owner-editor of *Everyman* and was therefore free from J.M. Dent's editorial interference.[15] In addition, during the early days of the German invasion of Belgium, Saroléa was in Paris and his wife and children were holidaying in the family villa at Middelkerke, near Ostende.[16] Whilst his family promptly returned to Scotland, Saroléa took their place in Belgium and installed himself as a war-correspondent as near to the front-line as he could get.[17] *Everyman* benefited, therefore, from Saroléa's first-hand experience of events in Belgium.

In the early months of the war, there were two facets to *Everyman*'s reportage. The first was discussion of the nature of the German invasion of Belgium. The second took the form of a Belgian relief fund for refugees who had been displaced by the Kaiser's army and found their way to Britain. Both these subjects were close to Saroléa's heart. Although he had known for many years that his native land would be inevitably drawn into any continental conflict, the German invasion nevertheless shocked Saroléa. A personal perspective on these events was, he freely admitted, unavoidable and he openly confessed to *Everyman*'s readers that he could not 'pretend to remain neutral or impassive' about the suffering of the Belgian people.[18] Saroléa had many family members who were permanently resident in Belgium, including his aged mother. Most were located in areas of Belgium that bore the brunt of the initial stages of the invasion.[19] Saroléa wrote of finding German troops 'quartered in my father's house, and my mother a prisoner in their hands'.[20]

Saroléa claimed, like many British, French and Belgian commentators in 1914, that the German army had perpetrated numerous atrocities against the Belgian people.[21] The 'barbaric Hun' had apparently indulged in an unprecedented level of violence and committed unspeakable outrages against civilians 'unequalled in the whole history of modern warfare'.[22] In Antwerp, for instance, the day after a German attack, Saroléa saw some gruesome sights, including a 'chamber of horrors, where every wall [was] bespattered with the entrails of women and children'.[23] Elsewhere he observed the 'endless vista of hospital wards', 'two hundred old men and women in a frenzy of terror' hiding in 'murky catacombs, oozing with moisture', and gravediggers busy on a battlefield [burying] the mutilated bodies of two farmers'.[24] Such images, he wrote, would haunt him 'till the end of his days'.[25]

Saroléa's revelations about the barbarity of the German invasion were closely connected to the setting up of the *Everyman* Belgian Relief Fund in August 1914. His graphic descriptions were intended to elicit the sympathy of his readers in order that they give generously to the fund. Such strategy apparently worked, and by September 1914 over £11,000 had been raised.[26] Further monies were raised in November 1914 with the appearance of a supplement to *Everyman*, the 120-page 'Special Relief Number'. The compiling of this publication was again a tribute to Saroléa's seemingly boundless energy and his commitment to the Belgian cause. It contained articles by a variety of well-known figures, including Chesterton and Belloc, Bernard Shaw, the historian H.A.L. Fisher and sociologist B.Seebohm Rowntree. Amongst its European commentators were Cardinal Mercier, Belgium's primate, Nobel Prize winner Maurice Maeterlinck and the former French minister of finance, Yves Guyot.

Many of the contributions in the 'Special Relief Number' responded to the early events of the war, and therefore added to *Everyman*'s general condemnation of the nature of the German invasion of Belgium. For instance, Émile Faguet, a French academic, accused the Kaiser's soldiery of devastating a nation that was the 'flower of humanity'.[27] G.K.Chesterton spoke of the 'triumph of the degenerate', and three illustrated supplements revealed in turn the 'wanton destruction, sacrilege and pillage', 'the brutality of the Huns' and the 'sad tale of the refugees'.[28]

Saroléa's contribution to the Special Relief Number revealed his own take on the war. His interest was not merely connected to fund-raising and, for him, there was a profound religious and moral significance to what had occurred in Belgium. This would have future ramifications for European civilisation. The land of his birth, he firmly believed, had performed a great sacrifice on behalf of its allies:

The Belgian tragedy touches every responsive chord, it calls forth every deeper feeling of human nature: sympathy for a small nation unjustly attacked, indignation for an odious international crime, determination for a gallant people, gratitude for those who have sacrificed themselves and did not count the cost.[29]

There was a spiritual dimension to the sacrifice the Belgian people had performed. Even in these early stages, Saroléa was thinking of the conflict as a 'holy war' and did not disguise this from his readers:

From the beginning the war was to the Belgian people much more than a national war; it became a Holy War. And the expression 'Holy' War must be understood in a literal and exact definition. The Belgian War was a crusade of Civilisation against Barbarism, or eternal right against brute force. In theological language Belgium suffered *vicariously* for the sake of Europe. She had to submit to barbarism in order that humanity elsewhere might be vindicated. She had to lose her soul in order to save the soul of Europe.[30]

This theme ran through *Everyman* for the duration Saroléa's editorship, and his attacks on Germany extended beyond the theatre of war. Moral and spiritual decay was at work throughout Prussianised Germany, from ordinary soldiers and their generals, to ministers of state and the Kaiser. It affected the German state, bureaucracy, armed forces and the church. A number of key figures played a central role in this degeneracy, including the unholy triumvirate of General Friedrich Von Bernhardi, historian Heinrich von Treitschke, and, somewhat inevitably, the philosopher Friedrich Nietzsche. As a result, Saroléa believed, there was no question that a 'slump in theology' had occurred in Germany. The Entente, fighting desperately to save 'civilisation' was doing so against the 'least Christian nation in Europe':[31]

The German people have ceased to believe in Christianity; but they have come to believe in his self-styled Anti-Christ Nietzsche. They have ceased to believe in God; but they still believe in His self-appointed vicegerent, the Kaiser. They have ceased to believe in the Holy Trinity; but they believe all the more fanatically in the New Trinity of Superman, Super-race and the Super-State. And it is this new fanatical belief that has brought about the war of the nations.[32]

Trinities regularly featured in the columns of *Everyman*, and were clearly intended as religious metaphors by Saroléa. He believed that in Germany, 'Father, Son and Holy Ghost' had been replaced by earthly idols. Nietzsche, Treitschke and Bernhardi made frequent appearances in *Everyman*.[33] A further trinity appeared in October 1915, after an event which, according to Saroléa, was the greatest demonstration yet of the 'depravity of the German soul'.[34] This was the execution of Nurse Edith Cavell, whose martyrdom cast 'a sinister light on the state of religion' in Germany.[35] This time the metaphorical trinity appeared as a sketch on the front page of *Everyman*, and comprised of Cavell, Florence Nightingale and Joan of Arc. The feminine, saintly and, above all, Christian virtues these women apparently possessed were, in Saroléa's mind, representative of all that was worth fighting for. The presence of Joan of Arc, in particular, was indicative of Catholic defiance and intent. These women were intended to stand in stark contrast to the masculine, barbaric, and satanic figures of Nietzsche, Treitschke and Bernhardi.

In the early months of the war, most of Saroléa's religious venom was directed rather generally at the protestant churches in Germany. No specific figure apparently shouldered the blame for the failings of Protestantism. This changed in 1916, when, quite suddenly, Martin Luther became Saroléa's next target. At the base of this grievance lay a fundamental disagreement with the structure of the church in Germany, largely the result of Luther's machinations, and especially with its close alignment to the state. Indeed, according to Saroléa, there existed in Germany such a 'confusion of temporal and spiritual power', the church had merely become a tool of government:

Christianity in a political sense has always meant the separation of the spiritual and the temporal powers. It is the essence of Anglo-Saxon Protestantism that it actually does protest. Prussian Protestantism has ceased to protest, and conforms to whatever is demanded by the state. The Lutheran parson is the obedient servant of the Hohenzollern.[36]

The role of the Lutheran church was to remain a grievance for the rest of the war. It was connected to Saroléa's long view of history, and reaffirmed his belief that the principal watershed in European history had occurred with the Reformation. In October 1917, a two-piece article directly confronted the part Luther and his church had played in Germany's spiritual degeneration.[37] It revealed that Lutheranism had, in Saroléa's words, broken the 'splendid unity of the European commonwealth' and destroyed the 'continuity of the Catholic religion'.[38] The 'Lutheran poison' had turned the German people into a 'submissive and unpolitical people' who had willingly and unquestioningly allowed themselves to be dragged into war.[39] It meant that the war being fought by the Entente was a truly righteous one.

Russia and Revolution

The part that Russia played in Saroléa's affections and worldview ensured that during the war it never strayed too far from his editorial pen. The war brought, however, numerous challenges to Saroléa's perceptions of the Tsarist Empire, and in contrast to his writings on Imperial Germany, he was not always preaching to the converted. Indeed, his views on Russia were mostly at odds with those held by the vast majority of his contemporaries. He believed, for instance, that Russia was benevolently governed by 'a paternal and religious monarchy', a notion that many others would have found hard to swallow.[40] For a long time in the west, particularly in France and Britain, Tsarist Russia had been regarded as a cruel despotism, arbitrarily governed by one man, and where stepping out of line meant an excursion to Siberia or being fitted with a 'Stolypin necktie'. In 1914, British and French commentators and politicians of every political hue found it difficult to reconcile an alliance with a nation that was apparently as oppressive as it had been a hundred years earlier. In the United States, despotic Russia was often cited as a justification for keeping out of the war.

Saroléa was well aware of the opposition to Russia that existed in Britain and France. It was frequently discussed amongst the intellectual circles in which he moved in the early years of the war.[41] He had first-hand experience, too, of U.S. resistance to Tsarist Russia. This he encountered during a 1915 lecture tour of the U.S. and Canada on behalf of *Everyman*'s Belgian Relief Fund.[42] As he often spoke in favour of the alliance with Russia, he sometimes found himself subjected to personal abuse.[43] In addition, Saroléa produced many pro-Russian articles for *Everyman*, all of which were directly aimed at Tsarism's detractors. He was determined to reveal the worthiness of Russia as an ally, whether in military, political, social and religious terms. He aimed, also, to ensure that when Russia was compared to Imperial Germany, the latter always appeared in an unfavourable light.

In an ambitious four-piece article entitled 'What the World Owes to Russia', Saroléa attempted to highlight to *Everyman*'s readers, and, no doubt, his other critics, the 'fallacy of the Russian peril'.[44] The central purpose of this piece was to contrast 'good' and 'bad' states in Europe, descriptions that must be understood from a religious perspective. The gulf between Protestant Germany and Tsarist Russia was amply emphasised, and it revealed that the Entente's eastern component stood for 'essential Christianity'.[45] Its people were the 'most religious' in the world, and their faith remained the 'regenerative influence of

Russian life'.[46] The soul of the Tsarist Empire was 'untainted by materialism, by the hypocrisy of western civilisation'.[47] Once again, a metaphorical trinity was used to highlight Saroléa's message. In contrast to the barbaric trio of Nietzsche, Treitschke and Von Bernhardi, the Tsarist Empire offered a literary triumvirate composed of Fyodr Dostoevskii, Lev Tolstoi and Ivan Turgeniev. Although these men were, in Saroléa's words, 'typical Russians', they were also 'equally good Europeans'.[48] Such a claim, though clearly somewhat tenuous, was a further demonstration of the central role Russia generally played in European civilisation, and not merely in the Entente.[49]

Saroléa made further assertions in regard to Russia's suitability as an ally, some of which must surely have been difficult for *Everyman*'s readers to believe. He claimed, for instance, that the Tsarist Empire stood for 'democracy and liberty' and was the 'liberator of oppressed nationalities'.[50] In this regard, Saroléa had in mind the liberation of those suffering under German occupation in Eastern Europe, and not those ordinarily living under Romanov jurisdiction, such as Poles and Jews. He also asserted that freedom in Russia was 'an elemental instinct, a fanatical passion which [created] martyrs, and [sent] its votaries to Siberia and the scaffold'.[51] The Russians, unlike their German counterparts, were not 'politically servile' and were prepared to fight to the death in the name of freedom.[52] He pointed to the peasant commune and the *Zemstvo* as proof of political representation and democracy in Russia. If *Everyman*'s audience remained unconvinced of Russia's desire for freedom and its healthy role in the Entente, it was assured that Britain and France would surely influence Tsarism both morally and politically. The close relationship of these three countries, forged as a result of war, would ensure that 'French and British institutions [would] mould the destinies of the Empire'.[53] The benefits of the alliance with Russia were not only being reaped in wartime, but would last far into the future.

Given Saroléa's support for the Tsarist regime, it might have been anticipated that he would oppose the February 1917 revolution that the toppled the Romanovs. He had, since the 1890s, explicitly backed autocratic rule in Russia. However, against these expectations, Saroléa actually spoke out in favour of the Revolution and in *Everyman* declared it a 'magnificent moral and political victory'.[54] It was 'conclusive proof' that the West had 'nothing to dread from the Russian people', and therefore a vindication for Saroléa's pro-Russian propaganda.[55] There were several reasons for Saroléa's apparent shift in allegiances, and his rejection of the autocracy. Like so many of his contemporaries, inside and outside Russia, Saroléa believed the gossip commonly proliferated in late 1916 and early 1917, that the Tsarina was actually a German spy.[56] The removal of the Romanovs therefore eradicated German influence at court. Such a belief was closely intertwined with Saroléa's hopes for victory in the war, undoubtedly his most important priority. Winning the righteous and holy war against Germany was a gaol to be pursued at all costs.

Saroléa's belief in a pro-German lobby within the highest echelons of the Tsarist government ensured that the events of February 1917 were greeted with evident relief. Henceforth, he assured *Everyman*'s readers, Russia would throw all its might against the enemy. Having replaced the Tsar and Tsarina, the Duma and the Provisional Government would become the 'organisers of victory'.[57] He was certain, also, that the Russian people's commitment to the

Entente's cause was even greater. The war was now 'twice sacred'.[58] It was, first of all, a sacred 'war of liberation against the Teuton', and, secondly, 'a war of liberation against an internal enemy'.[59] In April 1917, Saroléa described in detail the members of the Provisional Government, or, as he dubbed them, the 'Master Builders of the New Russia'.[60] These men, charged with responsibility for Russia's political destiny, had a profound duty to maintain a sacred task and keep Russia in the holy war against Germany.

Whilst Saroléa generally welcomed the Revolution, he nevertheless had some reservations about events in Russia. In particular, he was concerned with the composition of the Provisional Government. On the whole, Saroléa admired most of the men occupying significant posts in the new government, many of whom were intellectuals. But, in April 1917, he noted with some worry, the 'weakness of the labour element'.[61] Alexandr Kerenskii, Saroléa observed, was the only representative of Russia's labouring classes. In a prophetic moment, Saroléa predicted that such a shortcoming might prove the 'weakness of the cabinet'.[62] 'It is easy to foresee', he wrote, 'that, before many weeks are over, the extreme section of the revolutionary movement will demand a much stronger representation in the cabinet'.[63] The whole future of the government, Saroléa warned, depended on whether its 'bourgeois members, the princes and the professors and industrial magnates, will be able to cooperate' with the socialist parties.[64] He was undoubtedly accurate in these assertions. From the outset of the Revolution, Russia's former imperial capital was home to two centres of power: the Provisional Government and the Petrograd Soviet. Saroléa instinctively recognised that this was a recipe for instability, and from an early stage, as he predicted, the Soviet hindered the Provisional Government every move.

Throughout 1917, *Everyman* presented to its readers an exceptionally accurate and detailed account of the events unfolding in Russia. In May 1917, the optimism Saroléa had once felt for the Revolution was beginning to wane somewhat, and he recognised that 'Russian democracy [was] engaged in a deadly conflict with the forces of anarchy'.[65] In another perceptive moment of political prophecy, Saroléa wrote: 'Today Miliukov is overruled by Kerenskii; tomorrow Kerenskii may be overruled by Lenin'.[66] It was not long before such a prediction was apparently being fulfilled, and in August 1917 *Everyman* noted that 'a counter-revolution is imminent'.[67] A month later, Saroléa and his journal were predicting a civil war in Russia, and he urged the Russian people to 'chose between the civilian dictatorship of demagogues – which means anarchy, chaos and disaster – and a ruthless military dictatorship'.[68]

Masaryk and Austria-Hungary

Saroléa's accurate analysis of the February Revolution, the events of 1917 and their repercussion was largely the result of a friendship he established in late 1915 with Tomáš Garrigue Masaryk, future president of Czechoslovakia. At the time, Masaryk was an exile and living in London, from where he promoted the cause for Czech and Slovak independence. He was also a lecturer at the School of Slavonic and East European Studies, King's College London. Saroléa was present at Masaryk's inaugural lecture in October 1915, from which time the two men began a vigorous correspondence.[69] There were two important repercussions to this encounter. The first was Masaryk's influence on Saroléa's view of Russia. Even in his own time, Masaryk was regarded as an expert in Russian and eastern European affairs. Undoubtedly, Saroléa's relationship with Masaryk ensured he had an exceptionally insightful view of Russian politics. As we have already seen, such knowledge was to prove invaluable throughout 1917.

The second ramification of Masaryk's influence was Saroléa's conversion to the cause of Czech and Slovak independence. In the early years of the war, Austria-Hungary was noticeable only by its absence from *Everyman*'s war pronouncements and writings. Austria's alliance with Germany was a factor Saroléa ignored, or at least considered unimportant. The fact that Austria was a Catholic state may have played a role in Saroléa's disinterest. Catholic Austria-Hungary was difficult for Saroléa to incorporate into his notions of Holy War. It was only in 1916, that articles appeared in *Everyman* which were both anti-Habsburg and supported the dismantling of the Habsburg Monarchy. This was not a coincidence, and Saroléa's commitment to the anti-Habsburg cause resulted directly from his personal encounter with Masaryk.[70]

As already noted, Saroléa had long regarded Germany as the chief mischief-maker on the European continent. It must therefore have come as a surprise to his readers when in June 1916, Saroléa asked in *Everyman*, 'Is this an Austrian War or a German War?'[71] He noted that the British people had been told '*ad nauseam*, that we are fighting mainly to destroy Prussian militarism'.[72] Several readers must have raised an eyebrow at this comment. After all, Saroléa, too, had repeatedly presented the war as a confrontation between the 'good' (and mostly Catholic) states of the West and 'evil' Protestant Prussia. In a surprising twist, Saroléa revealed:

Austria has ever been a Pan-Germanic Power. It is Vienna which has dragged Berlin into this catastrophe. The Serbian quarrel was mainly an Austrian quarrel, and but for this quarrel, but for the Oriental ambitions of Austria, this War could never have taken place.[73]

Such a perspective was in tune with Masaryk's views on the origins and protagonists of the war.

Saroléa was taken very quickly into Masaryk's confidence after their initial meeting at the end of 1915. As a result, both Saroléa and *Everyman* benefited from a detailed insight into the affairs of Austria-Hungary and the future plans for a liberated Bohemia. In February 1916, for instance, Saroléa was permitted to read a secret memorandum Masaryk had prepared for the British Foreign Office.[74] Entitled *At the Eleventh Hour*, it would not be circulated at the F.O. until April 1916.[75] Many of Masaryk's opinions in the memorandum accorded with Saroléa's, particularly on the matter of German militarism.

It cannot be doubted that Saroléa and Masaryk shared a mutual antipathy towards Germany. This may have been the initial intellectual attraction in their friendship. Masaryk certainly held the same views as Saroléa on pan-German expansion, and was convinced that the Kaiser's war-plan was to extend the Empire's sphere of influence from Berlin to Baghdad. Unlike Saroléa's early pronouncements on German imperialist intentions, Masaryk believed that the Dual Monarchy was a crucial component of the *Drang nach Osten*. In *At the Eleventh Hour*, Masaryk wrote that Austria and Hungary were 'the tools and puppets of Pan-Germanism'.[76] In this regard, it was Berlin's ultimate aim to preserve the Habsburg Empire. Masaryk therefore urged the Allies to support the dismemberment of the Austrian Empire. Any scheme for the preservation of the Empire was, he believed, 'a direct form of travail pour le roi de Prusse'.[77]

Saroléa attempted to do as much as he could for Masaryk's cause in *Everyman*. In 1916, the two men struck up an agreement that would mutually benefit the Czech cause and *Everyman*. In return for giving publicity to the Czechs, *Everyman* gained financially. After two years of war, the journal had experienced financial hardship. A waning circulation and war-time restrictions on paper production had exacerbated the situation. The financial contributions that Masaryk managed to scrape together helped to keep *Everyman* afloat until the end of 1917.

From mid-1916, *Everyman* regularly featured articles on the Czech and Slovak problem. These included pieces by some of Masaryk's compatriots, Edvard Beneš, Vladimir Nosek and Štefan Osusky.[78] In July 1916, an interview with Masaryk appeared.[79] Here the Czech professor was permitted to air his opinions on the war, Germany, Austria-Hungary and the fate of the small nations of central Europe. Masaryk's concluding remarks no doubt gave Saroléa cause for some satisfaction, and reaffirmed their mutual desire to destroy Prussianism:

Realise what an independent Bohemia would mean! She would be a wedge driven in between Berlin, Vienna and Budapest. The dream of the Pan-Germans would be shattered. Bohemia would block the road to Bagdad. Germany would be reduced to the German continental territory. An independent Bohemia will ensure the downfall of Prussian ambitions, the future peace of Europe.[80]

This quotation from Masaryk adequately sums up Saroléa's own reasons for supporting the dismantling of Austria-Hungary. Undoubtedly, Saroléa viewed the dismemberment of the Habsburg Empire as the key to unlocking Prussia's dominance of Europe. It would assist in the defeat of Protestant Prussia. Once he realised the destruction of the Austrian Empire might turn the tide of Prussian ambitions, Saroléa was quick to jump on Masaryk's bandwagon.

Saroléa's Peace Proposals

By the end of 1917, the fortunes of *Everyman* were on the wane and its circulation of had been in decline for some time. In spite of frequent requests to readers for assistance in keeping *Everyman* afloat, times had remained hard. Moreover, on several occasions during the war, particularly during his visit to the U.S., Saroléa had handed over editorial and financial control to other people. These individuals, it has to be said, were responsible for a good deal of financial mismanagement, and a great deal of money was lost in a number of schemes, none of which had Saroléa's permission. Furthermore, with the departure of Masaryk for Russia in May 1917, Saroléa lost a vital source of funding for his journal. As a consequence, in late 1917 *Everyman* merged with another journal, *Foreign Opinion*. This was not sufficient to resurrect *Everyman*'s fortunes, and by December 1917, Saroléa decided to cut his losses and sold his interests.

In the latter months of *Everyman*'s life with Saroléa at the editorial helm, much of the journal's content concentrated on future moves for peace in Europe and regularly featured throughout late 1916 and 1917. Saroléa always believed that the Entente would defeat the Central powers, believing as he did in a 'holy war', 'good' would inevitably prevail over 'evil'. But in spite of his anti-German and anti-Austrian stance, he was not in favour of a punitive peace being imposed on these defeated states. There were aspects of the conflict, however, which had to be eradicated from the body-politic of Europe.

Throughout the war, Saroléa maintained his belief that the ideology of Prussianism, in its spiritual and political form, was to blame for the conflict. Once military victory was assured, it was necessary for the whole of Europe to make the destruction of Prussianism a priority. It was not only in Germany that Prussianism had to be defeated. It had to be chased from the psyche of the whole continent. 'Prussian militarism', he said, 'must be crushed everywhere, in Great Britain, in Finland as well as in Alsace-Lorraine, in Italy as well as Austria'.[81] At the same time, Saroléa continued to believe that the Germans were ultimately responsible for the war. They had 'planned' it and 'forced it on Europe'.[82] But the 'megalomania of the Teutons' was, in his view, just one of the longer-term causes of the war.[83] It would never have happened except for the 'universally accepted immorality of European foreign policy, writ large in Morocco and Persia, in China and Asia Minor'.[84] This was a change in his earlier attitude, when he had alleged that Germany bore sole responsibility for the conflict. By early 1917, Saroléa believed that the 'principle of nationality' in the foreign policy of the Great Powers had led to 'an aggressive imperialism'.[85] At the conclusion of the war, therefore, he thought it essential that such a principle be eradicated from the foreign policies of Europe's governments. 'The international principle', he wrote, 'must take the place of the national principle. Federalism and solidarity must take the place of tribal rivalry and national isolation'.[86]

Saroléa's early 1917 articles on the prospects for peace were direct responses to the utterings of President Woodrow Wilson, who had already presented a peace note to the world on December 21 1916.[87] Saroléa seemed agree in principle with much that the U.S. President had to say, and, indeed, proposed the creation of some kind of international organisation not dissimilar to Wilson's embryonic league of nations. Initially, Saroléa recommended the formation of a 'European Congress', that all nations had to join as signatories and guarantors of the peace settlement. This would include neutral states and the U.S.A.[88]

In early 1917, the setting up of a 'European Congress' was not Saroléa's sole concern in presenting his peace proposals. In harmony with his view that the war was a 'holy' one, he believed that the 'awful sacrifice of twenty nations [had] mainly been a vicarious sacrifice'.[89] Allied soldiers had died for 'the good of the enemy, as well as the good of Europe, [and] to make Germany and Austria free'.[90] In this context, the war was not a 'punitive expedition'.[91] It was Saroléa's belief that neither military nor political factors could end the war.[92] 'Moral factors alone', he wrote, would prove decisive.[93] This ethical stance was reflected in the manner in which the defeated Central Powers should be treated in the future:

Vengeance must be left to Almighty God. The punishment of the criminals must be left to the people themselves. Peace, if it is to be real, and if it is to be permanent, cannot be achieved by any vindictive policy. From the moment they enter the peace congress the belligerents cease to be belligerents, and become allies in a sacred cause - the reconstruction of the world. From the moment the Central Powers are admitted to cross the threshold of the Temple of Peace they are readmitted to the community of nations and they are admitted on equal terms.[94]

Such a response also reaffirmed the central role played by religion in Saroléa's world-view.

Almost two years before hostilities halted on the western front in November 1918, there were four essential ingredients to Saroléa's prognosis for a lasting peace. First of all, Prussianism had to be defeated, in all corners of the globe. Secondly, nationalities had to be 'liberated everywhere'.[95] Thirdly, the people of Europe had to be granted some sort of democratic representation and a league of nations. Perhaps the most important of all Saroléa's recommendations, was that peace had to be righteous, in every sense of the word. The sacrifice of millions of lives was not be wasted. It is not difficult to imagine Saroléa's response to the peace settlement that was finally signed in 1919.[96] As for his views on the 'holy war', it is clear that Saroléa continued to believe that 1914-1918 was part of the long pattern of history. Unlike many of his contemporaries, his world did not end in 1914, nor did it with the Treaty of Versailles. Undoubtedly, he did not fail to recognise the cataclysmic nature of the war and the Settlement on Europe and the rest of the world, but neither marked the beginning of the end of civilisation. Instead, for Saroléa, the 1917 Bolshevik revolution was to be the apocalyptic event of the twentieth century, marking the beginning of yet another holy war, one he would fight until the end of his days.[97]

NOTES

1. J.M.Winter, Propaganda and the Mobilization of Consent, in H.Strachan (ed), *The Oxford Illustrated History of the First World War*, (Oxford 1998), p.218.
2. This is not to say, of course, that religion, established or otherwise, ceased playing a part in the war after 1914. Evidently it did, and for soldiers in the trenches spiritual matters never seemed far away: examples of this include the Angel of Mons, and the image of Tsar Nicholas II blessing his troops with an icon.
3. For details on the publication, circulation, editorial process see files in the Saroléa Collection, in Special Collections, Edinburgh University Library (hereafter SAR): especially files 1-41, 102-135.
4. In the first year of publication, *Everyman* maintained a healthy circulation of around 120,000 copies per week. During the war, this fell around 40,000 per week, largely as a result of some financial mismanagement and paper shortages.
5. For Saroléa's involvement with publishers Thomas Nelson and Sons see: Peter France and Siân Reynolds, Nelson's Victory. A Scottish invasion of French Publishing, 1910-1914, *Book History*, Vol.3, (2000), pp.166-203.
6. Saroléa amassed a library of around 250,000 volumes, see: Samantha T Johnson, "One of the wonders of the world, not to say the monstrosities of the world". The Saroléa Collection at Keele University Library, 1954-2000, *Staffordshire Studies*, Vol.12, (2000), pp.109-119.
7. Charles Saroléa, The Ethical Foundations of Patriotism, *Everyman*, 6 December 1912, p.245.
8. Despite its title, *Everyman* was aimed at the lower middle classes and did not seek to embrace a readership amongst the working classes.
9. For a discussion of the views of the Chesterbelloc, see J.P. Corrin, *G.K.Chesterton and Hilaire Belloc. The Battle against Modernity*, (Athens, Ohio U.P., 1981).

10. Saroléa's francophile views are expressed in a number of articles and books, examples of which include: Charles Saroléa, Napoleon as a Socialist, *Everyman*, 13 & 20 December 1912, pp. 264-5, 298: *The French Renascence*, (Allen & Unwin, London 1916), *Le Réveil de la France*, (Allen & Unwin, London/ George Crès, Paris, 1916).

11. Corrin, *G.K.Chesterton and Hilaire Belloc. The Battle against Modernity*, p. 10.

12. Charles Saroléa, The French Renascence, *Everyman*, 29 November 1912, pp.207. Saroléa predicted a European war in a best-selling book of the period: Charles Saroléa, *The Anglo-German Problem*, (Thomas Nelson & Sons, London/Edinburgh 1912) – also published in France, U.S. and Russia. For Saroléa, and the Chesterbelloc, the terms 'Germany' and 'Prussia' were interchangeable, although Belloc usually could not bring himself to use 'Germany'.

13. It was quite difficult for Saroléa to accommodate Britain in his world-view, and, for the main part, he chose to ignore it. He had fundamental problems, for instance, with the British parliamentary system, its Empire and the Church. During the war, however, it seems that anyone was welcome in assisting with the routing of Prussianised Germany.

14. Saroléa visited Tsarist Russia three times before the First World War. In 1905, his first visit, he met the novelist Lev Tolstoy, who undoubtedly greatly influenced Saroléa's views, see: Charles Saroléa, *Count L.N. Tolstoy. His life and work*, (Nelson, London/Edinburgh, 1912).

15. Throughout his life, Saroléa often found it difficult to get on with those in authority and his relationship with Dent had been fraught with problems. According to a Foreign Office report, Saroléa had used *Everyman* for 'advertising himself', Dent had 'got sick of him and sold [their] interests', Foreign Office confidential internal file on Saroléa, Public Record Office, Foreign Office 395/223, 18 April 1918. Saroléa wrote a thinly-veiled attack on Dent: Charles Saroléa, Why is the Newspaperman Powerless in England?, *Everyman*, 1 August 1913, pp.485-86.

16. This villa was destroyed by Allied bombardment during the war, see letter from Charles Saroléa to *The Scotsman*, 6 March 1925, SAR 197.

17. Saroléa also reported for the *Daily Chronicle* in the early months of the war, and there is evidence that he got too close to the front line, particularly from the viewpoint of the British authorities. See Foreign Office memorandum on Saroléa, PRO FO 371/12382.

18. Charles Saroléa, The Moral Significance of the Belgian Campaign, *Everyman Special Relief Number*, Nov. 1914, p. 7.

19. Saroléa's family came from Liège, which was heavily bombarded by the Germans on 16 August 1914. His brother, Léon, was a surgeon in the military hospital at Louvain.

20. Charles Saroléa, Everyman's Belgian Relief Fund, *Everyman*, 21 August 1914, p.549.

21. For a discussion of the atrocity controversy, see J.Horne and A. Kramer, *German Atrocities, 1914: A History of Denial*, (Yale University Press, 2001).

22. Charles Saroléa, History in the Making, *Everyman*, 28 August 1914, p.562.

23. Charles Saroléa, Everyman's Belgian Relief Fund, *Everyman*, 28 August 1914, p.613.

24. Ibid., p.613.

25. Ibid., p.613.

26. The Committee members of *Everyman*'s Relief Fund included several Belgian government ministers: Émile Vandervelde, Henri Carton de Wiart and Paul Hymans.

27. Émile Faguet, The Belgian People, *Everyman*, Special Relief Number, November 1914, p.39.

28. G.K.Chesterton, The Triumph of the Degenerate, *Everyman*, Special Relief Number, p.10. In the same article he wrote: 'I do not know what the word "Junker" precisely means – something like "puppy" I imagine – but evidently what the North Prussians call an aristocrat is some sort of allotropic form of what we call a cad [...]. The very shape of his face is irreligious, "amen" sticks in his throat as in Macbeth'. For illustrations in Relief Number, see pp. 17-24, 41-48, 81-89. Some of the photographs used were taken by Saroléa and appeared in other editions of *Everyman*: see H.Bergson, The Moral Significance of the German Atrocities, *Everyman*, 5 February 1915, pp. i-viii.

29. Charles Saroléa, The Message of Everyman, *Everyman*, Special Relief Number, p.1.

30. Charles Saroléa, The Moral Significance of the Belgian Campaign, *Everyman*, Special relief Number, p. 8.

31. Charles Saroléa, A Slump in German Theology, *Everyman*, 20 August 1915, p.359.

32. Ibid., p.359.

33. Saroléa wrote a fuller article on Treitschke in 1917 which prompted a considerable amount of debate amongst *Everyman*'s readership: Treitschke and the Philosophy of Prussianism, *Everyman*, 15 June 1917, pp. 219-222. See also: Charles Saroléa, The Paradise of the Prussian Junkerthum, *Everyman*, 7 Jan 1916, p. 228, The German Menace after the War, *Everyman*, 11 Feb 1916 (pt 1), pp. 324-25, 25 Feb 1916(pt 2), pp. 365-66, The Father of Prussian Militarism, *Everyman*, 7 Apr 1916, pp. 483-84

34. Charles Saroléa, The Martyrdom of Nurse Cavell, *Everyman* 5 November 1915, p.36.

35. Ibid., p.36.

36. Charles Saroléa, Characteristics of the Prussian state, *Everyman*, Belgian Supplement, 31 March 1916, p.56.

37. Charles Saroléa, Lutheranism in Germany, *Everyman*, 12 October 1917, p.11, 19 October 1917, pp.34-5. These pieces prompted a great deal of correspondence from readers. See letters in edition of 26 October 1917, pp.57, 68-69. Saroléa also gave a lecture on this theme in Edinburgh in October 1917. It also prompted a great deal of correspondence to *The Scotsman*, October-November 1917. See SAR 184.

38. Saroléa, Lutheranism in Germany, *Everyman*, 12 October 1917, p.11.

39. Saroléa, Lutheranism in Germany, *Everyman*, 19 October 1917, p.35.

40. Charles Saroléa, A Propos du Message du Czar en Faveur de Désarmement, *Revue de Belgique*, Oct.1898, p.5.

41. This was certainly a topic for discussion amongst the Chesterbelloc, and Chesterton, for instance, often spoke out in favour of the alliance with Russia: see G.K. Chesterton, *The Barbarism of Berlin*, (Cassell, London 1914). See also the comparable views of H.G.Wells, *The War that will end War*,

(Palmer, London 1914), p. 63: 'It is evident that there is very considerable dread of the power and intentions of Russia in this country. It is likely to affect the attitude of British and American Liberalism very profoundly, both towards the continuation of the war and the ultimate settlement'.

42. For details of Saroléa's arrival in the U.S., see, for example, Will Visit U.S. on Official Belgian Mission, *New York Times*, 27 February 1915.

43. See: Dr Saroléa and Hyphenated Hecklers in San Francisco, *Everyman*, 9 July 1915, p. 47 of Belgian Supplement. Saroléa was described thus: 'like a slender toreador fencing with onrushing bulls, for he brought a rapier-like intellect to the fray and knowledge of European politics that confounded many of his questioners'. Further evidence can be found in the files of the Belgian Ministry of Foreign Affairs, microfilm P87-Pf98.

44. Charles Saroléa, What the World owes to Russia, *Everyman*, 23 July 1915, pp. 279-80, 20 July 1915, pp.299-300, 6 August 1915, pp. 319-20, 13 August 1915, pp.339-40. See also Russia and the War, *Everyman*, 1 October 1915, pp.479-80, Russia and Germany, *Everyman*, 19 November 1915, pp.71-74, The Future of Russia, *Everyman*, 19 November 1915, pp.78-9.

45. What the World owes to Russia, 20 July 1915, p.299.

46. Charles Saroléa, The Soul of Russia, *Everyman*, 24 March 1916, p.445.

47. Ibid, p.445.

48. What the World Owes to Russia, 13 August 1915, p.339.

49. That Russia was not Catholic, nor had played a part in the sixteenth century Reformation, was easily reconciled by Saroléa, and he never felt the need to explain this. But, for sure, the main point was that Russia remained untainted by Protestantism

50. What the World Owes to Russia, 20 July 1915, p. 299, 6 August 1915, p. 319.

51. Ibid, p.299.

52. Ibid, p.300.

53. Charles Saroléa, Russia and Germany, *Everyman* 19 November 1915, p. 74.

54. Charles Saroléa, The Meaning of the Russian Revolution, *Everyman*, 30 March 1917, p.503. Also: The Russian Revolution and the War, 20 April 1917, pp. 27-30. Many of Saroléa's 1917 *Everyman* articles appeared in his book published (in two editions) later that year: Charles Saroléa, *The Russian Revolution and the War*, (Allen & Unwin, London 1917). Saroléa later examined the Romanovs in detail: Some Characteristics of the Romanov dynasty, *Everyman*, 1 June 1917, pp.172-174.

55. The Meaning of the Russian Revolution, p. 503.

56. Charles Saroléa, 1789 and 1917, *Everyman*, 4 May 1917, p.77: 'Nicholas II was a victim of his German wife. Alexandra Feodorovna intrigued with the enemy for a separate peace'. For an examination of the 'German spy' phenomenon, see Orlando Figes & Boris Kolonitskii, *Interpreting the Russian Revolution. The language and Symbols of 1917*, (Yale University Press, New Haven/London 1999).

57. The Meaning of the Russian Revolution, p.503.

58. Ibid, p.503.

59. Ibid, p.503.

60. Charles Saroléa, The Master Builders of the New Russia, *Everyman*, 27 April 1917, pp.51-52.

61. Ibid, p.52.

62. Ibid, p.52.
63. Ibid, p.52.
64. Ibid, p.52.
65. Charles Saroléa, A Diagnosis of the Russian Crisis, *Everyman*, 11 May 1017, pp.99. See also: A Diagnosis of the Russian Revolution. An Open Letter to Prince Paul Dolgorukov, President of the National Liberal Congress, *Everyman*, 25 May 1917, pp.147-49. Saroléa participated in the official proceedings that accompanied a Duma delegation's visit to Scotland in May 1916, and possibly encountered Dolgorukov during this. See *The Scotsman*, 16-17 May 1916.
66. A Diagnosis of the Russian Crisis, p. 100.
67. Charles Saroléa, The Coming Counter-Revolution in Russia, *Everyman*, 31 August 1917, p.255. Saroléa proposed a federal solution on the U.S. model to Russia's problems in: The United States of Russia, *Everyman*, 8 June 1917, pp.197-8.
68. Charles Saroléa, What will Happen in Russia?, *Everyman*, 7 September 1917, p.517. See also: What is Happening in Russia?, *Everyman*, 14 September 1917, p.539. Saroléa also held a number of public meetings on Russia throughout 1917, in Edinburgh and Glasgow. Details of these appear in the *Glasgow Herald* and *The Scotsman*. See also the stenographic report of lecture entitled *The Russian Revolution*, delivered in Edinburgh's United Free Church Assembly Hall, 6 November 1917, SAR 185.
69. See D.Hájkova, T.G.Masaryk a Charles Saroléa. Československá Propaganda v Anglii 1915-1917, *Historie a vojenstvi*, (June 1998), pp. 35-57.
70. Saroléa has been credited, along with academic R.W. Seton-Watson and M.P. Frederick Whyte, with giving 'invaluable help' to the cause of the 'non-German and non-Magyar nationalities of the Dual Monarchy', Harry Hanak, *Great Britain and Austria-Hungary during the First World War*, (Oxford University Press, London 1962), p.279.
71. Charles Saroléa, Is this a German War or an Austrian War?, *Everyman*, 23 June 1916, pp.185-6.
72. Ibid, p.185.
73. Ibid, p.185.
74. Letter from Charles Saroléa to T.G.Masaryk, 1 February 1916, SAR 27.
75. *At the Eleventh Hour* can be found in R.W.Seton-Watson, *Masaryk in England*, (Cambridge University Press, 1943), pp.153-202.
76. Ibid, p.190.
77. Ibid, p.195.
78. A list of these articles can be found in V. Nosek, *Anglie a Náš Boj za Samostatnost*, (Prague 1926), pp. 51-53 and appeared in *Everyman* between June 1916 and Dec 1917. They include: [no author], Why Austria must be crushed: Part 1: Austrian pan-Germanism, part 2: The central European scheme, part 3: Austria at war against her own Slavs, *Everyman*, 4 Aug 1916, p.305, 11 Aug 1916, p.325, 18 Aug 1916, pp. 352-53: [no author], The Austrian Reichsrat, *Everyman*, 13 Apr 1917, pp. 3-5, V.Nosek, Panslavism and Pangermanism, *Everyman*, 25 May 1917, p.150, A striking Czech manifesto, 8 June 1917, pp.208-9, Professor Masaryk and free Russia, 15 June 1917, pp.231-32, The Austrian deadlock, 10 Aug 1917, p.421. Correspondence relating to this in T.G. Masaryk Archive, Prague (AÚTGM) f. TGM V/VIII

– 15i/111, -15c/84, -15c/101, 15i/135, 15d/2, 15c/145. Saroléa is also mentioned in Masaryk and Beneš memoirs: T.G.Masaryk, *The Making of A State: Memoirs and Observations*, (Allen and Unwin, London 1927), p. 98, E.Beneš, *Světová Válka a Naše Revoluce*, (Prague 1935), pp, 149,162

79. Charles Saroléa, The Future of Bohemia. Interview with Professor Masaryk, *Everyman*, 14 July 1916, p.245.

80. Ibid, p.245.

81. Charles Saroléa, Via Pacis, *Everyman*, 5 January 1917, p.223, 26 January, pp. 287-8. See also: The German Menace after the War, *Everyman*, 13 February 1916, pp. 324-5, 25 February 1916, pp. 365-6. Some of Saroléa's *Everyman* articles on Germany were collected and published as *German Problems and Personalities*, (Chatto and Windus, London 1917).

82. Saroléa, Via Pacis, 5 January 1917, p.223.

83. Ibid, p.223.

84. Ibid p.223.

85. Ibid, p.223.

86. Ibid, p.223.

87. T.J.Knock, *To End All Wars. Woodrow Wilson and his Quest for a New World Order*, (Oxford University Press: Oxford 1992), p.108. The note was written on 18 December 1916.

88. Saroléa, Via Pacis, 5 January 1917, p.224.

89. Ibid, p.223.

90. Ibid, p.223.

91. Ibid, p.223.

92. Charles Saroléa, The Catechism of Peace, *Everyman*, 9 February 1917, p.335.

93. Ibid, p.335.

94. Saroléa, Via Pacis, 5 January 1917, p.223.

95. Ibid, p.223.

96. For details of Saroléa's response to the Versailles Settlement and its accompanying treaties, see: Charles Saroléa, *Europe and the League of Nations*, (Bell and Sons, London 1919), also published in Germany.

97. Saroléa was vehemently anti-Bolshevik throughout the 1920s, and wrote prolifically on the matter. It was also the subject of numerous public speeches in the 1920s and 1930s. See: Charles Saroléa, *Impressions of Soviet Russia*, (Nash & Grayson, London 1924).

Chapter Five
DER MAGISCHE GÜRTEL (THE ENCHANTED CIRCLE, 1917) – A CASE STUDY IN FIRST WORLD WAR GERMAN FILM PROPAGANDA
Roger Smither

Although the Imperial War Museum's restoration of the 1917 German film Der magische Gürtel does indeed offer an interesting case history in First World War propaganda, honesty compels us to admit that this particular aspect of the film ranked fairly low in the original reasons for our embarking on the project. More important motives for selecting this particular film – from a strictly archival perspective – included the fact that, unlike most British films in the IWM archive, Der magische Gürtel survived in a form from which it was possible to try to recreate authentically the original tinting-and-toning colour effects seen by its first audience. Also important was the possibility that a project to restore a German film in Britain, with participation from archives in France and Germany, could attract funding from the European Union's short-lived but imaginative Lumière Project, a subsidiary budget of the first MEDIA programme designed to promote film preservation. The third important leg of the motivational tripod was the generous support of Lloyd's Register of Shipping, whose sponsorship for this project enabled the Museum to commission a new musical score to accompany the film – and to contemplate the publication of a viewing guide to accompany its video distribution. It was research for this viewing guide which finally opened our eyes to the propaganda interest of what we were doing. First, we discovered that the film we were working on was a valuable historical record of the German U-boat war; second, we discovered that it provided some intriguing insights into the possibilities and pitfalls of film propaganda.[1]

Der magische Gürtel was one of the titles produced by a German propaganda agency set up to counter a perceived British superiority in the field of film propaganda – a fact that itself offers a certain amount of enjoyable irony. It is a recurrent concern of the propagandist that 'the other side' is doing better than 'we' are, and that 'our side' is consequently missing a trick – the concern may be genuinely expressed or used as part of a campaign for increased resources, but it makes its presence felt just the same. The 'superiority' to which the Germans were reacting had itself come about because of British fears that the exact opposite was happening. Soon after the start of the war, following Lord Kitchener's ban on film and photography in the British front line, the cinema trade in the UK started to point out that film from the German side was, in contrast, apparently quite freely available – German material even found its way (suitably edited) onto British screens that were otherwise starved off suitable war coverage.[2] British fears that the Kaiser was winning the propaganda war were voiced in terms such as these:

The supreme War Lord (the Kaiser) keeps his people plentifully supplied with the constant changing of films and photographs of the war, assisted by lecturers, so that every German subject and child is taught what war means, and how their own flesh and blood are fighting for their country.[3]

These concerns led to the relaxation of Kitchener's ban, to the appointment of the first 'Official Cinematographers' by the War Office in late 1915, and so in less than a year to the production of the feature-length documentary record *The Battle of the Somme* which reached British cinema screens in August 1916. It was the huge success of *Battle of the Somme* both nationally and internationally which led the Germans in turn to the conclusion that it was now they who were losing the film propaganda war, and to react by the creation of BUFA, the *Kaiserliche Bild- und Film Amt* (Imperial Picture and Film Agency).

BUFA was officially created by decree of the Prussian War Ministry on 30 January 1917.[4] This date was, rather curiously, almost two weeks after the opening of its first production, *Bei unseren Helden an der Somme* (With Our Heroes on the Somme), which was a very deliberate attempted riposte to the successful pioneering British battle film, and which had the full benefit of a gala premiere – the first German propaganda film to be launched in this way. As that event showed, the new agency had the enthusiastic support of the German Army, and particularly that of the powerful Quartermaster-General, Erich von Ludendorff. Ludendorff provided the sum of 45,000 Marks – two thirds of BUFA's funding – from the High Command propaganda budget, and maintained frequent and direct communication with its head, *Oberstleutnant* von Haeften. BUFA employed more than 13 officers and 30 other ranks; it was constituted into three distribution sections (one each for foreign distribution, the armed services, and the home front) and two production sections – one for film and one for photographs.

By the end of its first year of existence, BUFA had grown dramatically. Its *Frontdienst* was servicing over 800 front-line cinemas, and its distribution catalogue listed more than 300 titles. Of these, the majority were general 'educational' films on non-military topics, but 111 titles had been made on various fronts by BUFA's own seven film units. Of these in turn, the majority focused on the Army, where the films came in for a pattern of critical reception that would have seemed very familiar to BUFA's British counterparts. Initial enthusiasm at a new product gave way to complaints that the material lacked excitement, containing too high a proportion of over-familiar 'behind the lines' footage, and not enough novelty and action.

These were criticisms that could not be levelled at *Der magische Gürtel*, which showed activities in a much less familiar environment, and could not be accused of skimping on the action. *Der magische Gürtel* is a record of a single 36 day voyage – 31 March to 6 May 1917 – by the German submarine *U-35*, operating from the Adriatic base of Cattaro under the command of Naval 'ace' *Kapitän-Leutnant* Lothar von Arnauld de la Perière. The material was filmed by a cameraman named Loeser (first name unknown) and released through BUFA in early September 1917.   On release, its 'presentation' was credited to Hans Brennert, an established scenario writer whose services had previously been used by the German High Command to promote *Bei unseren Helden an der Somme*. Although it was not the first BUFA production to include U-boat material (an earlier film called *Ein Besuch bei unseren Blaujacken* – A Visit to our Blue-jackets – had included footage of a submarine crash-diving, and showed the searching of a merchant vessel), *Der magische Gürtel* was the first to show U-boat combat. As such, it merits close attention as a document of that aspect of the First World War.

This is not the time or the place for a discussion of the development of submarine technology, but it is worth recalling that it was, together with aeronautics and the technology of the tank, one of several aspects of military science which evolved in a remarkably short period of time to become a definite war-shaping, and potential war-winning weapon during the First World War. The *Handelskrieg* (war on trade) was of great significance both for Germany and for her enemies.   In interrupting the flow of supplies to the enemy, the cards – in the shape of geography and naval supremacy – were overwhelmingly in the hands of the Allies.   Commerce raiding, particularly through the U-boats, was the only countermeasure available to the Central Powers. The implications of these broad ststements were of direct, day-to-day concern to the citizens of the combatant nations.

Germany's initial declaration of unrestricted submarine warfare on 4 February 1915 is now most notoriously associated with the sinking of the *Lusitania* on 7 May; this event is generally recognised as a propaganda disaster for the Germans, and the fact that the campaign was suspended on 20 September is sometimes the last that is said about this aspect of the War. The U-boats did not, however, go away in September 1915: the suspension was as much to enable the force to re-group as to bow to hostile neutral opinion, and when the campaign was re-launched in February 1917, it was extremely effective. In the single month of April 1917 (the month during which *U-35* was at sea on the voyage filmed for *Der magische Gürtel*) a total of 860,334 tons of shipping was lost to German U-boats – something like 13 ships a day. British effort had produced a total of 650,000 toms of new shipbuilding during the whole of 1916. At a time when fighting on land and surface sea engagements were costly and inconclusive, this sort of balance sheet could be quite compelling.

During this second cycle of the U-boat campaign, the Mediterranean offered particularly rich pickings for the Germans. The Mediterranean carried heavy traffic – military supplies flowed east to sustain the Allied campaigns in Salonika and the Middle East, and to support Italy, while raw materials flowed west to France and Britain from their empires beyond Suez – and all this traffic had to follow predictable routes with known bottlenecks. In the single voyage shown in the film, von Arnauld de la Perière, operating both in the Mediterranean and in the eastern Atlantic just beyond the Straits of Gibraltar, was able to sink 68,000 tons of allied and neutral shipping: 23 ships in all, 20 steamers and 3 sailing ships, 16 of them 'enemy' and 7 neutral vessels. Impressive as this tally was, de la

Perière was to surpass it: in a later voyage, in July/August 1917, he accounted for 54 ships, 91,150 tons.

The filmed record provided by *Der magische Gürtel* offers good historical evidence (with some limitations) of the actions it portrays. The events shown on screen for the most part closely match the written record in *U-35*'s *Kriegstegebuch* or log, which survives in the German military archives, and can be confirmed by British records. Ten of the sinkings brought about by the submarine on this voyage are recorded on film. The film illustrates the allied practice of arming merchant vessels, and records the preferred tactics of this highly successful German commander. It also demonstrates that the personality cult of the 'ace' was not confined to the still more romantic fighter pilots of the War's other new dimension – de la Perière is shown several times in his role as Captain charting the course, sending a signal, or joking with his crew as he crosses out the name of another victim from his copy of *Lloyd's Register of Shipping*. There are also other glimpses of more mundane aspects of the submarine crew's life, the sailors being seen coping with rough weather, going about their on-deck cleaning chores, bathing in the ocean, and so on.

Missing from *Der magische Gürtel* are long shots of the *U-35* herself, and film showing life and living conditions below deck. There may have been an element of censorship in this, but it is more likely that the main reason why every shot was taken from the deck or conning tower was more prosaically practical. Cameras at the time were large and cumbersome, and there was only one on board. The U-boat commander – and the cameraman – may not have wished to risk sending it off-ship in the dinghy to secure the necessary distant views. The technology of available filmstock and lenses would also have made it impossible to film with the light levels available below decks. It is an important part of the historian's ability to analyse the evidence captured on photograph, film or video to consider the technological capabilities of the recording devices used.

The film was, of course, not made for future historians. It may well have been made largely to satisfy simple curiosity among Germany's civilian population about what submarine warfare entailed, but its makers would certainly have had other objectives in mind. The ethics of the *Handelskrieg* were a major theme in the propaganda campaigns of the period. From the allied perspective, the issues were clear, though not always expressed in quite the terms used in this literally told-to-the-children extract from the oeuvre of Arthur Mee:

> There is no objection to Germany using her submarines, *only she must keep the rules, and the submarine cannot keep the rules*. There is no objection to playing cricket, only one side must not bowl with a bomb for a ball. We must play the game and keep the rules, and the submarine can do neither, because it must make haste to be gone, and cannot wait to make sure of its ship; and it has no means of saving the lives of the crews. Therefore, the only way in which the submarine can cut off supplies is to break all the rules and sink every ship in sight, whoever it belongs to, whatever its business is, and whatever happens to the people on board. When a British ship captures a German ship, it saves the life of every man on board; Germany proposes to sink the ship and drown the men. It is war on every ship at sea, war not against a nation but against humanity. It is going back to the days of the pirates.[5]

The Germans would, naturally, have rejected the charge of not playing cricket, if they had understood it; more seriously, they rejected the charge of piracy. Germany pointed out that the Allied use of neutral shipping made unrestricted warfare inevitable, and that it was the Allied practice of arming merchant shipping that made a policy of attack without warning a logical choice for U-boat commanders. Nonetheless, the charge of ungentlemanly conduct (emphasised by poster images of drowning women and children from the *Lusitania* sinking, as well as by language like that used by Mee) was one the Germans were anxious to counter, and it seems more than likely that this was one of the reasons why de la Perière and the U-35 were chosen as subjects for filming. De la Perière preferred to sink his targets on the surface – bringing them to a halt by gunfire, allowing the crews to abandon ship, and then completing the sinking by torpedo, gunfire or demolition charge. He thus offered a face of submarine warfare that was visibly more chivalrous, as well as being more filmable, than the tactics used by other U-boat aces such as Max Valentiner of U-38, who did indeed prefer to use torpedoes fired without prior warning.

In addition to demonstrating a new form of advanced technology warfare and countering enemy accusations of the way in which that technology was applied, the film undoubtedly had other propaganda objectives. An important goal was to provide comfort to a German home front, that had experienced the chronic food shortages of the notorious 'turnip winter' of 1916/17, by demonstrating that the English enemy – German propaganda almost invariably preferred the adjective 'English' to 'British' – was also being hit in the stomach: three of the seven cargoes specifically itemised in the intertitles when *Der magische Gürtel* describes the ships sunk by U-35's actions are wheat, sugar and salt herrings, and a fourth is coal. Another objective for the filmmakers seems likely to have been the portrayal of tangible military success: after the inconclusive outcomes of the land battles on the Western Front and the naval engagement of Jutland, the portrayal of clearly successful actions was obviously desirable. More tentatively, one may also speculate that a further possible motivation for the release of a film showing patriotic, disciplined naval fighting men going successfully about their business for the Fatherland could have been the wish to counter any tendencies to mutiny or unrest in the ranks: 1917 was, after all, the year in which the Russian Empire fell to a revolution in which disgruntled soldiers and sailors played an important role. Many of these messages – particularly those relating to German success and German chivalry – were of course aimed as much at Germany's allies and at the populations of neutral states as they were at the domestic audience.[6]

The film as originally issued appears, to judge from contemporary reviews, to have included some more literal 'messages' – these reviews refer to the film's having contained *Aussprüche von bedeutenden deutschen und englischen Staatsmännern und Heerführern* (quotations from important German and British statesmen and military commanders) which commented on the effcicacy of the U-boat weapon. No trace of these quotations was found in any of the German material assembled for the restoration (although the French version did contain one possible vestige of their inclusion), and without any clear guidance to their content, appearance or placement, it is not possible to comment on the possible efficacy or otherwise of this aspect of the film. One review speaks of the quotations being 'skilfully though rather too lavishly interwoven' with the pictures, so one may perhaps deduce that they were removed after initial screenings because audiences did not particularly appreciate them.

One such quotation would evidently have answered a question which might otherwise have bemused contemporary audiences – it certainly confused the Imperial War Museum's researchers: that of the film's rather curious title. The Museum's confusion was compounded by the discovery in those contemporary German film reviews of the assertion that the title had been taken from a speech by arch-enemy Winston Churchill. Although it may at first sight be difficult to imagine the former First Lord of the Admiralty saying anything so directly complimentary about the U-boats that it would lend itself to use by German propagandists in this way, the attribution proves nonetheless to be entirely accurate. In the concluding paragraph of an article with the title 'The Real Need of the British Navy' written for *The Sunday Pictorial* on 24th June 1917, Winston Churchill did indeed use a phrase the Germans were able to translate as *Der magische Gürtel*.

It is only when we are able to devise and carry into execution a method of aggressive naval war against the German that we shall find his weakness and our strength, that we shall liberate our splendid Navy from the enchanted circle the submarine has drawn around it, and compel our enemies to absorb themselves so much in the process of their own defence as to leave them no leisure to compass our ruin.

The phrase actually used by Winston Churchill, 'the enchanted circle', suggests a form of bewitchment that restricts the liberty and actions of whoever is enclosed by it, perhaps like the spell that enclosed the castle of the Sleeping Beauty in the classic fairy tale. In translating the phrase as *Der magische Gürtel*, however, the Germans turned it into one that conjures up a mental picture of a different form of magic familiar from many other kinds of fairy tale – a talisman that enhances the powers of the hero who wears it. Active heroism offered a stronger image for a German portrayal of U-boat warfare than static sorcery. The Imperial War Museum has reverted to Churchill's original words for the English-language title of *Der magische Gürtel*, to emphasise this surprising but accurate attribution.

The Germans themselves seem, however, to have been aware that the title risked being a little too obscure. Posters and advertisements at the time appear commonly to have associated the title with a more helpful subtitle or tag, such as *Deutsche U-Boote gegen* (or *wider*) *England* – German U-boats against England – or *Die Heldentaten von 'U 35'* – the heroic exploits of U-35.

In trying to judge the efficacy of *Der magische Gürtel* as propaganda, we are of course hampered by the usual problems of the absence of useful contemporary analysis of audience numbers, let alone of audience reaction. Contemporary press reviews do indicate, however, that German newspapers and journals at least were prepared to endorse nearly everything the film's makers would have wanted them to say about the film, as the following extracts will illustrate:

In Germany of course, but also and above all abroad where people are able to judge our submarine warfare without prejudice but have not yet believed to the full extent in its success, the film will be a powerful agent of propaganda for the concept of the submarine, for our heroes and for their achievement. (From Number 458 of *Vossische Zeitung*, 8 September 1917.)

The most powerful document from a war such as the world has never seen before is now written on the narrow strip of film, and in far off days it will tell of the potent weapon by which the German people – through their U-boats and the heroes who commanded them – were able to counteract England's criminal determination to starve them... Back and forth cruises the U-boat, outside the blockade zone as well. Now the Greek steamer India (2933 tons) travelling with 3883 tons of coal from Cardiff to Oran comes in sight. The explosives crew crosses by dinghy to board the India – the coal is being carried for the enemy and must be sent to the bottom: what the English foe denies to us we can also not allow to him. He who is not allowed to bring us grain should not bring the enemy coal... The British steamer Patagonia (3832 tons), which was supposed to bring sugar from Cuba to sweeten the Englishman's beloved tea and pudding, goes down... (From Number 424 of *Berliner Börsenkurier*, 11 September 1917.)

Reading in the newspapers about what these craft and our brave young men in blue achieve, and painting a picture of it in the imagination, however well it might be done, could not adequately conjure up the reality. And now comes cinematography which permits us to experience the activity of a U-boat. We are witnesses, we are present at the events... We have here an example of the very best photography which is still further enhanced by tasteful tinting. The Königliche Bild- und Film-Amt's previous releases were already in all the best senses sensational, but even so none was so triumphant as this 'Magische Gürtel'. There will scarcely be a cinema whose public will not demand to see this film. (From Number 559 of *Der Kinematograph* magazine, Düsseldorf, 12 September 1917.)

Here the undeniable testimony of the image takes the place of the word: clearly and plainly one sees through the deforming lies and perceives the picture that the evidence provides – that the German, in spite of danger and deception, and all allegations of his opponents to the contrary, knows how to conduct this dreadful economic warfare with the utmost propriety; indeed, that his heart bleeds over the values that he is obliged to ignore in the cause of self-preservation. This film, dazzlingly photographed, skilfully constructed, and with the most immediate effect on the spectator, is a document of which the German Reich itself, as much as the German cinema, should be proud. From Number 37 of *Der Film* magazine, 15 September 1917.)

Despite the confidence voiced by the journalists in some of the extracts just quoted, the film was not in fact as well received outside Germany as German propagandists would have hoped. A BUFA report from Constantinople, capital of Germany's ally, the Ottoman Empire, spoke of some 'Turkish ladies' walking out of a specially-screened matinee performance 'because they did not wish to watch this so-called German barbarism any longer', and screenings in neutral countries were initiated with great caution, to carefully vetted invited audiences only. This was because of experiences with a recent film on another aspect of the *Handelskrieg* – a filmed record of the exploits of the commerce-raider *Möwe* and her commander Graf Nikolaus zu Dohna-Schlodien with the title *Graf Dohna und seine 'Möwe'*. This production had backfired badly in a number of neutral countries, and *Der magische Gürtel* too obviously offered more of the ingredients that had upset the audiences for the *Möwe-Film* (as it was known for short).

The elements of the *Möwe-Film* that had alienated neutrals – including normally well-disposed citizens in Sweden and Switzerland – were the appearance of official satisfaction or pleasure at the destruction of valuable cargoes of food and of beautiful ships, and the absence of any attempt to explain why the German Navy was behaving in this way. A Swedish newspaper had expressed the opinion that 'one could not watch the disappearance of such huge assets without a certain feeling of anguish'. In Switzerland, the *Journal de Genève* for 27 May 1917 had carried an elaborately ironic article by 'Job' which for several paragraphs described the *Möwe-Film* as a piece of 'ingenious propaganda' on the part of the Allies (while expressing repeated bewilderment at how they could possibly have got hold of such damaging footage), before finally revealing that it was actually a case of highly counter-productive German propaganda, for which some psychological aberration must be responsible. An anonymous agent reporting to the German Admiralty after a visit to Switzerland confirmed the doubtful value of *Handelskrieg* propaganda, citing the following example:

> An eminent Swiss-German of largely pro-German sympathies said: 'My wife and I left this film feeling stirred up and enraged against the Germans. We knew that the Germans excelled in military technology and knew how to sink ships. This production, however, left us only with the impression of an indiscriminate lust for destruction. We deplored the loss of so much of irreparable value, and I personally sadly missed the justification for the German action that could so easily and effectively have been given at the same time. How easy it would have been to quote a few sentences from the Chancellor's speech in December, [7] in which he revealed who were the enemies to the progress of peace negotiations, and thus to remind the spectator, and make him understand that such sinkings are only the last resort of self-defence; a few reminders of this kind would also have been useful to complement psychologically the dry recitation of sunk ships and cargoes. It is twice as shocking for the spectator to see all these sinkings crammed together into one scant hour, since for the uncritical observer no guidance is given as to whether the *Möwe* had sunk one ship per day, or twenty.'

In the light of this fairly compelling, if anecdotal, evidence that *Handelskrieg* propaganda had backfired in the earlier case of the *Möwe-Film*, it seems inexplicable that BUFA should have made no effort to include in the intertitles for *Der magische Gürtel* any of the explanations or justifications that the earlier reports had suggested would be needed. The press inside Germany may have understood the message that the film was seeking to convey, but it was by no means certain that the audience in neutral countries would be equally convinced.

Endorsement of the ironic joke by 'Job' in Geneva, and confirmation of the double-edged nature of *Handelskrieg* propaganda, were both to be offered in the curious post-war afterlife of *Der magische Gürtel*. All three of the major western Allies – Britain, France, and the United States – issued their own versions of the film. First off the mark was the United Kingdom, where a film was released at the end of October 1919 with the title *The Exploits of a German Submarine (U.35) Operating in the Mediterranean*.[8] The Americans followed in January 1920 with a version entitled *The Log of the U-35*, and the French in February 1920 with *La croisière de l'U.35*. The British and the French at least both added sequences to the end of the film to emphasise the ultimate Allied victory,[9] and all three made changes to the language used in the intertitles. The British captions emphasised the resistance put up by the *U-35*'s targets, and questioned the fate of their crews, the Americans affected a legalistic, almost sermon-like presentation of evidence, and the French used the most emotive, anti-German language of the three. Despite these superficial changes, however, what is extraordinary in all three versions is how much of the original German film – and, indeed, how much of the language of the original German intertitles – is lifted without any alteration straight into a film with a diametrically opposite purpose.

The release of the British film was, quite literally, front-page news in the tabloid *Daily Sketch*, which on 22 October 1919 carried the headline 'U' CRUELTY FILMED FOR HUN APPLAUSE. The trade journal *The Cinema*, which had a week earlier carried a review and an advertisement for the film, editorialised on 30 October: 'It is an eloquent object-lesson in Hun Kultur that will do more to convince all who see it of the righteousness of the war waged by civilisation against a race of brigands than volumes of mere rhetoric. What makes the picture so impressive is that it was not only taken by the Huns themselves but was actually shown to neutrals as a proof of what a wonderful thing 'Kultur' is.'

The viewer of any of the versions of *Der magische Gürtel* thus finds that the film offers him or her an unusual and accurate (if incomplete) picture of a particular high-point and a key theatre of a vital but often neglected campaign in the First World War: its value as visual evidence is beyond question. But what does that viewer learn about the film's propaganda value? The film stands as an example of the best product that Germany's most advanced agency for film propaganda was capable of generating, and appears to have been loyally welcomed as such by the German press and, in all probability, the German public. At the same time, the film failed to deliver the expected propaganda benefits when screened to neutrals, because neutrals had difficulty in seeing the intended message of necessary German efficiency tempered by chivalry through the more obvious sight of elegant ships with valuable cargoes being sent to the bottom of the sea. The film later proved only too easy to translate into counter-propaganda in enemy countries. It is generally recognised that film propaganda works best when it confirms a sentiment that its audience is already predisposed to accept: film will reinforce an opinion far more often than it will change it.[10] The German home front, the neutrals, and the 'enemy' audience in Britain, France or the USA all knew what the U-boat war meant to them. *Der magische Gürtel* confirmed them in that opinion.

NOTES

1. Most of the contents of this paper derives from research carried out in preparing a viewing guide, published on behalf of the Imperial War Museum by Lloyd's Register of Shipping, London, 2000, as Roger Smither (editor), *First World War U-Boat: a guide published to accompany the video release of the films* Der Magische Guertel *(The Enchanted Circle) (1917) and* The Exploits of a German Submarine *(U.35) Operating in the Mediterranean (1919).*

2. S D Badsey, '*Battle of the Somme:* British war-propaganda' in *Historical Journal of Film, Radio and Television,* Vol. 3, No. 2 (1983), p. 101.

3. Distin Maddick, writing for the *Daily Mail,* quoted in David Welch, *Germany, Propaganda and Total War, 1914-1918* (London: Athlone Press, 2000), p. 53. Welch's book provides an excellent analysis of its subject – although its failure to mention *Der magische Gürtel* provides one of the justifications for the writing of the current article, which might otherwise be considered superfluous.

4. Information on *BUFA* comes from the essay 'BUFA and the Production and Reception of Films on the German *Handelskrieg*' by Martin Loiperdinger in Smither (*op. cit.*).

5. Arthur Mee, *Adventure of the Island: the Story of the Great War written down at the time for the children of the future* (London: Hodder & Stoughton, ca. 1919), p. 40. Mee is best known as the founder of the *Children's Newspaper* and editor of the *Children's Encyclopedia.*

6. The original print held by the Imperial War Museum is an 'international' version, with the intertitles supplied in three languages: German, French and Turkish, although the Museum's restored print has only the German titles.

7. This refers to Bethmann-Hollweg's address to the Reichstag on 12 December 1916, when he had said 'If, in spite of this offer of peace and reconciliation, the struggle should continue, then the four [Central] powers are determined to continue until victory, while solemnly disclaiming any responsibility before mankind and history.'

8. The British film is included, together with the German original, in the IWM/Lloyd's Register release of *First World War U-Boat.*

9. While complete copies of both the British and French versions were available to the IWM during its restoration, the only material from the American *Log of the U-35* that could be traced were a few extracts which, while giving a flavour of the film, did not convey its overall shape.

10. For an impressive historical survey of this subject, see Nicholas Reeves, *The Power of Film Propaganda: Myth or Reality?* (London/New York: Cassell, 1999).

Chapter Six
'THE MEDIATOR': IMAGES OF RADIO IN WARTIME FEATURE FILM IN BRITAIN AND GERMANY
Jo Fox

The documentary filmmaker Paul Rotha predicted that film would become the key medium for communication to the masses. In 1936, he identified film as 'a weapon that can mould the minds of the multitudes in any given direction without those multitudes being aware of what is happening'.[1] He argued that its potential for reaching the masses could only be matched by one other method of communication: radio. Rotha saw film and radio as an integral part of a total propaganda campaign, reaching every listener in their own home and every viewer in their place of entertainment and relaxation. The two media had a natural connection – both were relatively new forms for transmitting propaganda and both assumed primary importance during the Second World War because of their effectiveness as a means of conveying information and their popular appeal. It was, therefore, not unusual to find the two linked and, often, used together. The link was significant enough to be a central issue of comment and debate among contemporary observers. It was embraced by both radio and film producers and governmental propagandists, and publicised to a wider audience. Initially, this chapter seeks to outline the relationship between film and radio, particularly focussing on the two central adversaries in the Second World War, Britain and Germany, and discuss how this relationship functioned as both a means for mutual promotion and as an essential element of a total propaganda campaign. Media and methods of communication tend to be studied in isolation, and media's capacity for combined psychological assaults on the public consciousness can be overlooked. The dual operation of forms of media through diverse but focussed campaigns, can have a wide-ranging and deep impact on reception. The use of film in conjunction with a radio theme, not only promoted the film studio's production and output, but served to outline the diverse function of radio in wartime society and provided a visual identity to this popular form of media. As such, the central focus of this paper is the depiction of radio in feature film. Two films are particularly representative of this diversity: *Freedom Radio* (Great Britain, Anthony Asquith, 1941) and *Wunschkonzert* (Request Concert, Germany, Eduard von Borsody, 1940). These films fulfil different functions in their depiction of radio to the cinema audience, one being an instrument of resistance and the other an instrument of concensus. However, both films reflected radio as a form of communication used to develop a wider sense of community, and signified the link between film and radio in their mutual promotion in the public arena.

Film and Radio: the Natural Link

The natural link between film and radio, recognised and exploited by Britain and Germany during the Second World War, had already been well established in the United States with the popularity of the Lux Radio Theater. Adaptations of Hollywood classics such as *Casablanca, How Green Was My Valley, Now Voyager, Miracle on 34th Street* and *Wuthering Heights* were broadcast weekly on national radio at prime time on Monday evenings, with the show reaching 40 million listeners at its height. A main attraction for listeners was the appearance of many major Hollywood stars, performing alongside one another for the first time, unconstrained by studio contracts. Initially broadcast from New York, production of the Lux Radio Theater was moved to Hollywood in order to fit in with the stars' busy schedules. In its heyday, the show attracted some of the major film actors of the 1930s and 1940s, such as Marlene Dietrich, Bette Davis, James Stewart, Clark Gable, Rita Hayworth and, for many years, until 1944, the show's presenter, Cecil B. De Milne. The programme was well-financed, with a budget of $5,000 per show, a full orchestra and the luxury of five days rehearsal time.[2] The Lux Radio Theater had major benefits for the sponsor, radio and the film industry, with the studios using the popularity of the radio programme to promote stars and forthcoming productions. Not only did the relationship prove to be mutually beneficial for the radio and film industries, but, as Cecil B. De Milne observed, it created a sense of identification with the audience. Commenting on the popularity of the radio show, he noted that 'the great audience of the Lux Radio Theater was America... I spoke... to an ever increasing audience in homes across the whole broad country'.[3] Recognising the importance of the 'listening community', Cecil B. De Milne clearly understood the impact of communicating to the individual in their own place of relaxation. This technique proved valuable to Axis and Allied powers alike during the Second World War.

In Britain, the link between film and radio was also recognised, if not as fully exploited and integrated for commercial purposes as in the United States. In Spring 1941, *Sight and Sound*, a leading British film journal, encouraged producers of film and radio to forge a closer relationship, suggesting that radio talks could be tied up with film illustration, and noting that 'there is much to be said from every point of view for this alliance of film and radio. Some people profess to think that the two are mutually exclusive. They are nothing of the kind'.[4] The film industry were keen on exploiting the link between the two media. Aside from short films[5], a number of feature films such as *One of our Aircraft is Missing* (Michael Powell, 1942), *Fires Were Started* (Humphrey Jennings, 1943)[6] and *The Next of Kin* (Thorold Dickinson, 1942)[7] all owed their titles to well-known radio announcements, phrases and bulletins, which were easily recognised by cinema audiences. The BBC radio feature *Appointment with Fear* was scheduled to be converted into a feature film in February 1944, with P. and C. Producers Ltd. The planned production revealed significant co-operation between the film and radio producers, with John Dixon Carr, writer of the original radio series, scripting the film, and Martin C. Webster, a producer on the radio programme, acting as technical supervisor.[8]

Some wartime films were transformed into radio plays and, in addition, wartime radio provided features on the latest cinema releases. One such example was the conversion of Dickinson's 1942 production, *The Next of Kin*, into a radio play for broadcast on the BBC on Monday 6th July 1942 at 9:20 p.m. and starring some of the original cast.[9] Originally a military training film, the feature film for release in British cinemas and for distribution[10], detailed the fictional story of a British raid on a German held harbour on the French coast, which ended in disaster as a result of enemy infiltration, fifth column activity and careless talk. The film showed scenes of the failure of the raid and the resulting casualties, shocking audiences with its 'realistic' portrayal of conflict.[11] The radio adaptation was clearly intent on conveying the same message of security to the British public, but also served to provide publicity for the film and cast. Tom Harrison, of Mass-Observation, however, on listening to the radio adaptation, considered *The Next of Kin* to be of poor propagandistic value. In *The Observer* on 12 July 1942, he commented that the adaptation was 'unnecessarily uncomplimentary to officer intelligence'. [12] Dickinson, angered by Harrison's assertions about the film, replied to the review, taking care to draw a clear distinction between the radio and film version of the script. He chided 'it is a great pleasure to know that the *radio version* "got over" to you as entertainment. I merely want to suggest that before you begin to assess the propaganda value of the *film* to our allies, you should also see the film through yourself'.[13] Although Harrison criticised *The Next of Kin* for being 'difficult to follow', he noted that 'a little radio complexity forces the listener to concentrate to reach out beyond the soporific level of sedentary semi-attention'.[14] The union between British cinema and radio was not always a harmonious marriage, but a beneficial one for studio and film promotion.

In Germany, the *Reichsministerium für Volksaufklärung und Propaganda* (RMVP, Reich Ministry for Popular Enlightenment and Propaganda), with its somewhat more 'co-ordinated' system of publicity and propaganda, deliberately attempted to couple film and radio in order to produce a total mobilisation of propaganda methods through various media. In their study of German radio programming in 1944, Ernst Kris and Hans Speier, directors of the Research Project on Totalitarian Communication, drew attention to the link between radio and film, observing that:

> the press, film and radio publicise each other; films such as *The Voice from the Ether*, or *Request Concert* were devoted to popularising radio. The radio in turn frequently reports on newsreels and on films of political importance… In short, the propaganda effects of all three media are co-ordinated to attack the political independence and the reasonable judgement of their audience.[15]

This link was well publicised both on radio and in the film press. In August 1944, Hans Hinkel and Hans Fritzsche, the respective heads of film and radio broadcasting, were interviewed together on German radio to stress the union of the two media for total mobilisation.[16] Equally, as early as January 1940, film and radio were linked in their mutual promotion and support for the war effort. Rolf Marben, writing for *Filmwelt*, a popular German film magazine, observed that, once 'rivals' engaged in a long-term feud, film and radio had 'formed a close alliance'[17] under the direction of the National Socialists. In contrast to the fragmented media relations prior to 1933, Marben asserted that the former enemies now stood shoulder to shoulder, united as 'mutual friends and servants of the...nation'.[18]

Like Britain and indeed the United States, the link between the radio and film was evident in both cinema and film promotion. Marben reported that radio publicised the work of the studios by previewing forthcoming films, conducting interviews with authors, producers, film score composers, directors, actors, film set architects, in addition to updates from the studio floor on the progress of new films, visits to film complexes, reports from film premieres and features which went 'behind the cameras' to look at the world of film technology.[19] The trend of transferring films to radio was also reflected in Germany, with the film *Robert Koch – Bekämpfer des Todes* (Hans Steinhoff, 1939) broadcast as a radio play in its own right and by popularising film music, such as the score of *D III 88* (Herbert Maisch, 1939). *Filmwelt* claimed that a number of films had been inspired by radio plays and broadcasts, such as *Urlaub auf Ehrenwort* (Karl Ritter, 1937) and *Parkstraße 13* (Jürgen von Alten, 1939). Radio also became the focus of minor reports in the *Wochenschauen* (weekly newsreels) and short cultural films such as *Diener des Volkes*.[20] Both Britain and Germany, then, sought to stress the importance of radio through film, both media seeking to promote the other through a visual and aural identity.

The Propagandistic Function of Radio

Before turning to an examination of the image of radio in feature film, it is important to briefly establish the way in which radio was perceived by the propagandists of Britain and Germany during the Second World War. Radio can perform many functions: a weapon of aggressive home and foreign propaganda, a conveyer of news and information and a means of diversion and entertainment. In wartime, as at other times of crisis, there is a need to create unity or a unified community, to make the individual feel part of something greater. Radio played a key role key in bringing people out of isolation and integrating them with the mass. Alongside other media, radio could, and, arguably, still can, fulfil this function as a 'mediator' – an indirect, intermediate link between two or more parties, as witnessed by De Milne and others. However, for this to be effective, the individual listener needs to *feel* psychologically integrated with the wider community. As Jacques Ellul noted, '[t]he individual must never be considered as being alone... the listener to a radio broadcast, though *actually* alone, is nevertheless part of a larger group and he is aware of it'.[21] Ellul termed this phenomenon the 'lonely crowd'. He argued that 'the most favourable moment to seize a man and influence him is when he is alone in the mass: it is at this point that propaganda can be most effective'.[22] This 'feeling' of psychological integration needed to be created by the broadcaster, and believed by the listener. Radio offered its listeners a 'bridge' between the individual and the mass, and played an essential role in community building.

This function of radio was particularly important during war . Writing on the importance of radio for the war effort in 1942, Charles Siepmann observed that 'radio in wartime accentuates the need for unity'.[23] Like Ellul, he recognised that 'war calls for unity, for integrated action and purpose. The integration of each individual personality is as urgent as that of the nation as whole'.[24] In Germany, this concept had a particular resonance. Radio could embrace the ideological formation of the *Volksgemeinschaft* (people's community) and produce a rallying, uniting effect on the nation. Hans Fritzsche believed this to be one of the primary functions of Nazi wartime broadcasting, stating that 'the German radio... has managed to unite at certain hours, and for certain moments, Germans all over the world, welding them into one single listening community with one common purpose'.[25] The individual was to be integrated within the mass. The *Handbuch des Deutschen Rundfunks* informed broadcasters that 'the political use of the radio made masses out of individuals and a national community out of the mass'[26]. More importantly for the war effort, 'well prepared political broadcasts' were thought to be able to 'produce such a strong mental current that a community, a people and even groups of peoples may be induced to common action'.[27] In this way, radio built a bridge between isolated peoples, the government, and particularly in the case of Nazi Germany, the leader[28], and, during the war, between home and front. Propagandists in Britain also recognised the importance of the radio as a means of communication with the masses. The Ministry of Information (MoI), like the RMVP, saw radio as a diverse medium which was to be used for 'news, talk, announcement, feature [and] light entertainment'. [29] Walter Monckton, Director General of the MoI in 1941, extolled the virtues of the use of radio, emphasising that this was 'the first radio war'. Drawing comparisons with the modern revolution of the Great War, which he noted had extended the physical parameters of warfare, the Second World War had extended the battle to the media.[30] For Monckton, like his German counterparts, radio was 'at once the most public of services and the most private, the most universal and the most individual'.[31] Radio, then, for the Allied and Axis powers was viewed as a conduit between governments, the individual and the nation. It opened up an important channel of communication which not only gave the impression of one-to-one contact, but also created and reflected a wider listening audience. This was ultimately, as De Milne, Fritzsche and Monckton recognised, the power of radio.

Visualising Radio: the Depiction of Radio in Film

During the Second World War, film played a significant role in *visualising* this power and listeners' awareness of being united by the radio. In the 1940 German State sponsored feature film *Wunschkonzert*, the radio is portrayed as the bridge between individuals separated by war: mother and son, husband and wife, family and friends, lost lovers. Each individual is fully integrated into the mass. The role of the individual is stressed only as part of a national machine or consensus. The film conveys a sense of holism or, specifically, 'the community'. At the centre of this image is the radio. This prominence confirms the pre-existing experience of the audience who could both identify with being a listener and being a part of that 'listening' community. Film enables the individual listener to actually *see* that community, rather than simply 'feeling' a part of it, thus turning a rather vague sense into a substantive visual image. For the 1941 British film *Freedom Radio*, this awareness fulfilled a different function where isolated individuals are also seeking to relate to a wider community – but this time in *resistance*. Radio allows isolated individuals to come together, forming an oppositional grouping. Clearly, images of radio as a 'mediator' or 'bridge builder' had different emphases in the wartime film propaganda of Britain and Germany. These differences corresponded to the different national and wartime contexts of the two nations between 1940 and 1941. Although each film fulfils a different thematic purpose, both sought to use radio as a coalescent to bring the individual into the mass, creating a national, fighting identity.

Freedom Radio (Great Britain, Asquith, 1941): Radio as Resistance

Anthony Asquith's 1941 production, *Freedom Radio,* was one of the first major British feature films of the war years to reflect the link between radio and film. The film's central topic, the establishment of a resistance radio station broadcasting across Germany, was, by the time of the film's release, a popular media theme. In the initial years of the war, the press concentrated on the depiction of radio as an instrument of resistance and 'truth'[32], which connected well with early hopes that the Third Reich would suffer an internal collapse[33]. This was coupled with the growing realisation that radio could be used for the purposes of both state propaganda and small resistance movements alike; as Tom Harrison noted in 1943, radio '*make[s]* modern war... [A]ny Tom, Dick or Harry may start a freedom station'.[34] This interest was also reflected in popular literature, such as the 1939 novel *Freedom Calling!* The book bears a remarkable similarity to Asquith's film in its depiction of the freedom station as an instrument of truth and reason and in its promotion of the possibility of internal collapse.[35] The subject had also been seized upon by film producers, keen to capitalise on the subject's publicity. In October 1939, the British Board of Film Censors (BBFC) received a film scenario bearing the title *Liberty Radio* .[36] The BBFC recorded that the film was to be the story of 'how the secret "Liberty Radio" was brought about in 1934 in Germany, and of its aims and reception of its news by the public, and the subsequent action of the Gestapo'[37]. It was in this media environment that *Freedom Radio* was scripted and filmed. The film, made at the Sound City Studios in Shepperton , produced by Two Cities and costing £60,000 to make[38], began shooting just as Paris fell in 1940[39] and continued throughout the year. Its progress was reported almost weekly in 'This Week's Studio News' in the trade newspaper, *Kinematograph Weekly,* ensuring that its eventual release was keenly anticipated. Working under the titles 'If This Be Treason'[40] and 'This German Freedom'[41], the film was originally to be directed by Brian Desmond Hurst, director of the first major British war film, *The Lion has Wings.*[42] However, the choice of Anthony Asquith to succeed Hurst was critical. Asquith was a director with an interest in freedom of speech, censorship and liberal sentiments, as demonstrated in a number of his films.[43] His fascination with the importance of the media in undermining Nazism is reflected in *Freedom Radio.*

The film tells the story of Karl Roder (Clive Brook), an Austrian doctor, who, having observed the effects of Nazism on the German population, sets up an underground radio station, broadcasting the 'truth' to the German people in order to instigate a collapse of consensus, leading ultimately to the overthrow of the Nazi regime. Although Karl is eventually murdered for his attempt at resistance, the radio carries on through another freedom fighter, a touch the *The New Statesman* felt the director, Anthony 'Asquith[,] would have found more difficult to enforce in peacetime'.[44] The central moral of the film is that 'truth' will always prevail, and that the members of the resistance movement, no matter how few in number and isolated they may be, will strive to bring about the overthrow of tyranny. The function of radio in the film operates on three main levels: as a weapon of truth in wartime, as an instrument of Nazi tyranny and as a

communicator to and bridge between isolated individuals. Such themes fitted well
with British intentions for the depiction of the Allied War effort, outlined at the
beginning of the conflict.[45] The most striking observation about the image of
radio as presented in the 1941 film is the juxtaposition of radio as an instrument
for 'good' or 'evil'. The film simultaneously represents radio as a means of
communicating freedom, liberty and truth with the Freedom Station, and a device
of authoritarian powers to subjugate, disenfranchise and deceive the people of a
nation.

The image of Nazi radio in the film is confined to the function of
deception. This is emphasised by the fact that the cinema audience never sees the
face of the Nazi broadcaster, a technique which bars identification with the
character and which also stresses the unknown, and therefore untrustworthy,
source of the broadcast. Karl Roder, is spurred into resistance by the faceless
propaganda of the Reich. In the scene in which Karl decides to actively oppose the
regime, he is walking through the streets surrounded by dizzy images of Nazi
pageantry and militarism with the distorted national anthem playing in the
background. Images of Nazi atrocities swirl around his head: the destruction of
Jewish shops and businesses, book burning, the violence of the SA, the
indoctrination of his wife and the nation. His fragmented and chaotic thoughts are
suddenly sharpened by the high pitched interruption of the faceless Nazi
broadcaster, represented as a loudspeaker. Both Karl and the cinema audience are
united in their mistrust of the radio, steadily established throughout the film,
heightened by the anonymous identity of the voice. A similar image of Nazi
broadcasting was forwarded by the documentary filmmaker Humphrey Jennings in
his 1943 film, *The Silent Village*. Jennings used the image of the loudspeaker to
emphasise the difference between the dissemination of information in democratic
and authoritarian countries, stressing that 'the main feeling of oppression, the
existence of the invisible Germans, is carried in the film by a German speaker.
Sometimes he is speaking on a loudspeaker, sometimes from a radio – one voice'.[46]
The image of 'the new fangled loudspeaker, blaring culture invented by Dr.
Goebbels'[47] established a role for the portrait of radio in film as a means of further
emphasising oppression and censorship in Nazi Germany, promoting the Allied
war effort and warning the populace of foreign and unidentified information
conveyed over the airwaves.

The image of the Freedom Station not only corresponded to the publicity
given to the movement prior to the film's release, but also to the MoI's own image
of itself as the broadcaster of 'truth and justice'[48]. Outwardly, the MoI claimed
that British communications were to be guided by 'one hard and fast rule: always
to tell the truth... to tell the truth, nothing but the truth and (so far as is safe) the
whole truth'.[49] This perception was starkly contrasted to the German propaganda
methods which were, according to Monckton, designed to 'prevent [people]
thinking; ours is designed to help them to think, and think freely... embolden[ing]
them to act as free men'[50]. These same principles of propaganda were brought out
by Asquith's film, where Roder and his team took on the role of the British
'propagandist' and the champion of the 'free peoples' of Europe. The film is, in
this sense, a reflection of the perceived portrait of the principles behind British
propaganda during the Second World War, with the radio empowered as the
herald of truth. This was reinforced in the film by the fact that the audience could
identify the broadcaster. Roder and Hans (Derek Farr), the primary announcers on
the freedom station are steadily and deliberately established by Asquith as the

vehicles of truth. They are not, like the Nazi broadcaster, a faceless propagandist, but developed characters, who have already established a visual relationship with the cinema audience, transforming them into a trustworthy source of information. Sympathy with Roder and Hans is accentuated by the loss of their female companions to Nazism: Roder's wife, Irena (Diana Wynard) , who is converted to Nazism by flattery and deceit and Elly (Joyce Howard) who is physically attacked by an SS guard in the defence of Hans' grandmother and subsequently deported to a Concentration Camp. The differences in approach to radio broadcasting are emphasised and contrasted in the film, demonstrating the multiple facets of radio transmissions under democracy and authoritarianism. Nowhere is this more apparent than in the scene in which Frau Schmidt, Hans' grandmother, is reported to the authorities for listening to light- hearted music on foreign stations. The SS guard, having heard the French broadcast, bursts into her apartment and destroys her radio, symbolically stamping a shiny jackboot through the apparatus.

In the film, both democratic and authoritarian broadcasters alike recognise the power of radio in conflict and resistance activity. The freedom station is initially founded by Roder, not only as a means of communication, but also as a weapon of opposition, asserting that *'that's the only way we'll ever get them to listen. Loudpeakers blare at them all day. We've got to use their methods. And give them the truth'*. Throughout the film, the radio is referred to by terminology which confirms its status as a legitimate weapon of warfare; parts for the radio transmitter are termed 'ammunition', cables for the illegal broadcast on Nazi war aims are compared to 'bombs' and Roder is aware that his movement cannot defeat Nazism by conventional means and seeks to topple the Third Reich thorough psychological warfare, reinforcing the perception that propaganda is of equal importance in winning battles as field activities.

In addition to the perception of radio as a weapon of modern warfare, the film presents a conception of radio as a creator of a 'listening community' and a means of national or communal unity. In *Freedom Radio*, the sense of community is conveyed on three distinctive levels: as a united entity, bonded through the connection via the radio, working as a community for the construction of the freedom station apparatus in resistance to the oppressive regime and as a community with collective responsibility. Each level is carefully inter-linked, and is an important subtext in the film. The creation of an active community, rather than the 'false' construct of the *Volksgemeinschaft*, is emphasised in the manufacture of the radio transmission for the Freedom Station. In one scene, the community comes together to secret collect parts for the transmitter. Resistance is shown to be trans-generational and non-gender specific – the whole spectrum of the community are seen to be contributing to the resistance movement by smuggling parts through the local toy shop: a young boy trades a clandestine package for a spinning top and an older woman produces radio crystals hidden in a toy elephant. It is an effort of the people for the people, emphasising that the Reich is collapsing from within. The following scene, which is remarkably reminiscent of the community based scenes in the German production *Wunschkonzert*, gives the 'listening community' a visual identity. As the Freedom Station makes its first broadcast to the people of Germany, the camera quickly moves from the broadcaster to the listener, highlighting the diversity of the audience and stressing their common bond over the airwaves. Significantly, the transmission and the link to community is broken by the jamming of the station by the Gestapo, who are seen to atomise society, rather than bringing unity and notions of the collective mass. This is clarified later in the film, when Roder is congratulated for bringing the community together in resistance to Nazism, with his maid commenting that people '*have been calling up from all over the country*', to which Roder replies, '*well boys – all over the country – we've done it!*'. The subsequent montage sequence depicts the underground promotion of the freedom station across local and national communities, displaying that news and the 'truth' are reaching every corner of Germany, from urban to rural areas, further strengthening the audiences' recognition of this important function of radio broadcasting. This, then, is the community of the present, united by radio. But the film also warns of the prospects for the community of the future within Roder's final broadcast before his assassination. Collective identity is once again accentuated through the broadcasts, with Karl outlining to his fellow citizens the nature of collective responsibility:

> Over and over again you have been told that the democracies will not fight. We have certain proof that they will. But only if you force them to. For this thing rests with you. You cannot escape responsibility by blaming it on your leaders. If you allow this thing to happen, the blame is yours and you will earn the loathing of posterity. You gave this man his power. Your future is at stake. It is for action, united and courageous action, that from our hearts we appeal to you tonight... unless you act now, your chance is gone forever. Rise up and make your stand for freedom.

Here, as we shall see in the German film *Wunschkonzert*, the image is the means of providing a visual identity to the role of the radio as a community builder or as a bridge among peoples on various levels. Radio is presented as a unifying force in the community and creates a sense of collective identification. However, the nature of the particular images featured in each film were determined by the traditional assumptions of the national war cultures of Britain and Germany. It is unsurprising that the British representation of radio corresponded to a prevalent theme in their propaganda campaign: freedom and democracy. This was a device used in film propaganda to create identification with the audience, drawing on previous cultural assumptions.

That the audience did not react well to *Freedom Radio* was more a failure of timing than the rejection of these key ideological concepts.[51] By the time the film was released in January 1941[52], it had become clear that the Third Reich was not collapsing from within[53], and the gap between the propaganda image and the reality of the war situation affected the credibility of the film. In addition, the public had grown tired of anti- Nazi films, which were proving to be ineffective as a propaganda device for the MoI.[54] Individual reactions to *Freedom Radio* confirmed that cinema goers had grown weary, commenting that the film was 'yet another anti- Nazi picture. Surely this theme is threadbare... enough, please! No more anti- Nazi films – however good'.[55] The propaganda content of the film was out – of – step with public opinion, despite Two Cities' claims that the film was not intended as an overtly propaganda picture'.[56] Although the image of radio in *Freedom Radio* corresponded to a wider propagandistic aim, other factors prevented the film from making the impact the industry and the producers expected. Whereas Two Cities had poorly judged the potential audience reaction and empathy with the subject matter, the German film *Wunschkonzert* was timed to perfection, and represented the apotheosis of the functioning of the propagandistic impact of a combined assault by film and radio.

Wunschkonzert (Germany, von Borsody, 1940): Radio as Conformity through the Volksgemeinschaft

Wunschkonzert, released in 1940 as a state sponsored feature film, was an example of how German propagandists deliberately sought to combine the use of radio and film for mutual promotion, giving popular radio broadcasts a visual identity, and enabling the public to identify with the wider aims of the radio as a community builder. As we have seen, the relationship between film and radio was already relatively well established. *Wunschkonzert*, however, was the first major entertainment feature film to focus on the impact of radio on the *Volksgemeinschaft*. The film was based on a popular radio programme. The Request Concerts for the armed forces are regarded as the primary example of the power of German radio in the propaganda war. The programmes, which began on 1 October 1939, were initially broadcast twice a week, and, after a short break in the summer of 1940, were transmitted every Sunday at 3 p.m. After May 1941, the broadcasts took on a different format, but essentially fulfilled the same function: to forge a close link between the front lines and the homeland.[57] Strictly controlled in a joint operation between the propaganda ministry and the army,[58] the programme thrived on variety and contained a mixture of popular and military songs, concert and operatic pieces, comedy sketches, appeals for military welfare funds and messages between loved ones at home and on the front lines. Indeed, by December 1940, the Request Concerts claimed to have broadcast 44,634 messages.[59] The programme was considered to be an important source of 'relaxation and entertainment'.[60] There was a particular emphasis placed on the successful balance of music and humour, which Goebbels believed to be the best means of sustaining morale and strengthening the resolve of the population in the midst of war.[61] In this environment, entertainment fulfilled a specific political function. Contemporary observers noted that one of the most successful means of communicating with the individual and the mass was the careful combination of entertainment and propaganda, stressing that 'broadcast propaganda, if shrewdly interwoven with entertainment, will be listened to whether people like it or not'.[62] Kris and Speier argued that German musical radio broadcasts were 'not entirely lacking in political interest'.[63] It was recognised that 'light music and entertainment serve[d] as the bait of the political radio'.[64] Not only was this a clandestine method of concealing overtly political propaganda, but it equated to the audiences' own listening preferences. In 1942, analysis of the content of Nazi broadcasts found that the proportion of entertainment programmes had steadily increased until, by the beginning of the war, 69.4% of the schedule was centred on musical diversion. [65] This goes some way to explaining the popularity of the Request Concert. However, the essential link between home and front and the ability to pass messages directly to loved ones, without having to wait for the delays incurred through the field post, was undoubtedly the overriding factor in establishing high listening figures.[66] The Request Concert served as a bridge between those separated by war, allaying fears and sharing news. This function of the radio was later developed and expanded by the *Kameradschaftsdienst*, which broadcast daily messages to the front between 5:00 am and 6:15am, linking soldiers in the Soviet Union, across Europe, in Africa and at sea with family at home, wives, children, brothers and sisters, parents, friends and wounded comrades in the field hospitals.[67]

During the war, the RMVP stressed that the front and homeland were united, living together in an 'insoluble bond'.[68] Both propagandists and military leaders saw the inherent value of establishing a link between home and front and considered this 'bond' an important element of National Socialist propaganda in reinforcing the ideological 'consensus' of the *Volksgemeinschaft*. Praised by those involved in the RMVP and in the *Wehrmacht*, the Request Concert became a focus for uniting home and front. To General Dietl, commanding troops in Northern Norway, the Request Concerts were 'the soul of the front and the soul of the homeland and this inner bond is the secret of victory'.[69] As such, the Request Concerts came to embody the *Volksgemeinschaft* and the total mobilisation of the German people, creating a 'listening community', united in spirit over the airwaves. This accounts for its popularity with both listeners within the Reich and those away from home in the forces. According to an SD (*Sicherheitsdienst* or Security Service) report in April 1940, the programme was listened to widely by soldiers on the front lines, in the garrisons, and by the civilian population alike.[70] The Request Concerts, therefore, had a multiple propaganda function, providing for entertainment, consolation and empathy on both the front lines and at home. For those on the front lines, the programme became a means of staying in touch with loved ones, entertaining troops and, as the SD report noted, bringing a form of diversion to even the most remote soldier who was stuck somewhere in a bunker with his 'possibilities for entertainment [greatly] reduced'.[71] Hinkel noted that 'the comradeship and service of the German radio strengthens the personal bond of the individual soldier with his family...every night it tells the soldier about important events in his family and at home'.[72] For these reasons, he considered the Request Concert to be one of the best means of morale care for the troops.[73] For those at home, awaiting news from the Front, it served to comfort family and friends. Ilse Werner, the female protagonist of the 1940 film, recalled that, within the programme, the radio 'produced an intensive bond between the people at home and the soldiers away... Truth is nearly every family had a son, a brother, a father, a husband or a sweetheart at the front... worried about him, waiting for news'.[74] Hans Hinkel noted that radio had 'proved its value as a news instrument, as a propaganda weapon and as a "mediator" between the front and the homeland'.[75] This was, undoubtedly, the appeal of the Request Concert. Goebbels, however, felt that the Request Concerts had become dominated by sentimental message exchanges and declared in January 1940 that 'the main purpose for the Request Concerts should be to give the people very fine music. They are not to be turned into a family affair and "all talk" during the Request Concerts should be cut down'.[76] His desire to promote fine music, however, could not override the concerns of women on the home front fearing the fate of their men away on military duty.

The decision to produce the film almost certainly stemmed from the popular reaction to the broadcasts. Even before the release of the film, the SD reports confirmed that the radio programme was already one of the most popular items on the German radio, and would almost certainly guarantee a box office success for Ufa.[77] The film sought to give the Request Concert a visual identity, strengthening both the radio experience of the audience and cinematic portrait of the *Volksgemeinschaft*, already established prior to the film's release in 1940 and ingrained German war propaganda and culture. The link between radio and film was not only to be found in the theme of *Wunschkonzert*. As demonstrated by the success of the Lux Radio Theater, film and radio could act as a mutually promotional tool. The film and radio industries found that *Wunschkonzert* could, at the same time, trade on the pre-existing popularity of the Request Concerts, promote the radio broadcasts to a wide audience, establish a visual image for the radio show and act as a vehicle to publicise the activities of the major film, theatre and musical stars of the Third Reich. The Request Concerts were found to be, as in the Lux Radio Theater, a cost effective way of promoting new cinema releases, through music and sketches.[78] They featured some of the leading film stars, such as Zarah Leander, Ilse Werner, Heinz Rühmann, Marika Rökk, as well as leading theatre and musical personalities. The stars could be seen to be contributing to the war effort and, in addition, adding some prestige to the radio show. The 1940 film gave emphasis to this by featuring the performances of Rühmann, Rökk, Werner, Hans Brausewetter and Josef Sieber, amongst others. Bringing together such major stars of stage and screen for the first time promoted both the film and the radio broadcast, and epitomised the potential impact of a dual assault on public opinion, as evidenced by the American experience of the Lux Radio Theater. It represented a major feat for von Borsody to manage to negotiate screen appearances by the stars, who were often committed to other projects, filming and performing all over Europe. In the case of Rühmann, Brausewetter and Sieber, he had to wait three weeks until all of them were in Berlin at the same time and could spare a few hours to contribute to the film.[79]

The film depicts a series of relationships and individual tales, all told through the medium of radio. It opens with the relationship between Inge and a pilot, Herbert, who meet by chance at the 1936 Olympic games. Herbert is called away to fight in the Spanish Civil War. He promises to return and marry Inge. She hears nothing. Years pass and the radio announces the outbreak of the Second World War. Men from all walks of life are called up to serve their country: among them a young music student, a baker, a butcher, and a young teacher. The fate of these characters is then tracked through the Request Concert. News, messages and entertainment by well-known figures unite home and front lines. All news from home and front is passed through the radio: Inge is finally reunited with Herbert, the mother of the young musician mourns the loss of her son, and the young teacher learns that he has become the proud father of a baby boy, born while he was away at the front. The plot closely mirrored the functions of the Request Concerts on the radio, creating a sense of audience identification with the film's central theme.[80]

Their main method of communication and unity is the radio, which plays a pivotal role and, as in *Freedom Radio*, is the main protagonist in the film. The radio both creates and reflects the listening community such that the main characters almost forget that they are separated. The lines between home and front are blurred and the two communities are merged. Although the characters are living an individual existence throughout the day, each playing their specific role in helping the war effort, they unite every Sunday. This is either achieved by sharing and exchanging messages or through listening to the same piece of music. A number of montage sequences in the film, stress the diversity of war duties and at the same time reinforce the *Volksgemeinschaft*. The camera passes from men at the front, preparing for operations, women at home, looking after children, people at work in factories and workshops, producing for the war effort, to soldiers resting in the barracks, shaving and playing games. The *Volksgemeinschaft*, like the resistance community in *Freedom Radio*, is trans-generational, non-gender specific (except in the roles played within the community), urban and rural and diverse. The film stressed the role of the radio in bringing together these societal groupings into a homogenous and united community. In promoting the central aim of the film, the *Illustrierter Film-Kurier* eulogised: 'a magical bond embraces the front and homeland. In dugouts in France, in submarines on operational duties, on military airfields on the coastlines, in the still room of a mother, in thousands, hundreds of thousands of homes, everywhere, the sound... of words and songs and music... unites all Germans'.[81] In the film, the radio becomes the bridge between those kept apart by war and is the vehicle through which they may be re-connected. As the journal *Filmwelt* reported on 13 September 1940, 'the front and the home interrelate... greetings for the front personally reach the soldier at the most lonely post', with radio making it seem as if he 'just lived next door'.[82] The *Filmzeitung* reported in January 1941 that 'we all realise the importance of the Request Concert broadcasts by the German Radio: they are a kind of bridge between the home and the front'.[83] *Wunschkonzert* gave a visual identity to the sense of community created by the radio Request Concerts, strengthening the power of the broadcast and the sense of audience identification with the film.

In addition to creating a link between home and front, between family and friends, the film seeks to engender a similar connection to other 'comrades' in the community. In an emotionally charged scene, Frau Schwarzkopf, who has just lost her son, mourns his loss through the radio. He died saving his comrades. The scene stresses not only his own bravery but also her selfless sacrifice in giving up her son for the fatherland. Heinz Goedecke, the presenter of the Request Concerts, explains that her son has been killed in action and that his personal belonging have been returned to his mother. He explains that he loved a particular song, 'Good Night Mother' and she would like them to play it for her. As the lullaby resounds over the airwaves, it is clear to the audience that she is not mourning alone. The community mourns with her. While she is physically alone, the radio enables her to remain, at least, psychologically part of the mass. If this image was unclear to the audience, *Illustrierter Film- Kurier* reminded them that 'the sadness and joy of individuals, strangers, anonymous people, becomes the sadness and joy of the whole nation'.[84]

In this expression of emotions and separation, comfort is derived through a radio connection, producing the most significant message of the film: the building of the valuable bridge between home and front. As the key function of the radio in the film *Wunschkonzert*, it establishes a *collective experience*, and represents the role of radio in wartime Germany. Everyone in the cinema audience could relate to one of the characters in the film; whether it is Inge, missing her sweetheart and having to endure long periods of silence from him, whether it was the wives of those away at the Front who are having to run their husband's businesses or fulfil important war tasks in the factories and in the essential services, whether it is Frau Friederich, who has to go through her pregnancy and birth of her son without her husband or whether it is Frau Schwarzkopf, who shares her grief, after the loss of her son, with the wider community. To each individual, the radio is a source of comfort, providing an experience with which they could identify. The SD report claimed that the success of the film was due to its 'contemporary theme' and its depiction of 'present events'. The report noted that the inclusion of these themes made the film vivid and 'increased...[its] believability'.[85] The use of original newsreel footage triggered these memories and the interplay between 'real' events and a fictional subplot increased the audiences' perception that the film was 'true to life'. That the film discussed experiences which were shared and realistic was a contributing factor to its success, creating a high level of audience identification. The timing of *Wunschkonzert* was significant: it was released in 1940, when the public had not yet tired of contemporary themes, were in the midst of a victorious campaign, and when the images of war in the film were perceived by the audience to be realistic. [86]

The link between film and radio, already established prior to the outbreak of war in 1939, was one that contemporary observers recognised and film and radio producers embraced and publicised. In a commercial sense, the link was used to promote film and radio work, maximising publicity to the wider audience. Film stars became regulars on popular radio shows, enhancing the profile of radio broadcasting as a source of entertainment, and film studios were keen to exploit scenarios with a radio theme, to capitalise on the popularity of the radio, and to gain publicity for key productions by converting them into radio plays. The relationship was mutually beneficial, therefore, in a business sense. With the onset of war in 1939, this link was exploited for propaganda purposes, by both allied and axis nations alike. The image of radio in films confirmed its status as a weapon of war, either in clandestine broadcasting or as the vehicle for national unity and collective action against the enemy. The connection between the two media also underlined that allied and axis powers were striving to utilise all media as a part of a total propaganda campaign, aimed at the full spiritual and physical mobilisation of the nation. The propaganda campaign of total war needed to be all-encompassing in order to maximise input from the population. With two media working alongside and in conjunction with each other, the psychological impact of the message was deep and wide-ranging.

Although radio had many different functions during the Second World War, one of the most important was the edification of the wider, mass effort and the integration of every individual into the wider society, reinforcing national, indeed even global communities, at a time when the concept of community became more pronounced. It was essential to create and maintain united populations; united in thought, determination and action, to achieve the final goal of victory. Radio was but one element of attempting to achieve this. The image of radio in film served to crystallise this function, demonstrating how radio removed individuals from an isolated existence and brought them into a collective experience. It engendered this experience, and gave it a visual identity. Film provided an image for this sense of the 'lonely mass', solidified the vague notion of being a part of a listening community, capitalised on the popular and shared experience of the radio, whilst at the same time, visually promoted the propaganda message. In both Britain and Germany, radio was frequently portrayed as an instrument of unity and creator of communities. The most important function of the radio, as portrayed on the screen, in these early days of the war was its role as a bridge builder. Both the British and German propagandists recognised the need to 'show the interdependence of the individual and the community'.[87]

However, as we have seen, the image of radio portrayed and its reception depended very much on national circumstance. The individual images presented in Britain and Germany related to the specific 'national' function of radio. In Britain, *Freedom Radio* mapped onto war ideals created by the MoI, intended for transmission to a democratic society. As such, the image of radio emphasised free speech and the freedom of individuals, with the community functioning in order to achieve liberation from authoritarian dictatorship. It was anticipated that his concept would have greater resonance among a population whose liberal freedoms were enshrined in their traditional identity. In Germany, *Wunschkonzert* celebrated consensus and unity through the *Volksgemeinschaft*. This concept would have had specific meaning for German wartime film audiences, aware of the function of community spirit at a time of conflict and impressing upon them the importance of the all-encompassing sense of the *Volksgemeinschaft*, promoted as a central tenet of National Socialist ideology from an early stage. In each country, these notions were intended, either consciously or subconsciously, to increase audience identification with the films' central themes, mapping onto cultural traditions and inherent assumptions. The timing of the films' release was all-important. With an ever changing and fast moving cultural environment, the message and image contained in the films needed to correspond directly to the public's perception of the contemporary situation. If it did not, as in the case of *Freedom Radio*, the credibility of the propaganda message was lost, and its impact limited. As with other images in the Second World War, the central message to the war propagandists was to ensure that communication to the public was credible and realistic. With the changing fortunes of Britain and Germany from 1939 –1945, the initial German ascendancy in both military and psychological operations was lost to the Allies. An analysis of the image of radio in the films of the two main protagonists in the conflict offers some initial observations on how this ascendancy was achieved and finally relinquished, and how media were mobilised in unison to enhance the propaganda campaigns of total war.

Acknowledgements: The research for this paper has been completed with the kind financial assistance of the British Academy and Collingwood College at the University of Durham. I would like to offer my thanks to the following: The Trustees of the Monckton Papers, Balliol College Oxford, the Trustees of the Mass-Observation Archive, University of Sussex, Janet Moat of the Special Collections Archive at the British Film Institute, The Public Record Office, London, The Film Department of the Imperial War Museum, the National Film and Television Archive, London, the *Bundesarchiv*, and the German Historical Insitute. I would like to thank my colleagues at the University of Durham for their support in allowing me to take research leave in order to pursue the research for this project. I would like to thank James Chapman and Martin Doherty, whose questions at the conference inspired further research and particularly Jeffrey Richards, who kindly allowed me to look at his own research into the Lux Radio Theater.

NOTES

1. Rotha, Paul, 'Film and the Labour Party'. Address delivered at a special Labour Party Conference on Film Propaganda, Edinburgh, 3 October, 1936. Reprinted in Aitken, I., *The Documentary Film Movement. An Anthology.* (Edinburgh University Press, 1998), pp. 171-178. Here, 173.
2. All information in this section from 'Lux Radio Theater'. Written and produced by Jeffrey Richards for the Open University Unit 'Hollywood and Radio'. I would like to thank Jeffrey Richards for drawing my attention to the Lux Radio Theater and for sending me a copy of this programme.
3. Cecil B. De Milne, quoted in 'Lux Radio Theater'. Written and produced by Jeffrey Richards for the Open University Unit 'Hollywood and Radio'.
4. *Sight and Sound,* vol. 10, no. 37, Spring 1941.

5. Radio was taken as a central theme in the British film *Radio in War*, which did not explore the commercial radio, but looked at the 'empire and overseas broadcast and monitor service'. (Public Record Office – hereafter PRO -INF 1/ 251. HPC 11 December 1940). This was matched in Germany with *Rundfunk im Krieg.*

6. Taylor, P., *Munitions of the Mind. A History of Propaganda from the Ancient World to the Present Day* (Manchester University Press, 1995), 223.

7. British Film Institute Special Collections (Hereafter BFI Special Collections). Papers of Thorold Dickinson. Box 7. Notes on *Next of Kin* by Thorold Dickinson, October 1978. He stated that the title came from the radio announcement 'The next of kin have been informed', which he described as a 'grim chill for all' at the end of the radio programme.

8. 'Radio Thriller to be Filmed: "Appointment with Fear"', *Kinematograph Weekly*, 17 February 1944, 13.

9. Details of BBC Broadcast in BFI Special Collections. Papers of Thorold Dickinson. Box 7. Item 5. Film cast list with annotations from Box 7. Item 7. The cast featured in the radio production were Nova Pilbeam who played Beppie Leemans in the film version, Phyllis Stanley (Miss Clare), Guy Mas (Frenchman), Reginald Tate (Major Richards) and Stephen Murray (Mr Barratt).

10. Notes on the distribution to the United States can be found in Papers of Thorold Dickinson. Box 7. Item 7. Details of US Features and Serials Analysis from Library of Congress, Washington DC. LP 12020. 12 April 1943. Pci. No. F388.

11. Dickinson recalled an encounter with an hysterical woman, who having seen the film, confronted the director believing the footage to be real. Dickinson also recalled that Churchill requested alterations to the film, in the light of the St Nazaire raid of 1942. Details of these recollections can be found in BFI Special Collections. Papers of Thorold Dickinson. Box 48. Item 1. Original and unedited transcript of an interview for *Film Dope*. Printed in *Film Dope*, No. 11, January 1977. A discussion of Dickinson's claims and further recollections can also be found in Coultass, C., 'British Cinema and the Reality of War', in Taylor, P. M. (ed.), *Britain and the Cinema in the Second World War* (St. Martin's Press, New York, 1988), pp. 84-101. Here p. 84-87.

12. Tom Harrison in *The Observer*, London, 12 July 1942. Article in BFI Special Collections. Papers of Thorold Dickinson. Box 7. Item 4.

13. Thorold Dickinson to Tom Harrison, 12 July 1942. BFI Special Collections. Papers of Thorold Dickinson. Box 7. Item 3. Dickinson's italics.

14. Tom Harrison in *The Observer*, London, 12 July 1942. Article in BFI Special Collections. Papers of Thorold Dickinson. Box 7. Item 4.

15. Kris, E. & Speier, H., *German Radio Propaganda. Report on Home Broadcasts during the War* (Oxford University Press, 1944), 59.

16. 'Film und Rundfunk im Zeichen der totalen Mobilmachung', on 'Zeitspiegel am Sonntag', Reichsprogramm, 27 August 1944, 19:00. Text of interview in Wiener Library Cuttings Collection Reel P5/133.

17. Marben, R., 'Film und Funk', *Filmwelt*, 5 January 1940, 4.

18. *Ibid.*

19. *Ibid.*

20. All information here from Marben, R., 'Film und Funk', *Filmwelt,* 5 January 1940, 4.
21. Ellul, J., *Propaganda. The Formation of Men's Attitudes* (Vintage, New York, 1975. 1st ed. 1965), 7.
22. *Ibid.,* 9.
23. Siepmann, C., *Radio in Wartime* (Oxford University Press, 1942), 8.
24. *Ibid.,* 29.
25. Hans Fritzsche quoted in Kris, E. & Speier, H., *op.cit.,* 59.
26. *Handbuch des Deutschen Rundfunks,* 1938-1939. Quoted in Jacob, P. E., 'The Theory and Strategy of Nazi Short-Wave Propaganda', in Childs, H. L. & Whilton, J. B. (eds.), *Propaganda by Short-Wave* (Princeton University Press, Oxford University Press, 1942), pp. 49-108. Here 61-2.
27. *Ibid.,* 61.
28. As discussed in Kris, E. & Speier, H., *op.cit.,* 59 and Briggs, A., *The History of Broadcasting in the UK. Vol. III. The War of Words* (Oxford University Press, 1995ed.), 5.
29. PRO INF 1/ 251. Home Publicity Committee. 10 December 1940.
30. Walter Monckton. Draft Speech. 'Broadcasting and War' to the Manchester Luncheon Club. 6 February 1941. Monckton Trustees Papers. Bodleian Library, Oxford. MSS Dep. Monckton Trustess. Box 4.
31. Walter Monckton. Draft Speech. 'Broadcasting and War' to the Manchester Luncheon Club. 6 February 1941. Monckton Trustees Papers. Bodleian Library, Oxford. MSS Dep. Monckton Trustess. Box 4.
32. Articles on a 'freedom station' can be found, for example, ranging from *Manchester Guardian* (14th December 1939), or *Times* (8th July 1941, 'Wireless to Europe'), Wiener Library Clippings Collection PC5 / 209B / 140.
33. For British press promotion of the myth of 'internal collapse' see Wiener Library Clippings Collection PC5 / 113.
34. Tom Harrison, quoted in Briggs, A., *op.cit.,* 55-56. Harrison's italics.
35. *Freedom Calling! The Story of the Secret German Radio by the Representative in Great Britain of the Freedom Station* (Frederick Muller Ltd, London, 1939).
36. BFI Special Collections. Records of the British Board of Film Censors (scenarios). 1939. *Liberty Radio.* Submitted by C. Mann Ltd. 6 October 1939. It is not clear whether this film was later produced under the title *Freedom Radio,* although the author has not found evidence that this was ever suggested as a title for the Asquith film.
37. BFI Special Collections. Records of the British Board of Film Censors (scenarios). 1939. *Liberty Radio.* Submitted by C. Mann Ltd. 6 October 1939, 64.
38. *Kinematograph Weekly,* 9 May 1940, 21.
39. Cowie, P., 'This England', *Films and Filming,* vol. 10, no. 1, October 1963, 17.
40. *The Cinema,* 1 January 1941.
41. Mass-Observation Archive, University of Sussex (hereafter M-O). File Report (hereafter FR) 24 'The Cinema in the First Three Months of War'. January 1940. Also reproduced in Sheridan, D. & Richards, J. (eds.), *Mass-Observation at the Movies* (Routledge & Kegan Paul, London, 1987).
42. M-O. FR 24 'The Cinema in the First Three Months of War'. January 1940. Also reproduced in Sheridan, D. & Richards, J. (eds.), *op.cit.,* pp. 144-145.

43. For example, *Uncensored* (1942), which had a similar theme of resistance, the communication of the truth and the underground media, in its portrait of the distribution of a newsletter, *La Libre Parole,* in Occupied Belgium. As son of the Liberal Prime Minister, Herbert Asquith, Anthony was raised with strong political views which translated into his film work. Examples of Anthony Asquith's writings and speeches on censorship and film can be found in 'Film Censorship. Mr Asquith's Criticisms', *Manchester Guardian,* 20 April 1942 and in his papers, held in BFI Special Collections.

44. William Whitebait, *New Statesman and Nation,* 1 February 1941, Quoted in Noble, P., *Anthony Asquith* BFI Series, No. 5, 27.

45. PRO HO 199/434. 'Yardstick for the Measurement of Propaganda and Publicity'. September 1939. The ten key words of the campaign were to be 'right, strength, efficiency, sacrifice, effort, freedom, union, truth, happiness [and] victory'.

46. BFI Special Collections. Humphrey Jennings Collection. Item 8. '*The Silent Village*': Telephone Recording with BBC. 26 May 1943, 4:30 p.m. Also reproduced in Parkinson, D. (ed.), *The Humphrey Jennings Reader* (Carcanet Press, Manchester, 1993), pp. 67-75. Here, 74.

47. *Ibid.*

48. This can be seen in a paper by Walter Monckton , 'Matters of Moment', 31 March 1941. 1st draft. MSS Dep. Monckton Trustees Papers, Bodleian Library, Dept of Modern Manuscripts, Oxford.

49. *Ibid.*

50. *Ibid.*

51. Indeed the British Institute of Public Opinion Poll (BIPO) conducted in June 1941 noted that the majority (46%) of people questioned on 'what we are fighting for' replied 'for freedom, liberty and democracy'. PRO INF 1/292. Home Intelligence (hereafter HI) Report no. 41. 9-16 July 1941.

52. *Monthly Film Bulletin,* vol. 8, no. 85, January 1941, 1.

53. For a brief discussion of this genre of films, released between 1940-1941, see Coultass, C., *loc.cit.,* 86.

54. Much evidence for this can be found in the British tendency to draw a distinction between the German people and the Nazi leadership in propaganda, although this distinction was blurred at the height of the Blitz, 1940-1941. For more detail see PRO INF 1 /292. HI Report no. 86. 18-26 May 1942. Item 10; PRO INF 1 /292. British Institute of Public Opinion (hereafter BIPO). April 1943; M-O, FR 1104 'Private Opinion on the German People', 27 February 1942.

55. M-O Topic Collection (Hereafter TC) 17/1/B. Film Reports from Volunteers, 1939-1940. 'Freedom Radio'.

56. *Kinematograph Weekly,* 9 May 1940, 21.

57. Details here from Diller, A., *Rundfunkpolitik im Dritten Reich.* (Deutscher Taschenbuch Verlag, Munich, 1980), 341. See also Sington, D. & Weidenfeld, A., *The Goebbels Experiment. A Study of the Nazi Propaganda Machine* (John Murray, London, 1942), 196. The dates presented by Sington and Weidenfeld are slightly different to those cited in Diller.

58. *Ibid.,* 341-2.

59. 'Wunschkonzert: "Mahnung und Ansporn"', in *Der Montag,* Berlin edition, no. 47, 2 December 1940. Wiener Cuttings Collection, 101c.

60. *Ibid.*
61. *Ibid.*
62. Rolo, C., *Radio goes to War* (Faber and Faber, London, 1943), 32.
63. Kris, E. & Speier, H., *op.cit.*, 80.
64. Jacob, P. E., *loc.cit.*, 67-8.
65. *Ibid.*, 67.
66. The press claimed that, by December 1940, the Request Concerts reached an audience of 90 million. This figure needs to be treated with caution, as it was quoted in Goebbels' speech praising the work of the broadcast. 'Wunschkonzert: "Mahnung und Ansporn"', in *Der Montag*, Berlin edition, no. 47, 2 December 1940. Wiener Cuttings Collection, 101c.
67. 'Rufen Sie bitte dem Soldaten W. zu...' in *Hamburger Fremdenblatt*, no. 258, 17 September 1941. In Wiener Cuttings Collection, 210o. The *Kameradschaftsdienst* claimed to pass on 500 messages a day, as well as distributing donated items, such as games, musical instruments books, toothpaste, razors and cigarettes to soldiers at the front.
68. 'Front und Heimat' in *Filmwelt*, no. 22, 31 May 1940.
69. General Dietl quoted in Goebbels' speech on the 50th anniversary of the *Funkhaus*. 'Wunschkonzert: "Mahnung und Ansporn"', in *Der Montag*, Berlin edition, no. 47, 2 December 1940. Wiener Cuttings Collection, 101c.
70. 'Aufnahme der Wehrmachtswunschkonzerte bei der Bevölkerung und bei der Soldaten'. Nr. 71. 1 April 1940. Reproduced in Boberach, H. (ed.), *Meldungen aus dem Reich. Die geheimen Lageberichte des Sicherheitsdienstes der SS, 1938-1945*. Vo. 4 (Manfred Pawlak, Herrsching, 1984), 940.
71. *Ibid.*
72. *Bundesarchiv* (Hereafter BA) R56 I/ 104. Hans Hinkel *Der Einsatz unsere Kunst im Krieg*, 1940.
73. BA R56 I/ 104. Hans Hinkel *Der Einsatz unsere Kunst im Krieg*, 1940.
74. Werner, I., *So wird's nie wieder sein. Ein Leben mit Pfiff!* (Ullstein, Frankfurt am Main, 1996), 106-110.
75. BAR56 I/ 104. Hans Hinkel *Der Einsatz unsere Kunst im Krieg*, 1940.
76. Secret Meetings. 29 January 1940. In Boeckle, W., *The Secret Conferences of Dr. Goebbels, 1939-1943* (Dutton, London, 1970), 17.
77. BA R58/ 157 SD Report 17 February 1941. Also reproduced in Boberach, H. (ed.), *op.cit.*, 2007.
78. Sington, D. & Weidenfeld, *op.cit.*, 197.
79. Marben, R., 'Film und Funk', *Filmwelt*, 5 January 1940, 4.
80. Sington and Weidenfeld detail announcements made in the Request Concert, which closely match scenes in the film, such as the news that a baby has been born to a serving member of the armed forces. Sington, D. & Weidenfeld, A., *op.cit.*, 196.
81. *Illustrierter Film-Kurier*, nr. 3166. *Bundesarchiv, Filmarchiv*, Berlin, 19913.
82. BA R56 I/ 114. *Filmwelt*, Nr. 12. 13 September 1940.
     A. Schmidt in *Filmzeitung*, Munich Edition. 12 January 1941. Reproduced in Romani, C., *Tainted Goddesses. Female Film Stars of the Third Reich* (Sarpedon, New York, 1992), 138.
83. *Illustrierter Film- Kurier*, nr. 3166. *Bundesarchiv, Filmarchiv*, Berlin, 19913.
84. BA R58/ 157 SD Report 17 February 1941. Also reproduced in Boberach, H. (ed.), *op.cit.*, 2007.

85. *Filmzeitung* claimed that *Wunschkonzert* was 'a film of war and a film for the people, reflecting our times A. Schmidt in *Filmzeitung*, Munich Edition. 12 January 1941. Reproduced in Romani, C., *op.cit.*, 138. The emphasis on the appeal of realism can be found in Sander's thesis, which claimed that the film was voted 11th most popular film by the over 18s, primarily due to the film's realistic content. Sander, A. U., *Jugend und Film* (Franz Eher, Berlin, 1944).

86. PRO INF 1/ 533 'Propaganda on the Home Front'. HPC. 27 May 1940.

Chapter Seven
'TEMPERAMENTALLY UNWARLIKE': THE IMAGE OF ITALY IN THE ALLIES' WAR PROPAGANDA, 1943-45

Ilaria Favretto and Oliviero Bergamini

The purpose of this paper is to examine the image of Italy and Italians that underlay the Allies' propaganda in the period from July 1943 until the end of the war. The essay will investigate the efforts made by British and American propaganda agencies to reach a greater understanding of the new Italian war theatre confronting the Allies as a result of the landing in Sicily. Attention will be paid to the extent to which the perception and, on numerous occasions, misperception of Italy affected the propaganda material produced. Differences between individual agencies will be fully considered and analysed.

Propaganda during the Allied occupation in Italy has been a well-researched topic.[1] However, the literature's focus has so far been confined to the propaganda machine's organisational aspects and its role in military operations; very little attention has been paid to the image of Italy and Italians that informed the propaganda agencies' work. A far more systematic investigation of these aspects is crucial for a greater understanding of the impact and outcome of the Allied propaganda. It will also cast new light on the efforts made throughout the war period by the main Allied propaganda agencies to 'scienticize' their work and improve their research methods and means of investigation. Moreover, a deeper knowledge of the Allies' notion of Italy, will contribute to a greater comprehension of the factors that influenced Allies' policy in Italy during the period of co-belligerancy (i.e. their attitudes towards the Badoglio government, the anti-Fascist parties, the Resistance, etc).

The paper is based on material from the British PWE (Political Warfare Executive), the American OSS (Office of Strategic Services) and the OWI (Office of War Information). The latter was founded in June 1942 as a result of the expansion of the COI (Coordinator of Information), a body that had been established in July 1941. However, most of the research is based on the Record Groups of the PWB (Psychological Warfare Branch), the American-British joint propaganda agency that was created in the wake of Operation Torch in 1942, which was to remain operative up to December 1945. PWB depended on the Allied Headquarters in Algiers (AFHQ) and included members of the OWI, the OSS, the PWE and the British Ministry of Information (MOI). It might be worth remembering that, unlike France that, following the Darlan Clark agreement, was given back some degree of autonomy in the information sphere, the PWB played a crucial role in Italy's propaganda, and counterpropaganda efforts up to the end of the conflict.[2] The purpose of the PWB was to achieve a better co-ordination between British and American propaganda and avoid useless overlapping. However, both OWI and PWE remained fully operative. Not only was this a constant source of tension within the PWB but it also produced conflicting and inconsistent propaganda messages that on some occasions undermined the efficacy of the Allies' propaganda efforts.

Following the Allied landing in Africa in 1942, Allied propaganda agencies were put under great pressures to thoroughly revise their propaganda material in relation to Italy, that is to update it to the new war phase that the imminent landing in Sicily was to open up. From then on increasing efforts were made on both the British and the American side to reach a greater comprehension of Italy and her 'national character'.

Knowledge of Fascist Italy, in both Britain and in the US was extremely poor. With the exception of inter-war years coverage provided by quality papers such as *The Times* and the *Daily Telegraph*, there were hardly any books available in English on Italian Fascism in the United Kingdom. Jackson's *The Post-war World* (1935)[3] dedicated only fifteen pages to Mussolini's Italy.[4]

Americans in particular suffered from a considerable delay. Italy had until then been of a marginal strategic and military importance to US foreign policy. Moreover, the very ambivalence shown by the US towards their future role in Europe once the war was over, meant the former's interest in its enemies was in the early part of the conflict confined to issues that were strictly related to military operations with scant regard for domestic politics.[5] Last but not least, having entered the war later than the British, the US propaganda machine, unlike that of the Foreign Office, whose propaganda work on Italy started since Mussolini's declaration of war in 1940[6], was only fully operational in 1942.

After almost twenty years of 'isolationism' and little concern shown for European affairs, knowledge of countries such as Italy was fairly limited. As an OWI 1945 report read, the Fascist machine propaganda spent considerable sums to plant articles in foreign newspapers for the simple purpose of reprinting them at home, thereby giving the impression that foreign attention was great. Foreign newspapermen and writers were constantly invited to Italy and their output was reprinted at home as proof of foreign interest. However, the report went on, Italy did not arouse much attention and did not receive any particular space in the foreign press.[7] Furthermore, the little information available on the Fascist Regime had been scarce and inaccurate. The great majority of American correspondents from the most prominent newspapers were very close to Mussolini and the image of inter-war Italy they conveyed to their readers was, in most cases, one that, while pleasing to the Fascist oligarchy, was far from being a realistic one.[8] Italy was in 1942 something like a 'mystery' to the US.[9]

The need to fill the knowledge gap on this 'obscure' Mediterranean country within which the US was soon to operate, was therefore felt with great urgency. Staff numbers were massively increased and experts were recruited.[10] The OSS appointed for instance the late Harvard historian Stuart Hughes as Director of its Italy's Research and Analysis Department. [11]

On 30 September 1942, the first Joint American-British Plan for Psychological Warfare in Italy was produced.[12] In this very long and detailed report the PWB attempted to provide, as the introduction read, a 'more thorough and accurate appraisal of some of the dominant psychological and historical factors' affecting Italian morale and 'national character'.[13] Italians are described as 'temperamentally unwarlike' and not keen on violence: 'In no European country more than Italy, the home of the humanities, does human life have a higher value… except when in the grip of passion, the Italians instinctively hate killing, maiming, hurting'. They rather 'tend to be passive or "feninine" (sic)'.[14] It might be worth remembering that Italians' 'femininity' was one of the most recurrent stereotypes held by the Allies throughout the war period. In none of the propaganda movies produced by OWI, did Italians ever appear at the head of international spy conspiracies. Mussolini's military machine was always ridiculed and never depicted as a real 'threat' to the Allies. One of the very few British films on Italy's role in military operations, *Ship With Wings*, showed Italian soldiers making fun of their elegantly dressed and sophisticated superiors and their subservience to the Nazi ally's superiority. [15] The latter is an image that was recently perpetuated in the recently released Hollywood movie *Captain's Correlli Mandolin* where 'good', romantic and opera-singing Italians were contrasted with cruel, tough and resolute Nazi troops.

However, 'despite deceptive appearances', the PWB document continued, Italians 'have the "classic Mediterranean" temperament: they are realists, guided by clear-headed appraisal of self-interest':[16] '…the Italian does something for society because he gets something in return; he refrains from doing something against society because he will be punished'. After all, as the report put it, he grew up in a 'system of Catholic rewards and punishments'.[17] The above factors should not be ignored, the plan carried on, when rethinking the main guidelines of Allied propaganda. For two and a half years British and American psychological warfare in Italy, the document read, had taken a 'soft' line. It had operated on the theory that an attitude of consistent sympathy and implied friendliness toward the Italians would most effectively stimulate them to oppose the war. However, by sticking to this approach, propaganda had achieved very little: Italy had 'fallen short of producing her share of effective sabotage… both in the Army and in civilian life all but an infinitesimally small portion of the population have continued to make their allotted contributions to the war effort'.[18]

Time had come, the PWB suggested, for a 'tough' line to be pursued. Allies should on the one hand convey the message that they can 'really offer the Italians something'; and on the other hand, 'convincingly threaten them with something'. By so doing, Anglo-Americans, should persuade Italians that they were 'more to be feared than either the Fascists or the Germans'; but at the same time they alone presented 'the hope of salvation'.[19]

Italy was regarded as a nation lacking initiative and cohesiveness, a nation uniquely moved by opportunistic considerations. As the PWB plan read it, centuries of political disturbance had left the Italians with 'little national social sense, little social discipline and little social initiative'. This, it was argued, should not be confused 'with individualism, meaning by that a capability of autonomous and active action'. By contrast, Italians had always been in need of guidance and direction. For Italians it was not the nation which was capable of fostering 'passionate loyalty' and action, but rather small social groupings 'based on consanguinity or on physical contiguity or proximity': family first and foremost. Consistently, one reads, 'class-war and political revolutionary tendencies' were 'either weak or alien in Italy'.[20]

The PWB Report concluded that Allies could not expect and count on any self generated national insurrection as no credible leaders that had enough authority to unite antifascist forces seemed to be there. Allied intervention would fit in with the Italian historical pattern that saw foreign nations taking the initiative in 'helping the Italians free themselves'. For many centuries, it was argued, since the days of Ludovico il Moro, foreign nations had, for better or worse, participated in domestic Italian affairs: 'Italy became a nation in the nineteenth century because several foreign countries, for their own motives interfered in her affairs. Napoleon broke the power of the old feudal masters. Napoleon the Third helped the *Risorgimento* by battles on Italian soil. The Germany of Bismarck played a part. Liberation through temporary foreign invasion is no new story to Italy and psychological warfare can assign this role in a favourable light to the Unites States.'[21]

Comments on Italian familism, and Italy's weak civic culture reflect some familiarity with Italian society and political culture. In this respect, it should be remembered that the notion of 'amoral familism' was to become central to the work of post-war American anthropologists like Edward Banfield.[22] However, on the whole the document suffers from vagueness and a lack of accuracy. Remarks on Italians' opportunism and 'classic mediterranean temperament' seem to be drawn more from literature than from any social scientifically informed approach. Of greater significance, the point made about the absence of revolutionary tendencies is a grave mistake that testifies to a complete lack of knowledge of pre-Fascist Italian history.

Those in charge of propaganda were to show in the years to come a growing concern with the need for the elaboration of far more detailed and systematic investigations, particularly when it came to Italians' 'psychological situation'. From early 1943 the PWB staff began to lament the failure of the system of 'intelligence officers' in liberated areas to provide them 'with really reliable information about public opinion on which a sound propaganda or economic policy could be based'. A far more accurate analysis of Italian public opinion, it was argued, was of crucial importance to devise an effective propaganda. Greater efforts should be made to go beyond an 'impressionistic' approach and to 'scienticize' their means of investigation.[23]

In October 1943 the PWB proposed for a wide-ranging series of 'Gallup polls' surveys on issues such Italian feelings towards the Allies, 'radio listening habits', political orientations, the question of co-belligerancy, the impact of propaganda, news circulation, etc. The survey was to have been conducted in the period from October to December 1943 in the liberated territories. Under the supervision of the American sociologist Stuart C. Dodd, the operation entailed the recruitment of hundreds of Italian interviewers who were provided with a 'training course'.[24] Incidentally, those were to be the very first polls ever carried out in Italy since the presence of a dictatorial regime delayed the creation of a Gallup-like agency in Italy – that is the Doxa – up to 1946.[25]

American pollsters were soon to realise the difficulties in carrying out polls in a country that had long been unaccustomed to free expression and free thinking. The lack of trust which most of those interviewed showed was a constant source of frustration and suggested some second thoughts among propaganda agencies on the use of this method. In November 1944 Richard P. Stebbins, head of the OWI's Italian Office was asked to consider the possibility of carrying out a secret 'opinion poll' intended to single out the political orientations of the 'man in the street' in Rome. Stebbins rejected the proposal as unfeasible. He, in fact, pointed out the problem of securing a staff of properly trained and trustworthy interviewers. Furthermore, as he put it, 'it is highly doubtful whether "the man in the street" in Italy would be willing to express his opinions frankly for this purpose, even though Italian interviewers were employed. Public opinion polls among Italians in this country have encountered serious difficulties arising from the suspiciousness and reticence of the interviewees.'[26] As the OWI Long Range Plan drafted in December 1944 read, it was difficult 'to gauge Italian public opinion with any degree of precision'.[27]

For all the difficulties and obstacles encountered, the accuracy of the research background work produced by Allied propaganda agencies improved as years went by and reflected an ever growing familiarity with the country and its specificity. However, one should not underestimate the degree of continuity between later and earlier reports, i.e. the PWB September 1942 report we mentioned above. Some of the most significant ideas underlying it persisted unchanged up to 1945: the notion of Italy's complacent and ambivalent attitude towards Fascism was, for instance, to remain unchallenged throughout the war time period and, it could be argued, in post 1945 years too.

Both British and American propaganda agencies seemed to agree on the degree of consensus that the Fascist regime could rely on among the population. This was a view that, incidentally, was fully consistent with the notion of Fascism's 'inevitability' for a backward Italy, a view that had prevailed in both countries during the inter-war years.[28] The British Foreign office and the PWE in particular did not make any concession to the attempt of the old pre-fascist Italian political elite to present themselves as alien to the advent of Fascism: it is quite obvious, as a document drafted by the British Ministry of Information in September 1940 read, that the Fascist crisis started with the war, which, since the very beginning, was highly unpopular among the population; Italians' antifascism was dictated by nothing other than opportunism; this was why - the document continued- it would be highly unwise to insist in the propaganda on leitmotifs such as 'we are saving democracy'. This, would have 'no appeal except to very few Italians'.[29]

A consistently dismissive attitude towards the Resistance movement continued throughout the years from 1943 to 1945. Indeed military and political reasons did account for it; Allies, particularly Britain, aimed at confining and dismissing as much as possible the role played by the Communist-led Resistance in Italy's fight against the Nazi occupier so as to prevent its leaders from advocating a prominent role in Italy's reconstruction and post-fascist transition once the war was over. However, it also reflected a widespread reluctance among the British establishment to recognise any moral and political strength in the anti-

Fascist movement; the latter was always regarded as minority and, far from being representative of the country as a whole.[30]

The American propaganda agency OWI was also not prepared to make any concession to the 'myth' of the Italian people's hostility to the Fascist regime. As the OWI Draft Operational Plan for Italy of 12 February 1944 read, although 'one should welcome the signs of redemption that many Italians were showing, easy self-absolving tendencies should be firmly rejected'. One should not forget that 'the abolishment of Fascism was brought about not by the people but by national defeat.'[31] After 20 years of a Fascist regime, 'there is almost nobody left in Italy who is not in one way or another contaminated by Fascism.'[32] No exceptions were made: intellectual elites, writers, scholars and scientists had all 'been stymied and corrupted by the Fascist regime.'[33]

Nevertheless, the deep mistrust towards Italians had, for obvious reasons, to be concealed. Anglo-American propaganda, it was argued, should instead emphasise a clear-cut distinction between the people and the Regime. It was only by hinting that Fascists, not Italy, would pay the price that the Allies managed to sign a separate peace with the Monarchy. At the same time it was only by stressing the difference between a corrupted and evil regime on the one hand and the nation on the other – which Allied propaganda depicted as the very first victim of Mussolini's foolish ambitions – the Allies could hope to spark some internal reaction and get some support for their military operations within the population; the people would be eventually offered the chance to prove its estrangement from Fascism.[34]

The scepticism that the Allies held towards Italians, is well reflected in the little faith shown in the self-regenerative capacities of the nation when it came to discussing Italy's political future. The widespread consensus over Fascism among the population had been a further illustration, it was argued, of the lack of civic and democratic culture of Italians. Italy was a country unfit for democracy: It was going to be extremely difficult for the Italians 'to accept the idea of a democratic way of life, and much more difficult to translate the idea into practice'.[35] Italians were not in other words, 'sold on democracy'.[36]

As the literature on Italy's Allied occupation has pointed out, when it came to devising a strategy on how to deal with what was described as the 'sick man of Europe', the views held by Britain and the US differed quite substantially. This is well reflected in the guidelines produced by the Allies' propaganda agencies.

The OWI's recipe for a 'cure' or 'convalescence' urged a cathartic self-generated revolutionary process that Allies should help to promote in Italy. Fascism was a 'disease' which had infected most of Italians: '… after more than 20 years in the lazaretto (sic) of Fascism, a very large number of Italians have not escaped systemic infection; the twisted ideas and warped passions of the false doctrines we are determined to destroy are inextricably woven into the pattern of thinking and feeling of many Italians.'[37] The document carried on that only a revolution from below could eliminate Fascism's germs for good: '...Fascism cannot be removed bloodlessly as one peels the skin from an orange. Individuals must share and participate in the revolutionary purging of the State of which they have been made organic parts: catharsis of the whole is inconceivable without catharsis of the parts'. Hence Italians should be freed to 'carry out a real revolution for themselves in their own way... a counter-revolution against a counter-revolution, any form of static, frozen "order" imposed upon the Italians by alien soldiers will merely submerge the false doctrines we are pledged to destroy, and postpone a more dreadful day of reckoning'.[38]

Therefore, Italy was a 'sick' country but if well-directed and patiently guided – the paper refers to it as a long 'convalescence' – she could recover and purge herself for good. Unlike Germany and Japan, Italy was a country that Allies should not annihilate but rather punish and re-educate.[39] Under the influence of liberal, 'New Dealist' journalists and writers, OWI's propaganda was therefore markedly characterised by the production of highly didactic and pedagogic material aimed at proving the goodness of the American model.[40] On most occasions, not only did this 'American Democracy in Action'[41] material present a highly idealised picture of the American system but, more significantly in so far its impact and efficacy were concerned, paid very little regard to the peculiarity of the Italian case and the substantial differences in history and political culture that existed between Italy and the US. In this respect the OWI publication 'The Story of Alexandria' is extremely emblematic. The booklet was to be a presentation of the American way of life through the case of Alexandria, a tiny little town located in Indiana. The picture offered was one of a peaceful and harmonious community, uniquely populated by white, religious and affluent people, meeting regularly in public assemblies usually held in the local school.[42] The typically Jeffersonian emphasis on direct democracy and a system of highly empowered decentralised local governments, as an OSS report put it, disregarded Italy's lack of 'a vigorous tradition of local administration'.[43] However, Italians, as OWI officers optimistically and quite self-complacently noted in a report on 'Attitudes of the Italian People Towards other Nations', seemed very eager to learn and to be re-educated;[44] if only because they held a great sympathy and interest towards the United States, which – incidentally – contrasted with the deeply hostile feelings that Italians seemed to show towards the 'arrogant and ungenerous' British.[45] American soldiers reported the eagerness people showed to know more about this far away country in all respects: in economic, social, political and even more trivial terms.[46] US officers wrote of the enthusiasm of Italians for Hollywood films and their surprisingly well informed knowledge of Hollywood stars and their lives; the movies from the OWI's film section had proved highly popular among the population which enthusiastically filled the hundreds of reopened and newly set up cinemas all around liberated Italy.[47]

Italians expected from Americans 'information, guidance and leadership': they were not unaware that Communism was getting 'fashionable' but it was fairly obvious from the greed they showed for everything which was American that they looked at American thought as something which could 'rescue them from the quagmire of their own conscience.'[48] As the end of the war approached and preoccupation with military operations made way for concern over Italy's post fascist transition, educating Italians in democracy acquired increasing centrality within the OWI's propaganda.[49] The assumption was that by means of advise and education Italians could be eventually redeemed and morally rescued.

The biggest obstacles for a successful redemption were said to be Italy's ingrained tendency towards political fragmentation and divisiveness. It is again worth noting that the OWI underestimated what was to become shortly a veritable obsession of US foreign policy: that is the 'Red danger'. Unlike other sectors of the American establishment such as the OSS and unlike the British Foreign Office, for which the Communist threat would acquire growing centrality and importance after March-April 1944[50], Communism and Marxism were dismissed in OWI reports as a matter of fashion.[51] Consistently, OWI officers did not have any problems in co-operating with Italian communists, recruiting them for instance to work for Radio Italia, the OWI radio that from 1943 to 1944 targeted Italian partisans. Not surprisingly the radio's 'marxist and revolutionary' tones were often objects of fierce criticism and attacks. [52]

The policy advocated by American agencies such as OWI, their emphasis on a self-generated liberation sharply contrasted with the US State Department and the War Department; but most of all with the far more punitive and less idealistic approach pursued by the British Foreign Office and the (AMGOT) military command.[53] Italians' self-regenerative capabilities, it was argued, could not be trusted. As one reads in the reports which the PWE produced in the years from 1943-1945, democracy was just a 'word' and it did not have the meaning it held in the UK:[54] Italians, unlike the British, had always been cynical towards their political elite and institutions and after twenty years of Fascism they would feel even more detached and alien from the democratic process. The average Italian tends blindly to follow charismatic political figures with no distinction being made between different ideas and political parties.[55] Democracy would never come into life if left to the good will of Italians; Britain should rather establish firm political control of the country. [56]

The clash between the more realist approach urged by Britain and a more idealist one promoted by the American OWI was on some occasions at the origin of an ambivalent propaganda. It also produced a number of clashes between the US and UK agencies, as for example the 'King accident': after the removal and arrest of Mussolini on the 26 of July 1943, the OWI speakers described King Vittorio Emanuele on a radio programme as a 'moronic little king' and denounced his support for fascism. This clashed with the more supportive line towards the Monarchy pursued by the Allied Military command, which hoped to sign an armistice and which formally complained about OWI; some commentators in the US accused OWI of being a "Communist lunatic fringe."[57] Overall as an OWI's report lamented the operation in Italy was largely a 'British show'. This was for example quite apparent in the way partisans were pictured in the propaganda material. After an initial period (1943-1944) when insurrection was solicited, from 1944 onwards the policy of 'containment' of the Resistance movement pursued by the allies went hand in hand with a propaganda intended to dismiss its contribution and role in military operations[58]

The knowledge of Italy held by most of the officers in charge of propaganda aimed at the Italian theatre was in 1943 fairly limited and strongly influenced by a number of stereotypes that had developed during the inter-war years (i.e. the idea that Italy was unfit for democracy). As we argued, considerable efforts were made before and after the landing in Sicily in July 1943 to reach a deeper understanding of the country by recruiting scholars or adopting more 'scientific' tools of investigation, such as public opinion surveys. However, in many respects the analyses produced by the Allied propaganda agencies, while improving in accuracy as years went by, continued to suffer until the very end of the war, particularly on the American side, from a poor understanding of the Italian case. It will suffice to mention the emphasis on the lack of revolutionary tendencies, or the description of Communism as a fashionable and transitory phenomenon, to illustrate this fairly limited knowledge of pre-fascist Italian history.

Propaganda agents also showed some naïveté: one thinks of the idealist identification of Italians' enthusiasm for Hollywood films and American life style as a sincere interest in American thought and 'American democracy in Action', and not instead an interest in the prosperity with which the American dream was associated. The Messianism and the political idealism that characterised the work of many US agents, particularly from OWI, were often conducive to a type of propaganda that, while dismissing the difficulties in importing the highly decentralised American model of democracy in a country that had a completely different cultural, historical and political background, resulted in the production of material - such as the 'History of Alexandria' booklet- that hardly fit the Italian context and raise some doubts about the propaganda's efficacy.

One significant example of miscalculated propaganda is the use of gender-oriented leaflets. To the Allies' great disappointment and surprise, as a 1944 PWB report read, the leaflet 'Donne in Guerra (Women at War)' was met with indifference and suspiciousness by the majority of the population: 'Only disagreeable reaction we have found today concerned Donne in Guerra. People have not yet realised the feminine part in this war'.[59] Far from being discouraged, PWB officers, it was said, continued to produce material picturing the heroic role played in the war by 'nurses, British sisters, etc...'.[60] However, the insistence on gender-oriented material showed American ignorance of one of the main lines of anti-American Fascist propaganda, which emphasized the disruptive effects on American society of the widely extended freedoms that American women were said to be endowed with – notably easy access to contraception, the right to divorce, and abortion. This, it was argued, was conducive to the destruction of the traditional values and institutions that Italian cherished, above all the family unit.[61] The more prominent 'political' role Eleanor Roosevelt played next to her husband was often pictured by Fascist propaganda as an unforgivable betrayal of her femininity and the most glaring illustration of a country where 'everything could happen' and that Italians should look at suspiciously.[62]

One last factor that undermined the efficacy of the Allies propaganda was the number of tensions existing between UK and US agencies as well as between military and civilian bodies (i.e. OWI) regarding many far from marginal issues, such as the attitude towards the Badoglio government and the King, or the 'Read Threat'. The latter were often at the origin of conflicting messages that did not demonstrate the consistent and unified propaganda which the creation of PWB was designed to lead to.

After 1945, against the background of the Cold War, the US's interest and understanding for Italy was to significantly increase. However, some of the most distinctive themes underlying the Allies propaganda would not easily dissolve, i.e. Italy's unfitness for democracy. The latter underlay the US ambivalence throughout the post-war years towards far-right groups and authoritarian solutions when it came to dealing with the 'Communist threat'. As the long-range policy plan in 1945 had warned, the whole Italian culture was still 'contradictory and ambivalent on the subject of Fascism'. While the Italians did not want to reconstruct the Fascist Regime and were, by and large, 'averse to its symbols and its mythology', they had 'retained many of the psychological traits that made Fascism possible...'. Italians were an 'audience of sceptics, not anti-fascists; who, disappointed by Fascism, were afraid of being disappointed by democracy'.[63]

At the same time US foreign policy was to remain highly characterised by a great deal of Messianism. After all, as the 1945 OWI long-range policy plan put it, Italy was a country that had put her destiny in American hands. The end of the war was not to decrease expectations. The opposite was true: 'It is difficult to assess with any exactitude what the Italians expect from us. To take the broad view, we may say that they expect everything… concomitantly with our help, the Italians expect from us a manufactured dream world, a magnification of a Hollywood production (p. 5). As the report concluded, there was no doubt that 'Italian dependence on us is very great. The Italian people feel themselves alone in a totally hostile world, flanked by greedy neighbours, unwilling to forgive them for past sins for which the Italians feel they have already atoned. (p. 3). Against a context of 'total desperation' and a deep economic crisis, the United States seemed to be 'the only ray of hope' (p. 4) and were not in the position to let Italians down.[64]

NOTES

1. See for instance, Alejandro Pizarroso Quintero, *Stampa, radio e propaganda. Gli alleati in Italia 1943-1946* (Milan, Franco Angeli, 1989); Lamberto Mercuri, *Guerra psicologica. La propaganda anglo-americana in Italia* (Rome, 1983); Robert W. Van De Velde, *The Role of US Propaganda in Italy's Return to Political Democracy, 1943-1948* (Phd), Princeton University, 1950; M. Caprioli Piccialuti, *Radio Londra 1939-1945. Inventario delle trasmissioni per l'Italia* (Rome, Bari-Laterza, 1976); M. Caprioli Piccialuti, *Radio Londra 1939-1945* (Rome-Bari, Laterza, 1979).

2. See, A. Pizarroso Quintero, *Stampa, Radio e Propaganda*, op. cit., p. 18

3. J. Hampden Jackson, *The Post-War World. A Short Political History 1918-1934* (London, Victor Gollancz, 1935)

4. See on this also J. Diggins, *L'America, Mussolini e il fascismo* (Rome-Bari, Laterza, 1972)

5. Ennio Di Nolfo, 'Italia e Stati Uniti: un'alleanza diseguale', *Storia delle Relazioni Internazionali*, no.1/year 6 (1990), pp. 3-27, p. 8-9; See also Elena Aga Rossi 'Gli Stati Uniti e l'armistizio italiano', in R. H. Rainero, *L'Italia in guerra - Il quarto anno 1943* (Rome, Commissione italiana di storia militare, 1994), pp. 195-205 and Elena Aga Rossi, 'Politica estera americana e Italia nella seconda guerra mondiale', in G. Spini, G. Migone, M. Teodori, *Italia e America dalla grande guerra ad oggi* (Venice, Marsilio, 1976), pp. 159-177

6. Following Mussolini's war declaration, Italy was at the centre of a special meeting held at the Foreign Office gathering together representatives of the Ministry of Information, and of the Political Intelligence Department aimed at drafting the first operative guidelines for propaganda in Italy. A document titled 'Directive on British Propaganda for Italy' was drafted (20 September 1940) to be circulated among the Italian BBC World Service. In January 1941, the Italian Service went through a major re-organisation and staff, which had already increased from 3 to 10 in 1940, passed to 38. M. Caprioli Piccialuti, *Radio Londra 1939-1945*, op. cit., pp. 13, 23.

7. 'Long Range Policy Directive for Italy', 3 July 1945, National Archives Washington (hereafter NAW), Office of War of Information (hereafter OWI), Record Group 208 (hereafter RG 208), Entry 6G, Box 4.

8. See on this J. Diggins, *L'America, Mussolini e il fascismo* , op. cit., p. 51 e p. 22ss

9. See on this B. L. Mercuri, *Guerra psicologica. La propaganda anglo-americana in Italia*, op. cit.

10. Ibid. See also R. Faenza e M. Fini, *Gli Americani in Italia* (Milan, Feltrinelli, 1976), p. 7; Luigi Rossi, *Gli Stati Uniti e la 'Provincia' Italiana, 1943-1945. Politica ed Economia secondo gli analisti del servizio segreto americano* (Naples, Edizioni Scientifiche Italiane, 1990) and Max Corvo, *The OSS in Italy, 1942-1945: a personal memoir* (New York, Praeger, 1990)

11. Stuart Hughes was to become in the post-war years a leading scholar of European intellectual history. He also published a oft-quoted book on the relationships between Italy and the United States: Stuart Hughes, *The United States and Italy* (Cambridge, Harvard University Press, 1953; Italian edition: Stuart Hughes, *Italia e Stati Uniti : un secolo di storia italiana visto da un americano* (Florence, La Nuova Italia, 1956)

12. "Joint American-British Plan of Psychological Warfare for Italy', London 30 September 1942, NAW, OWI, RG 208, Entry 6G, Box 4.

13. Joint American-British Plan of Psychological Warfare for Italy', London 30 September 1942, p. 1, NAW, OWI, RG 208, Entry 6G, Box 4.

14. Joint American-British Plan of Psychological Warfare for Italy', London 30 September 1942, p. 1, NAW, OWI, RG 208, Entry 6G, Box 4.

15. L. Mercuri, *Guerra psicologica. La propaganda anglo-americana in Italia*, op.cit., p. 204. See also Gregory D. Black and Clayfon R. Koppes, 'Owi goes to the Movies: the Bureau of Intelligence's Criticism of Hollywood 1942-43', *Prologue* (Spring 1974).

16. Joint American-British Plan of Psychological Warfare for Italy', London 30 September 1942, p. 1, NAW, OWI, RG 208, Entry 6G, Box 4.

17. Joint American-British Plan of Psychological Warfare for Italy', London 30 September 1942, p. 2, NAW, OWI, RG 208, Entry 6G, Box 4.

18. Joint American-British Plan of Psychological Warfare for Italy', London 30 September 1942, p. 1, NAW, OWI, RG 208, Entry 6G, Box 4.

19. Joint American-British Plan of Psychological Warfare for Italy', London 30 September 1942, p. 1, NAW, OWI, RG 208, Entry 6G, Box 4.

20. Joint American-British Plan of Psychological Warfare for Italy', London 30 September 1942, p. 3, NAW, OWI, RG 208, Entry 6G, Box 4.

21. Joint American-British Plan of Psychological Warfare for Italy', London 30 September 1942, p. 3, NAW, OWI, RG 208, Entry 6G, Box 4.

22. See for instance Edward Christie Banfield, *The Moral Basis of a Backward Society* (New York, Free Press, 1958).

23. 'A Plan for the establishment of the PWB Opinion Survey Section', Allied Force Headquarters PWB, 15 October 1943, NAW, OWI, RG 208, Entry 6G, Box 4.

24. See on this also S. C. Dodd, A Manual of Social Surveying in 'Liberated Territories', American Documentation Institute, Washington DC 1944 and R. W. Van De Velde-Robert T. Holt, Strategic Psychological Operations and

American Foreign Policy, University of Chicago Press, Chicago and London, 1960, pp. 132-133

25. See on this Sandro Rinauro, 'The diffusion of Public Opinion Research in Italy between Fascism and Democracy', paper presented at the International Conference of the Freie Universitat of Berlin, 9-10 May 1997, 'Opinion Research in the History of Modern Democracies – Methods, Applications, Effects. And Sandro Rinauro, 'Il sondaggio d'opinione arriva in Italia (1936-1946)', *Passato e Presente*, year XIX, no. 52, 2001, pp. 41-66.

26. 'Proposed Public Opinion Survey in Rome', Richard P. Stebbins to Dr. Langer, 8 November 1944, NAW, Office of Strategic Services (hereafter OSS), Record Group 226 (hereafter RG 226), Entry 51, Box 3.

27. 'Long-Range Guidance Policy for Italy', 6 December 1944, p.7, NAW, OWI, RG 208, Entry 6G, Box 4.

28. See on this M. Berselli, *L'opinione pubblica inglese e l'avvento del fascismo (1919-1925)* (Milan, Franco Angeli, 1971), p. 149; Massimo De Leonardis, 'La Gran Bretagna e la Monarchia italiana (1943-1946)', *Storia Contemporanea*, Vol. XII, no. 1, 1981, pp. 57-134

29. 'Directive on British Propaganda for Italy', 20 September 1940, PRO, FO, R 7686/6600/22, in M. Caprioli Piccialuti, *Radio Londra 1939-1945. Inventario delle trasmissioni per l'Italia*, op. cit., p. cxi; see on this also David Ellwood, *L'alleato nemico. La politica dell'occupazione anglo-americana in Italia 1943-1946* (Milan, Feltrinelli, 1976), p. 69. On the British punitive attitude towards Italy see A. Varsori, 'L'atteggiamento britannico verso l'Italia (1940-1943): alle origini della politica punitiva', in A. Placanica (edited by), *1944 Salerno capitale istituzioni e società* (Naples, ESI, 1985), pp. 137-159 and A. Varsori, 'Gran Bretagna e Italia 1945-1956. Il rapporto tra una grande potenza e una piccola potenza?, in A. Varsori (edited by), *La Politica estera italiana nel secondo dopoguerra (1943-1957)* (Milan, LED, 1993).

30. See on this M. De Leonardis, *La Gran Bretagna e la Resistenza partigiana in Italia 1943-1954* (Naples, Edizioni Scientifiche Italiane, 1988).

31. 'Draft Operational Plan for Italy in the Ceres Phase', 12 February 1944, Appendix B, NAW, OWI, RG 208, Entry 6G, Box 4.

32. Ibid, p. 3.

33. Ibid., p. 10.

34. See the PWB Weekly Directives (Italy), NAW, RG 331, Entry AFHQ Microfilm, Box 156; see also 'Draft of General Directives for Italy for use of OWI in North Africa', Percy Winner to Robert E. Sherwood, 26 January 1943, p. 1, NAW, OWI, RG 208, Entry 6G, Box 4; and the 'Long-Range Policy Guidance for Italy, 6 December 1944, p. 2, NAW, OWI, RG 208, Entry 6G, Box 4.

35. 'Long-Range Policy Guidance for Italy', 6 December 1944, p. 2, NAW, OWI, RG 208, Entry 6G, Box 4.

36. 'Long-Range Policy Guidance for Italy', 6 December 1944, p. 2, NAW, OWI records, RG 208, Entry 6G, Box 4.

37. From Percy Winner to Robert Sherwood, 19 July 1943, NAW, OWI, RG 208, Entry 6G, Box 4.

38. From Percy Winner to Robert Sherwood, 19 July 1943, NAW, OWI records, RG 208, Entry 6G, Box 4.

39. See on this also G. Spini, G. Migone, M. Teodori (edited by), *Italia e America dalla Grande Guerra ad Oggi*, op. cit., pp. 197-221, p. 202

40. On OWI and the tensions that its 'liberal' stance produced both with others sectors of the US establishment and the British ally, see Allan M. Winkler, *The Politics of Propaganda: the Office of War Information 1942-1945* (New Haven, Yale University Press, 1978).

41. 'Long Range Operational Plan for Italy', March 6 1945, pp. 1-3, NAW, OWI, RG 208, Entry 6G, Box 4. See also 'Long Range Policy Directive for Italy', 3 July 1945, NAW, OWI, RG 208, Entry 6G, Box 4.

42. 'This is the story of Alexandria', NAW, OWI publications, RG 208, Box 21.

43. Donald C. McKay to William L. Langer, 'Report on the Political Situation in Liberated Italy', 16 February 1944, OSS, RG 226. The pressures exerted by some sections of the US establishment on the Italian post-1945 elite towards the adoption of a federal institutional model similar to that of the United States through the creation of regional governments were to persist unchanged up to the years of the *Costituente*, that is the democratically elected Italian Constituent Assembly that in the years from 1945 to 1946 drafted Italy's new Constitution. See on this James Miller, 'The search for stability: an interpretation of American policy in Italy: 1943-1946', *The Journal of Italian History*, Vol I, no 2, Autumn 1978, pp. 264-286, p. 270

44. Long-Range Policy Directive for Italy, 3 July 1945, p. 3, NAW, OWI, RG 208, Entry 6G, Box 4.

45. Ibid. In a survey carried out by DOXA in 1946 on Italians' attitudes towards Allies, 62.4 per cent of Italians expressed a preference for American troops with the British soldiers scoring a poor 12.2 per cent(Doxa, Bullettin no. 2, 1947, quoted in L. Mercuri, *Guerra psicologica. La propaganda anglo-americana in Italia*, op. cit., p. 223). See on this also A. Varsori, 'Gran Bretagna e Italia 1945-1956. Il rapporto tra una grande potenza e una piccola potenza?, in A. Varsori (edited by), *La Politica estera italiana nel secondo dopoguerra (1943-1957)* (Milan, LED, 1993); A. Varsori, 'L'atteggimento britannico verso l'Italia (1940-1943): alle origini della politica punitiva', op.cit., pp. 137-159; G. Filippone Thaulero, *La Gran Bretagna e l'Italia dalla conferenza di Mosca a Potsdam (1943-45)* (Rome, Edizioni di Storia e Letteratura, 1979); Peter Sebastiani, *I servizi segreti britannici e l'Italia (1940-1945)* (Rome, Bonacci Editore, 1986); Peter Sebastiani, *Laburisti inglesi e socialisti italiani. Dalla Ricostruzione del PSI(UP) alla scissione di Palazzo Barberini da Transport House a Downing Street (1943-1947)* (Rome, Quaderni FIAP, 1983); M. De Leonardis, La Gran Bretagna e la Resistenza partigiana in Italia 1943-1954 (Naples, Edizioni Scientifiche Italiane, 1988); AAVV, *Inghilterra e Italia nel 900. Atti del Convegno di Bagni di Lucca*, October 1972 (Florence, La Nuova Italia, 1977); Pietro Cavallo, *Italiani in guerra. Sentimenti e immagini dal 1940 al 1943* (Bologna, Il Mulino, 1997). P. P. D'Attorre, 'Sogno americano e mito sovietico nell'Italia contemporanea', in D'Attorre (edited by), *Nemici per la pelle: sogno americano e mito sovietico nell'Italia contemporanea* (Milan, Franco Angeli, 1991), p. 25.

46. From John Karl to Natt S. Getlin, Chief Mobile Unit Operation, 27 March 1944, NAW, OWI, RG 208, Entry 6G, Box 4.

47. [47] See on this 'Report on the film situation in Italy', by Louis Lober, Assistant Chief, Motion Picture Bureau, 19 March 1945, NAW, OWI, RG 208, Entry 6G Box 4. As the report read, 'It is estimated that the film section has shown

American feature movies in their custody to more than 13 million Italians, short subjects, newsreels, and documentaries to an audience that topped 52 million' (p. 4). As the report continued, reception of this material was to say the least enthusiastic: 'When "The Great Dictator" was shown in Naples for the first time, crowds were so large that Allied military police and Carabinieri.. had to be called out to keep order' (p. 5). The overall aim of this propaganda material –as stated in the report – was to influence 'the people against the Germans and for democracy'. See also on this 'Italian People Welcome American Films and ask about their stars', *New York Times*, 13 August 1944. And Christopher Duggan, 'Italy in the Cold War years and the Legacy of Fascism', in Christopher Duggan and Christopher Wagstaff (edited by), *Italy in the Cold War. Politics, Culture and Society 1948-1958* (Oxford, Berg, 1995), pp. 1-24, p 12.Ibid., p. 11.

48. 'Report on the film situation in Italy', by Louis Lober, Assistant Chief, Motion Picture Bureau, 19 March 1945, p. 11, OWI, RG 208, Entry 6G, Box 4.

49. Long Range Operational Plan for Italy, March 6 1945, p. 1-3, NAW, OWI, Entry 6G, Box 4.

50. See on this R. Filippelli, *American Labor and Post-war Italy 1943-1953. A Study of Cold War* (Stanford, Stanford University Press, 1989), p. 30 and M. Margiocco, *Stati Uniti e PCI 1943-1980* (Rome-Bari, Laterza, 1981). See on this Entry 73 of the OSS documents (Research and Analysis Branch), National Archives, OSS, RG 226, Boxes 1-8. On the OSS's activity in Italy and the 'containment' of the PCI see R. Faenza e M. Fini, *Gli Americani in Italia*, op.cit; Leopoldo Nuti, *Gli Stati Uniti e l'apertura a sinistra : importanza e limiti della presenza americana in Italia* (Rome, Laterza, 1999); Elena Aga Rossi, 'La politica estera americana e l'Italia nella seconda guerra mondiale', op. cit., pp. 162-163; B. Arcidiacono, *Le 'précédent italien' et les origines de la guerre froide. Les Alliés et l'occupation de l'Italie, 1943-1944* (Bruxelles, Bruylant, 1984); Bruno Arcidiacono, 'La Gran Bretagna e il pericolo comunista: gestione, nascita e primo sviluppo di una percezione (1943-1944)', in *Storia delle Relazioni Internazionali*, n. 1, 1985, pp. 43-44; Ennio Di Nolfo, 'La svolta di Salerno come problema internazionale', in *Storia delle Relazioni Internazionali*, no 1, 1985, pp. 5-28, pp. 23-24; and E. Di Nolfo, 'The Unites States and Italian Communism 1942-1946: World War II to the Cold War', in *The Journal of Italian History*, I, 1978, n. 1, pp.74-94. Lastly, see David Ellwood, *L'alleato nemico*, op.cit., pp. 78-79.

51. 'Long-Range Policy Guidance for Italy', 6 December 1944, NAW, OWI, Entry 6G, Box 4.

52. R. Filippelli, *American Labor and Postwar Italy 1943-1953*, op. cit., p. 30.

53. The telegram the Foreign Office sent to the Ministry of State at Cairo on 12 November 1943 is, in this respect, highly revealing: 'The last minute conversion of the Italians to democratic principles will not enable them to escape the consequences of their ill behaviour. Our acceptance of the Italians as co-belligerants by no means weakens the force of the armistice on which the relations with the Italian government continue to be based. When the time comes for a settlement, the claims or position of our Allies will in no way prejudiced by Italy's co-belligerancy'. NAW, OSS, RG 226, Entry 5, Box 2.

54. See David Elwood, *L'Alleato Nemico*, op. cit., pp. 99-100.

55. Ibid.

56. Ibid.

57. Allen Winkler, *The Politics of Propaganda: the Office of War Information 1942-1945*, op. cit., pp. 93-96.

58. On the Allies' policy towards the Italian Resistance and its purported role in the military operations, see M. De Leonardis, *La Gran Bretagna e la resistenza partigiana in Italia (1943-1945)*, op. cit., pp. 43-45; See also Carlo Musso, *Diplomazia partigiana: gli alleati, i rifugiati italiani e la delegazione del CLNAI in Svizzera, 1943-1945* (Milan, Franco Angeli, 1986).

59. 'Copy of the Report of Publications Department in Italy dated Dec 31 1943', p. 9, NAW, OWI, RG 208, Entry 6G, Box 4.

60. Ibid.

61. P. Cavallo, *Italiani in guerra*, op. cit., p. 192

62. Ibid., pp. 192-193

63. 'Long-Range Policy Directive for Italy', 3 July 1945, p. 3, NAW, OWI, RG 208, Entry 6G, Box 4.

64. Long-Range Policy Directive for Italy, 3 July 1945, p. 3, NAW, OWI, RG 208, Entry 6G, Box 4

Chapter Eight
HUMPHREY JENNINGS: THE POET AS PROPAGANDIST
Jeffrey Richards

For those generations born since the Second World War, the experience of life in Britain on the home front is now encapsulated in a series of black and white documentary images, endlessly recycled in film and television accounts of the conflict. Many of the most striking images are drawn from the films of Humphrey Jennings, who has been called Britain's greatest documentarist. His vision has become our vision.

One of the most notable developments of the war years was the way in which the documentary, its techniques and its ethos entered the mainstream of British film-making. Despite their critical acclaim, pre-war documentaries were regarded as 'box office poison', unable to attract the mass audience to the cinema. During the war, the cinema audience was prepared to turn out in large numbers to see films which told them how the war was being fought and if possible acted by the men and women doing the fighting. Films like *Target for Tonight* and *Desert Victory* achieved both critical and box-office success. There was an extraordinary cross-over as pre-war feature film directors like Carol Reed, Thorold Dickinson and David Macdonald turned to making documentaries and documentarists like Cavalcanti, Harry Watt and Pat Jackson became feature film directors. As Dilys Powell noted in 1947, there was:

> a new movement in the British cinema: the movement towards concentration on the native subject, the movement towards documentary truth in the entertainment film. The war both encouraged a new seriousness of approach by British producers and directors, and drove them to look nearer home than before in their themes... This

mingling of documentary technique and native character marks many British war films.... The British no longer demand pure fantasy from their films, they can be receptive also to the imaginative interpretation of everyday life.[1]

Realism became the dominant tradition in criticism as it was in film-making, and films were judged by how far they achieved that 'imaginative interpretation of everyday life.'[2]

Ian Dalrymple, head of the Crown Film Unit, attributed this wartime development to the existence of the pre-war documentary movement inspired by John Grierson which aimed to record episodes from real life with real people on real locations.[3] Humphrey Jennings' films did this but not in a way of which Grierson approved at all. Grierson, who was in Canada during the war running the Film Board there, was deeply contemptuous of Jennings' films. He saw the purpose of documentary as being to educate the mass population for participatory citizenship. In a fulminating article written in 1942 he described the documentary movement as fundamentally 'anti-aesthetic' and argued that films should be banged out simply and speedily to instruct the people. 'The penalty of realism is that it is about reality and has to bother for ever about not being 'beautiful' but about being right,' he declared with baleful self-righteous Scots Calvinist rigour.[4] Jennings' films committed the unforgivable sin of being beautiful. Interviewed by Elizabeth Sussex for her book *The Rise and Fall of British Documentary*, published in 1975, three years after Grierson's death, Grierson dismissed Jennings as a 'minor poet' and described his films as 'stilted' and patronizing: 'He was fearfully sorry for the working class, which is a kind of limited position to be in, you know,' he said.[5] During the war, the documentary purists writing in the house journal of the movement, *Documentary News Letter* regularly lambasted his films. Edgar Anstey described *Listen to Britain* in *The Spectator* as 'the rarest piece of fiddling since the days of Nero' and the *Documentary News Letter* denounced *Words for Battle* as 'an illustrated lantern lecture with Olivier's curate-like voice reverently intoning various extracts from poetry, verse and topical political speeches' and complained of *Fires Were Started* that from time to time Jennings goes 'all arty (in his worst *Words for Battle* manner.).'[6]

But audiences who saw these films seem not to have agreed with Grierson and the *Documentary News Letter*. Mass-Observation reporting on the popular reaction to Ministry of Information shorts in 1941 recorded: '*London Can Take It* was the most frequently commented on film, and received nothing but praise' and Helen Forman, who helped organize the 130 mobile cinema vans which took the films round to audiences in factories and canteens, recalled that:

> one of the NT (non-theatrical) films...which was liked and applauded was Humphrey Jennings' magical *Listen to Britain*. All sorts of audiences felt it to be a distillation and also a magnification of their own experience of the home front. This was especially true of factory audiences. I remember one show in a factory in the Midlands where about 800 workers clapped and stamped approval. Films got very short shrift if they touched any area of people's experiences and did not ring true.[7]

Jennings wanted his films above all to connect with the people. In a series of radio broadcasts in 1938 he argued that the modern poet had lost touch with the public and with everyday life. In the days, when the poet was in touch with the people, he was a kind of reporter. For poetry to connect again with the ordinary person it had to be 'as simple and as familiar with the things that he already has in his head.' One of the principal functions of a poet was to remind the community 'that there are still mysteries...and that these mysteries reside in the humblest everyday things.'[8] These beliefs informed his work as a film-maker.

It is of course true that Jennings, like the other documentarists, was working to the aims and objectives laid down by the Ministry of Information. These were summed up at the outset as: why we fight, how we fight and the need for sacrifice if the war is to be won. Emphasis was to be laid on British life and character, British ideas and institutions.[9] The idea that came to dominate all others was the projection of the war as 'The People's War'. But these were ideas that Jennings was only too anxious to put onto film.

He had his own distinctive and particular way of doing it. In one sense his films were intensely and deliberately personal, but in another, by addressing themselves to the nature of the nation, they were resoundingly public. In a succession of beautiful, moving and richly textured films, he managed both to express his deep love of England and to capture something of the soul of a nation at war. If you look at the films one after another in chronological order, *The First Days* (1939), *London Can Take It* (1940), *Heart of Britain* (1941), *Words for Battle* (1941), *Listen to Britain* (1942), *Fires Were Started* (1943), *The Silent Village* (1943), *The 80 Days* (1944) and *A Diary for Timothy* (1945) you get an account of the Home Front in all its different phases and moods. Take *A Diary for Timothy*, for instance, following the first months of the life of Timothy James Jenkins, born near Oxford on 3 September, 1944, the fifth anniversary of the outbreak of the war, explaining the war effort to him and expressing hopes for the future which will not involve a return to the bad old days of unemployment, division and deprivation. But it is a film, which despite its upbeat ending with news reports of American, Russian and British advances in 1945, is extraordinarily melancholy in tone, a mood underlined by Richard Addinsell's haunting and plaintive score. It embraces the news of the Arnhem disaster, the flying bombs, extensive bomb damage, queues, rain, and as commentator Michael Redgrave says of December 1944: 'death and darkness, death and fog...death came by telegram to many of us on Christmas Eve.' It conveys through its imagery, its commentary and its music an aching sense of war-weariness, a longing for it all to be over but underlying it a determination to see it through.

Jennings had an agenda and he had a technique. His agenda was a celebration of the people and the People's War. He had a very deep love of England and the English people. Jennings' love of England centred on three basic principles: his admiration for the common people, his instinctive belief in individualism and his love of English culture. The war had been a revelation to him in that it had shown him the real worth and strength of ordinary people. He wrote to his wife in 1940:

> Some of the damage in London is pretty heart-breaking but what an effect it has had on the people! What warmth - what courage! What determination!... Everybody absolutely determined: secretly delighted with the *privilege* of holding up Hitler. Certain of beating him; a certainty which no amount of bombing can weaken, only strengthen.[10]

It was this indomitable spirit that Jennings celebrated and honoured in his films; the ARP men and WVS women in *The Heart of Britain* who talk directly and simply and movingly about their work; the Welsh miners of *The Silent Village* refusing to submit to the Nazi yoke in the powerful and imaginative recreation of the Lidice massacre (transposed from Czechoslovakia to the Welsh village of Cwmgiedd); the fire-fighters of *Fires Were Started*; and the four central figures of *Diary for Timothy* whose lives intermesh in the last full year of the war - Goronwy the miner, Bill the engine driver, Alan the farmer and Peter the fighter pilot, all of them emblematic of different aspects of the national life and all doing their bit with courage and calmness. There is nothing patronizing or superficial about this. What comes through is an enormous sense of respect for ordinary people and their innate dignity. It is a very far cry from the portrayal of the working classes in 1930s cinema, in which they were for the most part depicted as comic characters. The poet Kathleen Raine wrote of *Fires Were Started* that it:

> remains one of the few of the innumerable contemporary works about the working-class which sincerely and convincingly depicts 'the people' in terms of heroic Churchillian glory, without sentimentality and without vulgarity. Such films had been made in Russia, but nothing comparable in England. Humphrey after the war said that it was a sad truth that only the situations of war could give the common people opportunities to show their finest innate qualities.[11]

Closely related to his feelings for the people was his belief in individualism. He saw it as integral to the English character, writing:

> The English travel in trains; not a company, but a collection of individuals; first turning each carriage into a row of cottages...and then sitting in each corner with the same blank denial of any other presence that the lovers show in the park. The English live in cities, but they are not citified; they very seldom produce, for example, that characteristic symptom of the city, the mob. They are urbane without being urban: creating their own environment within their own being.[12]

So in *Fires Were Started*, his leading characters are all firefighters and all men but each is uniquely himself. This was a cardinal point of British propaganda, given the stock image of the German as a faceless, heel-clicking, identikit automaton. The British, though they came together in the common task of defeating the enemy, remain individuals.

The picture is completed by Jennings' immersion in English culture. Kathleen Raine wrote that: 'in the tradition of Chaucer and Blake, Humphrey Jennings had a sense of the organic wholeness of English culture.'[13] Gerald Noxon amplified this point:

> In his formative years... Humphrey had been influenced particularly by certain English writers and artists of the past – by Shakespeare and Marlowe, of course, but more unusually perhaps by John Milton, John Bunyan, John Constable, and William Blake. The works of these men remained in Humphrey's background as a permanent frame of reference. Their kind of Englishness was Humphrey's kind of Englishness.[14]

To these we should certainly add Purcell, Handel, Elgar and Vaughan Williams. All three of these characterizing elements (love of ordinary people, belief in individualism, and a sense of the organic wholeness of English culture) are to be found in his films.

It has frequently been remarked that Jennings' approach to film-making was both poetic and painterly. He was after all both poet and painter as well as film-maker. Lindsay Anderson dubbed him 'the only real poet the British cinema has yet produced' and Kathleen Raine wrote of him 'Certainly no poet, since Blake has understood English history, and in particular the Industrial Revolution, with the two-fold intensity of observation and imagination that Humphrey Jennings brought to bear on it.'[15] She recalled 'many walks with Humphrey through the streets of London, which in his company always entered another dimension and became 'ideas of imagination' and she saw the dockside setting of *Fires Were Started* 'transformed by Humphrey's inimitable magic into Blake's 'spiritual fourfold London eternal' '[16] But she also wrote that 'he always regarded himself as, before everything else, a painter.' Jennings' Crown Film Unit colleague Pat Jackson recalled of his approach to film-making: 'It was terribly like a painter in a way; it wasn't a storyteller's mind. I don't think the dramatic approach to a subject, in film, really interested him very much. It was an extension of the canvas for him.'[17] What binds together his poetry and his painting in his film-making are two constant factors, to which he himself regularly referred: image and pattern. Charles Madge, the co-founder of Mass-Observation, in his tribute to Jennings wrote:

> I think it may help to understand Humphrey Jennings' paintings if one reconsiders what he meant by 'the image'. It was a meaning personal to himself and bound up with his early researches into poetry and painting. His use of 'image' is not far off from the way it is used in psychology, in literary criticism and in surrealist theory, but it is not quite identical with any of these. It has resemblances to the psychological concept of *gestalt*: 'the combination of many effects, each utterly insensible alone, into one sum of fine effect.'[18]

Then there is 'pattern'. Jennings, reviewing Sir Ernest Barker's book *The Character of England*, wrote that 'the English love of pattern, of order,' was 'one of their supreme qualities... This absorption in pattern is one aspect of the general power of absorption, of concentration, which the Englishman specially enjoys. It is possible that this has enabled him to pass into a civilization of streets without becoming a part of it.'[19]

The term 'pattern' recurs constantly in Jennings' work. In his grand synthesis on national identity, *Family Portrait* (1950), made for the Festival of Britain, he observed that the British loved public pomp and private domesticity and experienced variations in weather, landscape and race, but he saw the identity of Britain in the alliance of art and industry, science and agriculture, the mingling of poetry and prose. He concluded by looking out from Britain to Europe and the Commonwealth. The narrator says:

> We have become both inside the family of Europe, and the pattern overseas. We are the link between them. For all that we have received from them, and from our native land, what can we return? Perhaps the

very things that make the family, a pattern, possible – tolerance, courage, faith. A world to be different in – and free – together.

The technique which he employed equally in his paintings, his poems and his films was that of collage, the juxtaposition of different and distinct images to create something new and striking. It is significant in this regard that Jennings was one of the organizers of the International Surrealist Exhibition in London in 1936 and one of the founders of Mass-Observation in 1937. Both these movements employed collage, as is evident in the Mass-Observation volume on Coronation Day, *May the 12th*, which Jennings co-edited with Charles Madge. But as Mass-Observation moved under the influence of Tom Harrisson much more towards straight social anthropology Jennings lost interest in it. However, he employed the technique of collage triumphantly in his films.

It was in the process of editing that the ideas of image, pattern and collage were applied to film. On many of his films, Jennings worked with the Scottish-born editor Stewart McAllister – indeed *Listen to Britain* is credited to them jointly as director and editor. Ian Dalrymple recalled:

> Humphrey and McAllister had a strange effect upon one another. Humphrey was frightfully well-organized in shooting. He'd have the most marvellous luck, too, because he'd been a painter and in fact was still daubing with paint when he had a moment, but he has a wonderful gift for choosing the exact place to put the camera. So he'd go out and shoot madly and all the stuff would come in to McAllister, and McAllister would brood over it on the Movieola. When Humphrey had finished shooting, he would join McAllister in the cutting room and nothing would happen for weeks, apparently. You wondered when the hell anything was going to emerge... Then all of a sudden, overnight, somehow everything went together - doink. And there was what I thought a mini-masterpiece in each case.[20]

It is clear that the two men worked on the same wavelength. McAllister had written as early as 1933: 'It is agreed, I think, that our delight in all the arts depends greatly on what may be called 'pattern'.'[21]

In the cutting room, they set about giving their images a pattern. It has often been alleged that Jennings improvised his films when he was shooting. He was certainly willing to incorporate interesting details encountered during filming, like the penny whistle blower in *Fires Were Started*, but his films were carefully scripted and he had a good idea of what images he wanted. Several of the striking images in *Fires Were Started* shot in 1942, are already present in his 1941 poem *I See London*, and were visually 'realized' in the film: the dome of St. Paul's, 'the grey water of the Thames, unchanged, unruffled', the one-legged men crossing the fire on crutches.

Kathleen Raine wrote in 1975: 'Like Churchill, Humphrey saw England's present glory in the light of her past, of Pitt and Nelson, of Stubbs and Gainsborough, of Blake and Gray and Inigo Jones. He himself gave in his war films a last expression of a civilization specifically English.'[22] *Words for Battle*, saw Jennings giving expression to his belief in the nobility and relevance of England's cultural heritage and demonstrating it through collage. The film was constructed from existing film footage which was edited together to illustrate seven pieces of poetry and prose, read by Laurence Olivier, with extracts from Handel's 'Water Music' as the score.

It begins with passages from William Camden's *Britannia*, an account of the landscape and resources of England published in 1586 and we see as Olivier speaks the archaic language of Elizabethan England the cliffs, pastures, forests and towns of a peaceful and abundant land. Then a shot of the bust of John Milton introduces a reading from his *Areopagitica*. 'Methinks I see in mind a mighty and puissant nation rousing herself like a strong man after sleep... Methinks I see her as an eagle, mewing her mighty youth, kindling her undazzled eyes at the full midday beam,' declares Olivier over shots of air cadets gathering round a spitfire and then a low-angle shot of the spitfire taking off. When Olivier speaks of 'the whole noise of timorous and flocking birds, with those that also love the twilight flutter about, amazed at what she means,' Jennings cuts to a shot of Hitler and Goering strolling together in a dark wood, and on the words 'their envious gabble' to a shot of Goebbels.

A plaque on the wall recording the birthplace of William Blake introduces *Jerusalem*. 'Bring me my bow of burning gold, bring me my arrows of desire' is heard over high-angle shots of child evacuees gathering and on 'bring me my chariot of fire' Jennings cuts to a steam train pulling up to the platform to collect the children. Finally after 'I will not cease from mental fight nor shall my sword sleep in my hand, till we have built Jerusalem in England's green and pleasant land' we see shots of children playing happily on the river and in the woods, the image of the joyous and carefree future for the young that is one of the objectives of the war.

Then over shots of the sea, warships, the white ensign and a bust of Nelson come extracts from Robert Browning's *Home Thoughts from the Sea* with its mentions of Trafalgar and Gibraltar and the line 'here and here did England help me, how can I help, England, say.' A shot of the tombstone of Rudyard Kipling introduces his poem *The Beginnings*. 'It was not part of their blood, it came to them very late...when the English began to hate' is heard over shots of blitzed buildings, rescue workers struggling to free people from the ruins and a formal funeral procession with black-plumed horses pulling a hearse and civil defence workers marching behind.

Then comes Churchill's celebrated speech of defiance: 'We shall go on to the end...we shall defend our island whatever the cost may be...we shall fight on the beaches...we shall never surrender'. Each line is cut to a shot: of Churchill inspecting the troops, of a soldier with a sten gun at the ready, waves rolling up a beach, and St. Paul's Cathedral, still standing intact and defiant among surrounding ruins. When Churchill declares 'And even if this island were subjugated and starving, then our Empire beyond the seas...would carry on the struggle,' the screen fills with the marching troops of Australia and New Zealand. He concludes: 'until in God's good time the New World with all its power and might steps forth to the rescue and liberation of the Old,' and there is a shot of the statue of Abraham Lincoln to link seamlessly into the final passage, Lincoln's Gettysburg address: 'We here highly resolve that...government of the people, by the people and for the people shall not perish from the earth.' As the words are spoken we see tanks passing Lincoln's statue and moving through Parliament Square, the combination of Lincoln, Parliament and the tanks, indicating the resolve to fight for the defence of democracy, and implicitly urging America (then still neutral) to join the fight. The films ends with random shots of service men and women moving through the streets of London in various combinations.

In the space of a mere eight minutes, Jennings has succeeded in encapsulating a wealth of ideas: a peaceful England, the preparedness of the air force and the navy, orderly evacuation, the children as the hope for the future, the sinister nature of the enemy, the devastation wrought by the enemy, but also the resolution to resist, the inspiring leadership of Churchill, the support of the Empire, the communality of purpose between Britain and the United States in defending democracy, and finally the mobilization of the people for the people's war. The combination of the luminous images, the apposite readings, the impeccable delivery by Olivier and the extraordinary richness of the musical, visual and literary allusions fully justify the description 'this exquisite little masterpiece' bestowed on the film by Anthony Hodgkinson and Rodney Sheratsky in their study of Jennings.[23]

There is another vital aspect that we must add to Jennings' artistic vision. It gives a further dimension to the films, an extra layer to the image and an essential element of the pattern - music. The writer William Sansom, who played the newcomer Barrett in *Fires Were Started*, recalled:

> He always stressed the need for music in the film; and I think it is plain
> that, apart from any material music he used, his films were composed in
> the swelling-dying, theme and repeat-theme notation of a kind of
> musical composition.[24]

Even a cursory look at *Fires Were Started* or *The Silent Village* reveals a very definite three-movement structure, which gives the films something of their classical shape and feel. Sir Denis Forman interestingly compared *Fires Were Started* to a Mozart concerto.[25] The working title for *Listen to Britain* was *The Tin-Hat Concerto*.

Music was integral both to the content and to the structure of Jennings' films and it fulfilled several functions, often at the same time - which is what Jennings sought in his images. His choice of music ran the gamut from classical to popular. English classical music, particularly Handel, Vaughan Williams, Elgar and Purcell, were regular features of his films. But so too were hymns, folk songs, dance band music, music hall songs, popular songs. Music was continually in his mind and was part of his vision. In fact he made an entire film, *The True Story of Lilli Marlene* (1944), about the German song which had been appropriated by the British Eighth Army. He even appeared in it himself as the lyricist of the song. His letters are full of comments about the music he wants in his films. In 1948, he devoted several months to preparation for a documentary on the London Symphony Orchestra, and although it was never made, his notes 'working sketches of an orchestra' were published in 1954.[26] Jennings chose Ralph Vaughan Williams as one of his four representative Englishmen commenting on the state of the nation in *Dim Little Island* (1949).

How does music affect listeners? Anthony Storr in his important book *Music and the Mind* argues that music causes emotional arousal, 'a generally enhanced state of being' and that there seems to be a closer relation between hearing and emotional arousal than between seeing and emotional arousal. Music, he says, is 'a way of ordering the human experience,' finding patterns of tone and melody to which audiences can relate; providing order and structure, stimulating feelings. In fact it has always been designed for that purpose. Music began by serving communal purposes, notably religious ritual and warfare, and has ever since been used as an adjunct of social ceremonies and public occasions. Both at coronations and cup finals, singing connotes belonging. 'The music ensures that the emotions aroused by a particular event peal at the same time,' says Storr.[27]

It is reasonable to assume that each person in an audience will react to some extent differently according to personality, age, gender, experience, temperament. But music also functions within a shared culture and until the gramophone and the wireless created the possibility of the solitary listener, music was designed to be experienced communally and for the most part was, allowing for the emotion of a shared experience based on common denominators. It is striking therefore how much of the music in Jennings' films is communal, the music becoming the means by which individuals are integrated in the community or group. The use of the music can also heighten the emotions.

Music functions in three specific ways in Jennings' films. First there is background music, either specially composed or selected from the existing stock usually of British music which underlines, counterpoints or extends the argument of the image. Second, there is music performed within the film itself as part of the action. Finally, there is musical rhythm in the cutting. All three functions can be seen in operation in *The Heart of Britain.*

The Heart of Britain (1941), released in America as *This is England,* is a ten-minute film which also perfectly illustrates Jennings' love of the ordinary people, of England, of music and his desire to create a pattern and to integrate the disparate elements into a whole. Designed as a tribute to the workers in the North and the Midlands it incorporates footage of Coventry after the Coventry blitz, which occurred while he was planning the film.

Jennings begins with Elgar's *Introduction and Allegro* over scenes of moors and hills, Ullswater, Durham, Liverpool and Coventry cathedrals – the music of England's greatest composer and images of the eternal elements of England (landscape, faith). Jennings cuts to industrial areas (Sheffield, Lancashire, Liverpool, Coventry) and the testimony of ARP men and WVS women, simple, decent, dignified, determined. Mrs Hyde, head of Coventry WVS, air raid warden George Good, and a Lancashire mill foreman had recounted their experiences to Jennings and although their lines are scripted, they are based on these verbal accounts.

But then in Manchester, Sir Malcolm Sargent conducts the Hallé Orchestra in Beethoven's Fifth Symphony. This is one of Jennings' resonant multiple images, for of course the opening bars of the Fifth Symphony are the wartime V for Victory sign. The playing of Beethoven indicates the superior civilization of Britain for as the narrator says, 'In Manchester today they still respect the genius of Germany - the genius of Germany that was.' This is a recurrent theme in Jennings - represented by the iconic figure of Dame Myra Hess playing German music and in *Diary for Timothy* Tim is asked to consider the paradox that the Germans can create beautiful music and also wage a terrible war. But in *Heart of Britain* the Beethoven continues over a long eloquent panning shot across ruined buildings in Coventry. Words are not needed to tell us what the combination of the music and the image does: that the music of the Old Germany accompanies evidence of the devastation wrought by the New Germany.

Then in a change of music, the Huddersfield Choir sing the *Hallelujah Chorus* from *Messiah* by Handel, another resonant multiple images, for Handel was a German who chose to become an Englishman and created what became a British national institution - the oratorio *Messiah*. The enthusiastic participation of the singers leads the narrator to comment: 'People who sing like this in times like these cannot be beaten.' Once again, the inspiring music continues, this time over scenes of the workers building planes, and the final *Hallelujah* is heard over a shot of a warplane taking off. So the initial *Britain Can Take It* message is followed by one of *Britain Can Hit Back*.

The Elgar, the Beethoven, the Handel all play vital structural roles in the film. They strike chords, they evoke memories, they integrate with the people and the landscape both rural and urban in the kind of multi-layered organic whole that Jennings constantly sought. Jennings is perhaps the ultimate example of the poet as propagandist but his stated view of the role of the poet was as a reporter capturing for his audience what was inside their hearts and minds.

The classic example of his technique is *Listen to Britain* (1942), which many regard as Jennings' masterpiece. It is a sound picture of 24-hours in Britain at war, a film in which music, sound and image mesh perfectly setting up a host of related ideas in the classic Jennings mould. It integrates and accords equal respect to all elements of the population, men and women, adults and children, soldiers and civilians, factory workers and teachers, British and Canadians.

Along with the trill of birdsong, the roar of Spitfires, the rumble of tanks, the clip-clop of horses hooves, the hiss of steam engines, the clang of Big Ben and the pips of the BBC, there is music of all kinds, highbrow and lowbrow, folk and popular song, the music of the people engaged in the People's War. It is striking how much of this music is communal music. In the Tower Ballroom in Blackpool couples glide round to the dance band's playing of *Roll Out the Barrel*, aboard a train Canadian soldiers join in *Home on the Range* (a reminder of the contribution of the Empire to the war effort), in an ambulance station a lone woman sings and plays the plaintive folk song *The Ash Grove*, factory girls at their work stations cheerfully join in *Yes, My Darling Daughter* on the BBC's *Music While You Work*. But the most potent visual/aural link comes in the daring mix from the dying notes of Flanagan and Allen's *Round the Back of the Arches* in a workers canteen to Dame Myra Hess playing the Mozart piano concerto in G Major in the National Gallery. The popular and the classical are seamlessly and wordlessly integrated, the performers and the music accorded equal respect. But there is a host of related ideas in that sequence: Myra Hess playing German music, the Gallery stripped of its pictures (mute testimony to the barbarity of the New Germany in waging war), Myra Hess accompanied by the band of the RAF in uniform, the implication being that our warriors can still appreciate the great music of the past while fighting the battles of the present. And conspicuously amongst the off-duty service personnel and lunching office-workers, the Queen sitting beside Sir Kenneth Clark – the people's monarch sitting with her people absorbing a shared musical culture. The final shots of this sequence are cut to the beat of the music and it is eventually mixed with and drowned by the sound of machinery as the enjoyment of culture blends into the necessary business of war factory production to ensure a final victory, which is again signalled musically as the film ends with a choral version of *Rule Britannia*.

The film throughout captures that organic wholeness of people and culture in which Jennings believed so profoundly. There is no commentary in the film. This so worried the Ministry of Information that they insisted on the addition of an introduction in which a Canadian lawyer Leonard Brockington explained to the audience what they were about to see. There was absolutely no need for it, as the film spoke for itself. But the Ministry's uneasiness is eloquent testimony to the revolutionary nature of Jennings' vision.

What Jennings wrote in the introduction to his collage of documents relating to the Industrial Revolution *Pandaemonium* (1948) might also have been written of his films:

> And these images - what do they deal with? I do not claim that they represent truth - they are too varied, even contradictory for that. But they represent human experience. They are the record of mental events. Events of the heart. They are facts (the historian's kind of facts) which have been passed through the feelings and the mind of an individual and have forced him to write.[28]

But of *Fires Were Started*, William Sansom, who was a fireman and played the newcomer Barrett in the film, wrote: 'As a practising fireman I could say this: the film was true to life in every respect. Not a false note - if you make the usual allowances for the absence of foul language which was in everybody's mouth all the time.'[29] Fred Griffiths, who played the cockney Johnny Daniels and was also a fireman, said in 1954 at an NFT showing of the film: 'As you see it in the film, so it was.'[30] So are the films reportage, historical reconstruction, propaganda or personal poetic image? - they are all of these things simultaneously. There is a profound emotional truth about these films which combine observation and imagination. It is the reason they survive, where many another documentary is forgotten. They represent the lived experience of a nation at war.

NOTES

1. Dilys Powell, *Films Since 1939*, (London: Longman, 1947), pp.22, 29, 40.
2. John Ellis, 'Art, Culture and Quality', *Screen* 19 (Autumn 1975), pp.9-49.
3. Ian Dalrymple, *London Calling* 109 (October 1941), pp.6-7.
4. Forsyth Hardy ed., *Grierson on Documentary*, (London: Faber, 1966), p.249.
5. Elizabeth Sussex, *The Rise and Fall of British Documentary*, (Berkeley: University of California Press, 1975), pp.110,111.
6. *The Spectator*, 13 March, 1942; *Documentary News Letter* (May 1941), p.89; *Documentary News Letter* 4 (1943), p.200.
7. Jeffrey Richards and Dorothy Sheridan eds., *Mass-Observation at the Movies*, (London: Routledge, 1987), p.443; Nicholas Pronay and Derek Spring eds., *Propaganda, Politics and Film*, (London: MacMillan,1982), p.230.
8. Kevin Jackson ed., *The Humphrey Jennings Reader*, (Manchester: Carcanet, 1993), pp.260, 280.
9. 'Programme for Film propaganda' (INF 1.867), reprinted in Ian Christie ed., *Powell, Pressburger and Others*, (London: BFI, 1978), pp.121-124.
10. Mary-Lou Jennings ed., *Humphrey Jennings: Film-Maker, Painter, Poet*, (London: BFI, 1982), p.25
11. Kathleen Raine, *Autobiographies*, (London: Skoob Books, 1991), p.229.
12. *Times Literary Supplement*, 7 August, 1948.
13. John Grierson et al., *Humphrey Jennings: a tribute*, (London: 1951), p. 4.

14. *Film Quarterly* 15 (Winter 1961-2), p.21.
15. Mary-Lou Jennings, *Humphrey Jennings*, p.53 (Anderson) and p.51 (Raine).
16. Kathleen Raine, *Autobiographies*, p.232.
17. Elizabeth Sussex, *British Documentary*, p.144.
18. Mary-Lou Jennings, *Humphrey Jennings*, p.47.
19. *Times Literary Supplement*, 7 August, 1948.
20. Elizabeth Sussex, *British Documentary*, p.144. On McAllister, see Dai Vaughan, *Portrait of an Invisible Man*, (London: BFI, 1983).
21. Dai Vaughan, *Invisible Man*, p.137.
22. Kathleen Raine, *Autobiographies*, p.230.
23. Anthony Hodgkinson and Rodney Sheratsky, *Humphrey Jennings: More than a Maker of Films*, (Hanover and London: University Press of New England, 1982), p.57.
24. *Film Quarterly* 15 (Winter 1961-2), p.28
25. National Film Theatre Programme Notes, 1958.
26. Kevin Jackson, *Humphrey Jennings Reader*, pp.118-156.
27. Anthony Storr, *Music and the Mind*, (London: Harper Collins, 1992), pp.24-5, 187, 182, 30.
28. Humphrey Jennings, *Pandaemonium*, (London: Andre Deutsch, 1985), p.231.
29. *Film Quarterly* 15, p.29.
30. *Humphrey Jennings: The Man Who Listened to Britain*, Figment Television Production for Channel 4, 2001.

Chapter Nine
WAR REPORT (BBC 1944-5), AND THE BIRTH OF THE BBC WAR CORRESPONDENT
Siân Nicholas

From William Howard Russell and the young Winston Churchill to Kate Adie and Martin Bell, the public has looked to war correspondents to tell them about wars. Newspaper correspondents from the Crimean War onwards revolutionised public interest in war. In more recent times, television coverage of wars has likewise both illuminated and obscured the realities of war. In the Second World War it was of course radio that led the war coverage. But remarkably, as late as 1939 Britain had no such thing as a radio war correspondent.

During the Second World War the British Broadcasting Corporation (BBC) assembled from almost nowhere a complete news gathering organisation capable of reporting from the fighting line across Europe and beyond, straight into people's homes. As will be seen, the BBC war correspondents proceeded by trial and error, their task constrained by the press, the military, their technological limitations, and their own inexperience. Their efforts culminated in the nightly war news programme, *War Report*, which broadcast with scarcely a break from D-Day to VE-Day. One of the most vivid and eclectic war coverage operations of any of the belligerents, it represented a revolution in the aims and internal administration of the BBC. It consolidated a new kind of war reportage, mixing news and eye-witness 'actuality', brought to listeners by broadcasters who were already familiar voices in other contexts. Above all, it brought the front line into the home for the first time.

War reporting before 1939

Britain's earliest war correspondents were larger than life characters, as popular at home as they were mistrusted in the field. Their despatches tended to be self-publicising 'boys' own' tales of military (and their own) derring-do, and formed the basis of best-selling memoirs and widely tradable celebrity. Winston Churchill (*Morning Post*) and Edgar Wallace (*Daily Mail*) became household names as Boer War correspondents well before they achieved fame in other fields. Their relations with the military were fraught (General Kitchener, for instance, branded them 'outlaws'), and only during the First World War were they accepted as an unavoidable part of the modern war effort, formally accredited with honorary military rank, and given unprecedented military access in return for almost wholly uncritical front-line coverage.[1] In the 1930s, the public profile of newspaper war correspondents waned. Evelyn Waugh's novel *Scoop* (1938) confirmed a less favourable image: that of irresponsible and dissolute hacks.

From the turn of the century, a new dimension was added to war reporting. Newsreel, first used during the Boer War, provided some of the most enduring popular images of warfare in the early twentieth century. But newsreel cameras were cumbersome and unreliable; they could not follow a story without the logistical support of the military authorities. The iconic newsreel images of the Battle of the Somme, seen by millions of British cinemagoers in 1916/17, and indelibly imprinted on subsequent generations, were official pictures, shot at points out of immediate danger (mostly behind the lines, or in the aftermath of battle), by cameramen given the honorary military rank of lieutenant, and released to the public only after prior viewing by political and military leaders, some eight weeks after the start of the battle.[2] The news content of newsreels was negligible, captions providing only the briefest points of identification; the pictures themselves 'told the story'. Later sound newsreels characterised overseas conflicts essentially as visual tableaux of marching troops, strutting leaders and desolate civilians picking through rubble, the anonymous commentary strident but barely informative.

The contribution of broadcasting to twentieth century war reporting was less clear to predict. Certainly wireless offered advantages to newspapers themselves: in 1904 a *Times* correspondent attempted to set up a wireless link to cover the Russo-Japanese war.[3] And certainly, in theory at least, the new medium offered unprecedented immediacy—as the impact of the wireless relay to New York and beyond of the unfolding Titanic disaster in 1912 made clear. Yet newspapers ensured that this advantage was rarely developed. In the USA, for instance, after a brief mutual accommodation, American press interests successfully strangled the development of network radio news in the USA until as late as 1934 when—in the increasingly febrile international political climate-- the radio networks finally asserted themselves. American radio news owed its vitality in part to a self-imposed pledge that all news programmes would only be broadcast live, made to deflect press charges that they might use recordings to fake or distort news. This often made for inconvenient scheduling, but ensured a compelling urgency to news reports as well as an instant tradition of 'breaking' news. This reached a climax during the Munich crisis, when CBS, the pioneer in European news coverage, broadcast the latest news live from the capitals of Europe, Edward R. Murrow, William L. Shirer et al. bringing to millions of American listeners the breaking developments as well as the voices of the principal actors, from Hitler and Chamberlain to Benes and Masaryk. It also precipitated a different kind of crisis—the national panic caused by Orson Welles's War of the Worlds, broadcast on CBS on 30 October 1938, just a month after the Munich agreement was signed, would not have been so profound had not Welles so carefully mimicked the tone and style of his own network's news radio in the play's initial 'breaking news' sequence.[4]

Such a panic was less likely to have occurred in Britain, which had no live news broadcasting culture. British radio, though developing on ostensibly different, 'public service', lines, was likewise hamstrung by the press. The British Broadcasting Company's (1922-26) news bulletins were dictated (at first quite literally) by a consortium of the British news agencies in association with the Newspaper Proprietors' Association. Not until 1927 was the new British Broadcasting Corporation permitted to write its own news bulletins—and even then it was forbidden to gather its own news independently (required to rely instead on agency wires), or to broadcast any news at all until the early evening in order to preserve the priority of daily and evening newspapers in breaking news. A separate BBC News Department did not even formally exist until 1934. To distinguish itself from newspaper journalism, and in deference to the potentially fragile susceptibilities of its audience (of whom the BBC considered itself a 'guest' in the living room), BBC news editors followed a policy of rigorously ignoring most of the leading 'human interest' news stories of the day on the grounds that they were trivial, vulgar or morbidly sensational. BBC news was read by a team of announcers whose names were never mentioned on air, but who were well known to wear dinner jackets at the microphone. Over the course of the 1930s the BBC gradually but persistently stretched its restrictive bounds, for instance employing 'Topical Talks Assistants' (later renamed 'news observers') to provide 'eye-witness' reports (a limited number of which the BBC was permitted to broadcast each year). Here, the young former newspaper journalist Richard Dimbleby swiftly established himself an independent-minded, ambitious and eloquent reporter, most famously reporting live from a public telephone at the scene of the Crystal Palace Fire in 1936. But the BBC News department remained through this period a small and constantly frustrated operation.[5]

In fact it was the BBC Outside Broadcast (OB) Department that made the most of the 'eye-witness' loophole. Throughout the 1930s a talented team of OB commentators, employed less for their journalistic abilities or specialist knowledge than for their knack of describing live events so as to making listeners feel a part of them, broadcast events as varied as live musical performances and Saturday night entertainment (notably *In Town Tonight*, featuring Michael Standing's *vox pop* interviews 'Standing on the Corner'), sports commentaries (John Snagge, Howard Marshall and Canadian Stewart MacPherson were, respectively, the voices of the Boat Race, Test Match cricket and—oddly popular in 1930s Britain—ice hockey), and the broadcast of great public occasions, culminating in the Coronation of George VI in 1937. They brought their own personalities to their assignments: during the 1938 FA Cup Final Thomas Woodrooffe announced his intention to eat his hat if Huddersfield beat Preston North End, then did so on air after the final whistle. A year earlier he had made newspaper headlines with an audibly inebriated commentary of the Spithead Review ('The fleet's lit up … it's lit up with little lamps'). Both in London and the BBC regions outside broadcasting was at the forefront of technical innovation, from the development of mobile recording vans to the 'wandering microphone' set-up, i.e., stringing together a succession of live reports from different venues across the country, most effectively in the BBC's Saturday afternoon sports broadcasts. And OB Director S. J. de Lotbinière's own eyewitness commentary of the Crystal Palace fire, recorded in a mobile van, showed how outside broadcasts could complement and even rival news coverage.[6]

What the OB department could not and the News department did not cover was foreign affairs. The BBC accepted the need to follow Foreign Office advice when reporting international politics and conflicts, on the admittedly self-fulfilling argument that since a government-chartered and publicly-funded national broadcasting network such as the BBC would naturally be assumed by other regimes to voice the foreign policy of the British government, in order to prevent confusion or worse it had better do so anyway. BBC news reported the Spanish Civil War with the barest agency details. It steered clear of Germany as much as possible. Although its coverage of the Munich Crisis was the most detailed of any international crisis thus far (as a mark of its seriousness, and for the first time since the General Strike of 1926, it was also permitted to broadcast bulletins throughout the day), the 'conspiracy of silence' that had preceded it precipitated a crisis of confidence in the News Department, and a resolution to do better. In early 1939 Dimbleby was at last permitted to report from the Pyrenees on the Spanish Civil War, and—in one path-breaking broadcast—to describe, live, with gunfire in the distance, the retreat of Republican soldiers across the Franco-Spanish border.[7]

The 'phoney war' and after, 1939-41

When war was declared in September 1939, the American networks already had a strong presence in London and throughout Europe. The Canadian broadcasting network CBC rapidly set up a wartime Overseas Unit in London and sent their first war correspondent, Bob Bowman, over to England with the First Canadian Division. In stark contrast, the BBC began the war with no formal plans for war reporting, just two news observers, and one mobile recording car which Dimbleby had presciently lodged in an underground garage in Paris.[8] It had been understood that the function of BBC news in wartime would in any case be limited essentially to the transmission of official communiqués and a positive portrayal of the home front. The main wartime innovation was the introduction of regular news bulletins throughout the day— though to pacify the press a complex embargo system was instituted by which no news received after 5 p.m. could be broadcast before 7 a.m. the following day (i.e., after the daily newspapers had run the stories), and nothing received between midnight and 5 a.m. broadcast before 4 p.m. (i.e. after the first editions of the evening papers had hit the streets). Fleet Street, unmollified, managed to restrict the BBC's use of 'Eye-witness' (the single war correspondent permitted in France in the first weeks of the war), and ran scare stories about the lengths to which the BBC might go in reporting the war. When the *Radio Times* publicised that Dimbleby, accompanying the BEF with the courtesy rank of captain, had managed to record some battle sounds from the French lines, newspaper articles condemned BBC 'plans' to put microphones on the battlefields ('A more ghastly idea was never conceived', trumpeted the *News of the World*). The BBC hurriedly reassured listeners that, 'There will be no awful sound-glimpses of the battlefields where those we love are perhaps giving up their lives.... The bulk of the recordings ... will be made with troops resting or at headquarters'.[9] In the first months of the war, with military news subject to stringent censorship, even this was better than nothing.

With no precedents on which to draw, the first BBC war correspondents largely made up the rules as they went along. Dimbleby, for instance, saw his role as to 'establish ourselves as trusted observers....'; the way to do this was to 'fit ourselves into the landscape and conduct ourselves in accordance with the rank whose privileges we enjoy.' [10] To this end he dispensed hospitality liberally, broadcast the official line, and was soon bored. More innovatively, Edward Ward, a formerly undistinguished BBC announcer (and incidentally heir to the Sixth Viscount Bangor), who had joined the News department on the outbreak of war rather than being exiled to West Region, volunteered to go to Finland and report on the Soviet invasion. With no need to ingratiate himself with the services--and not allowed to take recording gear near the front--he decided early on to leave official communiqués to the news agencies and to concentrate on eye-witness reports, transmitted to London periodically from the nearest available Finnish radio station. His descriptions of the air raids on Helsinki and Viipuri, and especially his harrowing account of the battlefield of Suomussalmi, the 'Valley of Death' where two Russian divisions lay dead and frozen, made for arresting broadcasting. He even succeeded in breaking the news of the Finnish surrender, through an ingenious interview with the Finnish Minister in Sweden. [11]

In April 1940, Dimbleby was reassigned to the Middle East and replaced in France by Bernard Stubbs and Charles Gardner. However, within weeks, Gardner had led the return home of the RAF press corps in protest at the decision to replace independent newsgathering with official communiqués; a few weeks later Ward found himself reporting the fall of Belgium and France, and shortly after that Stubbs solemnly reported the sights and sounds of the Dunkirk returnees ('their spirit unbroken, and with faith in their cause undimmed'). [12] With the troops back home, and so little to report, listeners looked less to news than to Churchill and J. B. Priestley for their inspiration. One news broadcast however did capture the public imagination. On 14 July 1940 the BBC broadcast Charles Gardner's account, recorded live, of a dogfight over the English Channel. The 'sports commentary' style of the broadcast, in particular Gardner's schoolboyish excitement as a Junkers 87 went crashing into the sea, was as controversial as it was infectious: the BBC was both reviled and praised for such a lapse from its conventional reporting style, and the commentary itself was made into a best-selling record (with proceeds to the RAF Comfort Fund). But it was a one-off; the BBC's eyewitness reports during the Blitz were by contrast sober and retrospective in style. Shortly after, Gardner himself enlisted in the RAF.

A year into the war the BBC still had only two full time 'war commentators', Dimbleby and Ward, both now stationed in the Middle East. During the Blitz however, they were supplemented by several part-time commentators, including Godfrey Talbot (a News department sub-editor), Frank Phillips (an announcer), Robin Duff (newsreader and producer on the Empire service), and in Scotland Robert Dunnett (Talks assistant). In early 1941 they were formally accredited as BBC war correspondents, along with Alan Bell, Richard Sharpe, Michael Reynolds and A. P. (Patrick) Ryan (the MoI's liaison with BBC Home programmes, a former newspaper sub-editor and publicity manager of the Gas Light and Coke Co., who had become a surprising and increasingly influential advocate of the BBC itself). They were now entitled to wear uniform and go out on central sorties under War Office control. They were shortly joined by five regional war correspondents, mostly sub-editors or

Regional Publicity Officers, accredited on a similar standing to provincial newspaper men, tasked with covering local military matters, and on stand-by should the Germans invade.   These included Frank Gillard, a former schoolteacher and freelance broadcaster, Robert Reid, a former journalist and BBC Press Officer, and most illustriously the playwright Denis Johnston, before the war a BBC television producer, but now back home in Ireland as a reserve reporter for the BBC in case of German invasion. Between them they possessed just three camouflaged recording cars, with accompanying engineers.[13]

The full-timers' performance was by all accounts unsatisfactory. Dimbleby, living in opulent style in a houseboat on the Nile, was according to his own colleagues 'more rajah than reporter', sought after by 'every party-giver in Gezira and Zamalek' but rarely mixing with other correspondents.   His journalistic instinct was to go to the top for his information, to which end he ran up prodigious expenses which he justified as necessary to maintain the BBC's prestige among senior officers.   However his reliance on GHQ in Cairo made him increasingly unpopular with the military authorities in London, especially during Auchinleck's controversial tenure, with the troops on the ground themselves, and with BBC news editors who found it increasingly difficult to control or often even to locate him. Ward, unlike Dimbleby, had no recording gear, and his infrequent despatches were sent over Egyptian State Radio whenever he returned to Cairo from the front; his attempts to stretch the bounds of war reportage were consistently thwarted by military intelligence, notably a projected trip to Malta by Navy submarine, which was approved on condition that he didn't broadcast a word about it.   Dimbleby's recording engineer, Donovan, was rarely used; he had lost half his original gear in transit, then the replacements, and when Ward finally persuaded him out on an alcohol-fuelled sortie he nearly died of a stomach ulcer, was taken off active service and 'traded' for another recording engineer doing 'message home' programmes from Cairo. Ward was taken prisoner in November 1941 and spent the next three years in Italian and German POW camps; his replacement, Johnston, had to surrender his Irish passport lest his own capture compromise Irish neutrality.[14] A few months earlier Bernard Stubbs had become the BBC's first war correspondent fatality, lost on *HMS Hood* on 24 May 1941.

The part-timers at home fared better, if only because their task was easier.   Their assignments involved, variously, describing the aftermath of air raids, interviewing bombed-out families or shelter dwellers, reporting uncensored army and RAF stories, and recording some of the sounds of war. They were joined by OB commentators, who likewise spent the Blitz broadcasting from locations as diverse as tube stations and naval patrols, as well as commentating on what desultory sports fixtures remained.   The OB Department had been virtually broken up on the outbreak of war, with Lotbiniere and Snagge promoted to administrative posts, Marshall recruited as Public Relations Director for the Ministry of Food, Woodrooffe joining the Navy and MacPherson returning home temporarily to Canada.   However, the new OB Director, Michael Standing, took every opportunity to maintain output (even instituting 'Standing in the Shelter' in the revived wartime *In Town Tonight*), and made some important new appointments, for instance Wynford Vaughan-Thomas (seconded from Cardiff) and Raymond Glendenning.

The principal problem the BBC war correspondents faced was that the military authorities treated them as if they were no more than inferior press correspondents, with no need for special facilities (i.e., recording or transmitting equipment) of their own.[15] True, recording technology was brutally cumbersome, and 'front-line' recording itself a two-man operation, with an engineer cutting the news observer's commentary onto vinyl discs, using battery-driven equipment in so-called 'mobile' recording vans (more like heavy trucks). The discs were censored by further cutting, which if done carelessly could ruin the whole recording. Experiments were made putting recording equipment on anti-E-boat patrols out of Felixstowe, but the vibration of the boats made disc-cutting impossible.[16] Pressmen were easier to accommodate, and the BBC's correspondents had to fight for every concession. This raised another, related, grievance. For 'reasons of home morale', neither the BBC's news observers nor OB commentators were permitted to do what for reasons of overseas propaganda American network correspondents were allowed to do every night of the week: broadcast live the sounds of war. Ed Murrow's celebrated live broadcast from Trafalgar Square during a night raid galvanised public sympathies among listeners in the USA and Canada. Ironically, permission to transmit it was only granted through the efforts of the BBC's liaison, Roger Eckersley. It was only technically possible through the use of BBC sound equipment. Yet British listeners were not yet permitted to hear it, nor anything like it.[17]

Extending BBC coverage, 1942-44

In early 1942, the BBC found itself under attack from the Minister of Information, No. 10, and its own Board of Governors 'for not having a high enough standard of news observing'. It was a measure of their own despondency that both Ryan (in the new BBC post of Controller (News Co-Cordination)) and Standing agreed entirely with the criticisms. The only news observer who had emerged with credit since the war began was Edward Ward, from his time in Finland. The current complement of war reporters were 'men of varying degrees of competence. Not one of them is a first-class observer.' Some of the best broadcasters, such as John Snagge, had been promoted 'away from the microphone'. Front line reporting to date had lagged far behind both allied and enemy broadcasters: 'virtually confined to despatches and eye-witness accounts, all purely retrospective in treatment, and, except in a very few instances ... uncoloured either by the sound of battle or by any simultaneous description of it'. Ryan pinpointed the problem:

The combination of qualities wanted is not easy to find in one man. He must be able to broadcast, to get on with the Services, including the high-ups, on whose good-will he is considerably dependent, and to keep his feet in the rough-and-tumble of outside news gathering. Standing proposed a solution: they should 'make every effort to get the microphone as near as possible to the scene of operations'—and they should give OB commentators a chance.[18]

In fact, BBC correspondents were fighting back, in particular against the newspaper press. In the Western Desert Denis Johnston would send back to London marked 'Hold till required' seemingly innocuous descriptions of desert locations that intelligence suggested would be the scene of the next military action; when the battle commenced press correspondents on the ground found their reports held up by military censorship while BBC news ran Johnston's eyewitness description of the battlefield.[19] But the entry of the USA into the war provoked a new and explosive problem. If BBC war coverage remained this weak, and British military restrictions on BBC reporting remained this stringent, people in Britain, the Empire and overseas would lean their news of the war from the American networks.[20]

During 1942, therefore, Ryan begged the War Office to permit BBC representation for the first time on Combined Operations, stressing the value of 'the voice of an eyewitness' as opposed to a general communiqué. He was unmollified when the MoI reported that the American networks had offered the BBC reciprocal use of any reports of commando raids to which the one and not the other had been accredited ('To have to tell Home listeners about so eminently a British event through the mouth of an American observer, seems to have nothing to excuse it').[21] The BBC's coverage of the Dieppe Raid in August 1942 demonstrated the huge audience interest in such operations (news audiences rose a quarter, some three million listeners), the positive gloss put on the raid by news observer Frank Gillard and eye-witness (Lieutenant, RN) Thomas Woodrooffe amply demonstrating the BBC's 'reliability'. Ryan used this opportunity to plead again for serious news reporting facilities, including mobile and headquarters recording gear and headquarters transmission links to London. Permission to accompany the Forces on combined operations was granted in October, but no special provision was made for BBC recording equipment.[22]

Meanwhile, news of further American plans to publicise the activities of American servicemen in Europe ('if even a quarter of what one hears is true, it means that the Americans are fashioning a powerful trumpet for themselves, and are preparing to blow it hard as soon as they go into action') prompted Ryan to reopen the whole question of 'Second Front' coverage.[23] In October 1942, he discovered that accreditation had been given to two British press correspondents, and to representatives of the American networks--but not the BBC--to stand by to cover 'special' military operations. Appalled at the prospect of relying either on second-hand newspaper stories or 'the charity of the Americans', the BBC demanded equal treatment. Director-General Sir Cecil Graves himself argued with the MoI that they must 'put our national propaganda on a modern war-time basis'; unless the British government backed the BBC to at least the same extent as the press, 'there is a real danger that British prowess will be swamped by American stories'. Again, the development of transportable recording equipment was seen as crucial: the sophistication of the German front-line reporting facilities were already well known, and the BBC feared that the Americans, better organised and more farseeing, would 'steal a march on us'.[24]

El Alamein and after

The battle of El Alamein (October-November 1943) was a key moment in war broadcasting. The broadcaster concerned was an unlikely one. Godfrey Talbot had recently replaced Dimbleby in the Middle East, his over-optimistic summaries of the military situation having finally gone too far for London. Formerly a Regional Press Officer, Talbot had become a News department sub-editor on the outbreak of war, and got his first broadcasting break when he filled in during an early-morning news bulletin for an announcer who had overslept. Talbot's first attempts to record the sounds of the battle failed: his recording truck rocked so violently when the opening artillery barrage began that the cutter jumped from the disc. However, his recorded commentary of the tank advance through enemy lines on the night of 1-2 November (Talbot at the end of a microphone cable relaying to his engineer the sounds of the tanks passing just yards away) was one of the great sound coups of the war thus far.[25]

To Wynford Vaughan-Thomas in London, after Alamein 'the whole climate of war reporting changed'.[26] The huge impact of this broadcast with listeners confirmed the BBC's belief in the importance of front line sound reportage, as well as its views about its current shortcomings (to Standing, Talbot's commentary 'could have been made definitely more vivid and interesting by the application of OB technique').[27] With the front line opening up, the BBC's tentative discussions of 1942 hardened into far more urgent demands. The earlier arrangements, whereby single accredited reporters (with or without attendant engineers) were assigned overseas on an ad-hoc basis, treated like inferior pressmen and reliant on local Service goodwill for facilities, were now wholly inadequate; the BBC now demanded a new set-up whereby teams of multi-skilled broadcasters were formally accredited, with access and facilities suitable for broadcasting, their role acknowledged by the services, and their activities co-ordinated from London. Standing's proposal to accredit OB commentators as war correspondents was revisited: as a preliminary move Dimbleby was sent to the OB department for training in running commentary technique, Glendenning seconded to News in return, and Howard Marshall retrieved from the Ministry of Food and accredited as a 'Special War Correspondent' to the Tunis front. In late 1942 the BBC's joint Directors-General, Robert Foot and Sir Cecil Graves, personally approached the Minister of Information, Brendan Bracken, urging as a matter of 'vital importance' the drawing up of a clear and coordinated common plan of action, involving the BBC, the MoI, the British and American propaganda bodies the Political Warfare Executive and Office of War Information, and the British and American General Staffs.[28]

Again, Ryan and Standing put it most forcefully. Indicting the BBC's lack of will and resources thus far, its failure to secure adequate cooperation with the Services, and the dearth of broadcast outlets for 'authentic front-line war material', Standing recommended 'really drastic action': the immediate setting up some half-dozen cross-departmental reporting teams, comprising a news reporter, OB commentator, feature writer and recording engineer, all uniformed accredited war correspondents, each bringing their own particular expertise to war reportage, equipped with their own recording van and, as soon as possible, portable recording equipment. Teams should undergo both broadcasting and military field training. The material they produced in the field would be placed in 'some sort of regular news supplement period' that paid particular attention to 'actuality'.[29] Ryan underlined the importance of the distinct roles of news and commentary:

> ... anyone with practical experience of newspaper and of broadcasting work will see the point. A correspondent who can write quickly and well cannot in practice (nine times out of ten) tell his story direct and as it is happening into the microphone. On the other hand the man trained in this special technique—commentators like John Snagge, whose names are known all over the country—cannot sit down after the event and write. Nobody taking a realistic view of news and publicity would argue that the two jobs are not as distinct as chalk from cheese.

The main job of the BBC in 1943 would be to keep the exploits of the British fighting services 'vividly and justly' in the public mind in Britain, the Dominions, the USA and Russia, and worldwide. But if broadcasting were treated as if it were 'just another newspaper, the country must inevitably fail to receive from broadcasting the service to which it is obviously entitled. And 'with all friendliness to our American Allies', American publicity must not be permitted to eclipse the British war effort.'[30]

The pressure worked: the BBC was given permission to try out its new team system during Exercise Spartan, the biggest army manoeuvres ever held in Britain, held across central England in early March 1943. 'Spartan' pitted the 'Second British Army' (First Canadian Army), based in 'Southland', the Southern counties of England, against the 'German Sixth Army' (British forces), based in 'Eastland', or the counties North of the Thames and around London, with 'Westland' or the West of England neutral territory. The BBC correspondents were likewise divided into two teams, co-ordinated by Lotbinière and Standing respectively, each with a 'general coverage' man (Dimbleby/Reynolds), OB man (Vaughan-Thomas/MacPherson), feature man (Robert Barr/ John Glyn-Jones) and two engineers. Ryan's instructions to the BBC teams talked up the importance of their role ('The BBC's chance of getting the show to which broadcasting is entitled when the Second Front comes depends on how successfully this week's experiment is conducted....'), but was realistic about the BBC's relationship with the military ('keep clear of blitzes with the Soldiers).[31] Although militarily the results of the exercise were mixed (military vehicles jammed country lanes, angry farmers confronted trespassing enemy armies, and the 'Germans' did better than they were supposed to), as a broadcasting exercise it was largely successful. Over ninety recordings were made, including news updates, action commentaries, interviews, topical talks and background material for features, mixing straight reporting and colourful fantasy (bayonet attacks, the destruction of Caversham bridge, even interviews with 'liberated' Henley shopkeepers). Military liaison had been relatively smooth (three of the four military conducting officers had been helpful), as had censorship procedures. Suggestions for the future included better labelling of discs, better transport facilities (with BBC flags on them: 'the military mind responds to such insignia'), and portable typewriters and carbon paper 'for those who can type'. The most critical report came from Dimbleby himself, who suggested the OB man confine himself to reports of the '"here I am in a ditch" type', demanded that news men got a jeep and a military despatch rider, and criticised the BBC's selection of recording engineers ('At present they do not seem to realise that by donning the uniform, the correspondent is assuming automatically the status and most of the privileges of an officer').[32] Above all, the BBC had showed itself both careful and reliable; the following month the War Office gave the BBC permission to extend the experiment to actual operations. The BBC submitted a provisional Treasury estimate of £72,250 for two fully equipped war reporting teams, and on 14 May 1943 the BBC's front line reporting unit was formally christened the War Reporting Unit (WRU).[33]

Reports coming in from Robert Dunnett and Howard Marshall at the Tunis front underlined the case for a complete reorganisation of the BBC's war reporting operations. The BBC's efforts there had been hampered by military secrecy, lack of high-level military contacts (they were forced to rely on the interventions of the resident minister, Harold Macmillan), inadequate equipment, and the deliberately unhelpful attitude of the American broadcasting authorities who controlled the transmission facilities ('it is an illusion to believe they are in any way grateful to the BBC for past services'). The BBC recording unit had been sunk in a convoy, General Alexander was blaming the BBC for a censorship blunder, and the BBC was in danger of losing the confidence of the troops. Dunnett recommended the BBC establish independently functioning units with correspondents at both GHQ and the front line, with satisfactory transmitting facilities and above all a co-ordinated sense of purpose ('Every BBC man reporting a campaign should be part of the pattern of it before its begins and a force within it thereafter to tell its exploits roundly to the world'). Marshall's critique went further, to the heart of what the BBC was trying to do. Unlike newspapers, or the rival US broadcasters, the BBC should not compete for news scoops, but aim only 'to give the truth as completely as possible with the minimum of delay'. In a world where 'propagandists have systematically undermined the meaning and value of words', men no longer trusted newspapers, propagandists or politicians. The BBC was 'the last refuge of truth in a world which has lost its standards and values'; securing its reputation for truth would be 'the greatest contribution the BBC can make to the future of mankind'. However, he warned, 'The BBC must never become the official spokesman. It must ... gain the complete confidence of authority [but at the same time]... jealously preserve the integrity which may sometimes make the truth unpalatable to authority'.[34]

Recruiting the War Reporting Unit

The WRU was an entirely new departure in BBC administration, operating from within News Division but staffed by personnel from, and supplying material to, all the the BBC's departments, removed from the normal administrative channels, directly responsible to Ryan (now Controller (News)), and with direct access to the Directors-General and the BBC's new 'Editor-in Chief', newspaper editor William Haley, on matters of major importance.[35] Recruitment for the WRU commenced over the summer of 1943 and continued into 1944. Calls went out to every department in the BBC for outside broadcasters, feature writers, even dramatists, who were then sent for training: a three-day military course on intelligence, operations and administration; a short field censorship course at the MoI; a short divisional or battalion attachment; and a short course on OB running commentary technique. Correspondents were given the honorary rank of major (Vaughan-Thomas, Dimbleby, Barr and MacPherson) or captain. [36] Marshall was appointed its Director. Recruits ranged from the celebrated Canadian broadcaster Stanley Maxted, WWI veteran, war correspondent for *Stars and Stripes* and leading member of the BBC Overseas Services Division, to the poet Louis MacNeice, then a BBC features editor. Colin Wills, formerly in charge of the Press Section of the MoI Empire Division, and renowned for his ability to talk 'extraordinarily well about Australian aborigines and sheepfarmers, etc.', joined despite having a voice deemed 'unacceptable to Home News'.[37] Another Australian recruit, Chester Wilmot, was part-shared with the Australian Broadcasting Commission, for whom he had already reported from Greece and Tobruk. Former Shakespearean and West End actor Pierre Lefevre was recruited from the BBC European Service: he had joined the French army in 1939 and escaped to Britain in 1940. Guy Byam, also from the European Service, had served with the RNVR in Norway and the North Atlantic, been wounded on Combined Operations, and trained as a paratroop. Of the seventeen correspondents named in a pre-D-Day press release, eight had journalistic experience, ten had experience in radio production (mostly features), five had experience in outside broadcasting (mostly sports commentating), and four had been actors. Nine had war reporting experience. Two women were recruited: Audrey Russell, who sent vivid reports from 'Hellfire Corner' in Dover and Folkestone in October 1944, and Vera Lindsay, temporarily assigned to Paris in October 1944, but in the event never used as a broadcaster. The sole recruit of German origin, Rolf Sigler, failed to make the cut; so too did Louis MacNeice, after one too many accidents during his tank regiment placement. Support staff came from departments as varied as Overseas Presentation, Latin American News and Variety. Such were the WRU's personnel demands that Basil Nicolls, BBC Controller of Programmes, warned of a serious deterioration in programme quality across the board if WRU recruitment continued.[38]

The sending overseas of several teams of war correspondents raised all manner of logistical problems. This might be as apparently trivial as clothes: the shirts provided by the BBC supplier of choice, Moss Bros., tended to rot in hot conditions; meanwhile, whether or not to purchase mess uniforms caused anguish among some correspondents.[39] Salaries were decided on a surprisingly ad hoc basis. Richard Dimbleby, for instance, had started the war on £542 p.a., though Ward, on a 'special contract' received £1000. By 1941/2, overseas correspondents received in the region of £800, or around £1000 'if they showed outstanding capabilities', plus £100 active service bonus. £1000 remained the WRU top salary, received by Gillard, Johnston, Talbot and (from April 1944) Dimbleby—but Maxted retained an exceptionally high salary of £1400 from his previous post, and Marshall received £3000 as WRU Director.[40] Bonuses were given for exceptional work (for instance, £200 to Robin Duff in 1944 for his year reporting with the US forces). Increasingly well paid, BBC war correspondents found they were a tax anomaly: neither technically based abroad, nor in practice resident at home. (Some BBC war correspondents had apparently hoped to avoid tax altogether by going overseas.) Following Civil Service procedures, the BBC had always taken a 'notional tax deduction' from the salaries of permanent overseas staff. But the decision to extend this practice to WRU war correspondents in the field sparked such a fury among the correspondents themselves—the amount represented up to 50 percent of their salaries—that the BBC was forced to back down; the income tax 'deductions' were held instead in personal suspense accounts until either paid over to the Inland Revenue if required or returned to the correspondents themselves.[41] Rates of compensation for injury or death (including widow's pensions, allowances for children under 18, and discretionary pensions to any other dependents, such as parents) were based on equivalent army rates—the argument of some correspondents that they deserved more, since they would be running greater risks in the line of duty than their average army equivalent, was dismissed on the grounds that front line reporting traded extra risk for extra excitement. War correspondents would, though, continue to receive their full salaries if taken prisoner of war. Finally, correspondents were informed that subsistence rates would be fixed as soon after the opening of a campaign as possible. As for entertainment allowances, 'The best guidance that can be given is to remind you that you will be spending public money and you must therefore be concerned to spend it in the listeners' best interest.'[42]

Recording technology was still a problem. While the Canadians, for instance, were putting their efforts into developing more sophisticated recording vans (in effect high-fidelity mobile studios), the BBC (with an eye to the American networks) concentrated on portable broadcasting equipment, and were particularly concerned lest the Americans develop portable recorders before they themselves did. Experiments with the RCA Sound Camera had failed, an though in July 1943 the US Army provided the BBC with experimental sets of their new portable wire recording equipment, they never went into service.[43] There was, however, a boost for the existing technology in September 1943 when, at the invitation of the RAF, Wynford Vaughan-Thomas and his engineer Reg Pidsley made the BBC's first recording from inside a Lancaster bomber on a 300-bomber night raid over Berlin. Denis Johnston had already attempted to record a flight through an air raid over Tunisia, but the recording had been unusable. Dimbleby had made a bomber sortie (without recording equipment) in January 1943, but his account of his experiences had, through press pressure, been all but buried in the early morning bulletins. This time, with Vaughan-Thomas sitting with a microphone in the front of the plane beside the second pilot, and Pidsley sitting with the recording gear in the rear behind the navigator, they recorded a sound commentary of the raid as the plane flew through searchlights and flak ('we are running straight into the most gigantic display of fireworks in the world'), dropped its bombs on a Berlin in flames, shot down an attacking ME 110, and returned across the North Sea via Sweden. The crew landed home at dawn on 4 September; the recording went out to huge acclaim in the one o'clock news. [44]

The continued refusal of the military to acknowledge the BBC's technical requirements made the introduction of the portable recorder more urgent. A BBC team accompanying Exercise Pirate, the first full-scale battle practice for invasion, found themselves still treated like newspaper correspondents, allowed to observe from a distance but unable to record from the front line. Although in November the BBC was promised a place—with recording equipment--in the first landing barge that opened the Western Front (automatically giving them priority over the planned press ship), in December the War Office was still actively refusing to accredit BBC transmitting engineers or help the BBC acquire Army transport vehicles.[45] However in late 1943 the BBC's first portable wind-up disc recorders ('midget recorders') were at last introduced. They weighed 10-15 lbs and resembled portable gramophones; correspondents could crank them up and cut short despatches directly onto disc. They were not robust enough to record adequately the sounds of battle, but they proved excellent for voice recording. With them, a BBC correspondent could record despatches alone for the first time; he could thus circumvent the perennial problem of 'pooling', whereby only a single BBC correspondent and no recording engineer was permitted by the MoI and military, often at very short notice.[46]

The first test of the WRU team principle, the invasion of Italy, demonstrated what the BBC was still up against. The five American radio representatives effectively monopolised the press's Voicecast transmissions. The terrain was so difficult that it was impossible to operate the BBC recording trucks near forward lines. British troops were furious that the Americans were getting credit for British actions, for instance the capture of the beaches at Salerno, and resented being referred to as 'Allied forces' when Americans units were routinely identified by name.[47] In December Haley visited the Italian front at the direct invitation of General Alexander to discuss BBC facilities for news coverage, the importance of BBC news to troop morale, and in particular the BBC's losing battle 'to preserve the balance between British and American contributions to the war'.[48] Although the War Office appeared 'quite unconscious' of this particular twist in the propaganda war, support for the BBC came from an unexpected source. During his time in North Africa, the then General Montgomery had become very aware of the potential of broadcasting, using Denis Johnston to get his messages to the Eighth Army, for instance, and at one point persuading Godfrey Talbot to let one of his soldiers make a broadcast to his father. Now in Italy, he told Frank Gillard that he could not understand why the BBC didn't get proper representation and transport facilities: 'the BBC was the voice of Britain and that they should have a unit with each one of his divisions.'[49]

The BBC's Italy coverage raised other more practical problems. The decision to post Gillard at Army HQ, important in itself, meant the loss from the front line of one of the BBC's best reporters. Internally, the WRU was highly critical of its new team: Johnston deemed only 'tolerable', Vaughan-Thomas considered 'very much at sea as to news requirements', and Robert Beckwith dismissed as 'not a News man'.[50] This notwithstanding, the BBC's reporting of the Italy campaign was a triumph. Vaughan-Thomas made his mark again on 22 January 1944, carrying one of the first portable disc recorders onto the Anzio beachhead. The Allied advance towards Rome attracted unprecedented news audiences. The coverage culminated in Vaughan-Thomas' description on 4 June of the cheering crowds in St Peter's Square welcoming the Allied forces into Rome, accompanied by the sounds of church bells ringing the celebrations throughout the city. Two days later, D-Day launched the Second Front proper and *War Report* took to the air.

War Report

As late as March 1944 the WRU still had not chosen its final teams, set up OB transmission points on the south coast, or arranged air transport of discs. The WRU's control structure was still unclear, half the members of the Unit were still working part time for other departments, and a further round of training had to be set up to instil corporate spirit. Not until late April 1944 was it finally decided to establish a dedicated WRU broadcasting slot following the nine o'clock news, to act as 'the BBC's major daily war report to the nation'. Even so, the first edition of *War Report*, broadcast on the BBC Home Service on the evening of D-Day, 6 June 1944, passed into broadcasting legend.[51]

The first broadcast confirmation of the D-Day landings was announced by John Snagge at 9.30 a.m. on 6 June. The first WRU despatches (recordings made by Gillard, Dunnett, Dimbleby and MacPherson while awaiting embarkation the previous evening), went out in the one o'clock news. The first edition of *War Report* itself, introduced by Snagge at 9.24 p.m. after a statement from the King, was heard by over 60 per cent of the population. It featured statements from Generals Eisenhower and de Gaulle, sound recordings of the air force, navy and army in action (including Richard Dimbleby watching the paratroop planes taking off, John Macadam describing, on his return from a towing plane, how the gliders had set off for France, and Howard Marshall's famous extempore transmission, 'I'm sitting here in my soaked-through clothes with no notes at all. All my notes are sodden. They're at the bottom of the sea', broadcast live from Fareham after his return from Normandy, where earlier that day, as part of the first assault waves, his landing craft had hit a mine), and ended with a recording of Montgomery's final message to his troops ('Good luck to each one of you—and good hunting on the mainland of Europe'). Except for a six-week break in early 1945, *War Report* would broadcast virtually every night for half an a hour after the nine o'clock news to approximately half the British population until the end of the war in Europe.

In the early weeks, almost every edition of *War Report* seemed to offer something new. On June 8 Byam became the first correspondent to beam his report directly from France. From 11 June, when the press and broadcasting companies for the first time instituted separate pools, BBC listeners to *War Report* could regularly hear, not only their own correspondents but also their American, Canadian and Australian counterparts, reporting on British and Allied operations.[52] On June 18 Gillard was the first correspondent to broadcast live into *War Report* by direct transmission from Normandy—this became a much fought-over privilege. And despite all previous assertions to the contrary, scoops were noted with glee, from the advance on Cherbourg on 19 June, to the attempted assassination of Hitler on 20 July, to the Allied crossing of the Rhine on 23 March 1945. After D-Day, in fact, it became impossible to enforce the press's priority in news-breaking and the old embargo system was simply ignored.

Inevitably, not everything ran smoothly. From the first, there were problems with getting reports back: with apparently 1.85 correspondents to every mile of the Western Front, there was simply no room for them all to get their material back from France, and until landing strips were finally operating from which discs could be flown home, BBC correspondents found themselves entrusting discs to anyone they could find on a boat heading to England.[53] The BBC's first transmitters in France played up constantly. As the allies advanced, the distance between the correspondents on the front line and the transmission bases stretched sometimes to breaking point. In a delay over censorship on 16 June, the material due for broadcast at 9 p.m. was only cleared at 8.58.[54] Some days were better for material than others: 29 July 1944 was, for instance, a 'very thin day', when the programme was only saved by some material from the American networks. On 13 August nothing came in till 8 p.m., when three messages in rapid succession saved the day. By contrast, on 21 August so much came in from Rome in the evening that the telephone system jammed and not one despatch got through in time to be used. Meanwhile, the second wave of BBC correspondents was delayed, due, Ryan was convinced, to press interference ('There are gentlemen dressed in uniform who are more concerned to keep sweet with Fleet Street than to get good world-wide reporting for the real soldiers'). There were other more immediate problems: in the first six weeks dysentery was widespread among troops and correspondents alike.[55]

The amount of material processed by the WRU was immense. The WRU London Traffic Room worked 24 hours a day, seven days a week, with a staff of 24 transcribing, checking, censoring and distributing an average weekly load of 212 transmitted despatches, 56 discs and 196 service messages, plus a host of miscellaneous special material, for the Western Front alone. The BBC maintained lists of inaccuracies and instances of 'undesirable presentation', and Ryan, himself accredited as 'special correspondent with SHAEF', maintained a day-to-day watch on all WRU output. By 1 July 1944 36 correspondents were operating; by January 1945 the BBC had eight recording trucks, fourteen utility vehicles and 38 midget recorders in use in Britain and across Europe. The WRU alone provided 90 percent of the material broadcast in *War Report*, 98 percent of material broadcast in the Allied Expeditionary Forces Programme's *Combat Diary*, 50 percent of *Radio Newsreel*, and 80-90 percent of the North American Service's

Morning Special and General Forces Programme's own *War Report*, as well as background material for features, drama and talks across the BBC.[56]

Broadcast after broadcast made history. One of the BBC's greatest scoops of the war was Robert Reid's extraordinary commentary from Notre Dame, Paris, on 26 August 1944, as General de Gaulle came under sniper fire during the Service of Thanksgiving for the liberation of France. Reid had been commentating when the shooting began, and his recording cable had been broken by the surge of the crowd. Reconnected, and describing what had just happened, he found himself commentating as further shots rang out and then as the captured snipers were led away. By a miracle the recording proved broadcastable, and it went out the next night, not just on the BBC, but in the USA, first on NBC and then an hour later on CBS, completely contravening their traditional prohibition against recorded material.[57] MacPherson took special pride, as a Canadian, in reporting the taking of Dieppe by the Canadian Second Division on 11 September, two years and two weeks after the Dieppe Raid. On 29 September, an outstanding special edition on Arnhem featured sober reports from Gillard, Byam (who had swum the Rhine with his recordings of the retreat) and Maxted (who had bumped into his own son, a Canadian paratrooper, there). [58] On 15 April Edward Murrow shocked listeners across the Allied nations with his account of Buchenwald concentration camp, followed on the 19th by Richard Dimbleby's even more hard-hitting report from Belsen. And on 25 April Gillard reported, 'The forces of liberation have joined hands', as Soviet and American troops met at Torgau on the Elbe. Edward Ward, liberated from a German POW camp just weeks earlier, had hoped to file a further report from Torgau; unfortunately, the recordings made by himself and Reg Pidsley during celebrations with carousing Soviet and American officers ('we've all had a very big lunch … and everything is … BEAUTIFUL') proved too incoherent to use.[59]

The military authorities seem to have been rather disconcerted by the immediate success of *War Report*. Gillard reported that, while SHAEF bulletins often caused much anger among the front-line forces, approval for *War Report* itself was widespread. The BBC benefited from Gillard's close friendship with Montgomery, who regularly used the BBC to broadcast to his troops, though this did not save Chester Wilmot from temporary expulsion when an embargoed recording of Montgomery was unwittingly broadcast too early.[60] Unfortunately, the American high command deplored British coverage of the Western Campaign in general and the 'slavish hero devotion' of Montgomery in particular.[61] In August 1944 General Bradley suggested at a press conference that the BBC had cost the lives of American soldiers by announcing prematurely the closing of the Falaise gap. His statement ('naturally much relished by the American news men') was, Robert Dunnett reported back to London, 'calculated to undermine the confidence of his Staff and his Armies in the BBC news'. In September, Gillard and Maxted were taken to task for attributing the American Second Army's success at Nimjagen to the rearguard actions at Arnhem of the First British Airborne Division. In December, accusations that American servicemen had been killed entering towns that the BBC had erroneously reported were liberated prompted BBC correspondent Cyril Ray to suggest that *War Report* rely in future on its front-line despatches rather than the 'ever-enthusiastic briefings at SHAEF'. During the Battle of the Bulge, Bradley apparently stopped listening to BBC news altogether because it made him so angry.[62] A succession of complaints by SHAEF in the early months of 1945 culminated in a formal protest from

Brigadier-General Frank A. Allen Jr. (Director of SHAEF Public Relations Department) to the BBC Governors that the BBC had broken by 45 minutes SHAEF's news embargo (imposed 'at the request of the heads of the Allied States') on the link up of American and Russian troops at Torgau. In fact, as Haley tersely pointed out, the BBC had done no such thing; Allen had misread Double British Summertime on the embargo as Greenwich Mean Time (two hours later).[63]

BBC relations with American broadcasters, however, were generally good, with a good deal of material shared around. By now, the American networks had discovered that reporting the war on a 'live only' basis was practically impossible; ironically, the recording and mobile transmitting facilities in American areas were so poor that the BBC had to lend them three recording units and engineers, and two mobile transmitters.[64]

Above all, *War Report* was a success with listeners at home. The programme's audience figures (between 10 and 15 million) varied with the news coming in, but its overall popularity never wavered. The compelling mix of situation reports, eye-witness commentary, sound actuality and live broadcasts, brought the fighting front into the home with a directness and immediacy never before experienced. Though the sounds of battle themselves apparently soon palled, the voices themselves (of correspondents, servicemen, liberated citizens, even occasionally celebrities visiting the troops—Reid, for instance, managed to interview Fred Astaire) were what listeners responded to most. And while the programme presented an gratifyingly international cast of correspondents reporting on Allied (though inevitably mostly British) exploits, it was those well known voices from peace time, flung into the front line, that had the strongest following. The programme's one great failing perhaps was the paucity of its coverage from other fighting fronts. Though the WRU sent a team to the Far East in early 1944 (its MoI liaison one Squadron Leader Charles Gardner), its meagre output, further compromised by unsatisfactory communiqués from Mountbatten and by the devastating effect of humidity on the BBC's recording equipment, failed to dent the widespread British perception, which *War Report* implicitly endorsed, that the war *was* the Western Front.[65]

Personnel problems persisted. Colin Wills resigned from the WRU after accusations that he was buying his material by dint of spending four times as much as any other correspondent on entertainment. Denis Johnston, it was concluded, lacked the news instinct, and was reassigned to gather material for Features. Stewart MacPherson ('a reckless individual') was forced to arrange his own transport after wrecking two BBC vehicles. Dimbleby proved characteristic to the last: as late as January 1945, having cultivated yet another 'excellent relationship', this time with Bomber Command, he was still disappearing on his own ventures, 'more often than not on the very day that we want to get hold of him'. However, the physical and mental strain was telling: by January 1945 MacPherson was on sick leave, and Gillard, Wilmot, Vaughan-Thomas and Barr were all clearly exhausted.[66] More tragically, two correspondents, Kent Stevenson and Guy Byam, were killed in action. However, in spring 1945 the BBC correspondents assembled in strength to report the crossing of the Rhine, before following the Allied armies to Berlin. On 4 May 1945 Wilmot broadcast what was, even by the standards set by *War Report*, a coup: a recording of the surrender of the German generals to Montgomery earlier that day. An unfortunate technical hitch panicked the studio manager into cutting off the broadcast mid-recording; however, Haley personally intervened to secure an unscheduled rebroadcast of the full surrender an hour later. On the same evening, Vaughan-Thomas sent his last war report, from William Joyce's (Lord Haw-Haw) own microphone at Radio Hamburg, from a desk littered with the drafts of Joyce's final broadcast and an empty gin bottle.

On 5 May, its 235th edition, *War Report* went off the air for the last time. On 8 May, VE-Day, key members of the WRU, including Marshall, MacPherson and Dimbleby, fronted a nationwide link up, *Victory Report*, from London, telling the world how Britain was celebrating victory, and commentating on the celebrations in the capital for all the BBC home and overseas services throughout the day and long into the night. On 31 May the WRU was formally disbanded, save for three correspondents, engineers and mobile recording cars in Germany, four correspondents in Italy, one in the Far East and two in the Pacific Theatre. The Traffic Room was closed down at midnight. On 9 June 1945 the BBC Governors sent their formal congratulations to all those who helped in the success of *War Report*.[67]

After the war

The BBC's war reporters were a new kind of war correspondent. They had to negotiate new technical challenges, and evolve a new kind of relationship with the military authorities. Their variety of backgrounds, wide range of broadcasting experience, and different attitudes to their job, were co-ordinated through the WRU to produce an often uneven but at its best an uniquely vivid and immediate new kind of war coverage, marrying news and outside broadcast techniques, that brought the war into people's homes in a way that was both compellingly strange and reassuringly familiar. They were not, of course, 'objective'--in this kind of war one could hardly have expected it—but their institutional commitment to 'truth' (as Marshall stated, not just for the duration, but in trust for the post-war world) distanced them in important respects from their more news-hungry media competitors. And above all, setting aside their largely uncritical support of the Allied war effort, they were fierce partisans of the British and Empire war effort against the similarly partisan American publicity machine.

Yet for most of the WRU (and like most of their listeners), their wartime careers were a once in a lifetime experience. None returned to war reporting; indeed most did not even stay in news, choosing instead to return to the professions outside the BBC or Departments within the BBC from which they had been originally recruited (teaching, administration, feature-writing, etc.).[68] Michael Standing went from the WRU to become the BBC Head of Variety. Robert Barr returned to Features production, then to BBC Television when it relaunched in 1946. Denis Johnston (awarded the OBE after the war for services to war reporting) also returned briefly to BBC TV, then to writing, and an academic career in the USA. Stewart MacPherson became a radio compère on such popular programmes as *Ignorance is Bliss*, *Twenty Questions* and *Down Your Way*, and returned to sports commentary. Stanley Maxted, the chronicler of Arnhem, became compère of *Housewives Choice*, and returned to acting on stage and television.

Godfrey Talbot (likewise OBE), the 'accidental' newsman, was one of the few BBC war correspondents to stay in the news department; indeed he was made Chief Reporter, with the task of building a full home news team; however, in 1946 he was appointed the BBC's first 'accredited' royal correspondent, the start of a 30-year association with royal reporting. Edward Ward (despite succeeding to the title of 7ᵗʰ Viscount Bangor in 1950) remained as a BBC foreign correspondent until 1960. Richard Dimbleby (OBE), the BBC's first news observer, resigned from the BBC staff in 1945 but remained with the BBC as a freelance broadcaster, like MacPherson in popular radio series like *Down Your Way* and *Twenty Questions* (as a team member), and then as the face of BBC TV current affairs in *Panorama*, but most famously (and not without a certain irony) as the BBC's principal commentator on royal and state occasions. Wynford Vaughan-Thomas (Croix de Guerre) also became one of the BBC's 'royal' commentators (including the Royal Commonwealth Tours, the 1947 Royal Wedding and the 1953 Coronation); he became Director of Programmes at Harlech Television, and a Governor of the British Film Institute. Frank Gillard (OBE) rose highest of all in the BBC, eventually becoming Director of Radio. Patrick Ryan (CBE), largely the inspiration behind the BBC's war reporting effort, remained as editor of the BBC news services until 1947, then joined the *Times* as Assistant and Literary Editor. Howard Marshall, Director of the WRU, left the BBC altogether and for the next twenty years was head of corporate public relations, Richard Thomas and Baldwin's Ltd. It was a new generation that took on the challenge of war broadcasting in the 1950s.

NOTES

1. Phillip Knightley, *The First Casualty: the War Correspondent as Propagandist, Hero and Myth-Maker* (London, 1975, and subsequent editions) remains the best account of early war reportage. For First World War, see Martin J Farrar, *News from the Front: War Correspondents on the Western Front 1914-18* (Stroud, 1998).
2. See Lieut. Geoffrey Malins, OBE, *How I Filmed the War: A Record of the Extraordinary Experiences of the Man Who Filmed the Great Somme Battles, etc.* (London, [1920] 1993), in particular the introduction by Nicholas Hiley.
3. *The Times*, 22 December 2000.
4. See Erik Barnouw, *The Golden Web: A History of Broadcasting in the United States, vol II: 1933-1953* (New York, 1968), pp. 74-83. As Sperber notes, the voice of the reporter in *War of the Worlds* describing the destruction of New York City until his microphone too went dead might have been Murrow himself. Ann M. Sperber, *Murrow, His Life and Times* (London, 1987), pp. 132-33.
5. For BBC news 1922-39, see Siân Nicholas, 'All the news that's fit to broadcast: the popular press *versus* the BBC, 1922-45', in Peter Catterall, Colin Seymour-Ure and Adrian Smith, eds., *Northcliffe's Legacy: Aspects of the Popular Press, 1896-1996* (Basingstoke, 2000), pp.123-138; also Paddy Scannell and David Cardiff, *A Social History of British Broadcasting: Vol. I: Sound and Vision, 1922-1939* (London, 1991).
6. For BBC OB dept in the 1930s see Asa Briggs, *The Golden Age of Wireless* (London, 1965), pp. 76-7, 112-13 and passim; Wynford Vaughan-Thomas, *Trust to Talk* (London, 1980). For Woodrooffe see John Snagge and Michael Barsley, *Those Vintage Years of Radio* (London, 1972), pp. 68-69. Scannell and Cardiff, *Serving the Nation*, rightly highlights the role of the regions in developing outside broadcasts.

7. Dimbleby, *Richard Dimbleby*, pp. 85-6.
8. Stursberg, *The Sound of War: Memoirs of a CBC Correspondent* (Toronto, 1993), p. 24; Draft press release, 'Richard Dimbleby', nd., BBC Written Archive Centre, Caversham (hereafter, BBC WAC), File R44/609.
9. *News of the World*, 1 October 1939; *The Listener*, 12 October 1939, p. 706. For full discussion of BBC news broadcasting during the war, see Siân Nicholas, *The Echo of War: Home Front Propaganda and the Wartime BBC, 1939-45* (Manchester, 1996), Ch. 6.
10. Quoted in Dimbleby, *Richard Dimbleby*, p. 92.
11. Edward Ward, *Number One Son: an Autobiography* (London, 1969), pp. 120-29.
12. BBC WAC Home News Bulletins 33, 31 May 1940.
13. Note on BBC War Correspondents, 3 April 1941; Ryan to C(H) 25 April 1941, BBC WAC R28/277; Robert Reid, *War Correspondent* (Broadcast Echoes No. 31, Leeds, nd.), pp. 9-11. I am indebted to Jeremy Crang for lending me this account.
14. Godfrey Talbot, *Permission to Speak* (London, 1976), p. 47; Denis Johnston, *Orders and Desecrations: the Life of the Playwright Denis Johnston* (Dublin, 1992), p. 122-23; C(H) to SNE 14 May 1941, BBC WAC R28/277; Ward, *Number One Son*, pp. 151-75.
15. As late as July 1942 the War Office withdrew permission for a BBC recording car to accompany the defending forces in the event of a German invasion of Britain, on the ground that they would be an encumbrance. Cockburn to C(NC), 29 July 1942, BBC WAC R28/277.
16. See Howard Marshall, *Over to Tunis: the Complete Story of the North African Campaign* (London, 1943), p. 61; Vaughan-Thomas, *Trust to Talk*, p. 149.
17. See Sperber, *Murrow*, pp. 144, 162-64. For more details of the BBC's blitz coverage, see Nicholas, *Echo of War*, pp. 124-27; for American coverage, cf. Nicholas J. Cull, *Selling War: The British Propaganda Campaign Against American 'Neutrality' in World War II* (Oxford, 1995), Ch. 4.
18. C(NC) (Ryan) to DG (Graves), 3 April 1942, BBC WAC R13/432/1; DOB to C(P), 13 August 1942, R28/280/1.
19. Johnston, *Orders and Desecrations*, pp. 124-25.
20. AC(OS), to C(OS), 8 April 1942, BBC WAC R13/432/1; DOB to C(P), 13 August 1942, R28/280/1.
21. Ryan to Major-General the Hon. E. F. Cawson (War Office), 8 January 1942; Francis Williams (MOI) to Ryan, 12 August 1942, and Ryan reply 13 August, BBC WAC R13/432/1.
22. Ryan to Squadron-Leader F. C. Gillman, 23 Sept 1942; Note from Controller, Press and Censorship, MOI, 15 Oct 1942; Ryan to DG (Foot), 20 October 1942; Report of Meeting on BBC Raids Requirements, 29 Oct 1942, BBC WAC R28/279.
23. Supervisor of Overseas Planning and Liaison to C(OS), 14 August 1942, BBC WAC R13/432/1.
24. C(N) to DG (Graves), 10 October 1942; Graves to Radcliffe (MOI) 2 October 1942; C(OS) to Graves, 6 Oct 1942, BBC WAC R28/280/1. The fear that the Americans would 'steal our thunder' recurs throughout BBC internal correspondence; see too Pres.D (Snagge) to C(P) 5 Feb 1943, R28/280/2.

25. Jean Stroud, *Special Correspondent* (London, 1969), pp. 24-8. See too Godfrey Talbot, *Speaking from the Desert: A Record of the Eighth Army in Africa* (London, 1944).
26. Wynford Vaughan-Thomas, *Trust to Talk* (London, 1980), pp. 148-49.
27. AC(N) to Barker, 5 November 1942, BBC WAC R28/280/1.
28. AC(N) to Dimbleby, 3 December 1942; Draft memorandum from Joint DGs to Minister of Information, nd. (between 20 November 1942 and 8 January 1943), BBC WAC R28/280/1.
29. DOB to C(P), 19 January 1943, BBC WAC R28/280/2.
30. Ryan memo, and Foot to Bracken, 8 February 1943, BBC WAC R28/280/2.
31. 'To all BBC War Correspondents', n.s., n.d. (March 1943?), BBC WAC R13/432/1.
32. For complete Exercise Spartan despatches, see BBC WAC R28/280/2; see also Stursberg, *Sound of War*, p. 71-4. For internal BBC post-mortem, see 'Broadcasting Exercise', 15 March 1943 ns., (Ryan?); HNTE to C(N), Spartan Exercise--March 1943, 15 March 1943; Dimbleby to C(N), Report on Spartan Exercise, 15 March 1943, R28/280/2.
33. Draft letter to Minister of Information (ns), 23 April 1943, BBC WAC R28/280/3; Ryan to Lotbinière, 14 May 1943, R13//432/1. Lotbinière had held out in vain for 'Warcasting Unit'.
34. Dunnett report, 16 Feburary 1943, BBC WAC R28/280/2; Marshall to DG (Foot), War Reporting in North Africa – (1) Proposals, 28 May 1943, his underlinings; C(N) to DG (Foot), 1 June 1943, R28/280/3. Inevitably, Marshall's *Over to Tunis* (1943), published during the war, presents a more positive view.
35. DG to Controllers, 17 March 1944, BBC WAC R13/432/2.
36. DWR to AC(N), 25 November 1943, BBC WAC R13/432/2; AOND to WRU members, 7 July 1943, R13/432/1.
37. Lotbinière to C(N) 26 May 1943, BBC WAC R28/280/3; ASDB to Mr Cameron, 9 April 1940, R34/213/2; Empire News Editor to C(N), 14 May 1943, R28/280/3.
38. Draft press release, 'War Reporting Unit', nd., BBC WAC R13/432/3; Editor War Report, 10 Oct 1944, R28/222/2; R. D. Sigler to Miss Boland, nd., R44/609; Jon Stallworthy, *Louis MacNeice* (London, 1995), p. 317; Manager WRU memo, 22 June 1944, R13/432/3; C(P) to AC(N), 8 Nov 1943, R13/432/2.
39. See AOND to Chief Buyer, 2 September 1942, and reply 4 September, BBC WAC R28/277; AOND to Major G. Helder (War Office), 25 May 1943, R13/432/1. CBC correspondents, on the other hand, were splendidly outfitted by Burburry (Stursberg, *Sound of War*, pp. 57-8).
40. Salary details appear throughout BBC WAC files R13/432/1-3. See for instance, DPA (Rose-Troup) to GEO, 28 November 1940, R13/432/1; Salary note, nd. (December 1943?), R13/432/2; AOND to DDG 28 April 1944, R13/432/3.
41. AOND to Ryan, 17 September 1943; Rose-Troup to Ryan, 19 August 1943, BBC WAC R13/432/1; War Correspondents: Salaries and Income Tax: Note on points agreed at a meeting in DG's room on 12th October, 2 November 1943; Allport to Rose-Troup, 12 Nov 1943, and reply, 13 December 1943, R13/432/2.

42. Lotbinière, 'Attached "Terms of Service"', 8 July 1943; Lotbinière to DSA, 4 August 1943; AOND to WRU members, 7 July 1943, BBC WAC R13/432/1.

43. Stursberg, *Sound of War*, pp. 54-6, 290; C(OS) to Graves, 6 Oct 1942, BBC WAC R13/432/; RPD to AC(N) 27 October 1942; 14 January 1943, Supt. Eng. (Recording) to C(N), R28/280/1; Lotbinière to Major Howard Nussbaum (US Army Public Relations), 9 July 1943, R28/280/3.

44. Johnston, *Orders and Desecrations*, p. 124; Vaughan-Thomas, *Trust to Talk*, pp. 149-57; Stroud, *Special Correspondent*, pp. 29-31; Gilliam (ADF) to C(P), 24 Sept 1943, BBC WAC R28/280/4. In fact Murrow would soon trump this achievement by broadcasting *live* to the USA from a Berlin bomber. But Haley, mindful that news announcers had been accused of using 'gloating' tones to report air raids over Germany, refused all BBC requests to do likewise: 'for reasons of home psychology' the bombing of Germany was 'not to be stunted'. See AONTE to AC(N), with EONB addendum, 29 March 1944; Haley to AC(N) 6 April 1944, R28/280/5.

45. Marshall to C(N), 19 Oct 1943, BBC WAC R28/280/4; P.51/43 Note of Meeting held on 3rd November 1943, R13/432/2; Allport to DWR, 17 December 1943, R28/280/4. The only suitable vehicles were available only on Army contract through the Ministry of Supply.

46. Stursberg, *Sound of War*, p. 117; Foreign News Dept to AC(N), 24 Jan 1944, BBC WAC R28/280/5, re Nettuno landings. Stursberg, a war correspondent with CBC, believed these portable recording units had been devised in part out of snobbery: i.e., in order that the BBC might dispense with sound engineers, who were not (*pace* Dimbleby) considered appropriate to receive honorary officer rank.

47. This was War Office policy. Arnell (Gillard's recording engineer) to Marshall, 1 Dec 1943, BBC WAC R28/280/4.

48. Ex. PPM 21.12.43 No. 353, BBC WAC R13/432/2; Alexander to Haley, 15 Dec 1943, R28/280/4; EONB to AC(N), 25 Jan 1944, R28/278/2.

49. Marshall to Brig. A. G. Neville, MOI, 26 October 1943, BBC WAC R13/435; Talbot, *Permission to Speak*, p. 48; Arnell to Marshall, 1 Dec 1943, R28/280/4.

50. AC(N) to DWR, 12 January 1944, BBC WAC R28/280/5.

51. AOWR to AC(N), 6 March 1944, BBC WAC R13/432/2; ADF to CP, 25 April 1944, R28/280/5. For more details of *War Report* from day one, see Nicholas, *Echo of War*, pp. 211-219; Desmond Hawkins, *War Report: D-Day to VE-Day* (London, 1985); Snagge and Barsley, *Vintage Years*, pp. 191-203. See too Reports on Western Front Material (June–December 1944), R28/222/1-2.

52. H. T. Abady (MOI) to C(N), 10 June 1944, BBC WAC R28/280/5.

53. Brig. A.G. Neville (21st Army HQ, London) to Ivone Kirkpatrick (Foreign Office), 6 July 1944, BBC WAC R28/280/5.

54. DDWR memo, 6 November 1944, BBC WAC R28/280/6.

55. See BBC WAC file R28/258, passim.; C(N) to C(Eur.S), 1 July 1944, R28/280/5; Stewart MacPherson, *The Mike and I* (London, 1948), p. 73.

56. War Reporting Unit (Western Front), 26 Jan 1945, BBC WAC R13/434/2.

57. Reid, *War Correspondent*, pp. 56-61; G. D. G. Perkins, WRU Manager, thought it 'one of the biggest broadcasts, I think, of all time.' Perkins to Reid, 7 September 1944, BBC WAC R28/282.
58. MacPherson, *The Mike and I*, p. 77; Snagge and Barsley, *Vintage Years*, pp. 197-98.
59. Ward, *Number One Son*, pp. 244-46.
60. Gillard to HNTE, 12 July 1944; Gillard to ?, 13 July 1944, BBC WAC R28/280/5; see Dimbleby to C(N) 18/19 July 1944, Marshall to C(N), 18 and 19 July 1944, Neville to Ryan 19 July 1944 and Wilmot to Ryan 28 July 1944, R28/280/5. Gillard and Montgomery even had a bet on when the war would end (Montgomery lost). Alistair Horne with David Montgomery, *The Lonely Leader: Monty 1944-45* (Basingstoke, 1994), p. 314.
61. Major Chester B. Hansen diary, quoted in Norman Gelb, *Ike and Monty: Generals at War* (London, 1994), p. 392, also p. 247; cf. Nigel Hamilton, *Monty—The Field Marshall 1944-1976* (London, 1986), p. 301.
62. Dimbleby to C(N), 24 August 1944, BBC WAC R28/258; BBC WAC Home News Bulletins 119, 29 September 1944; Cyril Ray to Ryan, 4 and 5 December 1944, BBC WAC R28/258; Gelb, *Ike and Monty*, p. 392.
63. Allen to The Governors, BBC, 29 April 1945; Haley to Allen 3 May 1945, BBC WAC R28/258. There is no reply from Allen to Haley's letter in the BBC file.
64. DDWR memo, 6 November 1944, BBC WAC R28/280/6.
65. Nicholas, *Echo of War*, pp. 217; Reid, *War Correspondent*, p. 37. For BBC reporting from South East Asia Command, see BBC WAC file R28/253.
66. AOND to C(N) 1 December 1944, BBC WAC R28/280/6; Frost to Ryan 19 Jan 1945, R13/434/2; ONTE to DDWR 13 January 1945, R13/435.
67. Snagge and Barsley, *Vintage Years*, pp. 119-200; Vaughan-Thomas, *Trust to Talk*, pp. 186-87; MacPherson, *The Mike and I*, pp. 98-99; C(N) to DG 23 May 1945; DG to C(N) 9 June 1945, BBC WAC R28/280/7.
68. Talbot, *Permission to Speak*, p. 69.

Chapter Ten
CINEMATIC PROPAGANDA DURING THE COLD WAR: A COMPARISON OF BRITISH AND AMERICAN MOVIES
Tony Shaw

Politics, propaganda and film have always been intertwined, not least in times of national crisis and war. Going back to the Victorian era, the 1899-1902 Boer War is best known nowadays in propaganda terms for Winston Churchill's controversial dual role as a publicity-hungry soldier-correspondent and the damage inflicted on Britain's international reputation by the foreign press's exposure of the use of concentration camps.[1] Less often remarked upon but of equal importance, however, is the fact that the Boer War also represented the first time military censorship had to contend with a professional war cameraman (the Englishman Joe Rosenthal) and that the conflict produced the twentieth century's first faked wartime atrocity film – a British newsreel showing the Boers attacking a Red Cross tent, shot with actors on Hampstead Heath.[2] A century, and countless similar filmic fabrications later, movies remain one of the most powerful instruments of political propaganda. In the aftermath of the air attacks on New York and Washington, D.C. on September 11, 2001, Hollywood responded quickly to requests from President George W. Bush to boost American morale as part of the White House's 'War on Terrorism'. The stars of a new film, Steven Soderbergh's *Ocean's 11*, visited American troops in Turkey, while Oscar-winning director Chuck Workman made *The Spirit of America*, a three-minute, rapid-fire montage film shown on more than 9,000 American cinema screens alongside feature trailers in December. This short featured clips from 110 of Hollywood's best-loved movies and was designed, as producer Michael Rhodes put it, to celebrate the United States 'in all its diversity ... [and] to find a way for people to feel good again'.[3]

The Cold War stands out as the most enduring international political conflict of the twentieth century, occupying either three-quarters or one half of it, depending on whether the war is dated from 1917 or 1945. Propaganda inevitably played a vital role in this most ideological and psychological of conflicts. Moreover, unlike in other, shorter wars of the century, the uses to which propaganda were put grew in number and sophistication as the Cold War progressed, keeping pace with the global social and technological developments which the twentieth century brought. The most important of these developments concerned the available means of mass communication and information, the cogs in all propaganda wars. At the time of the Bolshevik Revolution, for instance, large proportions of the mainly peasant populations of Eastern Europe - a region that stood at the very epicentre of the Cold War - could barely read newspapers and had not even seen a radio or film. In contrast, by the late 1980s, the people of this region took these media for granted. Many of them also had access to computers, video and satellite television, some supplied from the West for propaganda purposes.[4] The recent 'cultural turn' in Cold War studies reflects the importance scholars now attach to the part that mass media and propaganda had not only in causing the eventual collapse of communism in Eastern Europe, but also in helping to make the Cold War a cultural as well as a political phenomenon.[5]

There is a considerable body of work on Cold War cinema, much of which concentrates on Hollywood during the notorious McCarthy era, roughly 1948-54.[6] This chapter builds on previous scholarship by comparing the treatment of the Cold War by the American and British film industries, with particular emphasis on feature films made between the late 1940s and mid-1960s. This was arguably the most crucial phase of the Cold War, when the territorial, political and rhetorical boundaries of the conflict were established and the machinery of propaganda was constructed. It was also during this period of the Cold War that cinema's potential for public influence was at its peak because it was the dominant visual mass entertainment form in both countries and elsewhere. Moreover, because these two film industries, particularly Hollywood, had a significant share of overseas markets, they were also able to project Cold War images internationally.[7] The chapter first offers a set of general comments about cinema's role in the Cold War. Sections two and three then explore the similarities and differences between the approaches towards the Cold War taken by the American and British film industries. This is done both in terms of output - the types of films produced and Cold War subjects covered - and by examining whether the well-documented political pressure on Hollywood during this period was in any way mirrored in Britain. I will argue that, despite the overall strong resemblance between British and American Cold War cinema, the two industries also showed signs of being at odds with one another - economically, stylistically and ideologically. This contrasts with the more homogeneous approach towards the Cold War taken by Eastern bloc filmmakers during the same period. The final section of the chapter looks briefly at how television's challenge to cinema led to a new phase in the Cold War from the early 1960s onwards, one in which visual propaganda could achieve even greater immediacy and intimacy.

Cinema and the Cold War: an overview

The cinematic world did not wait for the start of the Cold War proper - that is, after 1945 - before contributing to the conflict. From 1917 onwards filmmakers in both the East and the West played a central role in the cultural and ideological struggle between communism and capitalism. Tightly controlled by the Communist Party from the outset, early Soviet cinema projected an imposing set of politically and aesthetically revolutionary images in which the new workers' paradise fought valiantly against evil priests, spies, landowners, officers and capitalists.[8] In Hollywood, silent films like D.W. Griffith's *Orphans of the Storm* (1921), which drew comparisons between the excesses of the French revolutionary Jacobins and contemporary events in Russia, set the tone for other inter-war American movies by depicting the threat of Bolshevism in strikingly ghoulish terms.[9] Early Cold War British films were less lurid than their American counterparts. They were, nonetheless, equally clear as to the alien nature of communism. One, Phil Rosen's 1934 melodrama, *Forbidden Territory*, told the story of the daring rescue of an English baronet's son from a Soviet prison camp, and portrayed Stalin's 'new Russia' as economically backward, politically paranoid and socially cheerless.[10]

However, the high point of Cold War cinema in the USA and Britain can be dated to between 1948 - when the first full-blown Hollywood Cold War movie, William Wellman's *The Iron Curtain*, appeared - and 1964, the year which saw the release of perhaps the best known of all 'anti-Cold War' films, Stanley Kubrick's seminal black satire on nuclear deterrence theory, *Dr Strangelove*.[11] This 16-year period saw the release of approximately 300 British and American feature films which commented *directly* in one way or another on the Cold War.[12] It was also during this period that the British and American governments – together with others in the East - put the greatest effort into using the cinema as a Cold War propaganda instrument because of its perceived power relative to other mass media.[13] From the early 1960s onwards cinema began to take a back seat to television on the propaganda front. East-West détente notwithstanding, movies about the Cold War continued to be made but their various tales of espionage, subversion and nuclear war tended to echo films of an earlier generation without much innovation ideologically, thematically or technically. Thus, it might be said that the zenith of wartime cinema in general can be dated to the fifty-year period between 1914 and 1964 – taking in the First World War, the Second World War, and the First Cold War. Following this line of thought, the Cold War perhaps rank as the longest and last of all the great international cinematic propaganda wars.

Throughout the Cold War books, newspapers and the radio were constant sources of information and persuasion. The advantage that cinema had over these mass media was of course its ability to capture and project events and issues visually. From the perspective of Western audiences, this lent film great power in relation to the Cold War in two particular ways. Firstly, newsreels, documentaries and feature films managed to 'open a window' on conditions behind the Iron Curtain, that mysterious 'sub-universe' virtually cut off from the West after 1945. Far more than press or radio reports, these images, sometimes enhanced by location footage, actually allowed people in the West to 'see' how their counterparts lived in the East and thus to learn what communism had to offer them. Cinema's second chief strong point was its capacity to evoke and provoke people's feelings about a subject that most governments tried to render taboo – nuclear war. It is in these two areas especially - the depiction of life in the East on the one hand, and the implications for the world of nuclear science on the other - that the cinema excelled, providing some of the most compelling and lasting images of the Cold War. Excellent examples of the former are *The Third Man* (1949) and *The Man Between* (1953), two British-made espionage-cum-crime thrillers shot by Sir Carol Reed on location in Vienna and Berlin respectively. Typical of the latter category are the US-made post-World-War-Three Australian drama *On the Beach* (Stanley Kramer, 1959) and science-fiction classic *The Day the Earth Stood Still* (Robert Wise, 1951).[14]

The Cold War is often thought to have inflicted serious damage on the film business at a time when, given the competition from other parts of the flourishing post-Second World War leisure industry, it could least afford it. This belief largely derives from the vociferous complaints made by several Hollywood studio owners in the late 1940s about being forced to make so many overtly anti-communist movies at the behest of politicians. Audiences had always shunned politically oriented films, the owners argued, and the likes of R.G. Springsteen's *The Red Menace* (1949) and George Sherman's *Spy Hunt* (1950) proved to be no exception.[15] Looked at differently, however, the Cold War might have brought the film industries on both sides of the Atlantic commercial benefit. Like all wars, with their customary moral polarities and sensationalised accounts of bravery and death, the Cold War was easy to exploit both in fact and fiction cinematic forms. This was especially the case when combat units went into action – Hollywood made 52 films about the Korean War alone in the 1950s, for instance.[16] The Cold War also gave established genres involving traitors, spies and scientists especially a new lease of life, while family melodramas, Westerns, Imperial adventures, science-fiction and horror yarns were readily adaptable to Cold War situations (as we shall see). It might be argued that certain directors owed their living in large part to the Cold War. These include Sam Fuller, the fervently anti-communist Hollywood director of two Korean War movies, *Steel Helmet* and *Fixed Bayonets* (both released in 1951), the atomic secrets melodrama *Pickup on South Street* (1953), the Alaskan-based anti-Chinese atomic thriller *Hell and High Water* (1954), and an early Vietnam War film, *China Gate* (1957). Similarly, a number of actors had the Cold War to thank for helping to make them stars. These include Michael Caine, courtesy of his role as the downbeat MI5 agent Harry Palmer in the British-made *The Ipcress File* (Sidney J. Furie, 1965), *Funeral in Berlin* (Guy Hamilton, 1966) and *Billion Dollar Brain* (Ken Russell, 1967); and the American actors Sylvester Stallone and Chuck Norris, who became household names during the Second Cold War of the 1980s through their roles as muscle-bound Vietnam War veterans in the *Rambo* and *Missing in Action* trilogies respectively.[17] Finally, while the markets of the communist world remained largely closed off to American and British films during the Cold War for political reasons, aggressive cultural diplomacy conducted by state-run Cold War propaganda organisations like the United States Information Agency helped open up other markets in Western Europe, Latin America and Asia which had previously been less accessible. The longer the Cold War went on, the longer and more powerful Hollywood's reach grew.[18]

The role played by the USIA in promoting film for economic and political purposes during the Cold War was by no means unique. Each belligerent in the conflict in some fashion or other operated official propaganda strategies incorporating film. The Cold War was a total war, especially in terms of the importance of propaganda. Unlike the First and Second World Wars, however, in which war had been officially declared, the British and American governments were less free to control the mass media overtly. Indeed, the difference between the freedom given to media in the West and their suppression under communism stood at the very heart of the official American and British propaganda campaigns. An important theme of analysis is, therefore, how London and Washington sought to exert a subtle influence on cinematic output during the Cold War, and how far they succeeded.

American and British Cold War cinema: similarities

Between 1948 and 1964 the American and British film industries followed a similar pattern of Cold War coverage. This can be broken down into three stages. Stage one, 1948-1952, saw most films concentrate on the threat posed to democracy and national security by communist fifth columnism. During this period Hollywood produced a bevy of 'red-baiting' A- and B-pictures that achieved almost instant notoriety among critics for their transparently propagandistic portrayal of the CPUSA's villainy, sabotage and murder. Now often seen affectionately as eccentric period pieces, movies such as Howard Hughes's witch-hunting *The Woman on Pier 13* (AKA *I Married a Communist*, 1949) and Leo McCarey's paean to Catholicism *My Son John* (1952) feverishly reflected the political traumas that characterised so much of Cold-War America in the 1940s and 1950s.[19] Britain's first Cold War movie, Victor Saville's *Conspirator* (1949), told the story of a traitorous Guards officer selling secrets to the Soviet Union. Two years later, in Roy Boulting's *High Treason* (1951), a thriller about a Moscow-inspired plot to cripple Britain's electricity supply as the prelude to a coup d'etat, communists appear to have infiltrated not just the military but corner shops, music clubs and Parliament.[20] To an extent these movies simply amounted to a retooling of Second World War plot lines, in which communists played the new Nazi infiltrators with identikit personality flaws, false idealism and brutal methods. In some cases the 'Red-fascist' totalitarian link was made explicit. In Hollywood's *The Whip Hand* (William Cameron Menzies, 1951), for example, Otto Waldis stars as a former Nazi scientist since converted to communism who is carrying out germ warfare experiments in middle-town America.[21] The subversion theme also doubtless resonated strongly with audiences on both sides of the Atlantic all too familiar with the recent unmasking of real-life Soviet spies like Julius and Ethel Rosenberg, Klaus Fuchs, and Guy Burgess and Donald Maclean.

Stage two, the mid-1950s, saw the threat from the enemy within give way to the threat from the enemy without. As the highly-charged domestic Red Scares fizzled out in Britain and the United States, and filmmakers looked to exploit the Cold War's increasingly global reach, so a number of movies focused on communism's presence in the growing Eastern bloc or on the ambiguities of colonial 'liberation' in the Third World. Hollywood's Indian star, Sabu, and Johnny Weissmuller (formerly 'Tarzan', now the hunter 'Jungle Jim') fought communist rebels in tropical islands in Hollywood's *Savage Drums* (William Berke, 1951) and *Savage Mutiny* (Spencer G. Bennet, 1953) respectively. Britain's much-loved 'Cinema of Empire' was given a Cold War makeover with the appearance of left-wing troublemakers in *Simba* (Brian Desmond Hurst, 1955) and *Windom's Way* (Ronald Neame, 1957).[22] At the same time, the Cold War began in other films to take on a more institutionalised appearance, with stories of the East and the West settling down into their own mutually exclusive ways of life. Other movies showed how Cold War tensions could be invoked as much for narrative as for ideological purposes. A good example of this was Robert Aldrich's US-made film noir classic *Kiss me Deadly* (1955). Here the hero, private detective Mike Hammer (Ralph Meeker), prevents crooks from stealing a case of radioactive material, but his motives have less to do with patriotism than with his desire to turn a profit and wreak personal vengeance.[23]

Stage three, in the late 1950s and early to mid-1960s, witnessed a significant shift on the part of a small body of filmmakers towards a more critical approach towards the Cold War. These movies tended to fall into three categories: those, like Hollywood's *North by Northwest* (Alfred Hitchcock, 1959) and Britain's *The Deadly Affair* (Sidney Lumet, 1966), that exposed the cynicism of Cold War spying; satirical swipes at anti-communist paranoia, like Charlie Chaplin's *A King in New York,* made in Britain in 1956, or US consumerism, like Hollywood's Berlin-set *One, Two, Three* (Billy Wilder's, 1961); or films that translated the anxieties about nuclear science expressed in earlier sci-fi horror movies like Gordon Douglas's *Them!* (USA, 1954) into actual criticism of the nuclear arms race or the world being created under the Bomb's umbrella, such as Joseph Losey's *The Damned* (Britain, 1961).[24] It must be emphasised, however, that such films were very much in the minority throughout our whole period, and that the vast bulk of British and American Cold War films made from the 1940s to the 1960s (and beyond) projected Orthodox Western values. In other words, British and American audiences overall had access to a cinematic view that depicted the Cold War confrontation in simple black-and-white terms of good versus evil, that represented the West as morally, economically and politically superior to the East, and that portrayed the West's military and intelligence agencies as capable, trustworthy and rational.

If the two industries shared a similar Cold War trajectory politically, they were almost equally versatile in terms of their utilisation of genres and film styles. Reference has already been made to genres normally associated with war – combat films and espionage thrillers. I have also mentioned the Cold War's particular suitability for cinematic representations of The Other – either in science-fiction forms (for example, radioactive monsters), or in dramatic or melodramatic depictions of life on the other side, behind the Iron Curtain. But Cold War messages were also transmitted, consciously and unconsciously, in comedies: for example about Russian tourists in Britain (Gordon Parry's *Friends and Neighbours,* [Britain, 1959]) or uranium immunity (Leslie H. Martinson's *The Atomic Kid* [USA, 1954]); in religious films or Biblical epics: Peter Glenville's *The Prisoner* (Britain, 1955) and Cecil B. DeMille's *The Ten Commandments* (USA, 1956); in historical films and biopics: Gordon Douglas's *Rogues of Sherwood Forest* (USA, 1950) and Irving Pichel's *Martin Luther* (USA/Germany, 1953); and in Westerns: John Ford's *Rio Grande* (USA, 1950) and Fred Zinneman's *High Noon* (USA, 1952).[25] Both British and American cinema were to some extent characterised by a new realism after the Second World War, a factor which arguably helped bring a greater sense of authority to dramas or docu-dramas that portrayed communism within the workplace, like *I Was a Communist for the FBI* (Gordon Douglas, 1951) and *The Angry Silence* (Guy Green, 1960). Furthermore, technical innovations in the cinema in the 1950s allowed for the creation of potentially more powerful propagandistic images. CinemaScope's wide-screen format, for instance, lent considerable force to films like *The Robe* (Henry Koster, 1953) and *The Damned.*[26]

The third notable feature that the two film industries had in common was the breadth of Cold War subjects they addressed. Soviet cinema, in contrast, was in this sense far more constricted, especially during Stalin's later years.[27]

Hollywood and British films depicted the threat of communist subversion, including, interestingly, by highlighting their country's weak points – namely Britain's class system and America's racial divisions;[28] they acted out political situations based on actual events, such as the 1956 Hungarian Uprising;[29] they highlighted the differences between communism and liberal democracy by depicting lifestyles and conditions on both sides the Cold War divide, mainly in Europe but also in Asia;[30] they satirised politicians and events;[31] they created imaginary military and espionage engagements among Cold War enemies;[32] and they depicted nuclear war scenarios.[33] It should be noted of course that this is only the tip of the iceberg for, as indicated above, Cold War subtexts were embedded within a range of seemingly unrelated genres. Indeed, it might be argued that it was via movies like the celebrated comedies made in the late 1940s and early 1950s by the highly patriotic Michael Balcon at Britain's Ealing Studios, or Hollywood's extravagant musicals of the same period which, in the words of Peter Biskind, 'taught us to stop worrying and love the Fifties', that Western values were projected most powerfully. Recognising this is vital given the given the apparently apolitical nature of so much of the West's Cold War culture compared with that in the more controlled East.[34] The chief Cold War subject that both British and American cinema conspicuously did not cover in anything like the depth of the others above was what World War Three might look like and the chances of surviving it. Even *Dr Strangelove*, for instance, one of the very few films made in which a nuclear disaster is not averted, effectively ends when Major 'King' Kong (played by Slim Pickens) rodeo-rides his bomb into oblivion. Government-sponsored nuclear civil defence shorts did appear regularly but, by teaching children to duck-and-cover, for instance, these sought to allay fears about the holocaust's impact rather than explain all its horrors.[35]

The final similarity in this section relates to the connection between the film industries and the machinery of government propaganda. Unlike in the Soviet Union, in the United States and Britain during the Cold War cinema was not an instrument of the state. There were no state-run studios or any central state administrative body for cinema (Goskino in the USSR). Nor was there any direct equivalent of the British Ministry of Information or American Office of War Information, organisations set up in the Second World War to ensure that media output accorded with 'the national interest'. During the Cold War most American and British filmmakers tended to support the fight against communism and the Soviet Union out of conviction and economic self-interest, rather than because of direct control by the state. That said, there was common scope for political and official influence in both countries, identifiable in four ways.

First, socially and politically conservative censorship bodies within the industries – the British Board of Film Censors and the US Production Code Administration - acted as gatekeepers for the status quo, discouraging, cutting or banning films they deemed 'controversial'. The well-established links between these bodies and government were augmented during the Cold War by the policing roles of key individuals and organisations. J. Arthur Rank, for instance, who owned more than half of Britain's movie studios in 1945, frowned upon any film projects that undermined his Conservative and Christian values.[36] In the United States the Catholic National Legion of Decency, the guardian of the big screen's moral and political rectitude since the 1930s, continued to wield considerable power in Hollywood into the 1950s. This militantly right-wing pressure group was joined in the post-1945 period by another, Hollywood's own

Motion Picture Alliance for the Preservation of American Ideals. Formed by reactionaries like Eric Johnston, president of the Motion Picture Producers' Association, and Roy Brewer, the fiercely anti-communist leader of International Alliance of Theatrical Stage Employees, this group issued regular advice to filmmakers on how they might best express their patriotism. In 1948 it distributed *A Screen Guide for Americans*, replete with chapters calling on studios not to 'smear the free enterprise system' or 'deify the common man'.[37]

Second, this predisposition towards the 'containment' of radical or left-wing tendencies within the film industries was strengthened by outside political pressures. As is well documented, in the United States this came mainly in the form of the Committee on Un-American Activities of the House of Representatives, whose investigations of Hollywood in 1947 and 1951 helped lead to the blacklisting of dozens of real and suspected communists in the film community into the 1960s. J. Edgar Hoover's Federal Bureau of Investigation worked alongside HUAC, condemning as dangerously subversive those filmmakers, like Charlie Chaplin, whose patriotic credentials they considered not up to the mark, and hiring industry insiders like the post-war Screen Actors Guild president, Ronald Reagan, as undercover agents.[38] By contrast, the British film industry was neither publicly investigated for evidence of communist subterfuge nor coerced by politicians into making anti-Soviet films. However, the traditionally close ties between Whitehall and the industry, made even firmer during the Second World War, meant that many filmmakers were fully aware of the government's anti-communist measures in the late 1940s and early 1950s, including Prime Minister Clement Attlee's creation of a special Cabinet Committee on Subversive Activities. Many also knew of the BBC's informal blacklisting of real or alleged communist employees, an exercise overseen by MI5. Certainly, no actor, cameraman or director could afford to be smeared as a communist when jobs became increasingly difficult to find once audiences started to plummet in the 1950s.[39] These political pressures overlapped with the fears held by many at the higher levels of both film industries during this period that the film trade unions were too powerful and communist-dominated. Indeed, historians have tended to overlook the fact that at least some of the anti-communist movies made during the 1940s and 1950s were as much a reflection of politics *within* the film industry as outside it.[40]

Thirdly, government also acted in more constructive ways, that is by openly sponsoring or lending assistance to films which supported the official Cold War consensus. These films might or might not have been seen as official propaganda, depending on the audience's alertness and frankness of the movie credits. Both the US Pentagon and the British War Office assisted filmmakers in the form of bases, equipment and film clips, often in exchange for the approval of scripts. The resulting extraordinarily strong presence of the military on screen during the First Cold War took various forms. On one level, films like the short documentary about the Berlin Blockade released by British Movietone News in 1949, *Berlin Airlift*, and Hollywood's sentimental flag-waver about the United States's nuclear strike force, *Strategic Air Command* (Anthony Mann, 1955), sent a clear message to cinema-goers: that the Cold War required bravery, teamwork, even the ultimate sacrifice.[41] On another level, the retelling of the 'good war' against Fascism in scores of British and American films of the 1950s helped audiences to recognise the importance of military preparedness and the dangers of trusting extremist, dictatorial regimes in general. (The lesson was even easier to learn when the Red Army's contribution to the defeat of Nazi Germany was excised, as was the case with most of these Second World War films.)[42] On a slightly different tack, the British Treasury and Central Office of Information regularly sponsored short films calling for greater economic productivity and co-operation between trade unions and management, partly to avert strikes and partly to advertise the benefits of increased affluence to all.[43] The FBI helped script docu-dramas like *Walk East on Beacon* (Alfred Werker, 1952) which extolled the virtues of Hoover's G-men outsmarting Soviet spies.[44] And the Motion Picture division of the USIA produced high-quality documentaries for the international market on, among other things, American racial desegregation and the space race.[45]

In more creative ways still, government also established a covert alliance with a large number of powerful filmmakers in order to communicate the official Cold War line more discreetly. Organisations like the USIA, the Psychological Strategy Board, which co-ordinated US Cold War psychological warfare in the early 1950s, and the Information Research Department, the British Foreign Office's anti-communist propaganda arm, all served as a link between official propagandists and the film community, advising filmmakers on how to transmit negative and positive images about the Cold War. The best example of this was the so-called 'Militant Liberty' campaign of the 1950s, which secretly brought together CIA officials and a consortium of Hollywood actors, producers and directors who were willing and able to insert into films 'the right ideas with the proper subtlety' for domestic and overseas audiences. The legendary studio owner and director Cecil B. DeMille, who was appointed as the USIA's chief film consultant, director John Ford, and the actor John Wayne were among the most enthusiastic participants in this campaign.[46] The CIA even placed agents within the film community to alter film content. One of them, the head of censorship at Paramount Studios, Luigi Luraschi, developed industry-wide powers, persuading heavyweight producers like Darryl Zanuck at 20th Century-Fox to 'kill' anything that resembled a 'commie picture' and cajoling the Academy of Motion Picture Arts and Sciences to prohibit or promote awards favourable to US interests abroad. These sorts of efforts help to explain Hollywood's pronounced on-screen affirmation of big business and classlessness during the early Cold War.[47] Finally, British and American government propaganda bodies worked in unison on film projects, establishing secret joint Anglo-American enterprises. One example of this is the CIA's and IRD's heavy involvement in the big screen adaptation of George Orwell's novel *Animal Farm* (1945) in 1954.[48]

American and British Cold War cinema: differences

It should come as little surprise to learn that British and American filmmakers covered the Cold War in a similar fashion and that they were both relatively easily co-opted into government propaganda strategies. After all, both film industries were highly centralised and capitalised, they shared the same characteristics of genre production, and they each had an established tradition of deferring to authority during times of war. Their strong support for government policy, mixed with some increasing evidence of anxiety about where the Cold War was leading, also corresponded closely with wider political and mass media opinion within each country.[49] The differences between the two cinemas' approaches towards the Cold War are less obvious than their similarities and are largely concerned with matters of style. Nevertheless, they are significant as they have implications for the Cold War battle for hearts and minds overall.

The first point of contrast relates to the bluntness of the propaganda message. British-made Cold War films were generally less crude or didactic than their American counterparts in presenting the Soviet threat and the differences between communism and capitalism. To be sure, both industries were capable of producing equally fanciful story lines. Compare, for instance, Hollywood's *Attack of the Fifty Foot Woman* (Nathan Hertz, 1958), which sees a giant radioactive Californian wreaking vengeance on her unfaithful husband, or *Red Planet Mars* (Harry Horner, 1952), in which a religious revival in Russia is prompted by the discovery that Mars is a Christian civilisation, with Britain's *The Little Red Monkey* (Ken Hughes, 1954), which pits the police Special Branch against a villainous primate trained by Maoists to murder Eastern bloc defectors.[50] But no British film was as virulently anti-communist or as anti-liberal as, for example, Hollywood's *Big Jim McLain* (Edward Ludwig, 1952), which alleged Soviet use of bacteriological warfare in Hawaii and equated Cold War dissent with treason, or *Five Gates to Hell* (James Clavell, 1959), in which Vietnamese communists crucify a nun and ration out captive female nurses as the spoils of war.[51] This not to say that British films were less politically motivated, rather that their ideological coloration shone less brightly. Unlike Hollywood movies, for instance, very few British Cold War films actually mentioned communists by name. Instead, audiences were left to reach their own conclusions about the source of organised domestic political deviancy and economic disruption, albeit after many clear signals. It might be argued that by playing off against the insensate hatred of Hollywood's more extreme Cold War fare, British films faithfully reflected that society's more moderate self-image. Certainly, Britain's Cold War cinema was less arrogantly nationalist than Hollywood's, parts of which suggested that the United States had unique democratic credentials and consequently a missionary-like duty to save the world from communism. Some American government propagandists did indeed believe this and so it is not surprising to see such views in American movies. For their part, official British propagandists tended to criticise their American colleagues for being too bullish, preferring instead to take what they saw as a scalpel rather than a hammer to the task of persuading people of the superiority of Western values over those of the East.[52]

This difference of opinion between London and Washington over the tone and technique of Cold War propaganda leads us to another point: that of the competition between the British and American film industries during the Cold War. Rivalry not only manifested itself in terms of a fight for the share of their own and overseas markets, but also over which images and plot lines best served the West's propaganda cause. Close analysis of British and American Cold War movies shows that there was more than one way of selling democracy. As might be expected, American films tended to promote the benefits of Western consumerism and materialism more stridently than their British counterparts. Indeed, in some films the luxuries of fine clothing and fast cars were depicted as one of the West's key weapons – to induce defectors from the Eastern bloc, for instance, in Josef von Sternberg's *Jet Pilot* (1957). In contrast, British films were more inclined than Hollywood to extol the virtues of social democracy, implying even that Britain's reputation for progressive pragmatism married to liberal conciliation stood as a 'third way' between American-style capitalism and Soviet communism. The best example of this is Bernard Miles' *Chance of a Lifetime*

(1950), which sees shop-floor employees and management take joint ownership of a small firm of agricultural engineers.[53] American films also placed a greater emphasis than British movies on the superpower confrontation, downplaying London's role in the Cold War in the process. This is perhaps only natural given Washington's military and economic superiority, but it does illustrate how certain aspects of the Cold War could be accentuated over others, aspects that might have militated against feelings of Anglo-American solidarity for some in the audience. Some films saw British and Americans working together, such as the British-made *Highly Dangerous* (Roy Baker, 1950) and the US-made *Tangier Incident* (Lew Landers, 1953). Others pointed to the weaknesses of their ally, for example Hollywood's *The Red Danube* (George Sidney, 1949), which took a swipe at the British military.[54] Thus, British and American films exemplify the less straitjacketed approach taken towards film propaganda in the West compared with in Eastern Europe, where the Soviet Union's wishes tended to dominate and the solidity of the Warsaw Pact was not questioned. The different cinematic interpretations of democracy also highlight how elastic it and other terms like 'freedom' and 'totalitarianism' were that stood at the heart of the West's information crusade.

It is via the greater latitude given by the state to filmmakers in the West than in the East that a third difference between British and American Cold War cinema emerges – the production in Britain of proportionately more films that questioned official Cold War values than in the United States. Historians have identified signs of Cold War dissent in a range of Hollywood movies made in the 1950s. Lary May, for example, argues that the film noir of left-wing directors like John Huston and Billy Wilder, by asking its audience to side with criminals and by celebrating the dignity of populist communitarianism, amounted to a subtle critique of the ethos of liberal capitalism that so suffused Cold-War America.[55] Be that as it may, Hollywood produced only a handful of films from the mid-1950s to the mid-1960s that could be read categorically by audiences as direct critiques of either American Cold-War society or US Cold War strategy. These include *Storm Center* (Daniel Taradash, 1956), *The Manchurian Candidate* (John Frankenheimer, 1962) and *Fail Safe* (Sidney Lumet, 1964).[56] In contrast, in the same period the British film industry produced a steady stream of movies that questioned the West's reputation for liberty and tolerance (*The Young Lovers*, Anthony Asquith, 1954), lampooned the British secret services (*Our Man in Havana*, Carol Reed, 1959), or raised the spectre of a nuclear Armageddon (*Dr. Strangelove*, Stanley Kubrick, 1964). This difference can be explained to some extent by the fact that British filmmakers suffered far less political coercion than their American counterparts – there was no equivalent to the jailed Hollywood Ten in Britain, no loyalty oaths were imposed among film Guilds, and there was no outright blacklisting. Indeed, several Hollywood blacklistees' found work in Britain and contributed to Cold War dissent, including Carl Foreman in *The Mouse that Roared* (1959), a satire on Cold War politics and the Bomb, and Joseph Losey in his afore-mentioned *The Damned*.[57] It was also easier for films made in the communist bloc to gain an export licence and be exhibited in Britain compared with in the United States.[58] This said, cinematic dissent was marginalised almost as effectively and certainly more discreetly in Britain where there was no talk of McCarthyite censorship at all. Just as they always had, leftist filmmakers had great difficulty getting money from the all-powerful cinema magnates, especially from the likes of 'King Arthur' Rank and Sir Alexander Korda. Not one pro-Soviet or pro-communist mainstream feature film was made in Britain or the United States during the whole of the First Cold War.[59]

Television takes over from cinema: a new age of visual propaganda

In 1965 television documentary-maker Peter Watkins finished work for the BBC on a film about the after-effects of a nuclear attack on Britain. After taking advice from the government, senior BBC officials decided not to show *The War Game* on the grounds that it was 'too horrifying for the medium of broadcasting'. Instead, the BBC agreed to allow the British Film Institute to distribute the documentary in the cinema. The fact that ministers, the BBC and the press had fewer qualms about *The War Game* being shown at the cinema than on television - it was eventually televised in 1985, to mark the fortieth anniversary of Hiroshima - is a good measure of the diminished influence of the former compared with the latter by the mid-1960s. This episode also helps to reveal the emergence of a new dimension in the Cold War propaganda conflict, one dominated by the special qualities of the ubiquitous, apparently omnipotent small screen in the corner of the living room.[60]

Television and the Cold War grew simultaneously in the United States and Britain in the years following the Second World War, influencing and feeding off each other in important ways. The Cold War provided attractive, often sensational subject matter for the television companies, and the medium shaped the way that American and British people perceived and responded to the Cold War. Television not only offered these people a cheaper way of watching the Cold War than the cinema. It was also able to render experience of the conflict more immediately and with greater intimacy. This was particularly so in respect to news, for which television had become the most relied-upon source in the United States by the end of the 1950s and in Britain by the mid-1960s. For instance, the viewers of daily television broadcasts could actually feel that they were with 'their boys' in Korea in the early 1950s far more than by catching weekly snippets of the war via the cinema newsreels. A decade later, during the 1962 Cuban Missile Crisis, millions of people were glued to television sets around the world awaiting their fate as Khrushchev and Kennedy went to the brink of war.[61] Television's greater power to evoke and provoke emotional responses was just as strong when it came to Cold War entertainment programming, a vast industry that took in dramas, science-fiction shows, situation comedies, children's adventures, talk shows, soap operas and Westerns.[62] Early evidence of this in Britain came in 1954, when BBC Television screened an adaptation of one of the central texts of the Cold War, George Orwell's *Nineteen Eighty-Four* (1949). Many viewers wrote to the corporation to say how shocked and appalled they were by the play's dystopic images, and its 'sadistic' interrogation scenes in particular, beamed straight into their homes. One housewife reportedly died of a heart attack, setting off a heated national debate about television censorship and the relationship between television and violence.[63]

Along with immediacy and intimacy, television's relationship with the Cold War was also more interactive than that of the cinema. Edited images helped set the national and international agenda and programmes sometimes shaped the terms of debate about Cold War policies. For instance, the weekly satire show *That Was the Week That Was*, which ran on BBC Television and the US National Broadcasting Company in the early to mid-1960s, helped set the tone for some of the criticism voiced in the Sixties about the nuclear arms race.

In the United States televised pictures of spectacular rocket launches and views of Earth from outer space helped generate popular enthusiasm for space exploration and the public's consequent willingness to allocate funds for the military space race. Conversely, television coverage of North Vietnamese soldiers occupying the American embassy in Saigon during the 1968 Tet Offensive is often said to have encouraged many Americans to doubt US strategy in South East Asia.[64] Given the power of these and other images, gaining influence over television became the critical aspect of the Cold War propaganda conflict for government. In one important respect this task was easier than guiding the cinema, for there were far fewer television networks than film studios: by 1960 there were three American and two British networks. Research hitherto conducted on the 1940s through to the 1960s suggests that government efforts to control television output – allied to the networks' commercial interests and journalists' predominantly anti-Soviet views – played an important role in the medium's endorsement of prevailing attitudes towards the Cold War in the United States and Britain. Recent work has also focused on the domination of the international market for television programmes by the giant television industries of the United States, Britain and West Germany during the Cold War. By the end of the conflict the United States alone was selling approximately 150,000 hours of television programmes annually. One major contributory factor in the collapse of the wall between West and East Germany in 1989, writes H. Hanke, was the daily dose of television images of 'conspicuous consumption' that the East Germans could view in the context of their own relatively drab lifestyles courtesy of television programmes beamed from the West. [65]

A combination of television's remarkable rise, a drastic cut in cinema attendances, a decline in the Cold War's marketability, and the advent of a period of détente all meant that, by the late 1960s, the golden age of Cold War cinema had come to an end. Nevertheless, millions of people on both sides of the Atlantic remained movie addicts, and filmmakers continued to plunder the Cold War for profit and instruction until the end of the conflict. In keeping with the political fall-out following the United States' defeat in Vietnam, the Watergate scandal and the escalation in the number of high-profile Eastern defectors, in the 1970s films tended either to focus on the world of espionage and double agents or to expose Western complicity and corruption.[66] The latter type of film represented the first and only concerted attempt by mainstream cinema in Britain and the United States to turn conventional wisdom on the Cold War in the West entirely on its head. The Greek-born, US-based Constantin Costa-Gavras was perhaps the best exponent of this school, through such movies as *State of Siege* (1973) and *Missing* (1982), both of which dramatised the United States's involvement in repressive South American regimes.[67] With the renewal of Cold War hostilities following the Soviet invasion of Afghanistan in 1979 and Ronald Reagan's succession to the US presidency in 1981, in the 1980s British and American movies often played quite different tunes. Some British films, like the James Bond vehicle *Octopussy* (John Glen, 1983), were unequivocally anti-Russian, but others such as Chris Bernard's comedy about unemployed Liverpool girls falling in love with a Russian sailor, *A Letter to Brezhnev* (1985), looked forward to the end of the conflict. The majority of American movies, on the other hand, hawkishly invoked Reagan's rhetoric of an 'Evil Empire' centred in Moscow, vilifying the Soviet war in Afghanistan (Kevin Reynolds's *The Beast*, 1988) and glamorising the life of US navy pilots (Tony Scott's *Top Gun*, 1986). Others like

John Milius's *Red Dawn* (1984), in which a Soviet-Cuban invasion of the USA is defeated by a group of American teenagers, were a throwback to the hysterical paranoia the early 1950s.[68] In the mean time, Hollywood continued throughout this period to be a powerful projector overseas of Western affluence, acting in concert with television to penetrate the developing world and the increasingly accessible Eastern bloc.[69]

Hollywood's last major contribution to the Cold War was John McTiernan's *The Hunt for Red October*, a $30 million adaptation of Tom Clancy's novel about a Soviet naval officer (played by the former James Bond, Sean Connery) who defects with his country's state-of-the-art nuclear submarine. When the film went into production in 1989, Russia's underwater fleet posed one of the most critical and immediate threats to the United States. By the time the film was released in 1990, Moscow's hold over Eastern Europe had collapsed and Soviet leader Mikhail Gorbachev had famously declared, in December 1989, that his country no longer considered the United States its enemy. Despite being out of date, *The Hunt for Red October* was a huge commercial success on both sides of the Atlantic, where presumably it was greeted with a mixture of relief and celebration - World War Three had been averted and the West had won the Cold War.[70]

NOTES

1. See Phillip Knightley, *The First Casualty: From the Crimea to the Falklands: The War Correspondent as Hero, Propagandist and Myth Maker* (London: Pan, 1989), pp. 65-78.
2. Rachael Low (with Roger Manvell), *The History of British Film, Volume 1: The History of the British Film 1896-1906* (London: Routledge, 1997), pp. 65-6; Knightley, *The First Casualty*, p. 75.
3. http://www.natoonline.org/spirit.html; The *Guardian*, 18 December 2001, p. 3. The full list of 110 films is printed here. The Guardian also reported that, while The Spirit of America was neither commissioned nor paid for by the White House, it won the backing of Karl Rove, George W. Bush's chief political adviser, who had had a series of meetings with leading lights in the entertainment industry to enlist their services in support of the 'war on terrorism'.
4. Philip M. Taylor, *Global Communications, International Affairs and the Media since 1945* (London: Routledge, 1997), p. 51.
5. For recent examples of this 'cultural turn' in Cold War studies, see, for instance, Frances Stonor Saunders, *Who Paid the Piper? The CIA and the Cultural Cold War* (London: Granta, 1999); Noam Chomsky, *The Cold War and the University* (New York: New Press, 1998); Paul N. Edwards, *The Closed World: Computers and the Politics of Discourse in Cold War America* (Cambridge, MA: MIT Press, 1996); Woody Haut, *Pulp Culture: Hardboiled Fiction and the Cold War* (London: Serpents Tail, 1996); Uta G. Poiger, *Jazz, Rock, and Rebels: Cold War Politics and American Culture in a Divided Germany* (Berkeley, CA: University of California Press, 2000); Jessica Wang, *American Science in an Age of Anxiety: Scientists, Anticommunism and the Cold War* (London: University of

North Carolina Press, 1999); Arch Puddington, *Broadcasting Freedom: The Cold War Triumph of Radio Free Europe and Radio Liberty* (Lexington, KY: University Press of Kentucky, 2000); Esko Salminen, *The Silenced Media: The Propaganda War between Russia and the West in Northern Europe* (New York: St. Martin's Press, 1999); Paul Lashmar and James Oliver, *Britain's Secret Propaganda War, 1948-1977* (Stroud: Sutton, 1998); roundtable on 'Cultural Transfer or Cultural Imperialism', *Diplomatic History*, Vol. 24, No. 3, Summer 2000, pp. 465-535; Kenneth Osgood, 'The Unconventional Cold War', *Journal of Cold War Studies*, Vol. 4, No. 2, Spring 2002, pp. 85-107.

6.   See, for example, Peter Biskind, *Seeing is Believing: How Hollywood Taught Us to Stop Worrying and to Love the Fifties* (London: Pluto, 1984); Nora Sayre, *Running Time: Films of the Cold War* (New York: Dial Press, 1982); Larry Ceplair and Steven Englund, *The Inquisition in Hollywood: Politics in the Film Community, 1930-1960* (London: University of California Press, 1979); Patrick McGilligan and Paul Buhle, *Tender Comrades: A Backstory of the Hollywood Blacklist* (New York: St. Martin's Griffin, 1997); Victor S. Navasky, *Naming Names* (New York: John Calder, 1980); *Film History*, Vol. 10, No. 3, 1998, 'The Cold War and the Movies'; *Film and History*, Vol. 31, Nos. 1 and 2, 2001, 'The Cold War, Parts 1 & 2'.

7.   For cinema attendance figures in the United States and Britain between 1945 and 1965 see Douglas Gomery, 'Transformation of the Hollywood System', in Geoffrey Nowell-Smith (ed.), *The Oxford History of World Cinema* (Oxford: Oxford University Press, 1997), pp. 443-51; Stuart Laing, *Representations of Working Class Life, 1957-1964* (London: Macmillan, 1986), pp. 109-111; John Spraos, *The Decline of the Cinema: An Economist's Report* (London: Allen and Unwin, 1962), p. 14. On the international reach of the British and American film industries see Kerry Segrave, *American Films Abroad: Hollywood's Domination of the World's Movie Screens from the 1890s to the Present* (Jefferson, NC: McFarland and Co., 1997); Geoffrey Macnab, J. *Arthur Rank and the British Film Industry* (London: Routledge, 1994), pp. 219-220; Christine Geraghty, British *Cinema in the Fifties: Gender, Genre and the 'New Look'* (London: Routledge, 2000), pp. 116-7.

8.   On the main themes of early Soviet cinema see Richard Taylor, *Film Propaganda: Soviet Russia and Nazi Germany* (London: I. B. Tauris, 1998), pp. 50-62.

9.   David Manning White and Richard Averson, *The Celluloid Weapon: Social Comment in the American Film* (Boston: Beacon Press, 1972), p. 21.

10. See Tony Shaw, 'Early Warnings of the Red Peril: A Pre-History of Cold War British Cinema, 1917-1939', *Film History*, Vol. 14, No. 4, 2002 (forthcoming).

11. On *The Iron Curtain* see Daniel J. Leab, 'The Iron Curtain (1948): Hollywood's first Cold War movie', *Historical Journal of Film, Radio and Television*, Vol. 8, No. 2, 1988, pp. 153-188. On *Dr. Strangelove* see John Baxter, *Stanley Kubrick: A Biography* (London: HarperCollins, 1997), pp. 165-94; Gary K. Wolfe, 'Dr. Strangelove, Red Alert, and the patterns of paranoia in the 1950s', *Journal of Popular Film*, Vol. 5, No. 1, 1976, pp. 56-67; Lawrence Suid, 'The Pentagon and Hollywood: Dr. Strangelove or: How I learned to Stop Worrying and Love the Bomb', in John E. O'Connor and Martin A. Jackson (eds.), *American History/American Film: Interpreting the Hollywood Image*

(New York: Ungar, 1979), pp. 219-35; George W. Linden, 'Dr. Strangelove or: How I learned to Stop Worrying and Love the Bomb', in Jack Shaheen (ed.), *Nuclear War Films* (Carbondale and Edwardsville: Southern Illinois Press, 1978), pp. 58-67.

12. The figure of 300 feature films has been calculated from two main sources. In 'Hollywood's Cold War', *Journal of Popular Film*, Vol. 3, No. 4, Fall 1974, pp. 334-50, 365-72, Russell E. Shain calculates that there were 156 US-made Cold War feature films released between 1948 and 1962, accounting for approximately 4 % of the total American releases for that period. In my book, *British Cinema and the Cold War: The State, Propaganda and Consensus* (London: I.B. Tauris, 2000), I calculate that 130 British-made Cold War feature films were released between 1945 and 1965, accounting for roughly 6 per cent of the total British releases for that period. See Denis Gifford, *The British Film Catalogue*, Volume 1: Fiction Film, 1895-1994, 3rd edition (London: Fitzroy Dearborn, 2000), pp. 527-755. Shain and I have used similar criteria for defining what constitutes a Cold War movie, namely any film that portrays or evokes something relating directly to the conflict, irrespective of genre. The main difference is that Shain largely omits those science fiction films that could easily be interpreted as Cold War allegories. I should stress that neither of us have included in our calculations the scores of other feature films which commented on Cold War issues indirectly, by, for instance, supporting or undermining traditional pro-capitalist values such as private ownership, free trade, maintaining the status quo, and law and order. These more subtle or unconscious aspects of Cold War cinema will be touched on later in this chapter. A film is categorised as American if made in the country, the same with Britain.

13. On Soviet cinema during this period see Peter Kenez, *Cinema and Soviet Society, 1917-1953* (London: I.B. Tauris, 2001), pp. 185-221; Dmitry Shlapentokh and Vladimir Shlapentokh, *Soviet Cinematography, 1918-1991: Ideological Conflict and Social Reality* (New York: Aldine de Gruyter, 1993), pp. 121-45; Maya Turovskaya, 'Soviet films of the Cold War', in Richard Taylor and Derek Spring (eds.), *Stalinism and Soviet Cinema* (London: Routledge, 1993), pp. 131-41; Graham Roberts, 'A cinema of suspicion or a suspicion of cinema: Soviet film 1945-53', in Gary Rawnsley (ed.), *Cold War Propaganda in the 1950s* (London: Macmillan, 1999), pp. 105-24.

14. G. Tom Poe, 'Historical Spectatorship around and about Stanley Kramer's On the Beach', in Melvyn Stokes and Richard Maltby (eds.), *Hollywood Spectatorship: Changing Perceptions of Cinema Audiences* (London: BFI, 2001), pp. 91-102. In his *Science Fiction in the Movies: An A-Z* (London: Frederick Muller, 1978, p. 22), Roy Pickard calls The Day the Earth Stood Still the first film to deal intelligently with the dangers of international nuclear aggression.

15. Daniel J. Leab, 'How red was my valley: Hollywood, the Cold War film, and I Married A Communist', *Journal of Contemporary History*, Vol. 19 (1984), pp. 62-4.

16. Shain, '*Hollywood's Cold War*', p. 348, note 3. For further details of Hollywood's Korean War films see Susan L. Carruthers, 'Redeeming the captives: Hollywood and the brainwashing of American prisoners of war in Korea', *Film History*, Vol. 10, No. 3, 1998, pp. 275-94; Rick Worland, 'The

Korean War film as family melodrama: The Bridges at Toko-Ri (1954)',
Historical Journal of Film, Radio and Television, Vol. 19, No. 3, 1999, pp. 359-77.

17. Phil Hardy, *Samuel Fuller* (London: Studio Vista, 1970); William Hill, Arise Sir
Michael Caine: *The Biography* (London: John Blake, 2001), pp. 113-36.
Stallone starred as John Rambo in three films: *First Blood* (Ted Kotchoff,
1982), *Rambo: First Blood Part II* (George Pan Cosmatos, 1985) and *Rambo III*
(Peter MacDonald, 1988). Norris starred as Colonel James Braddock in
Missing in Action (Joseph Zeto, 1984), *Missing in Action 2 –The Beginning* (Lance
Hool, 1985), and *Braddock: Missing in Action III* (Aaron Norris, 1988).

18. See, for example, Segrave, American Films Abroad, p. 204; Reinhold
Wagnleitner, *Coca-Colonization and the Cold War: The Cultural Mission of the
United States in Austria after the Second World War* (London: University of North
Carolina Press, 1994); Nezih Erdogan and Dilek Kaya, 'Institutional
intervention in the distribution and exhibition of Hollywood films in
Turkey', *Historical Journal of Film, Radio and Television*, Vol. 22, No. 1, 2002, pp.
47-59.

19. Compare, for instance, Stephen J. Whitfield, *The Culture of the Cold War*
(London: Johns Hopkins University Press, 1996), pp. 136-40, with the more
light-hearted account of Hollywood's early Cold War aimed at the nostalgia
market by Michael Barson and Steven Heller, *Red Scared! The Commie Menace
in Propaganda and Popular Culture* (San Francisco: Chronicle Books, 2001), pp.
74

20. *I Married a Communist* was first released in late 1949 before being pulled and
re-released a few months later as *The Woman on Pier 13*. Though directed by
Robert Stevenson, the film's real creator was Hughes, head of RKO.

21. Stephen Guy, 'High Treason (1951): Britain's Cold War fifth column',
Historical Journal of Film, Radio and Television, Vol. 13, No. 1, 1993, pp. 35-47.

22. *The Whip Hand* review, *Monthly Film Bulletin*, July 1952, p. 92.

23. http://www.mergetel.com/~geostan/mutiny.html; http://www.powell-
pressburger.org/Reviews/Sabu/Rediff.html; Raymond Durgnat, *Mirror for
England* (London: Faber, 1970), p. 81; *Films and Filming*, Vol. 1, No. 6, March
1955; Geraghty, *British Cinema in the Fifties*, pp. 120-32.

24. Biskind, *Seeing is Believing*, pp. 55-6.

25. For more on these films see Donald Spoto, *The Dark Side of Genius: The Life of
Alfred Hitchcock* (London: Plexus, 1983), pp. 404-9; Robert Murphy, *Sixties
British Cinema* (London: British Film Institute, 1992), pp. 221-7; *Monthly Film
Bulletin*, October 1957, p. 123; *Sight and Sound*, Vol. 27, No. 2, Autumn 1957,
pp. 78-9; John McCabe, *Cagney* (London: Aurum Press, 1998), pp. 320-3;
Sayre, *Running Time*, pp. 192-3; Shaw, *British Cinema and the Cold War*, pp. 182-
6.

26. For more on these films see *Monthly Film Bulletin*, December 1959, p. 158;
Mick Broderick, *Nuclear Movies* (London: McFarland and Co., 1991), pp. 11-
12; Tony Shaw, 'Miracles, Martyrs and Martians: Religion and Cold War
Cinematic Propaganda in the 1950s', *Journal of Cold War Studies*, Vol. 4, No. 3,
2002, pp. 3-22; Gary Wills, *John Wayne: The Politics of Celebrity* (London: Faber,
1997), pp. 181-9; Whitfield, *The Culture of the Cold War*, pp. 146-50.

27. Shaw, *British Cinema and the Cold War*, pp. 160-6; Sayre, *Running Time*, pp. 86-
91; John Belton, 'Technology and Innovation', in Nowell-Smith (ed.), *The
Oxford History of World Cinema*, pp. 259-67.

28. Kenez, *Cinema and Soviet Society*, pp. 185-221; Roberts, 'A cinema of suspicion or a suspicion of cinema'; Josephine Woll, *Real Images: Soviet Cinema and the Thaw* (London: I.B. Tauris, 2000).

29. See, for example, Robert Tronson's *Ring of Spies* (Britain, 1963) and Mark Robson's *Trial* (USA, 1955). Murphy, *Sixties British Cinema*, p. 220; *Films and Filming*, Vol. 10, No. 8, May 1964; Daniel J. Leab, 'From even-handedness to red-baiting: The transformation of the novel Trial', *Film History*, Vol. 10, No. 3, 1998, pp. 320-31.

30. See, for example, review of Peter Maxwell's *The Long Shadow* (Britain, 1961) in *Monthly Film Bulletin*, September 1961, pp. 129-30.

31. See, for example, preview of Sydney Gilliat's *State Secret* (Britain, 1950), set in 'Vosnia' (a composite of Franco's Spain and Tito's Yugoslavia), in *Sight and Sound*, Vol. January 1950, pp. 10-12 and review of Elia Kazan's *Man on a Tightrope* (USA, 1953), set in communist Czechoslovakia, in *Monthly Film Bulletin*, June 1953, p. 86.

32. See, for example, Nora Sayre's analysis of George Kaufman's screwball comedy about a bumbling and corrupt US senator, *The Senator Was Indiscreet* (USA, 1947), in *Running Time*, pp. 54-5. See also review of Peter Ustinov's satire on great-power politics, *Romanoff and Juliet* (USA, 1961) in *Monthly Film Bulletin*, July 1961, pp. 95-6.

33. See, for example, review of Steve Sekely's, *Blue Camelia* (USA, 1954) in *Monthly Film Bulletin*, April 1955, p. 56 and Compton Bennett's *Beyond the Curtain* (Britain, 1960) in *Monthly Film Bulletin*, June 1960.

34. See, for example, analysis of Val Guest's *The Day the Earth Caught Fire* (Britain, 1960) in Shaw, *British Cinema and the Cold War*, pp. 135-6 and review of Arch Obeler's Five (USA, 1951) in *Monthly Film Bulletin*, November 1951, p. 356.

35. See Biskind, *Seeing is Believing*, pp. 1-6 especially. On Ealing's projection of a progressive, social democratic consensus during the early Cold War years see Shaw, *British Cinema and the Cold War*, pp. 85-9.

36. On American and British civil defence propaganda see Guy Oakes, 'The Family under Nuclear Attack: American civil defence propaganda in the 1950s', in Rawnsley (ed.), *Cold War Propaganda in the 1950s*, pp. 67-83; Duncan, Campbell, *War Plan UK: The Truth about Civil Defence in Britain* (London: Burnett Books, 1982); Spencer R. Weart, *Nuclear Fear: A History of Images* (London: Harvard University Press, 1988).

37. Macnab, *J. Arthur Rank*, pp. 164, 170, 189.

38. Frank Walsh, *Sin and Censorship: The Catholic Church and the Motion Picture Industry* (New Haven: Yale University Press, 1996); Lary May, *The Big Tomorrow: Hollywood and the Politics of the American Way* (Chicago: University of Chicago Press, 2000), p. 202.

39. Ibid., p. 194, 201-2; Ceplair and Englund, *The Inquisition in Hollywood*; McGilligan and Buhle, *Tender Comrades*; Navasky, *Naming Names*; John A. Noakes, 'Bankers and common men in Bedford Falls: How the FBI determined that It's a Wonderful Life was a subversive movie', *Film History*, Vol. 10, No. 3, 1998, pp. 311-19.

40. Public Record Office, London [hereafter PRO], CAB 130/71/GEN377 Committee on Subversive Activities' minutes, August-September 1951; John C. Tibbets, 'After the fall: revisiting the Cold War - A report on the XVIIth

IAMHIST conference, 25-31 July 1997, Salisbury, MD', *Historical Journal of Film, Radio and Television*, Vol. 18, No. 1, 1998, p. 116.

41. May, *The Big Tomorrow*, pp. 180-9; author's interviews with Roy Boulting about *High Treason*, 30 March and 5 May 1998.

42. Shain, 'Hollywood's Cold War'; PRO INF 6/55 Berlin Airlift; Biskind, *Seeing is Believing*, pp. 64-9.

43. On the different readings of the movies made about the Second World War see, for instance, John Ramsden, 'Refocusing the "people's war": British war films of the 1950s', *Journal of Contemporary History*, Vol. 33, No. 1, January 1998, p. 59; Roger Manvell, *Films and the Second World War* (London: J. M. Dent, 1974); Thomas Doherty, *Projections of War: Hollywood, American Culture, and World War II* (New York: Columbia University Press, 1999).

44. Shaw, *British Cinema and the Cold War*, pp. 146-7.

45. Author's correspondence with Borden Mace, President of RD-DR Corporation (owned by Louis de Rochement, producer of *Walk East on Beacon*) in 1950s, 28 March 1998; review of *Crime of the Century* (British title of *Walk East on Beacon*), *Monthly Film Bulletin*, September 1952.

46. Nicholas J. Cull, 'Auteurs of Ideology: USIA documentary film propaganda in the Kennedy era as seen in Bruce Herschenson's *The Five Cities of June* (1963) and James Blue's The March (1964)', *Film History*, Vol. 10, No. 3, 1998, pp. 295-310.

47. Saunders, *Who Paid the Piper?*, pp. 284-6; Scott Lucas, *Freedom's War: The US Crusade against the Soviet Union 1945-56* (Manchester: Manchester University Press, 1999), pp. 118-21, 224, 269-70, 275.

48. May, *The Big Tomorrow*, pp. 203-4; David N. Eldridge, '"Dear Owen": The CIA, Luigi Luraschi and Hollywood, 1953', *Historical Journal of Film, Radio and Television*, Vol. 20, No. 2, 2000, pp. 149-96.

49. Shaw, *British Cinema and the Cold War*, pp. 91-114.

50. On the coverage of the Cold War by other elements of the mass media in Britain and the United States during the 1940s and 1950s see, for example, Nancy E. Bernhard, *U.S. Television News and Cold War Propaganda 1947-1960* (Cambridge: Cambridge University Press, 1999); Michael Curtin, *Redeeming the Wasteland: Television Documentary and Cold War Politics* (New Brunswick, NJ: Rutgers University Press, 1995); James Aronson, *The Press and the Cold War* (Indianapolis: Bobbs-Merrill, 1970); Richard A. Schwartz, Cold *War Culture: Media and the Arts, 1945-1990* (New York: Checkmark Books, 2000); Alan J. Foster, 'The British Press and the Coming of the Cold War' in Anne Deighton (ed.), *Britain and the First Cold War* (New York: Macmillan, 1990), pp. 11-31; Tony Shaw, 'The British Popular Press and the Early Cold War', *History*, Vol. 83, No. 269, Jan. 1998, pp. 66-85.

51. *Monthly Film Bulletin*, February 1958, p. 31; *Monthly Film Bulletin*, October 1952, pp. 140-1; David Quinlan, *British Sound Films: The Studio Years, 1928-1959* (London: Batsford, 1984), p. 339.

52. *Monthly Film Bulletin*, December 1952, p. 165; *Monthly Film Bulletin*, January 1960, p. 7.

53. Lucas, *Freedom's War*, p. 49; Lashmar and Oliver, *Britain's Secret Propaganda War*, p. 42.

54. *Monthly Film Bulletin*, December 1957, p. 147; May, *The Big Tomorrow*, p. 275.

55. Shaw, *British Cinema and the Cold War*, pp. 69-70; *Monthly Film Bulletin*, May 1953, p. 76; *Monthly Film Bulletin*, February-March 1950, pp. 30-1.

56. May, *The Big Tomorrow*, pp. 215-56.

57. Sayre, *Running Time*, pp. 176-7; Greil Marcus, *The Manchurian Candidate* (London: British Film Institute, 2002); Robert Cole, *Propaganda in Twentieth Century War and Politics: An Annotated Bibliography* (Pasadena, CA: The Scarecrow Press, 1996), p. 326.

58. Durgnat, *Mirror for England*, p. 86; *Monthly Film Bulletin*, January 1960, p. 4; Shaw, *British Cinema and the Cold War*, pp. 123-4, 177-86.

59. Shaw, *British Cinema and the Cold War*, pp. 186-91; Segrave, *American Films Abroad*, p. 232; Baruch Hazan, *Soviet International Propaganda* (Ann Arbor, Michigan: Ardis, 1982), pp. 66-9.

60. On the slow and halting development of an oppositional film movement in Britain post-1945 see Margaret Dickinson (ed.), *Rogue Reels: Oppositional Film in Britain, 1945-1990* (London: British Film Institute, 1999).

61. BBC Written Archives Centre, Caversham [hereafter BBC WAC]: T56/266/1-2 *The War Game* - Research files; T56/265/1 The War Game post-production script; T16/679/1 TV Policy *The War Game* file 1a (1963-5) and 1b (1966-68).

62. On the Korean War and television see Bernhard, *U.S. Television News and Cold War Propaganda*, pp. 94-149 and Howard Smith, 'The BBC Television Newsreel and the Korean war', *Historical Journal of Film, Radio and Television*, Vol. 8, No. 3, 1988, pp. 227-52. On television during the Cuban missile crisis see Thomas Sorenson, *The Word War: The Story of American Propaganda* (New York: Harper and Row, 1968), pp. 197-213; Geoffrey Cox, *See it Happen: The Making of ITN* (London: Bodley Head, 1983), pp. 151.

63. See, for instance, Fred J. MacDonald, 'The Cold War as Entertainment in 'Fifties Television', *Journal of Popular Film and Television*, Vol. 7, No. 1, 1988, pp. 3-31 and Schwartz, *Cold War Culture: Media and the Arts*, pp. 306-28.

64. BBC WAC: AC T5/362/2 Television Drama Nineteen Eighty-Four (1954), File 2; Press Cuttings P6555, Book 14a Television Programmes, 1953-4; Transcript of *Panorama*, 15 December 1954; Jason Jacobs, *The Intimate Screen: Early British Television Drama* (Oxford: Oxford University Press, 2000), pp. 139-55.

65. Asa Briggs, *The History of Broadcasting in the UK: Volume 5, Competition* (Oxford: Oxford University Press, 1995), pp. 350-76. For the debate surrounding the effect of the media coverage of the Tet offensive on US opinion and government policy see Daniel C. Hallin, *The 'Uncensored War'* (Berkeley, CA: University of California Press, 1989), pp. 168-73.

66. See, for example, Briggs, *Competition*, passim; Bernhard, *U.S. Television News and Cold War Propaganda*; Michael Curtin, *Redeeming the Wasteland*; Garth Jowett and Victoria O'Donnell, *Propaganda and Persuasion* (London: Sage, 1999), pp. 144-7; H. Hanke, 'Media culture in the GDR: Characteristics, processes, and problems', *Media, Culture, and Society*, Vol. 12, No. 2, 1990, pp. 175-193.

67. Nicholas Pronay, 'British film sources for the Cold War: The disappearance of the cinema-going public', *Historical Journal of Film, Radio and Television*, Vol. 13, No. 1, 1993, pp. 7-17 and microfiche.

68. On Missing see Robert Brent Toplin, *History by Hollywood: The Use and Abuse of the American Past* (Chicago: University of Illinois Press, 1996), pp. 103-26.
69. James Chapman, *Licence To Thrill: A Cultural History of the James Bond Films* (London: I. B. Tauris, 1999), 200-17; Pronay, 'British film sources for the Cold War', microfiche; Schwartz, *Cold War Culture: Media and the Arts*, p. 101.
70. Taylor, *Global Communications*, pp. 53-4; Segrave, *American Films Abroad*, pp. 186-279.
71. Lee Pfeiffer and Philip Lisa, *The Films of Sean Connery* (New York: Citadal, 1993), pp. 238-41.

Chapter Eleven
'THE MAN IN ED MURROW'S SHOES': CARL T. ROWAN AS DIRECTOR OF THE UNITED STATES INFORMATION AGENCY, 1964-65
Nicholas J. Cull

The Cold War was a war of ideas: a mutual struggle between the USA and the USSR and their clients for the minds of the opposing public and for the imaginations of the non-aligned peoples of the world. The chief agent for the United States in this battle was the United States Information Agency (USIA), known overseas as the United States Information Service (USIS): a massive international publicity and propaganda operation created in 1953 to unite such diverse activities as Voice of America radio, embassy press and cultural programmes and overseas film, TV and printed propaganda under a single institutional roof. During the Kennedy presidency USIA had expanded its activities in the developing world especially under the leadership of the former CBS-journalist Edward R. Murrow, but by late 1963 Murrow was ailing with lung cancer. The assassination of President Kennedy on 22 November 1963 turned general questions over Murrow's imminent departure into a crisis. The new President, Lyndon Baines Johnson faced the same problems of international image control as Kennedy – the Cold War, the escalating conflict in South Vietnam and internal struggles over African American Civil Rights – but compounded by the brutal shock of Kennedy's death. Johnson had to reassure the world that the United States would remain both a sound ally and, no less significantly, a formidable opponent under his stewardship.[1] He needed a capable replacement for Murrow, and quickly. He selected a man whose very appointment would be propaganda: the talented African American journalist, Carl T. Rowan.

Carl Rowan's appointment projected the image of Civil Rights reform around the world (and no less significantly at home), moreover, as an African

American, he personally embodied the opportunities available within the United States. His tenure at USIA – revealed here with access to newly declassified documentation including tapes of President Johnson's telephone conversations – casts an intriguing light on the development of US Cold War propaganda. It gives the propagandists perspective on events such as the Civil Rights movement, the Kennedy assassination and events in the developing world; it demonstrates Johnson paying significant attention questions of international image. During his two years as director of USIA Rowan demonstrated the strategic value of propaganda, deftly handling the Congo crisis and delivering timely support for the US government's military intervention in the Dominican Republic in 1965. But Rowan's tenure also underlines the structural problems within the US information machine, particularly the perennial difficulty of combining the political need to manipulate information with the ethical emphasis on accurate news demanded by Voice of America. Rowan's career also displays the way in which an individual can sway the operation of a bureaucracy. His personal eagerness to boost the USIA's profile included agitation to increase the role of USIA in South Vietnam. Rowan got his wish and the agency's role in the Vietnam conflict escalated in tandem with the US military activity. By the summer of 1965 the consequences of his eagerness were becoming clear.

Rowan's background and appointment

Carl T. Rowan would later comment that white Americans saw his life as a *Horatio Alger* story. Born into poverty in Tennessee in 1924, Rowan's war service with the navy opened unexpected educational opportunities and after the war he became a journalist with the *Minneapolis Tribune*. In 1951, he made a swift reputation with a series of articles on segregation: 'How far from Slavery?' A book followed with the provocative title: *South of Freedom*. As Rowan moved into foreign correspondence – his stories included coverage of the Bandung Conference of 1956 – he made himself useful to the cause of American propaganda overseas. He lectured for USIA in India and elsewhere. In 1961 Rowan joined the Kennedy administration as Deputy Assistant Secretary of State for Public Affairs, a key appointment in the presentation of US foreign policy. His duties included 'bear leading' Vice President Johnson on a world tour. By his own account he showed a willingness to 'talk back' to Johnson, which, he claimed, impressed the Texan greatly. Kennedy promoted Rowan to the post of Ambassador to Finland, but Johnson asked Rowan to take on an even more substantial task.[2]

Rowan was not Johnson's first choice of USIA director. Like Kennedy, Johnson's favoured his friend and President of CBS, Frank Stanton. Stanton declined, but faced with a bout of the famous LBJ arm-twisting agreed to serve in the supporting capacity as chairman of the President's Advisory Commission on Information.[3]   The vacancy at USIA provided Johnson with a golden opportunity for a prestigious black appointment.[4] As Johnson explained to Roy Wilkins of the National Association for the Advancement of Colored People, although not a cabinet post *per se*, by convention the USIA director sat on the National Security Council, and Rowan would have the added kudos of succeeding Murrow.[5]   Privately the President conceded that the appointment was all that could be done at the time. He told Louis Martin of the Democratic National Committee: 'I want a nigrah in the cabinet but I haven't got a place.'[6]

Johnson's old Georgia friend Richard Russell immediately expressed doubts about the appointment of Rowan. He fretted over what would happen when the USIA 'pitches in and gives the South hell' in its coverage of Civil Rights. Johnson assured Russell that Rowan understood the Southern way of doing things: 'he's a Tennessee boy and he's got more sense than that.'[7] Tactfully, the President also called the potentially troublesome Democrat Senator John McClellan of Arkansas, chairman of the Senate committee of Government Operations, to warn him of his intentions. He feared that the segregationist Senator might rebel against the surprise appointment of a black man and, as Johnson put it, 'operate with a knife' at the appropriations hearing, and send Rowan back from the Hill 'without his Peter'.[8] LBJ announced the appointment on 24 January, confident that he could count on the world to be impressed by his promotion of a black American, and on that black American to be grateful and hence to 'rock-the-boat' less than a white East Coast liberal.[9]

Projecting Civil Rights

Even as Johnson arranged Rowan's appointment, USIA slipped into controversy over the issue of Civil Rights. The agency's willingness to depict the Civil Rights struggle overseas had long been an irritant to Southerners on Capitol Hill. In 1958 the Agency had been forced to withdraw elements of an exhibition dealing with the problem of segregation from the Brussels World's Fair because of objections from Southern Senators. Now their dissent focused on a documentary about the March on Washington of August 1963: *The March*, directed by liberal filmmaker, James Blue.[10] The President felt that the film had something to commend it telling Russell on the phone that 'it shows that the nigrah has a right to be heard...and has a voice and can petition and doesn't get shot.' Key Southern Senators, however, objected. McClellan complained about USIA 'just throwing money away' on a film 'showing the worst side of America.' Others around Washington felt uncomfortable about a brief sequence showing an inter-racial couple, while Robert Kennedy demanded that the film be re-edited to mention his brother. Some hinted at a further problem. When the head of the USIA's motion picture branch, George Stevens Jr., screened the film at a closed session on Capitol Hill, Representative John Rooney of New York asked him 'did you get a security clearance on your star?' which was to say, Martin Luther King.[11]

Johnson saw the film as a trap. He told the Texas Governor John Connally, that if USIA withdrew *The March* 'every nigrah's gonna get mad because it looks like its a reflection on him' and that the 'son-of-a-bitch *Washington Post*' would cry censorship.[12] But positive responses from the field convinced USIA that the film had immense propaganda value. The agency re-released the film with a prologue by Rowan, which pulled the film into line with its usual approach to Civil Rights. Sitting uncomfortably in front of the camera he intoned:

I believe that this demonstration of both whites and Negroes *supported by the Federal government and by President Johnson and the late President Kennedy* is a profound example of the procedures unfettered men use to broaden the horizons of freedom and deepen the meaning of personal liberty.[13]

With this prologue the film became a staple of agency work around the world, playing in cinema, on television and at film festivals to great acclaim. Rowan had weathered his first storm.[14]

Rowan soon learned exactly why Representative John B. Rooney had raised questions about Martin Luther King. At a meeting to prepare for the forthcoming budget round, Rooney warned Rowan away from making too much use of King in its projection of the USA. The Congressman explained that J. Edgar Hoover suspected King of Communist connections. These fears evidently centred on King's left-wing advisor Stanley Levinson. Hoover had used lurid auguries on the theme of the 'Negro Revolution' to boost the FBI budget. But beyond this, Rooney went on to recount how the FBI director had played him a surveillance tape of what Hoover described as 'an orgy' in King's suite at the Willard Hotel, in Washington DC. Rooney had been particularly disturbed by a graphic piece of dialogue in which the saintly Dr. King apparently invited his fellow churchman and Civil Rights organiser Ralph Abernathy to: 'Come on, you big black motherfucker and let me suck your dick.' As Rowan recalled in his memoirs, he listened while Rooney read this dialogue from a transcript and assured the Congressman this could just be the sort of comradely banter typical of Black men in the South. But Rowan left this meeting profoundly troubled. Clearly world opinion was not the only thing that Johnson expected him to influence. The President had already asked Rowan to generate talking points for his meeting with the influential Black magazine mogul John H. Johnson. As Rowan expected, when King began to criticise the Vietnam War, Johnson asked him to warn the Civil Rights leader away from friends and statements that made it harder for the President to help Black Americans. Rowan duly delivered the warning together with news of Hoover's lurid claims. King responded by promising to distance himself from Levinson. Although abhorring the FBI's campaign against King, which included an attempt to use their surveillance tapes to blackmail King into suicide, Rowan regretted King's statements on foreign policy. His memoirs record his admiration for Lyndon Johnson's refusal to 'blame all blacks, or abandon the Civil Rights movement, because of his irritation with King'. Martin Luther King would not figure prominently in the portrait of America drawn by Carl T. Rowan's USIA. In the USIA version the Federal Government rather than individual black leaders was the hero of Civil Rights.[15]

In early April 1964 all USIS posts received a summary of priority themes including a list of the aspects of American life to which President Johnson attached particular importance. The list included economic strength and opportunity but at the head read 'Racial and Ethnic progress'. The directive stressed the American 'melting pot' and the access of all to the fruits of American life: 'Negro Americans are now actively in the process of full integration. Progress will not always be easy, but with the support of the Federal Government and a majority of the citizenry, will continue until the process in complete.'[16] In the summer of 1964 USIA had good news to report: the imminent passage of the Civil Rights act. In preparation for Johnson's signing the bill on 2 July, Rowan prepared a worldwide campaign to explain the bill's meaning, including a thirty-minute television roundtable, featuring Roy Wilkins of the NAACP and other African American leaders.[17] Using British opinion as a barometer, the USIA felt satisfied that the agency message had got through. Although 53% of people asked still believed that Black Americans lived in inequality, 60% felt that the US government was at least working hard to correct matters.[18]

The Kennedy Assassination

Race was of course only one of the priority themes engaged by Rowan. In the wake of the Kennedy assassination the USIA had launched a major campaign to explain the event and memorialise the dead president. Ed Murrow rose from his sick bed to personally prevail on the Congressional appropriations sub-committee to grant USIA an additional $8 million to cope with the crisis.[19] The president himself helped set the agenda for this publicity. LBJ wanted to prove to the world that the assassination had been the act of a lone gunman and not a conspiracy involving either, as he feared, the Soviet Union or the homegrown extreme right. Johnson assigned the task of settling the specific questions raised by the assassination to the Warren Commission. USIA had, in due course, to introduce the findings of the Warren Commission to the world, but in the meantime had to introduce the new President to world opinion while still memorialising Kennedy.[20]

By the time Rowan took office the USIA's campaign around the assassination was already well advanced. Rowan took over longer term projects such the completion and distribution of the magnificent documentary obituary film, directed by Bruce Herschensohn: *John F. Kennedy: Years of Lightning, Day of Drums* released for the first anniversary of Kennedy's death. Other activities included a massive push to translate and distribute books about Johnson. On 1 February, just three weeks after an updated version of Booth Mooney's 1956 biography *The Lyndon Johnson Story* appeared in America, USIA released subsidised editions in French and Arabic translations which sold in North Africa and the Middle East for as little as 25 cents each. Cheap editions in other languages followed.[21] But such activities could not, of course, resolve the wider publicity issues generated by the Kennedy assassination. The suspicious murder of Oswald just two days after Kennedy's death laid the foundation for doubt.[22] As early as the spring of 1964 the USIA noted a growing global conviction that Kennedy had been the victim of a right-wing conspiracy. Writers in all regions complained about delays to the Warren Commission report, its closed hearings and the membership of a former CIA director. The agency 'furnished all US missions with all the facts available on the public record' but still 'found overseas observers difficult – and in some cases, impossible – to persuade.' Rowan hoped that the eventual publication of the Warren Commission report might ease matters.[23]

When the Warren Commission report finally appeared on Sunday 27 September 1964, the USIA added a full array of supporting materials, including special VOA features in thirty-seven languages. USIA distributed printed commentaries, placed highlights on the wireless file, sent out special film and television materials, and arranged international transmission for a two-hour CBS documentary on the Commission's findings. Each USIS library received all twenty-six volumes of the report.[24] USIA noted that the Warren Commission impressed Australia and the Philippines, reassured editors in Britain, Latin America, and to a lesser extent in India, Italy and Germany. But French, Belgian and Austrian editors remained unconvinced.[25]

A succession of investigative books kept the issue alive. The third anniversary of Kennedy's death brought Rowan's successor Leonard Marks face to face with a second wave of conspiracy stories: a 'second gunman' story ran on the front page of the London *Times*, tales of missing witnesses in *Le Monde* while the Italian media gave much coverage of a *Life* magazine call for a new investigation. The USIA instructed 'all field officers not to engage in a debate on this issue but to provide the media with those portions of the Warren Commission report refuting the rumours and outlining the extensive evidence which was taken.'[26] The campaign proved futile. However hard USIS field officers worked, the conspiracy theories refused to die, more especially when

Moscow's propaganda machine could not resist stoking the embers from time to time. On 12 June 1968 *Isvestia,* commenting on the assassination of Robert F. Kennedy, reported: 'There is in America a well-financed syndicate of political murder which not only cleverly covers up traces of the crime, but misleads the public.'[27]

The Soviet Union

Despite Soviet mischief making around the matter of the Kennedy assassination, the Rowan era saw a marked improvement in relations with the USSR. The cessation of jamming in the USSR in the summer of 1963 presented an immense opportunity for the VOA Russian service. 'The crucial factor in attracting and holding listeners within the Soviet Union' Rowan wrote in May 1964, 'is now content of programmes.' VOA responded with a major 'revamp' of its Russian programming, mixing lively current affairs programming mixed with jazz and popular music shows, with news 'on the hour.' Rowan also noted that: 'The tone of the content is also being modified to make it less polemical' although he assured President Johnson that broadcasts remained 'at the same time clear and firm in the enunciation of American policy, in the exposure of the weakness and duplicity of Communism.'[28]

The thaw apparent from the end of jamming also took USIA's deputy director Don Wilson to the USSR in June 1964, on a mission to increase Soviet-American cultural exchanges.   In the process he spoke to numerous Soviet scholars and students and evaluated USIA's cultural operations to date. He noted the success of the touring exhibition 'Graphic Arts USA', which had attracted one and half million visitors. But his sources asked for more intellectual depth in *Amerika* magazine. VOA listeners, complemented Wilson on the station's news and jazz programming, but complained about VOA propaganda in presenting an inflated picture of life in the US. Wilson believed that the new initiative at the Russian branch had eased these objections.   Finally, Wilson observed that although many Russians believed that that Kennedy had been killed by a conspiracy, they liked Lyndon Johnson. Wilson attributed this not to Johnson's charm but to Soviet censorship.   *Pravda* printed only the President's most conciliatory statements on foreign policy. The Soviet media had begun to prepare its people for what became détente.[29]

The USIA position in the Soviet Union had improved partly because the United States was no longer the sole object of Soviet antipathy. The Sino-Soviet quarrel had deepened. On 30 July 1964 the Soviets began to broadcast loud music on Radio Peking's Russian language channel. Radio Moscow then shifted its domestic programming onto Radio Peking's European frequencies.   The Chinese tried in vain to evade the Russians by shifting their signal. [30] International propaganda had become a three-handed game. USIA responded with further overtures to promote cultural exchange with the Soviets, improved the VOA signals to the Chinese mainland and prepared to wage ideological war with the clients of the two Communist superpowers in the developing world.

The Developing World

Rowan's USIA remained a key tool of American foreign policy in the developing world. It worked in an increasingly hostile environment. The USIA had been designed to transmit American ideas to the outside world. By the end of 1964 the outside world had begun to use the USIA to communicate with

Washington DC, by the most brutal method: riot. 1964 saw attacks on nine USIS posts in Latin America, six in Asia, and two in the Middle East. In Sukarno's Indonesia, Nasser's United Arab Republic and Nkrumah's Ghana, students protesting against American 'imperialism' burned USIS libraries. Rowan noted the 'fad' for such acts and refusal of the host governments to censure the rioters, but insisted that the USIA could not abandon these counties, and maintain information activities to 'contact and influence the future leaders of Asia, Africa and Latin America.'[31] In 1965 the agency withdrew from Indonesia, donating the remaining stocks of USIS books to university libraries as a resource for the future.[32]

In Latin America USIA continued to pay particular attention to the teaching of English. The agency noted that the spread of the English language brought an increased demand for explicitly political agency publications, and swelled the audience for USIS lectures and American film screenings. The global English language teaching programme received a major boost in June 1965 from National Security Action Memorandum 332, a statement of 'US Government Policy on Teaching English Language Abroad.' NSAM 332 pledged the various agencies involved overseas – USIA, AID, Defense, Peace Corps, and Health, Education and Welfare – would respond to the global demand for English teaching and cooperate in their language programmes, under the leadership of the Assistant Secretary of State for Education and Cultural Affairs. The document noted: 'English has become one the most important world languages. The rapidly growing interest in English cuts across political and ideological lines because of the convenience of a *lingua franca* increasingly used as a second language in important areas of the world.' Testament to this came from the Soviet propagandists who, as the *New York Times* noted in 1966, began to use and even to teach English as the language of political communication in Chile.[33]

Rowan's USIA also played a key part in the emergency operations of the era. The Congo had concerned Rowan since his diplomatic work for Kennedy. By 1964 he feared that its on-going troubles could escalate into a conflict with propaganda needs equivalent to those of Vietnam.[34] Over a five-day period in the winter of 1964 US airborne troops evacuated Americans and civilians from some twenty other countries from advancing Communist rebels. Agency officers worked hard to explain the emergency action to the world. Rowan gave orders to 'play-up evidence of rebel atrocities, callous disregard for lives of Congolese and other non-combatants' and 'defiance of worldwide condemnation.' He assured the President in a secret memorandum, that USIA could 'rely heavily on rebel brutality as a means of influencing world opinion.' Accordingly the USIS post in Leopoldville became a clearing-house for images of outrage. Although the action attracted criticism from many African observers (mobs attacked USIS libraries in Bujumbura, Nairobi and Cairo as a result) Rowan's deputy director for policy and plans, Tom Sorenson believed that the atrocity line worked well to undermine not only the rebel's credibility but also that of their Chinese backers.[35]

Choices in Vietnam

The cracks in Rowan's tenure at USIA began in Vietnam. As the President's obsession with the conflict deepened Rowan recognized his agencies contribution to that conflict as an ideal way to build up the standing of the Agency (and its director) in Washington DC.[36] The USIA role in Vietnam grew along side the rest of the American presence. As with the army the commitment, the USIA began with advisory operations, mounted to support South Vietnamese 'counterparts'. But by 1965 the United States seemed to be running its own propaganda war in South Vietnam.

Soon after becoming USIA director Rowan conducting a personal review of all USIA information activities within South Vietnam. He toured the country and, in a memo of 21 April, he informed Johnson that '*the weakest part of the war operation, both on our part and that of the Government of South Vietnam, is in the field of information and psychological warfare.*' Rowan called for the United States to develop South Vietnam's propaganda capability at home and abroad, in such fields as filmmaking and radio broadcasts to the North. Turning to the US mission in Vietnam, he stressed: '*the information effort will fail, no matter what resources we pour into it, unless it has the clear direction of a single individual.*' He nominated the USIA's recently appointed public affairs officer in Saigon, Barry Zorthian, as the ideal head for such a combined operation and insisted that USIA play a role in planning in Washington DC.[37]

Rowan immediately began to target North Vietnam with the Voice of America, increasing Vietnamese language programming from one and a half to six hours daily, comparable to the Voice's six-and-a-half hours in Russian and seven-and-a-half hours of Mandarin. Rowan also developed new medium wave transmitter sites in the South and relocating suitable short wave transmitters to the Philippines, and stepped up the programme to distribute radios in South Vietnam.[38] But larger issues remained unresolved until the key architects of US policy including Rusk, McNamara, General Taylor, General Westmoreland and Rowan met in a grand conference on Honolulu on 2 June 1964. Proceedings included a panel dedicated to the three key information issues: the 'right and need' of the US people to know about events in Vietnam; the need for thorough briefings from the US military and need to respect the sovereignty of the South Vietnamese government. Specific questions included the presentation of napalm and defoliant use and the participation of US crews and hardware in air combat and reconnaissance missions.[39]

The Honolulu conference agreed with Rowan that the US needed a single 'communications tsar' in Saigon to act as principal public affairs adviser to Ambassador Lodge and the new Commander, US Military Assistance Command, Vietnam: General Westmoreland. It also agreed that Barry Zorthian was the best man for the job. Zorthian now wore two hats in Saigon: his embassy role as Minister Counselor for Information and his duties as director of USIA operations 'in the country', including its developing psychological warfare activities.[40] Zorthian worked well with General Westmoreland, who made improved press relations a key element in his approach to command. On 7 July the State Department issued a directive calling for 'Maximum candour and disclosure consistent with the requirements of security.' Zorthian and Westmoreland were happy to oblige. However, as William Hammond has noted the 'maximum candour' policy grew from an assumption that the South Vietnamese would provide positive news of sustained victories to be reported. In the short-term relations between the US mission and the media improved, but the reform ensured that any downturn in the war would be as visible as the expected successes.[41]

In August 1964 Lyndon Johnson took the next step towards a major US commitment to the Vietnam War. When two US naval vessels in the Gulf of Tonkin reported apparent North Vietnamese attacks, Johnson launched his first retaliatory air strike on the North. He then pressed Congress to accept the 'Gulf of Tonkin resolution': a legislative blank cheque allowing him full power to escalate the US role in the war. The USIA noted mounting doubt in the world's press at the President's response, but Rowan mobilized all channels to disseminate his justification speech. Twenty-seven VOA transmitters with a combined power of 4 million watts carried Johnson's words live to the countries of Asia, with supporting material in English, Chinese and Vietnamese. Related programmes followed in thirty-nine VOA languages.[42]

Rowan prepared to increase USIA's role in Vietnam in response to Johnson's wishes. In the months following Honolulu the USIA budget and staffing in South Vietnam virtually doubled to 54, with a further 200 military and AID personnel working on propaganda under their guidance. From 13 August the agency had a 50,000-watt medium wave antenna in the central Vietnamese city of Hue, angled towards the North. The VOA's medium wave signal now covered as much a 70% of the country by day and 90 per cent after dark. In September 1964 Rowan reported to the President that 'the structure and staffing for a country-wide psychological program are essentially complete.' Unfortunately, despite US advice, the South Vietnamese government had yet to deliver sensitive handling of the press, effective economic development or 'military victories over the Viet-Cong'.[43]

The Communist enemy proved well able to respond to any psychological or military victory by the South Vietnamese and their American allies, more especially as the North Vietnamese stepped up their 'infiltration' of fresh forces. American analysts detected a marked shift in the origin of enemy fighters from interviews with prisoners and captured weapons. The war now seemed increasingly international rather than internal to South Vietnam. In February 1965 the State Department published a White Paper entitled *Aggression from the North*, presenting evidence for North Vietnamese infiltration. USIA publicised its findings with associated materials including a swiftly-produced fifteen-minute TV programme, *Report from Vietnam* and a similarly named half-hour documentary film: *Report on Vietnam*, which followed in 1966. The foreign nature of the fighters in South Vietnam became a major theme in USIS Saigon's approach to the correspondents covering the war.[44]

In early 1965 the United States stood at a crossroads. Johnson now assumed that a sufficiently punishing campaign against North Vietnam could turn off the war the war in South Vietnam like a switch and planned Operation Rolling Thunder, an escalating series of air strikes against North Vietnam. The project required a substantial number of US ground combat troops to protect the airbases and turn the tide in the guerrilla war. An ideal opportunity for this escalation came on 7 February, when the Viet Cong attacked a series of major US targets including a barracks in Pleiku in the Central Highlands. US bombers flew reprisal missions, but the wider question of escalation still hung in the balance. The Pleiku attacks ushered in the last phase of debate before the wholesale Americanisation of the Vietnam War. February 1965 became the last point at which Johnson could have withdrawn from Vietnam. Rowan, who up to this point had like Murrow been a passive member of the National Security Council, did not intend to be left out of this debate.

Since the 1950s USIA had kept a careful watch of the shifting tide of world opinion, and the agency understood the growing disquiet over US involvement. In the days following Pleiku, however, Carl Rowan used USIA research data to justify a continued American commitment to the war. Pleiku coincided with the start of a major debate in the Senate over US policy in Vietnam, initiated by, among others, the Republican Senate minority leader Everett Dirksen. Personally, Dirksen supported Johnson's policy, but on 7 February he raised the tricky question of exactly what would happen if, instead of escalating in Vietnam, the US withdrew. Both Pleiku and Dirksen's question found Carl Rowan smarting from being excluded from the first rank of policymaking. He had gained admission to the NSC only to find that decision making confined to an inner circle around the President. Rowan felt compelled to participate in the debate over Pleiku and, despite being ill in bed with flu, drove over to the emergency NSC held on Sunday 7 February regardless.

In a secret memo to Johnson written on Monday 8 February, Rowan presented a digest of USIA research and warned Johnson away from all thoughts of climbing down. He predicted unbridled Communist influence in the Asian region, with pro-Communist regimes in Vietnam and Laos and a decline in the 'Thai will to maintain an anti-Communist posture.' Rowan spoke of 'sheer unalloyed joy at what would be interpreted as a glorious victory' in Communist nations 'with heavy I-told-you-so overtones concerning the unmasking on the "US imperialist paper tiger."' An attached USIA Research Service report noted that withdrawal would devastate 'flagging' Taiwanese morale, breed doubt over their US alliance in Japan and drive India into the arms of the Soviet Union. Rowan argued in terms of public opinion for a policy that would destroy the international standing of the United States for a generation. Johnson had no reason to change his mind.[45]

Within the month Rowan presented evidence suggesting a caution. On 27 February Rowan sent Johnson a survey of opinion in Long An province, just thirty miles south of Saigon. The report noted that 'the population is largely apathetic and is primarily interested in ending the twenty years of war; they care less as to which side will win, although there appears to be a substantial degree of approval of the Viet Cong.' This was not what Lyndon Johnson wanted to hear. The escalation continued regardless.[46]

With the US committed to escalation Rowan prepared to maximise the USIA's role in the conflict. He toured South Vietnam in March and presented the South Vietnamese government with a twelve point plan to revitalise their approach to their own population and the world, including a distinct South Vietnamese *credo* and dedicated central 'psywar' ministry.[47] Rowan returned eager to take up the challenge of Vietnam. His report to President stressed the need to direct the propaganda effort, and proposed consolidating all information machinery in Vietnam under the leadership of USIA, which he characterised as 'this country's greatest reservoir of trained psywar manpower'. Rowan also noted the need for a fresh initiative to develop the propaganda activities of the South Vietnamese government. The NSC approved this agenda in early April 1965 under National Security Action Memoranda 328 and 330. In so doing it reaffirmed the primacy of USIA in information matters in both Saigon and Washington DC.[48] On 1 July 1965, the fruit of two years planning came into being: JUSPAO, the Joint United States Public Affairs Office in Saigon, under Barry Zorthian and comprising 153 Americans (civilian and military) and 400 Vietnamese. Rowan's empire had a new addition, but even in the flush of success a new crisis opened at the most highest profile component: Voice of America.[49]

The Crisis at Voice of America

Throughout the Kennedy years the USIA and the VOA had been on a collision course over the issue of the agency's control over Voice output. In 1960 the Voice had acquired a charter, which emphasised its responsibility to deliver balanced news. Ed Murrow had proved surprisingly unsympathetic to this project and expected the Voice to toe the policy line. Now the Pleiku attack brought the issue to a head. President Johnson's retaliatory strike coincided with the visit of the Soviet premier Kosygin to Hanoi, and hence the President insisted that the raids avoid the city and US presentation of the event avoid humiliating or confronting the USSR. Rowan identified what he thought to be unnecessarily confrontational passage in a VOA commentary and forbade its use. He insisted on 'very tight control over everything said about the Viet-Nam situation except for straight, authoritative news.' The agency informed the White House that 'All commentaries, news analyses, features, correspondents' reports, etc.' were now 'read in advance' by Rowan or one of his deputy directors.[50] Rowan also feared that speculation on the imminence of negotiations over Vietnam might prevent their actually happening. But old hands at the Voice complained that the level of political control.

In late February the Voice and the USIA clashed over a second issue: the reporting of criticism of Vietnam policy. The USIA policy office forbade VOA from mentioning two editorials criticising the war in *La Monde* and *The New York Times*. One VOA-insider complained to Mary McGrory of the *Washington Evening Star*. 'We are getting so afraid to be honest, we can't even reflect any diversity or discussion.' Another compared the USIA's policy to Radio Moscow. Even coverage of Senate debates became moot. USIA pushed VOA towards heavy coverage of Senator Thomas Dodd's (D-Connecticut) two-and-half-hour defense of Johnson's Vietnam policy on 23 February 1965 but restricted coverage to Senator Frank Church's (D-Idaho) criticism until the administration had responded.[51]

Rowan noted the growing dissent and suspected that the long-serving VOA director Henry Loomis had manipulated the issue in order to build the case for VOA independence. Rowan speculated 'a young, black boss' might seem an ideal chance for Loomis to 'pull off a coup.' By his own account Rowan informed Loomis that 'If you can't understand that the President and I determine the editorial content of what goes out over Voice of America, your ass is gone.'[52] Within a month, Loomis found other employment as the number two at the Department of Education.[53] On the morning of 4 March 1965, Henry Loomis made a farewell address to staff of the Voice of America, after seven years of service as director of the Voice. He spoke movingly of the need to maintain a commitment to broadcasting 'truth' even when that truth did not flatter the United States. With deliberate irony he cited Carl Rowan's eloquent defense of VOA coverage of the Civil Rights issue to support his case. Above all Loomis defended the VOA charter of 1960:

> the charter is a statement of the principles which guide our decisions. It is not a substitute for judgement, nor is it a password or a mystical rite revealed only to members of the broadcasting fraternity. It must be the common yardstick by which you, your colleagues in USIA and your listeners make value judgements and measure the success of your endeavours. It is my hope – it is my belief – that the charter, like the Constitution is so fundamental and so represents the realities of the

world and the moral principles that undergird this nation; that the charter will endure for the life of the Voice.[54]

Loomis' departure attracted the attention of the press. A piece by Mary McGrory in the *Washington Evening Post* set out the entire catalogue of VOA complaints over the issue of Vietnam. With Rowan away on another visit to Vietnam, Don Wilson managed the crisis and rebuked the departing Loomis for airing his grievances in public. In commenting on the dispute in a memo to Bill Moyers at the White House, Wilson stressed that the VOA's complaints stemmed from 'continued steps' taken by both Murrow and Rowan to 'make Voice of America more responsive to the policy directions of the United States government.' He argued that the objections raised in the McGrory column could actually be read as 'a somewhat angry indication of the success of that work.'[55] Before the situation could be resolved a new emergency seized Rowan's attention. It would open the breach with VOA still wider.

The Dominican Intervention

Rowan's success in persuading the president to place USIA at the core of strategic propaganda work in Vietnam owed much to the events of April and May 1965 and the support which he provided for Johnson's decision to send 23,000 troops from the US and Organisation of American States to end a rebellion in the Dominican Republic. The military dictatorship in Santo Domingo had little to commend it, and the rebels claimed to be loyal to the more attractive figure of the exiled liberal writer and former president, Juan Bosch. Johnson feared that without US intervention the Dominican Republic would turn to Communism and become a second Cuba on his doorstep. His special envoy to the island Ambassador John Martin warned that any use of troops could be compared to the Soviet intervention in Hungary in 1956. Johnson risked a propaganda disaster.[56] The President maintained tight personal control over the crisis acting, as one Senate staffer recalled, as 'his own Dominican desk officer' for its duration. He did not consult Rowan about the wisdom of this move but rather prevailed on him to send a USIA team in with the second wave of US troops. Johnson's obsession with detail required multiple 'Psychological Situation Reports' from USIA throughout the crisis. These arrived at the White House two or three times a day. [57]

The intervention presented a major challenge for USIA. The agency needed to justify the act to the people of the Dominican Republic and Latin American opinion in general. Both proved to be up hill tasks. Early regional editorials deplored Johnson's unilateral action and his crass disregard for the provisions of Organisation of American States, and challenged his claim that the rebels were Communists. Rowan suggested that Johnson stress his humanitarian motives and attempt to enrol regional leaders to 'push' the issue of anti-Communism and regional security. Johnson preferred to continue the anti-Communist theme himself in a speech on 2 May, but looked to USIA to handle the situation on the ground. The direct role of USIA began on 1 May. Rowan dispatched a small USIA taskforce to the island to organise all psychological operations, led by his Associate Director and former Assistant Director for Latin America, Hewson Ryan, who had participated in plans for the intervention. The Kennedy-era Public Affairs Officer in Santo Domingo, Serban Vallimarescu, went to coordinate press relations with one further USIA assistant and two VOA staffers to supervise the relay of broadcast material. The agency's deputy director, Don Wilson, who had been point man during the Cuban Missile Crisis of October 1962, represented the agency on the crisis committee in Washington.[58]

The first group of 500 US Marines landed in the Dominican Republic on 28 April and began to establish a 'security zone' ostensibly to protect US citizens. The USIA team arrived late on 1 May. Initial problems included limited printing facilities and disrupted communications with the outside world. Working with the existing USIS staff on the island the team took over a small print shop and set about producing leaflets explaining the US presence. The mission then commandeered a medium wave radio station in their zone of occupation which then began to relay VOA Spanish transmissions.[59] The VOA could also be heard at night from a medium wave transmitter in Florida, on six Puerto Rican medium wave stations, and the usual VOA short-wave signal. Soon estimates of the medium wave audience exceeded half a million, with a further 60,000 Dominicans in the interior able to receive the short wave broadcast. Of course the VOA needed solid news to pass on to this audience, and that was not easy find in the chaotic first days of the rebellion.[60]

Cable and wireless communications with Santo Domingo remained uncertain throughout the crisis. The VOA news correspondent, Harry Caicedo, covering events shared a single telephone link with one hundred other journalists. The VOA engineering team in Santo Domingo rigged a radio antenna in a tree near the embassy and established contact in Morse code with friends in the Potomac Valley Radio club back home in the USA. Their club-mates set up a round-the-clock watch on their frequency, and transcribed the VOA correspondent's reports as they came through. At the main Voice of America newsroom the Latin American desk worked in worked in rotation for thirty-three days straight covering the story largely from these transmissions. Thanks to the Potomac Valley volunteers, events in Santo Domingo could be on the VOA and thereby known all over the Dominican Republic within hours. This, the news room believed, worked to prevent unfounded atrocity stories, such as those heard in the early days of the crisis, gaining hold, and to dissuade either the rebels or the military junta from mounting reprisals. The VOA version of events proved so reliable that the USIA placed the news text on its daily wireless file for distribution to all agency posts worldwide.[61]

Despite the synergy of USIA and VOA operations in the field, the Dominican intervention widened the breach between the agency and its radio station still further. Rowan insisted on dictating news commentaries during the crisis and even tried to write a commentary himself. As during the Cuban Missile Crisis a representative of the USIA Policy Office (Burnett Anderson) took control of all VOA news output and insisted that the Voice staff should: 'damn well do what the people who pay your salaries say you should do.' The VOA had no intention of playing a partisan game and complained bitterly.[62]

Meanwhile on the island the USIA team proved their value in the field. By 3 May, the agency had prepared thousands of leaflets and posters to explaining the US action, dropped 10,000 leaflets on key areas of the capital and, using resources from the US army begun loudspeaker appeals from two planes, one helicopter and four trucks. A second medium wave transmitter maintained by the VOA engineers began to broadcast locally produced appeals featuring Dominican voices. Owing to power shortages the rebels only reply came over a feeble, shifting ham radio signal 'Radio Constitution'. The junta, in contrast, controlled

Radio San Isidro and aired a diet of strident anti-rebel propaganda punctuated by 'The Stars and Stripes Forever'. As the US claimed to be independent from the junta, and certainly had no wish to be associated with extremism, these broadcasts seemed a mixed blessing.[63]

On 5 May the USIS mission began broadcasting on a 5,000-watt medium wave transmitter provided by the US army. This station -- Radio in the Security Zone, and later Voice of the Security Zone -- carried VOA news, information regarding food and medical supplies, and devoted 10 minutes an hour to 'Operation Families', a project to allow Dominicans to send and receive messages about the welfare of family members separated by the crisis. Peace Corps volunteers manned three phones to maintain contact with the public. [64] Leaflets stressed 'known' Communists in the rebel camp, citing the country – Cuba, China or elsewhere – in which they had been trained.[65] Rowan drew satisfaction from loud rebel protests against their propaganda operations, although similar objections from the OAS Commission seeking to resolve the crisis remained, for a while, politically 'thorny'. [66]

The USIA operation ran into one major difficulty. The problem, as Rowan reported to the President, was the 'cynical disbelief' on the part of the 100-strong international press corps on the island that the rebels were Communist controlled. The press officer Vallimarescu hammered on with the Washington line regardless, denying that the US was in cahoots with the junta.[67] The more conservative Latin American papers soon accepted that the rebels had Communist links and accepted that one could not insist of diplomatic niceties when faced with a Communist threat.[68] Meanwhile Rowan sought to rally regional and world opinion by sending a television crew to the island to capture politically useful images: the humanitarian effort in food distribution, aid to refugees and Peace Corps work. USIS field officers achieved some success in placing images and specially produced radio features with local news media around the region.[69]

By the second week of the intervention the rebels had begun broadcasting radio and television propaganda over Radio Santo Domingo, a located outside the US-controlled zone. Responses included a rival TV signal from the Dominican navy, which included USIA films documenting Cuban subversion in the hemisphere.[70] As the intervention the junta put forward a new president, Brigadier General Antonio Imbert Barrera, the propaganda battle on the island settled into a familiar pattern of sniping between rebel, US and junta stations. The USIS team launched a two page daily newspaper in Spanish called *Voice of the International Security Zone* with a print run of 75,000.[71] Leaflet drops continued, though during the third week the accuracy of rebel small arms fire forced the USIS team to briefly suspend all daylight airborne operations. Increasingly frustrated the US resorted to the illegal expedient of jamming Radio Santo Domingo and at last enjoyed some success. On 18 May Rowan informed the President that the rebel signal was now weak and sporadic.[72] By 21 May Radio Santo Domingo had passed to the control of the new Imbert government.[73]

During the final weeks of May the USIS team on the island worked hard to reshape the intervention as a joint enterprise of the OAS. On 29 May the USIS team converted its own broadcasting efforts into 'Voice of the OAS' and began to offload the rest of its information work, including its newspaper into OAS hands.[74] The shift of the information effort away from explicitly US propaganda significantly eased the situation within the country. 1966 brought free elections, which returned Joaquín Balaguer, who had opposed the junta from exile, but seemed conservative enough to reassure the USA. The crisis had passed.

The USIA had fared well during the Dominican Crisis. The agency's chief on the island, Hewson Ryan, had proved well able to direct the US army propagandists from the 82nd airborne and Fort Bragg's First Psychological Warfare Battalion in the field. Ryan soon found himself chairing the inter-agency PYSOPS group. He had demonstrated the value of civilian information specialists in a psychological warfare situation. His tactical success in the Dominican Republic justified the emerging role of the agency at the fore of US propaganda and psychological warfare in South Vietnam.[75] However any triumph would be short-lived for Rowan.

The End of Rowan

By June 1965 the crisis in the Dominican Republic had passed, but VOA disquiet over Rowan's behaviour during the episode had not. Resentment smouldered on. Rowan's apparent inability to handle the situation at the Voice enraged Johnson, more especially as criticism spilled over into the press. In the first week of June *Newsweek* ran a stinging piece describing Rowan's administration on the USIA as 'ham-handed'. Don Wilson frantically drafted a rebuttal for the President's press conference in which Johnson would deny that he ordered Rowan to broadcast anything but 'the truth' over VOA. In the event the press corps asked other questions, but Rowan's days at USIA were numbered.[76] Only the *Chicago Daily News* attempted to defend Rowan's approach. The paper noted that the tougher policy controls had actually been introduced by Murrow.[77] As Johnson turned against Rowan for his inability to manage the Voice, the director felt increasingly tempted by the prospect of a triumphant return to journalism as the nation's first syndicated black columnist.

The final blow came in the summer of 1965, when President Johnson angrily refused to allow Rowan to travel to Thailand to personally conclude the vital VOA transmitter deal: 'Project Teak'. Johnson made disparaging remarks about key officials travelling because they 'liked to buy carpets'. Carl Rowan recognised a slight and resigned forthwith. Rowan claimed in his memoirs that Johnson apologised and begged him to remain at USIA, but archival record suggests that the President lost no time recruiting Rowan's replacement. Rowan's formal letter of resignation came on 8 July 1965. In order to protect the agency it spoke only of 'personal and family reasons'. By the time Rowan left the agency on 31 August 1965 he held lucrative contracts from the Publishers Newspapers Syndicate and *Readers Digest*. His position as the first syndicated black columnist in US press history was secure.[78]

Johnson's next director of the agency would be a trusted Johnson insider: his friend and lawyer to the family communications business interests: Leonard Marks. The VOA job went to John Chancellor of NBC. Johnson weathered the problem of loosing his only senior African American appointee and in January 1966 delivered the first black cabinet appointment: Robert Weaver, Secretary of the newly created Department of Housing and Urban Development. Johnson continued to regard USIA as a mechanism for steering world opinion. He paid little or no attention to Marks in matters of policy formation and ended the practice of commissioning a grand survey of US standing in world opinion, assuming that the news would be bad. In 1969 the

Nixon administration removed the agency director from the NSC completing the drift to complete separation of USIA from the policy making process. VOA continued to resent USIA intervention in the news but in 1976 in the aftermath of Watergate achieved the additional protection of having their charter underwritten by law.

Carl Rowan's undoubted talents as a communicator found far better use outside government service. He flourished as a liberal journalist and commentator. He became a regular contributor to television programmes such as *Inside Washington* and his syndicated column ran three times a week ran for over thirty-five years in 75 newspapers across the United States. The *Washington Post* dubbed him 'the most visible black journalist in the country.' In 1987, Rowan founded Project Excellence, a program to encourage black high school students to excel in their use of the English language. His causes in print included gun control, which left him vulnerable to criticism when in 1988 he wounded an intruder at his Washington home with a gun belonging to his son. Political enemies (specifically the Major of Washington, Marion Barry) had a field day, but Rowan's career survived. In November 1999 the National Press Club presented him with its Fourth Estate Award honouring 'a lifetime of achievement for his outstanding contributions to journalism.' When he died in September 2000 President Bill Clinton wrote: 'He was without a doubt, one of our nation's most eloquent voices for human rights and racial justice. His gentle, civil tone only heightened the power of his commentary; and he felt a special obligation not only to inform his readers but to enrich them with new ways of thinking.'[79] In his memoirs, published in 1991, Rowan looked back on his time at the helm of US Cold War propaganda with pride but conceded that he 'erred' in his eagerness to expand propaganda in Vietnam:

> I had believed that we could mount some propaganda campaign that would impel Vietnamese, North and South, to denounce political slavery, slaughter and tyranny, but I underestimated the factors of anti-colonialism, nationalism, hatred of racism, anger over economic exploitation for generations.[80]

The price of this misjudgement was paid by his successors at USIA in a decade of unnecessarily intimate involvement with an un-winnable war.

NOTES

1.   For recent studies of the early years of USIA see Scott Lucas, *Freedom's War: The US Crusade Against the Soviet Union, 1945-1956*. (Manchester: Manchester University Press, 1999); Walter Hixson, *Parting the Curtain: Propaganda, Culture and the Cold War, 1945-1961*. (Basingstoke: Macmillan, 1997). On Murrow's tenure see *Alexander Kendrick, Prime Time: The Life of Edward R. Murrow* (Little, Brown and Co., Boston, 1969); A. M. Sperber, *Murrow: His Life and Times* (Michael Joseph, London, 1986) and Nicholas J. Cull, 'The Man Who Invented Truth': The tenure of Edward R. Murrow as director of the United States Information Agency during the Kennedy Years.' *Cold War History*, forthcoming 2003.

2. For survey of Rowan's life see Carl T. Rowan, *Breaking Barriers: A Memoir* (Little, Brown: Boston, 1991).

3. LBJL tape WH6401.17, PNO 4, LBJ/Murrow, 20 January 1964; WH6403.02, PNO 12, LBJ/Feldman, 3 March 1964; WH6403.04, PNO 1, LBJ/Jenkins, 6 March 1964; Interview (telephone): Louis T. Olom, 3 April 2001; Interview: Frank Stanton (28 July 2002)

4. The appointment was not out of step with the emerging profile of USIA as one of the more integrated federal agencies. Between 1960 and 1963 the number of Black Americans in USIA's foreign service doubled. By the end of the Kennedy years Black people held one in ten of all senior and middle grade USIA career posts, serving especially in African posts see LBJL, Panzer papers, box 469, USIA, summary memo: 'United States Information Agency', 1 October 1963.

5. LBJL tape WH6401.15, PNO 2, LBJ/Rusk and WH6401.15, PNO 4, LBJ/Wilkins, both 16 January 1964.

6. LBJL tape WH6401.15, PNO 13, LBJ/Martin, 17 January 1964.

7. LBJL tape WH6401.17 PNO 12 and 13, LBJ/Russell, 20 January 1964.

8. LBJL tape WH 6401.15 PNO 6, LBJ/McClellan, 16 January 1964.

9. LBJL WHCF Ex FG296/A USIA, box 316, Statement by President and Rowan, 24 January 1964.

10. For background and analysis of the film see Cull, 'Auteurs of Ideology: USIA Documentary film propaganda in the Kennedy Era as seen in Bruce Herschensohn's The Five Cities of June (1963) and James Blue's The March (1964).' *Film History*, Vol. 10, 1998, pp. 295-310. On the Brussels World Fair debacle see Michael L. Krenn, 'Unfinished Business': Segregation and US diplomacy at the 1958 Worlds Fair', *Diplomatic History*, 20:4, Fall 1996, pp. 591-612.

11. LBJL tape WH6401.17 PNO 13, LBJ/Russell, 20 January 1964; WH 6401.15 PNO 6, LBJ/McClellan, 16 January 1964; WH602.05, PNO.11, LBJ/Rusk, 4 February 1964 and WH6402.06, PNO 14, LBJ to Wilkins, 6 February 1964. Interview: George Stevens Jr.

12. LBJL tape WH6402.10, PNO.5, LBJ/Connally, 8 February 1964.

13. Rowan's introduction survives on the National Archives print of the film, the emphasis is added.

14. Interview: George Stevens Jr.

15. Rowan, Breaking the Barriers, pp. 254-261. See also David J. Garrow, *The FBI and Martin Luther King, Jr.* (Yale University Press, New Haven, 2001). The talking points for the John H. Johnson meeting are at LBJL WHCF Ex, box 2, HU2 Equality and Race, Rowan to President, 28 January 1964. More typical of Rowan-era Civil Rights publicity was Charles Guggenheim's documentary about the lives of the nine black students who had broken the colour line to attend a previously white High School in Little Rock, Arkansas in 1957: Nine from Little Rock, which presented racism in America as a local issue being addressed by a benevolent Federal Government. Nine from Little Rock became one of the most successful USIA films, seen in ninety-seven countries and seventeen languages. In April 1965 it won the Academy Award for best documentary short. LBJL WHCF Ex, box 314, Ex FG296, Rowan to President, 8 April 1965; NA MPSVB, RG 306.5160, Nine From Little Rock.

16. LBJL Leonard Marks papers, box 27, USIA media priorities, Sorenson to all staff, 6 April 1964.

17. LBJL NSF Agency, USIA, box 73, vol. 2/2, doc. 92, Rowan to President, 30 June 1964.

18. LBJL WHCF CF, box 135, CF USIA 1965, Wilson to President, 13 July 1965.

19. Sperber, Murrow, p. 685.

20. On the establishment of the Warren Commission see LBJL Moyers papers, box 55, memos re. Death of President Kennedy, Katzenbach (Deputy Attorney General) to Moyers (White House), 25 November 1963, recommending a commission to cut off speculation on motives and conspiracies, and because 'the public must be satisfied that Oswald was the assassin' and acted alone. On Johnson's fears of a Soviet plot see Carl T. Rowan, *Breaking Barriers: A Memoir* (Little, Brown: Boston, 1991), p. 233. Murrow's post-assassination priorities for USIA were 1) The Pursuit of Peace; 2) Strength and Reliability; 3) Free Choice; 4) Rule of Law; 5) United Nations, see LBJL Leonard Marks papers, box 27, USIA Media Priorities, Murrow to Staff, 20 December 1965.

21. LBJL Salinger papers, box 1, agency reports for the President, Wilson to President, 4 February 1964; WHCF CF, box 135, CF USIA, Rowan to President, 24 March 1964.

22. LBJL Bill Moyers papers, box 55, Death of President Kennedy file, Wilson to President, 25 November 1963.

23. LBJL WHCF CF, box 135, CF USIA, Rowan to Johnson, 28 April 1964.

24. USIA HB USIA 23rd Review of Operations, 1 July to 31 December 1964, pp. 12-17 also in LBJL WHCF Ex, box 314, FG296, filed at 10/1/64-12/3/64.

25. LBJL NSF agency, box 73, USIA Vol. 2/2, doc 125, Rowan to Johnson, 30 September 1964.

26. LBJL WHCF CF, box 52, CF FO6-3 Publicity, Marks to President via Kintner, 29 November 1966.

27. For example on 12 June 1968 Isvestia reported that the newly assassinated Robert Kennedy himself believed in a conspiracy and had pledged to find out the truth, telling New Orleans District Attorney Jim Garrison: 'If I am elected President, I shall prosecute those who are guilty.' See LBJL WHCF CF, box 135, CF USIA, Marks to President, 19 June 1968.

28. LBJL WHCF CF, box 33, CF FG296-1 VOA, Rowan to President, 2 May 1964. Radio Liberty remained subject to jamming. Most Soviet bloc countries also relaxed their jamming of VOA and RFE at this time see LBJL Salinger papers, box 1, agency reports, Wilson to President, 14 January 1964.

29. LBJL NSF Agency, box 73, USIA Vol.2/2, doc 128A, Wilson to Rowan, 1 June 1964.

30. LBJ NSF Vol. 2/1, doc. 63, Rowan to President, 4 August 1964.

31. LBJL WHCF CF, box 33, CF FG296 USIA, Rowan to Rusk, 31 December 1964.

32. LBJL NSF Agency USIA, box 74, vol. 3a, doc 23, Rowan to President, 16 March 1965.

33. LBJL WHCF CF, box 52, CF FO6-3 Publicity, Marks to President via Kintner, pp. 2-3, 29 November 1966. LBJL NSF, NSAM 332, 11 June 1965

as   of   10/2002   available   online   at:
http://www.lbjlib.utexas.edu/johnson/archives.hom/NSAMs/nsam332.asp

34. LBJL WHCF CF, box 12, CF CO312 Vietnam (1964-65), Rowan to President, 19 June 1964.

35. LBJL NSF Memos to the President, box 2, file 7, doc. 9, Rowan to President, 21 December 1964, Sorenson, *The Word War*, pp. 259-260.

36. For an example of LBJ's personal feelings LBJL WHCF Ex, box 314, Ex FG296 USIA, President to Sec. of State et al. 6 June 1964 in which the President offers to write personally to any doubting official to convince them of the value of taking an assignment in Vietnam.

37. FRUS, 1964-1968, Vol. I, Vietnam 1964, doc. 122, Rowan to President, 21 April 1964, italic in original; doc. 124, 528th meeting of NSC, 22 April 1964.

38. FRUS, 1964-1968, Vol. I, Vietnam 1964, doc. 177, Rowan to President, 26 May 1964. For issues of broadcast content see doc. 88, Rowan/Rusk phone conversation, 17 March 1964. LBJL WHCF CF, CO312, Wilson to Reedy (White House), 22 July 1964.

39. NA RG59 CPF 1964-66, box 417, INF 8 US-Viet S., Ball to Saigon, 2144, 1 June 1964.

40. FRUS, 1964-1968, Vol. I, Vietnam 1964, doc. 189, Meeting, Honolulu, 2 June 1964; doc. 192, McGeorge Bundy to President, 3 June 1964, doc. 197, Rowan to President, 4 June 1964; doc. 203, Rusk to Saigon, 6 June 1964. Johnson agreed an equivalent concentration of responsibility within the US under Robert Manning at the State Department see doc. 219, NSAM 308, 22 June 1964.

41. Zorthian to author, 1 September 2001; Hammond, *The Military and the Media*, pp. 80-85.

42. LBJL NSF Agency, USIA Vol. 2/1, box 73, doc. 60 & 61, Rowan to President, 7 August 1964.

43. LBJL WHCF CF, box 12, CF CO312, Wilson to Reedy (White House), 22 July 1964; WHCF CF, USIA, box 135, Rowan to President, 8 September 1964.

44. FRUS, 1964-1968, Vol. I, Vietnam 1964, doc. 450, Ball to Saigon, 19 December 1964; NA RG59 CPF, 1964-1966, box 446, circular 1698, Rusk to posts, 15 March 1965; Interview: Zorthian. For follow-up publicity see LBJL WHCF Ex ND19/CO312, box 214, Wilson to President, 'USIA pamphlet on North Vietnamese arms shipment' 8 March 1965, with booklet: The Evidence at Vung Ro Bay'. See also NA MPSVB, RG 306.5438, Report on Vietnam, 1966.

45. LBJL NSF Agency, USIA Vol. 3 A, file 2, box 74, docs 83 a to n., Rowan to President, Secret, 8 February 1965, and attached documents. For Rowan's disgruntlement at being excluded from policy meetings see Rowan, *Breaking Barriers*, p. 267. The best analysis of Johnson's decision making at this time is Frederik Logeval, *Choosing War* (California, 2000).

46. FRUS, 1964-1968, Vol II, Vietnam January-June 1965, doc. 172, Rowan to President, 27 February 1965.

47. FRUS, 1964-1968, Vol II, Vietnam January-June 1965, doc. 178, Defense to Saigon Embassy, 2 March 1965; NA RG59 CPF 1964-66, box 417, INF 8 Viet S., Saigon TOUSI 625, Rowan to USIA, 9 March 1965.

48. LBJL NSF Country, Vietnam, box 190, Rowan to President, 16 March 1965; FRUS, 1964-1968, Vol II, Vietnam January-June 1965, doc. 203, McGeorge Bundy to President, 17 March 1965. The plan received approval under NSAM 328 and 330 see doc. 242, 6 April 1965 and doc 246, 9 April 1965.

49. FRUS, 1964-1968, Vol III, Vietnam June-December 1965, doc. 110, 554th meeting of NSC, 5 August 1965, note 3, p. 322; 'Pyswar', Newsweek 4 October 1965, p. 40.

50. LBJL WHCF CF, box 33, CF FG296-1 VOA, Wilson to Moyers, 5 March 1965; Rowan, Breaking Barriers, pp. 268-271.

51. Mary McGrory, 'Voice chiefs chafe at curbs', Washington Evening Star, 5 March 1965.

52. Rowan, Breaking Barriers, pp. 270-271. Loomis's new job is mentioned in the AP story, Lewis Gulick, 'American Radio Policies Overseas Discussed.' Washington Post, 7 March 1965.

53. Rowan claims he fired Loomis as a result of the McGrory article, but this piece included news of Loomis' transfer.

54. Tufts University, Murrow Papers, reel 45, Loomis departure speech, 4 March 1965.

55. LBJL WHCF CF, box 33, CF FG296-1 VOA, Wilson to Moyers, 5 March 1965.

56. Abraham F. Lowenthal, The Dominican Intervention (Johns Hopkins University Press, Baltimore, 1995) p. 123.

57. Gaddis Smith, The Last Years of the Monroe Doctrine, 1945-1993 (Hill and Wang, New York, 1994), p. 129.

58. LBJL NSF Agency box 74, USIA Vol.4, 4/65, #2, doc. 58, 59 and 60, all Rowan to President, 1 May 1965. Association of Diplomatic Studies and Training oral history, Georgetown University Library (hereafter ADST Oral History): Hewson Ryan interview.

59. Interview (telephone) Al Laun, 18 January 2001, Sorenson, The Word War, pp. 265-267.

60. LBJL WHCF CF, box 70, CF ND19/CO 62, Dominican Rep., Situation Reports, Rowan to President, 4 May 1965.

61. Interview, Bernie Kamenske, 6 December 1995.

62. LBJL WHCF Ex, box 317, Ex FG 296-1, VOA, Wilson to Reedy, 1 June 1965. Interviews: Kamenske; Anderson; 'His Master's Voice', Newsweek, 7 June 1965; '"Voice" policies disturb aides', NYT, 5 June 1965; 'America's Voice' NYT, 11 June 1965.

63. LBJL WHCF CF, box 70, CF ND19/CO 62, Dominican Rep., Rowan to President, 3 May 1965; WHCF Ex, box 314, Ex FG296 USIA, Rowan to President, 3 May 1965.

64. LBJL WHCF CF, box 70, CF ND19/CO 62, Dominican Rep., Psychological Situation Reports, Rowan to President, Confidential, 4 May 1965 and Confidential, 11 am, 6 May 1965.

65. LBJL WHCF CF, box 70, CF ND19/CO 62, Dominican Rep., Psychological Situation Report, Confidential, Rowan to President, 5 May 1965.

66. LBJL WHCF CF, box 70, CF ND19/CO 62, Dominican Rep., Psychological Situation Reports, Rowan to President, Confidential, 4 May 1965, Confidential, 11 am, 6 May 1965.

67. LBJL WHCF CF, box 70, CF ND19/CO 62, Dominican Rep., Psychological Situation Reports, Rowan to President, Confidential, Secret 2.30pm, and Tom Secret, 7.00 pm, 5 May 1965, and Secret, noon, 7 May 1965.
68. LBJL NSF Agency box 74, USIA Vol.4, 4/65, #2, doc. 52, Daily Reaction Report, Rowan to Johnson, 5 May 1965.
69. LBJL WHCF CF, box 70, CF ND19/CO 62, Dominican Rep., Psychological Situation Reports, Rowan to Johnson, Secret, 5 pm, 11 May 1965.
70. LBJL WHCF CF, box 70, CF ND19/CO 62, Dominican Rep., Psychological Situation Reports, Rowan to President, Confidential, 5 May 1965; Confidential, 11 am, 6 May and Secret, noon, 7 May 1965.
71. LBJL WHCF CF, box 70, CF ND19/CO 62, Dominican Rep., Psychological Situation Reports, Rowan to Johnson, Secret, 5 pm, 11 May 1965.
72. LBJL WHCF CF, box 70, CF ND19/CO 62, Dominican Rep., Psychological Situation Reports, Rowan to Johnson, Secret, 4.30 pm, 17 May 1965, Secret, 18 May 1965.
73. LBJL WHCF CF, box 70, CF ND19/CO 62, Dominican Rep., Psychological Situation Reports, Rowan to Johnson, Secret, 24 May 1965.
74. LBJL WHCF CF, box 70, CF ND19/CO 62, Dominican Rep., Psychological Situation Reports, Rowan to Johnson, Secret, 29 May 1965.
75. LBJL WHCF Ex, box 317, Ex FG 296-1, VOA, Wilson to Reedy, 1 June 1965; ADST Oral History, Hewson Ryan.
76. LBJL WHCF Ex, box 317, Ex FG 296-1, VOA, Wilson to Reedy, 1 June 1965. Interviews: Kamenske; Anderson; 'His Master's Voice', *Newsweek*, 7 June 1965; '"Voice" policies disturb aides', *NYT*, 5 June 1965; 'America's Voice' *NYT*, 11 June 1965.
77. Peter Lisagor, 'Voice of America stirs some static' *Chicago Daily News*, 9 June 1965 see also Wilson's response to criticism in a *Newsweek* story: LBJL WHCF Ex, box 317, Ex FH 296-1, VOA, Wilson to Reedy, 1 June 1965.
78. Rowan, *Breaking Barriers*, pp. 275-278; LBJL WHCF name, box 305, Rowan to Valenti, 19 July 1965.
79. http://www.blackjournalism.com/carl.htm and http://www.cnn.com/2000/US/09/23/obit.rowan.ap/index.html both accessed 15 October 2002.
80. Rowan, *Breaking Barriers*, pp. 262-63

Chapter Twelve
AMERICAN TELEVISION COVERAGE OF THE VIETNAM WAR: THE LOAN EXECUTION FOOTAGE, THE TET OFFENSIVE (1968) AND THE CONTEXTUALIZATION OF VISUAL IMAGES
David Culbert

The Vietnam War is of considerable interest to those who study the impact of visual images on political decision-making, though there is little certitude as to how one incorporates still photographs or television news reports into the process. For example, the 2003 edition of a widely-used college text, *American Public Opinion*, offers this safe conclusion: 'Media messages can influence opinion in several ways, but the effects are generally modest.'[1] Textbook prose is notorious for avoiding controversy in favor of platitudes, but students of propaganda have every reason to wonder about the oft-noted problem of the so-called 'magic bullet': does a single powerful photograph or television news programme actually have the capacity to alter public attitudes about a particular government policy. (See illustration number 1. Eddie Adams won the 1969 Pulitzer Prize for his photograph of Col. Nguyen Ngoc Loan executing a Vietcong suspect, downtown Saigon, 1 February 1968, at the start of the 1968 Tet Offensive. Loan's act was also captured by two American television crews, memorably by NBC's cameraman, Vo Suu. The image and newsfilm continue to provide scholars with a 'zone of contested meaning.' Source: Associated Press.)

As a general proposition, the answer is no. Media more often reinforces the decisions of those in power, or trivializes information policy by focusing on the irrelevant. Newsreels were notorious for the amount of space given, for example, to bathing beauties. American television news coverage of the Vietnam War for the most part offered little of visual significance, and more often

Figure 1: Colonel Nguyen Ngoc Loan executing a suspected Vietcong member

Figure 2: Media needs to see action – assault landing

Figure 3: Military move Media by Chinook helicopter

Figure 4: Tony Blair visits Oman

reinforced or followed elite opinion than attacked the status quo, as Daniel Hallin has demonstrated persuasively.[2] It is inaccurate to remember America's Vietnam War as a so-called 'living-room war,' in which nightly images of violence turned viewers from hawks to doves. Most shots were taken far from the scene of an actual fire fight, and there are far more instances of helicopters taking of and landing than of close-range fighting.

The beginning of the 1968 Tet Offensive is an important exception. In the fall of 1967 President Lyndon Johnson's popularity began to decline sharply, thanks to the continued unpopular war in Vietnam. Johnson called home the American field commander, General William Westmoreland, and ordered the general to travel around the United States, announcing that American policies were working—that there was, as the phrase of the day put it, 'light at the end of the tunnel.' Westmoreland did as he was told.

The North Vietnamese countered with the most sustained uprising of the entire Vietnam War, the January-April 1968 Tet Offensive, which began on the last day of January 1968, with uprisings which extended into downtown Saigon, the capital of South Vietnam, all-too-close to hotels where foreign television crews stayed. The terrorist arm of North Vietnam, the Vietcong, was brought into the open, in hopes that the populace of South Vietnam would embrace a new North Vietnamese government. The populace did no such thing. The Vietcong was decimated. The North Vietnamese suffered a major military setback. In military terms, the North Vietnamese suffered a severe defeat at the time of the Tet Offensive.[3]

From a psychological point of view, however, the Tet offensive ended up helping the North Vietnamese cause in a profound way. Images of violence in downtown Saigon, including Vietcong terrorists who blew a hole in the wall surrounding the American Ambassador's compound and got into the Ambassador's residence for some hours, made American television viewers—to say nothing of a number of foreign policy-makers in Washington, DC—fear that all Vietnam had been overrun by the North Vietnamese. For a time, visual images of disaster numbed Lyndon Johnson into inaction, in spite of what his National Security Advisor, Walt Rostow, insisted to be evidence of a serious North Vietnamese military disaster.[4]

Complicating this difficult situation was a still photograph and television newsfilm taken of a single violent event in downtown Saigon, on 1 February 1968, the execution by Colonel Nguyen Ngoc Loan, head of the South Vietnamese police, of a Vietcong terrorist. The event was captured by two American television news organizations, as well as Associated press photographer Eddie Adams, who won a Pulitzer prize in 1969 for his notorious photograph. The still photograph was shown on the leading nightly American news programme, the *Huntley-Brinkley Report*, on the night of 1 February. The next night, 2 February 1968, the color newsfilm of the broadcast was shown to the same large national audience. If one is to make the case for how a single news photograph or visual news story can have an identifiable impact on policy-making, it is with this particular photograph and this particular news story, remembering to take into account the uncertainty so many Americans felt – both elite and non-elite – about what policy American should adopt in terms of supporting or not supporting the Vietnam War.

America became a truly televisual society in the 1960s. American, with a total population of some 202 million, had 78 million television sets. By 1968, television had emerged as the principal source of news for a majority of Americans. Three networks offered nightly thirty-minute news programmes–the American Broadcasting Company (ABC), the Columbia Broadcasting System (CBS), and the National Broadcasting Company (NBC). In 1968 NBC's *Huntley-Brinkley Report*, with commentators Chet Huntley and David Brinkley, was the leading programme, enjoying a nightly audience of some 20 million viewers. CBS's Walter Cronkite as slightly behind in the ratings. ABC was a terribly-distant third, in fact so far behind in the ratings as to be little more than a courtesy news source, a situation far removed from what obtains today. It was a day before cable or satellite offered competition. And a day in which no newspaper in American was able to reach a national daily audience, given the vastness of the country and the inability to print the same edition from more than a single east-coast source. *The New York Times* was the paper of record then as now, but the central news source for a national audience was evening news, for thirty minutes, five times a week. Such broadcasts were heavily larded with commercials, so that viewers had at best perhaps eighteen minutes of actual news and news commentary in a typical programme.

The Eddie Adams photograph was shown on all three network evening news broadcasts on Thursday, 1 February; the next morning it could be seen on the front pages of newspapers the world over, including both London dailies and British television news programmes.[5] At no other moment in the entire Vietnam War did one event receive such visual reinforcement on television – the Loan photograph on Thursday evening; the colour newsfilm of the same event the following evening. NBC had no idea on 1 February that one of its camera teams had filmed the gruesome event. In fact, NBC had two cameramen covering the event, one with a sound camera, one with a silent one. An American military transport plane few the footage to Tokyo, where it was developed in a laboratory before being sent by satellite transmission to NBC headquarters in New York City. A cable from Tokyo to New York alerted NBC producer Robert Northshield as to what the footage consisted of. The actual footage was not transmitted to New York until a few minutes before the beginning of the 6.30 EST broadcast on Friday, 2 February.[6]

Some television viewers simply could not believe the violence of the newsfilm, particularly if they saw it in color. Professor Bruce Southard, a graduate student in 1968, said he had prepared a modest dinner, consisting of a fried hamburger over which he had poured some catsup. What he was eating suddenly suggested what he was seeing:

> I was just watching the news. General Loan pulled his gun and shot the man, and at first I could not believe that it was happening. It was unlike anything that I had seen before, and then I saw the blood coming out of the guy's head....It really turned my stomach. I didn't throw up but I came close to it. After that I decided what we were doing in Vietnam was wrong. I could not conceive of the callousness with which one person executed another with no pretense, with no trial, with no evidence...After that I became active in the antiwar movement.[7]

Of course not every viewer enjoyed precisely so basic a repast, and not every viewer was moved in the same way with the visual violence. Peter Braestrup, whose two-volume *Big Story* remains the most comprehensive analysis of media coverage of the Tet Offensive, is very uneasy about emotional attempts to read a moral meaning into either the Adams photograph or the NBC newsfilm:

> In journalistic terms, it was fantastic. It is not often that a television cameraman, or a still cameraman for that matter, gets on film happening right there before your eyes one man blowing another man's brains out....It was kind of the supreme melodrama....a kind of super pornography. It evoked strong reactions among those who saw it apparently....It was a kind of ultimate horror story that you captured in living color. But in terms of information it told you almost nothing. That's the chronic problem especially for television and for the still photos, the difference between drama and information.[8]

At one level, Braestrup's statement is unanswerable. What seems to be the execution of one human being by an authority figure may fail to upset some viewers. Indeed, the limitation of all true documentary photographs is precisely the inability to move every viewer in exactly the same way, or even at all. Some undergraduates study the NBC newsfilm in terms of how much gore is presented, and compare its violence with what has been achieved in some recent Hollywood blockbuster. Nor would one want to suggest that a refined aesthetic sensibility was required for images of violence to achieve maximum effect. Professor Southard still has a vivid memory of the Loan image; Peter Braestrup was proud to remind his friends that he was a combat veteran of the Korean War, and projected a tough journalist's persona in his later career, a lit cigar at the ready to make everyone know that he was a tough guy.

Selected obituaries for Nguyen Ngoc Loan, the police chief who pulled the trigger, remind us that the impact of the photograph and newsfilm has not yet been established. In London, *The Independent*'s Dale Hopper said the Adams photograph 'stunned the world' and 'became a haunting image of the Vietnam War.' The *Washington Post*'s Bart Barnes says the photograph 'stunned millions of readers' and that the combination of photograph and newsfilm 'contributed to increased popular disillusionment with the war and opposition to the U.S. involvement.' *The New York Times* is of two opinions. Robert McG. Thomas Jr. notes an immediate impact:

> when the film was shown on television and the picture appeared on the front pages of newspapers around the world, the images created an immediate revulsion at a seemingly gratuitous act of savagery that was widely seen as emblematic of a seemingly gratuitous war.

But Thomas then notes that 'for all the emotional impact, the episode had little immediate influence on the tie of American involvement.' *The New York Times*, Richard Bernstein takes a rather different view in a piece published a few months later. There the Adams photograph is captioned: 'This execution is credited with turning public opinion against the war.' He cites with approval the conclusion of Tom Buckley, that the Loan execution was 'the moment when the American public turned against the war.'[9]

A recent *New York Times* public service advertisement about the dangers of drug abuse has a headline which is relevant to the loan image: 'If you don't want something to be true, does that make it PROPAGANDA?' The North Vietnamese felt the photograph was a propaganda success for them during the

Tet Offensive. Eddie Adams reports that when he returned to Ho Chi Minh City (as it was then called) in 1983, he was met at the airport by a North Vietnamese journalist who wanted to thank him: 'We have your photograph in the center of our War Museum.'[10]

What about contextualizing the Loan execution, something not understood by the vast majority of those who saw the film and photograph at the time, to say nothing of those who in retrospect attempt to study the same imagery. We know whom Loan shot, we know that the victim's widow thinks officially, we know where the gun came from, and we know what Loan and Adams think about what they did. Tom Buckley, a *New York Times* reporter who had interviewed Loan in Saigon several times, came to speak with Loan again in 1979, by which time Loan was running a restaurant in a shopping centre south of Washington, DC. Loan's gun, given to him by an American intelligence officer, was a short-barrel .38 Smith & Wesson Airweight. Loan knew personally the man he shot:

> They tell me that he had a revolver, that he wounded one of my policemen, that he spit in the face of the men who captured him. They say that they know this man. He is not a nameless civilian, as the press says. He is Nguyen Tan Dat, alias Han Son. He is the commander of VC sapper unit.[11]

In 1985, NBC's John Hart interviewed the widow of the slain man in Ho Chi Minh City; she dismissed Loan as one of the 'slaves for the imperialists who killed my husband.'[12] Her appearance suggests that she shared her late husband's ideological fanaticism.

In 1979, I spent three hours with Loan at his home in Burke, Virginia, close to his restaurant. Loan offered some additional contextual details, albeit in not quite idiomatic English:

> I didn't think about the film-oh the hell with film-next day some American friend say 'what about film'-I had to go to Hue. I have big mouth-sometimes get me into trouble. Accordingly to Southeast Asian philosophy-if you can die it is good-otherwise you have to live. The unit commander of the Vietnamese who should have done it is now in the United States. He called me on phone-he was hesitating-so I did it. We had joint US-Vietnamese teams of MPs. 'You have your responsibility of course'-my wife asked-but why do it?' I did what I shouldn't do. For me I accept the consequences of my act. How about my daughter, day and night, day and night-my daughter getting married in the near future-how will husband's family respond?[13]

The problem of American television coverage of the Vietnam War has been analysed carefully by Daniel Hallin in his *The Uncensored War*. He reminds readers that what someone remembers is not the same as what happened. He concludes that before February 1968 American television coverage was 'lopsidedly favorable' to Administration policy. He believes that television's 'turnaround' was related to many other changes, a reflection of those changes not an explanation for those changes. He goes yet further: 'there is no way to measure the impact of television's changing images of the war.'[14]

George Herring, author of a widely-used textbook on the Vietnam War, is more insistent: 'A direct link between television reporting and public opinion cannot be established.' Not every scholar agrees. For example, Melvin Small notes that 'Most Americans were shattered by the first television accounts of the 'invasion' of Saigon....above all, film of the assassination of a suspected Viet Cong infiltrator in cold blood....Tet was the turning-point in the battle for the hearts and minds of Americans.'[15]

Consider the impact of the violent imagery on some senior aides to Lyndon Johnson. For example White House Counsel Harry McPherson says this about the impact:

> I saw that event on the screen and in the newspapers with two powerful impressions....I knew that the impact of that footage on television and on the American people would be tremendous, that it would hit them very hard, and it gave me all the more a feeling that I should do whatever I could to help us get out as quickly.[16]

Television images of disaster were very much in his mind as he wrote drafts for Johnson's television address on 31 March 1968, the speech where Johnson withdrew from trying to be re-elected as President.

Secretary of State Dean Rusk understood the impact of the Loan footage, shown on the third day of the Tet Offensive. As he watched on Friday night, 2 February, he felt the footage would 'give critics a cause celebre.' Assistant Secretary of State William Bundy also watched that Friday evening. He reportedly felt 'horror and dismay,' claiming it 'cost the government side an 'unnecessary roughing' penalty at a time when it could least afford it.'[17] Congressman Henry S. Reuss of Wisconsin sent an angry letter to General Earle Wheeler, Chairman of the Joint Chiefs of Staff, after seeing the Loan photograph. Nothing, Reuss insisted, could 'justify or excuse actions by the United States or allied forces which sink to this level. Murder or torture of prisoners is horrible and un-American.' The next day, Wheeler replied to Reuss; his letter was immediately leaked to *The New York Times*, by Reuss, an outspoken opponent of the war. Wheeler agreed that Loan's act was dreadful, but that it had occurred 'in a flash of outrage rather than 'in cold blood.' '[18] It would be inaccurate to insist that every senior White House official was shaken by violent television images. For example, National Security Advisor Walt Rostow was proud of ignoring television news, which he considered a waste of time. Rostow told me that Lyndon Johnson had installed three television monitors in his White House office so Rostow could watch the three evening news broadcasts simultaneously, but that he had made a point of not watching. He claimed to have an alleged Chinese Emperor's maxim under the glass on the top of his desk: 'There are some orders of the Emperor which *must* be disobeyed.' Rostow, to be sure, was an avowed hawk, and had access to important battlefield information from the White House Situation Room which was unavailable to members of the media, and which in fact did indicate that television images of destruction hardly served as representative of the entire Tet military situation. But surviving 16mm color film shot of Rostow in the Situation Room during the first days of the Tet Offensive, hardly suggests a figure of Olympian calm either.[19]

Clearly, historians and journalists are of two minds as to what to do with including visual images, still or moving, as part of the decision-making process, and not just for Vietnam. Nobody who sees the Adams photograph or the NBC newsfilm forgets it. But one might argue that this is not the same as making the case for its connection to historical causation. Unfortunately, for the demands of visual history, many American scholars have simply deleted the loan footage and photograph from accounts of the Vietnam War. These days, the Vietnam War may not quite be free of its emotional resonance in the minds of many Americans of a certain age, but by now a greater concern is whether or not alleged battle heroes have manufactured their battlefield heroism. 'On a Mission to Sniff Out the Fakers With Medals,' is the continuation headline for a front-page story in *The New York Times*, August 10, 2001. The reporter notes that fraud hunters have increased in number thanks to a 'surge of wartime fabrication.' The article reminds readers of Pulitzer Prize-winning historian Joseph Ellis, who regaled his students with stories of Vietnam battlefield heroism, when in actual fact he taught history at West Point and got no closer to Saigon that the Hudson River in New York.[20]

And Vietnam remains, as Robert McMahon indicates in his 2001 presidential address to the Society of Historians of American Foreign Relations, fertile ground for 'contested memory.' McMahon, speaking to those who teach American diplomatic history at the college level, points out our society's inability to reach a consensus as to what is or is not the 'lesson' of the Vietnam War. His thoughtful comments about memory are well-taken, both by those inside America, and scholars abroad who hope to place the Vietnam War within an appropriate historical context. Unfortunately, for those interested in media images, McMahon is more willing to speak of blockbuster Hollywood films than of television. Indeed, it seems that McMahon is only prepared to mention the continued relevance of a thirteen-part Public Broadcasting System series, *Vietnam: A Television History*, produced many years ago, in conjunction with a companion book by Stanley Karnow.[21] McMahon slips past the shortcomings of the PBS series by relegating criticism to two slight articles which suggest that the critics of the series are simply crackpots-the proof being a connection with Accuracy in Media, a conservative media organization which lot is purpose with the collapse of communism.[22]

The question of media impact has great significance for students of policy-making, for whom the presumed 'lessons' of the Vietnam War have considerable attraction. It is not true, for example, that in general television news reports were unfavourable to an Administration point of view. Most television coverage of the war was visually uninteresting; television's impact was overrated; the 'living-room war' is a remembered fiction. Television followed elite opinion; it did not lead.

But there is an exception to the rule, and that is the Loan execution photograph and newsfilm. It is impossible to separate the one from the other, particularly since television in America and Britain ran the still photograph and on NBC the still photograph appeared one evening; the color newsfilm of the same incident the next night. The loan execution is the most visually significant footage to come out of the war; it merits careful attention precisely because it defines the potential of the medium for influencing elite and mass opinion. Its' meaning is not simply found in, as it were, the aesthetic qualities of violence. Its impact is found by placing these images of violence within a particular context in which these images first appeared.

In early 1968 American citizens, Administration leaders, and elite opinion had become uneasy about Johnson's ill-conceived public relations campaign. Johnson needed progress; he has fighting an undeclared war, and public opposition was growing, as suggested by the March on the Pentagon in October 1967. There had to be 'light at the end of the tunnel' or the 'credibility gap' would turn into a chasm. The disbelief was already there. Into this critical situation came the dramatic North Vietnamese military action we remember as the Tet Offensive. It seemed that rosy prognostications were totally incorrect. It seemed that all South Vietnam was about to fall to the North Vietnamese. And the military action was particularly obvious in down Saigon, the largest city in all of Vietnam, the South Vietnamese capital city, and the place where all news organizations housed their employees. In this moment of doubt and uncertainty, a visual microcosm purporting to show the actual practice of justice by the government of South Vietnam offered persuasive-albeit misleading-evidence which gave people looking for factual reasons to justify a change in policy an opportunity to do so. The loan footage and photograph legitimized the moral arguments of the anti-war movement. In this moment of crisis, a television news story and a still photograph became part of the foreign policy-making process for the average person, for the politician looking for dramatic images with which to clothe his election-year promises, and for policy-makers, both military and civilian. There is a visual component to the Vietnam War in early 1968. American policy became clear with Johnson's 31 March 1968 speech. The unique confluence of extraordinary visual imagery and extraordinary policy uncertainty makes the Loan photograph and newsfilm a significant part of America's move from hawk to dove in early 1968. It is a part of contested historical memory which historians simply must confront.[23]

NOTES

1. Robert S. Erikson and Kent L. Tedin, *American Public Opinion: Its Origins, Content and Impact* (6th ed.; New York, 2003), conclusion, p.228.
2. Daniel C. Hallin, *The 'Uncensored War" The Media and Vietnam* (New York, 1986). Hallin's analysis of network television is based on Department of Defense kinescopes, 1965-68, now at National Archives II, College Park, MD.
3. See Peter Braestrup, *Big Story: How the American Press and Television Reported and Interpreted the Crisis of Tet 1968 in Vietnam and Washington* (2 vols.; Boulder, CO, 1977). Don Obderdorfer, *Tet!* (Garden City, NY, 1971) is a fine contemporary account of the crisis.
4. James J. Wirtz, *The Tet Offensive: Intelligence Failure in War* (Ithaca, NY, 1991), in particular pp. 246, 172-3.
5. See George A. Bailey and Lawrence W. Lichty,: Rough Justice on a Saigon Street: A Gatekeeper Study of NBC's Tet Execution Film,' reprinted in Braestrup, *Big Story*, II, pp. 266-81.
6. Robert Northshield, Producer, The *Huntley-Brinkley Report*, interview, Chapel Hill, NC, February 1978. This interview was filmed as part of a conference marking the 10th anniversary of the Tet Offensive, held at the University of North Carolina, Chapel Hill. This interview appeared in Peter Rollins and David Culbert, *Television's Vietnam: The Impact of Visual Images* (80 min.;

Humanitas Films, 1982). An ideologically recast version of this film, narrated by Charlton Heston, was shown nationally over PBS.

7. Interview with Professor Bruce Southard, *Television's Vietnam*.

8. Interview with Peter Braestrup, *Television's Vietnam*.

9. Dale Hopper, 'South Vietnamese executioner dies,' *The Independent*, 16 July 1998, p.14; Bart Barnes, 'Nguyen Ngoc Loan dies at 67; South Vietnamese General: News Photograph and TV Film of His Execution of Vietcong Prisoner in 1968 Fueled Opposition to War,' *Washington Post*, 16 July 1998, p. D6; Robert McG. Thomas, Jr., 'Nguyen Ngoc Loan, 67, Dies; Executed Viet Cong Prisoner,' *The New York Times*, 16 July 1998, p. C24; Richard Bernstein, 'In Vietnam the Pen Was as Mighty as the Napalm,' *The New York Times*, 1 December 1998, 0. B2.

10. *The New York Times*, 9 December 2002, p. A11; Eddie Adams, 'The Pictures That Burn in My Memory,' cover story, *Parade Magazine*, 15 may 1983, p.6. Adams feels that he destroyed Loan's life by taking a photograph of something that often occurs in war, but not with an Associated Press photographer ready to snap a picture. Adams spoke with Loan and visited Loan at the latter's home in Virginia. Eddie Adams filmed interview, *Television's Vietnam*.

11. Tom Buckley, 'The Villain of Vietnam,' *Esquire*, 5 June 1979, p.64.

12. On-camera interview with Jim Hart, NBC television broadcast, 11 April 1985, quoted in *AIM Report*, May-B, 1985, n.p.

13. Interview with Loan, 25 July 1979, Burke Virginia. At the time Rep. Elizabeth Holtzmann-NY, tried to have loan deported as an undesirable alien. Loan's lawyer urged Loan to talk to me; I came with video equipment so he could see what Eddie Adams had said about Loan in an interview filmed a few days earlier at Adams' home outside of New York City.

14. Hallin, '*Uncensored War*,' pp. 106, 110, 163.

15. George C. Herring, *America's Longest War: The United States and Vietnam, 1950-1975* (2d. ed.; New York, 1986), p. 203; Melvin Small, *Johnson, Nixon, and the Doves* (New Brunswick, NJ, 1998), pp. 132, 134.

16. Harry McPherson, filmed interview, *Television's Vietnam*. This interview was filmed in Baton Rouge, LA; the technician was Steve Soderbergh, at the time a student employee at Louisiana State University's media center.

17. Oberdorfer, *Tet!*, pp. 170-71.

18. William M. Hammond, *Public Affairs: The Military and the Media, 1962-1968*, (Washington, DC, 1988), pp. 351-52.

19. Walt Rostow, film interview, *Television's Vietnam*. Steve Soderbergh also helped film this interview at the Johnson Library, Austin, TX. For information about the monthly 16mm color movies made throughout the Johnson presidency, see David Culbert, 'Johnson and the Media,' in Robert A. Divine, ed., *The Johnson Years, Volume One: Foreign Policy, the Great Society, and the White House* (Lawrence, KS, 1987), pp. 214-48.

20. Pam Belluck, 'A Sworn Mission to Unmask Pretenders to Military Glory,' *The New York Times*, 10 August, 2001, p. A1 *et seq.*

21. Robert J. McMahon, 'Contested Memory: The Vietnam War and American Society, 1975-2001,' *Diplomatic History*, 26:2 (Spring 2002), pp. 159-84. McMahon's defense of the PBS series as 'balanced and objective' is found on p. 180.

22. *Ibid.*, p.180. McMahon cites as evidence two slight contributions by Robert l. Ivie and Philip Wander and Melissa Kane, both in Richard Morris and Peter Ehrenhaus, eds., *Cultural legacies of Vietnam: Uses of the Past in the Present* (Norwood, NJ, 1990), pp. 27-38, and 39-52.

23. David Culbert, 'Television's Visual Impact on Decision-making in the USA, 1968: The Tet Offensive and Chicago's Democratic National Convention,' *Journal of Contemporary History*, 33:3 (July 1998), pp. 419-49, which includes a series of sequential frame enlargements from the NBC newsfilm of the Loan execution. For another powerful still photograph with iconic significance to the Vietnam War see Denise Chong. *The Girl in the Picture: The Story of Kim Phuc, the Photograph, and the Vietnam War* (New York, 2000), and Elaine Sciolino, 'A painful Road from Vietnam to Forgiveness,' *The New York Times*, 12 November 1996, p. A1 *et seq.* One scholar has recently attempted to integrate the impact of the atypical violent visual image into the literature of decision-making. See Piers Robinson, 'World Politics, Media Influence and Theories of Media-State Relations,' *European Journal of Communication*, 16:4 (2001), which explicitly discusses the Loan execution newsfilm and photograph.

Chapter Thirteen
VIETNAM'S TET OFFENSIVE (1968) ON BRITISH TELEVISION: AN OVERVIEW
Christine Whittaker

It can be somewhat daunting to try to determine what was shown on British television, January-March 1968, relating to the Vietnam War, even for someone who has made a career as a film archivist for the BBC. There is information, to be sure, in the BBC written archives at Caversham, as well as the archives for Independent Television, ITV. Catalogue systems for the late 1960s include only shot-lists of film inserts, often mute, so it is difficult to determine what commentary originally went with which inserts. Actual television news bulletins were not recorded, as is the case today. It is much easier to know if a film insert exists, then to know for sure when and how it was first used. This is also a problem for students of American television who study the late 1960s.

It may be helpful to remember who television was organised in Britain in the late 1960s. There were three channels-BBC-1, BBC-2, and ITV. The BBC was in the process of changing from black and white to colour. BBC-2 launched its colour transmissions at the end of 1967; BBC-1 in 1969; so in 1968 there was a mixture of black and white and colour. ITV did not start transmitting in colour until the following year. Reports from location, as opposed to reports from a studio, were shot on film, and that film had to be flown back to London for editing and transmission. That was true for stories shot by and for the television companies' own reporters. ITV and BBC had journalists in South Vietnam, reporting from the battle front, but they also had arrangements with the American networks and would show stories from CBS, NBC, and ABC on a regular basis.

BBC-1 had several news bulletins during the day, the main one at 8:50 in the evening, lasting 15 minutes. BBC-2 had a thirty-minute programme called *Newsroom* at 7.30 pm, plus a summary at 11:20pm. The two main current affairs programmes on the BBC were *Panorama* – a fifty-minute programme analysing major political topics, which went out on a Monday evening at 8.00 pm, and *24 Hours* the nightly current affairs magazine programme which went out around 10.00 pm on weekdays, both on BBC-1. ITV had a thirty-minute news programme every night produced by ITV – *News at Ten* – as well as an earlier bulletin at 5.55 pm. ITV's main current affairs programmes were Granada's *World in Action* and Rediffusion's *This Week*. Later in 1968, with the creation of Thames Television, *This Week* continued to enjoy considerable success as a Thames Television programme. In sum, there was a lot of opportunity for the British public to see current events on television.

Not only was news very important in the schedules, the Vietnam War was certainly big big news. From the end of January 1968 until the beginning of March, the war featured in almost every news bulletin. On ITV's *News at Ten* it was the lead story every single day until 5 February, when a Hull fishing boat went missing off Iceland. This domestic tragedy took the lead for a few days, but Vietnam became the lead story again on 9 February, when Prime Minister Harold Wilson went to Washington DC, for talks with President Lyndon Johnson. Vietnam was high on the agenda. 1968 was a leap year: ITV news carried Vietnam stories on 28 of the 29 days in February.

BBC reveals a similar pattern. The Vietnam War was considered the most important topic for viewers, night after night. The attacks at Da Nang, Khe Sanh, Saigon, and Hue were described in detail, including the use of stills, film, and sometimes audiotape to illustrate. Casualties were listed, and the plight of refugees and the Vietnamese people was emphasized. Reactions and statements from Washington were followed with care. Anti-Vietnam War demonstrations became increasingly frequent as news stories. ITV showed demonstrations in Berlin and Lakenheath on 17 February; in Rome and London on the 18th, culminating in the large, violent protest at the American Embassy in London on 17 March, a major story.

Granada's *World in Action* made an award-winning programme about the same demonstration which was shown on ITV on 18 March. ITV's other major current affairs programme, *This Week*, devoted one complete programme on 22 February, to an American documentary opposed to the war, *Vietnam: The Year of the Monkey*. Viewers saw black American soldiers burying their colleagues, as well as South Vietnamese soldiers looting the dead bodies of the Vietcong – painful and emotional stuff.

British viewers witnessed horrific scenes from Vietnam, many having already appeared on American television. Of particular interest is NBC's footage of General Loan executing a Vietcong sympathizer in downtown Saigon, 1 February 1968, as well as the still photograph of the same event taken by Associated Press photographer Eddie Adams, a photograph which won the Pulitzer Prize in 1969. The footage seems not to have been shown on British television at the time, though it was certainly shown in later years. Written records reveal the footage was filed through to Visnews on 3 February. The Eddie Adams photograph was shown, and led to a strong reaction in the British Press. Here is the script from BBC News's 7.30 pm bulletin, on 2 February. John Timpson is the newsreader talking about the photographs:

> When the fighting's all over in Vietnam-if that ever happens-two men will be remembered for their small part in the events, and the brutality of the last few days. One, a Viet Cong officer, his uniform a check shirt and

black shorts. His name? – no one knows. The other, the man who shot
him, coldly and in public. His name is known – he's South Vietnam's
national police chief, General Loan. Both Vietnamese, but enemies.
Now their personal war is over – another nasty page in a very nasty
story.

The tragedy of the Vietnam War, the horrors and the suffering, had
been a regular part of British television for some time. British reporters like the
BBC's Julian Pettifer, Anthony Lawrence and Michael Charta, and ITV's Sandy
Gall had been sending back films from the battle front for several years; the
public was used to images of war. But the coverage of the Tet Offensive was
more concentrated.

Viewers were kept aware of the importance of events. On 29 January,
Michael Aspel, in the BBC 8.50 pm news studio, announced that the Americans
and their South Vietnamese allies had suddenly cancelled the planned thirty-six-
hour truce marking the Buddhist New Year. Aspel said that it was called off just
an hour before it was to begin, thanks to a reported massive Communist build-up
in the border area, especially around Khe Sanh. Coverage the following few days
emphasizes the bitterness of the fighting, the attack on downtown Saigon, and
high casualty figures. Here is a statement from the 7.30 pm BBC news on 31
January: 'General Westmoreland's troops in Vietnam are tonight fighting a
shadowy enemy, who's already penetrated to the heart of American military
power.' The whole of BBC's Europa programme that evening was devoted to
Vietnam.

Reactions in Washington were followed carefully. On 1 February, *24
Hours*, the BBC's nightly current affairs magazine programme, included an item
showing a peace demonstration in Washington, along with an interview with Judy
Collins. On 3 February, the 11.20 pm newsreader noted: 'The Johnson
administration's expressed confidence that the Vietcong have failed, has provoked
skepticism throughout the nation. Officials are showing more concern than they'll
admit on the record. Our Washington correspondent says there are grave doubts
whether the White House can be trusted any more.'

On 5 February both *Panorama* and *24 Hours* carried long stories on
Vietnam. *Panorama* the BBC's very traditional, rather staid flagship current affairs
programme, concentrated on reactions in America to fighting in Vietnam,
including excerpts from NBC interviews with Secretary of State Dean Rusk and
Secretary of Defense Robert McNamara. *24 Hours* showed a film report by Julian
Pettifer in the midst of the battle for Saigon.

Differing British attitudes to the war can be seen as preparations were
made for Harold Wilson's visit to Washington. On 5 February BBC news
announced: 'The Leader of the Opposition, Mr. Heath and the whole of the
Shadow Cabinet tonight tabled a motion in the Commons urging the Prime
Minister to make clear to President Johnson the British Government's support for
the Americans in Vietnam.' Two nights later, on 7 February, BBC news reported
that 'over ninety Labour MPs' were urging Mr. Wilson to disassociate the
Government from American policy.'

Details of the fighting and the escalation of the war continued
throughout February, with a mixture of on-the-spot reports from British and
American journalists. Captured film of Vietcong operations. An Englishwoman
from the Saigon embassy who was staying with Vietnamese friends in Hue when

the city was attacked, described her experiences. There was a report by Anthony Lawrence about a British team working in a children's hospital in Saigon, as well as interviews with American soldiers under siege at Khe Sanh.

Coverage of the war continued into March, but no longer as the lead story. On 11 March *Panorama* reported on the candidates and issues at the start of America's presidential race, showing an excerpt from NBC's *Meet the Press*, featuring Dean Rusk and Robert McNamara. On 17 March the anti-Vietnam War rally in central London was the main item of the news, as it had turned into a violent clash between police and demonstrators.

Vietnam coverage for the remainder of March focused on opposition to the war within Britain, including reports on demonstrations on 23, 24, and 26 March, as well as growing interest in political turmoil in Washington. There was speculation about Lyndon Johnson's address to the American people on 31 March 1968. The BBC's Charles Wheeler reported from Washington on 31 March, before the President spoke, that it seemed that Johnson would favor a middle-of-the-road approach, offering something to both hawks and doves. *Panorama* on 1 April included a long extract from Johnson's speech, including the President's dramatic announcement that he was calling a halt to most of the bombing of North Vietnam and that he would not seek another White House term. The main feature of the programme, it marked an end to two months of intensive coverage of the Vietnam War on British television.

If viewers in Britain lacked on-the-scene nightly stories of bloody carnage, they did not lack for a larger perspective. British television noted the turnaround in official American policy, with Johnson's 31 March speech, and attention given to anti-Vietnam War protest within Britain made it clear that there was no mass consensus on both sides of the Atlantic as to what the war meant in relation to the parameters of the Cold War.

Chapter Fourteen
CONTESTING WAR: BRITISH MEDIA REPORTING AND THE 1982 SOUTH ATLANTIC WAR
Klaus Dodds

Nothing I did as a Government information officer was more difficult, more nerve-wracking, and ultimately more rewarding than trying to maintain relations between the Government and the press, radio, television during the Falklands campaign.[1]

We learned our lessons from the Falklands war.[2]

The management of the British media during the 1982 Falklands according to Philip Knightley 'will go down in the history of journalism as a classic example of how to manage the media in wartime'.[3] In complete contrast to living rooms being bombarded with images of American servicemen perishing in the unforgiving jungles of South East Asia, the South Atlantic campaign was not a 'television war' as relatively few images of the unfolding drama reached their interested audiences lying over 8,000 miles from the battleground. Instead radio reporters such as Brian Hanrahan and Robert Fox who covered the conflict in the Falklands became household names.[4] As the war photographer Martin Cleaver famously noted, 'It wasn't a news war [in the sense of television], it's as simple as that. It was in the wrong place'.[5] By the time the Falkland Islands were retaken in June 1982, after a 74-day occupation by Argentina, only three batches of film had reached London. Over the last twenty years, evidence has steadily accumulated how both the British military and politicians were in favour of this extraordinary absence of visual material. According to Robert Harris this conflict really was 'the worst reported since the Crimea' in the nineteenth century.[6] Unlike later campaigns, images of the British armed forces in action were absent for fifty-four days of a seventy-four day campaign. Subsequent to the South Atlantic conflict, political and military leaders embroiled in the US invasion of Grenada, Panama and Operation Desert Storm in Iraq have approvingly referred to events between April-June 1982 as an example of 'good practice' [as opposed to Vietnam] in terms of media-political management. As Philip Knightley concluded with reference to the British government's management of news material:

The MOD [Ministry of Defence] were brilliant - censoring, suppressing, and delaying dangerous news, releasing bad news in dribs and drabs so as to nullify its impact, and projecting their own image as the only real source of accurate information about what was happening.[7]

While the absence of visual material and the containment of the media characterised Prime Minister Thatcher's political management of the Falklands crisis, little attention has focussed on the almost universal geographical ignorance of the Falkland Islands in 1982. After securing cabinet and parliamentary approval for the despatch of the task force, the Falklands were going to be defended regardless of the fact that geography had cruelly located the islands 8,000 miles away from the shores of the British Isles. Unlike the former Yugoslavia, this was not a place that members of the British public had visited on holiday and thus could not conjure up images of the islands let alone locate this British territory. Moreover, the Falklands were invaded by a violent and unstable military regime rather than a democracy so inevitably it was easier to justify a possible conflict. As a case study of media-political management, the Falklands conflict exemplifies an era, which defies the claim that television coverage is the most significant factor in determining a government's response to international crises. The crisis was also unusual for other reasons such the involvement of a member of the Royal Family [Prince Andrew serving as a Royal Navy helicopter pilot] and there were only a few weeks of actual fighting. This paper examines the circumstances surrounding the crisis in April 1982 and the response of the Thatcher government to the news that the Argentine armed forces had occupied the disputed Falkland Islands and South Georgia. The obstacles facing the media on the home and battlefront are then considered together with the paucity of basic transmitting facilities, the hostility of the armed forces to the taskforce journalists and the geographical distance of the Falklands from London. The penultimate section of the paper returns to the geographical dimension of the crisis and considers how unfamiliarity and remoteness of the Falkland Islands affected media reporting and conspired to create fantasies. Finally, the implications of the Falklands conflict are considered in a Post-Cold War era when television viewers are simply invited by some military and political figures to admire the professionalism of the armed forces and the precision of their weapons.

The Background to the 1982 Falklands Crisis

When the Argentine military regime invaded the disputed Falkland Islands in April 1982, British defence and foreign policy suffered arguably its worst crisis since the 1956 Suez campaign.[8] No one in the Foreign and Commonwealth Office was prepared for a small colonial war in a far flung corner of a diminishing empire. While the islands have long been an object of dispute between Argentina and Britain, a 1968 Memorandum of Understanding set out the terms for a transfer of sovereignty to Argentina once the 'interests' of the Falkland Islands community were secured. In the intervening period, successive

British governments prevaricated on the sovereignty question and pressurised by an increasingly vocal 'Falklands Lobby' in Parliament and the media premised the transfer to be conditional on the 'wishes' of the small community.[9] Unfortunately for those who wished to dispose of the Falklands from the imperial portfolio, the Islanders did not 'wish' to relinquish their claims to British citizenship and Argentine frustration mounted as the British showed little inclination to implement the provisions of the Memorandum of Understanding. After fourteen years of meetings and proposals, the Argentine military controlling the Republic began to contemplate a more radical action for solving this territorial dispute. In January 1982, a new military junta headed by the General Leopoldo Galtieri undertook a fundamental review of the Falklands/Malvinas question in a climate where there was considerable public pressure for a resolution prior to the 150th anniversary of the British occupation of the Falkland Islands.

While the South Atlantic was a comparatively neglected corner of the British Empire, successive post-war Argentine governments both military and civilian identified the Falklands question as one of the most important issues facing Argentine foreign policy. The symbolic importance of the Islas Malvinas cannot be under-estimated. Since the presidency of Juan Domingo Perón in the 1940s and 1950s, all school children were instructed of the pressing necessity for the Argentine Republic to recover these lost islands.[10] Argentina would never be totally free of the constraints of colonialism and dependency as long as the Malvinas as well as other disputed islands such as South Georgia remained in the hands of perfidious Britain. A major diplomatic victory for Argentina was achieved in 1965 when United Nations resolution 2065 was adopted and called for both parties to seek a settlement 'bearing in mind the interests of the population of the Falkland Islands (Malvinas)'. While the British agreed to initiate discussions on the matter in January 1966 the goals of both parties were very different. In contrast to Argentina's single-minded pursuit of restoring territorial integrity, British interests in the South Atlantic were diluted by the need to balance NATO responsibilities with the limited financial resources available for defence and foreign policy commitments. While some progress in improved contact between Argentina and the Falkland Islands, the hostility of the Islanders to an eventual settlement in favour of Argentina was a major stumbling block.

A major review of the economic potential of the Falklands and South Georgia in 1976 failed to further progress because the British neither agreed to fund the major economic priorities identified as necessary to improve the parlous condition of the local economy nor facilitated the transfer of sovereignty to Argentina. When the new government under Prime Minister Thatcher took power in 1979, the Falklands question remained insoluble whereas a post-colonial settlement for Rhodesia/Zimbabwe and Belize was implemented. As if to reinforce British disinterest in the South Atlantic, the high profile deployment of HMS *Endurance* was to be recalled after the results of the 1981 Defence Review were published. As the official inquest headed by Lord Franks into the Falklands crisis concluded, political muddle in combination with financial expediency had combined to send a series of ambiguous signals to the Argentine military regime that Britain was no longer really interested in retaining the Falkland Islands. Significantly, the Franks report did not blame the British government for not having predicted the invasion.

In Argentina too a series of circumstances helped to precipitate the Argentine invasion of the Falklands in April 1982. Since 1976, the military occupied political office in Argentina with the intent of pursing a number of territorial disputes involving Chile and Britain. The controversy with Chile over control of islands south of the Beagle Channel hinged on the belief that they were vital for access to Antarctica and South Atlantic. The Football World Cup hosted by Argentina in 1978 ultimately prevented an invasion of Chile because the military junta did not wish for further bad publicity following repeated accusations of human rights abuses. After an uneasy truce with Chile had been secured by the external arbitration of the Vatican, attention turned once more to the Falklands question. Unlike earlier regimes, the new junta under General Galtieri included Admiral Jorge Anaya whose ambition and well-established determination to recover the disputed islands for Argentina was no secret. While the symbolic value of the Malvinas was undisputed, the Argentine regime also believed that the Falklands were strategically important as a 'gateway' to Antarctica and the resource rich South Atlantic ocean. Aggrieved by the Vatican's decision to favour Chile in the Beagle Channel arbitration case, the military regime could not accept that the Falklands question remained unsettled. As Freedman and Gamba-Stonehouse concluded in their review of the Falklands crisis, 'Britain was far away from the South Atlantic. From the perspective of Buenos Aires it had no substantial strategic or economic interest in the Falklands, while the local population was small and declining. The Islands seemed to fall exactly into the category of old colonies that had been abandoned in the previous few decades'.[11]

The trigger for the Falklands invasion has been traced to the activities in the southern hemispheric summer of 1981 to an Argentine scrap metal merchant team working on a contract to recover materials at an abandoned whaling station in the disputed island of South Georgia. Before completing the contract, the Argentine party hoisted their national flag and claimed the island for the Republic.[12] Meanwhile plans were put in place in Buenos Aires for a military invasion in case new negotiations with Britain over the Falklands failed to deliver progress on sovereignty. National Security Directive 1/82 was drawn up by the military, which detailed the Junta's plans to recover the territories of the Falkland Islands, South Georgia and the South Sandwich Islands. Argentine patience was running out with a British policy, which appeared trapped on the one hand by defending the 'wishes' of Islanders and on the other hand by persistent pressures to achieve financial savings in overseas commitment. After inconclusive New York-based talks in February 1982, plans were set in motion for an invasion of the Falklands and in April 1982 Operation *Rosario* was implemented. Last minutes crisis negotiations involving the United States failed to dissuade the Argentine regime from military action in the belief that the Reagan administration would at worst only be a benign observer. After overcoming short but determined resistance from the 67 Royal Marines stationed on the Falkland Islands, Argentine forces successfully completed their mission and the Malvinas were once more part of the Republic's national territory. The Governor of the Falkland Islands, Rex Hunt, was instructed to pack his bags and leave the Governor's Residence in civilian clothing and await evacuation to Uruguay.

The news of an Argentine invasion reached London shortly after the occupation of the islands and provoked the most severe political crisis in the Prime Minister's eleven-year occupation of Downing Street. Meetings with military figures including one famous one involving the First Sea Lord, Admiral Sir Henry Leach, assured Mrs Thatcher that the launch of a task force was feasible to recover a British territory, which had been illegally invaded contrary to the principles of international law and self-determination.[13] Nevertheless, the British government was in some difficulty and arguably without the decision to proceed with the task force, Thatcher might have been forced to reconsider her political position. With the support of United Nations Resolution 502 condemning Argentina for violating Article 51 of the UN Charter, the British delegation in New York under Sir Anthony Parsons pushed for further pressure to be placed on Argentina to withdraw forthwith from the Falkland Islands. In order to consolidate political support, the government argued that they were upholding international law and principles such as 'aggression must not succeed' rather than understandably confronting more troubling issues such as colonialism and the complete failure to pursue a consistent policy towards the Falklands questions. Mrs Thatcher's credibility hung in the balance and only the success of the task force would convey the image of a government firmly in control of a crisis whose origin lay in part with British indecision and procrastination.

Media-Political Relations and the Reporting of War

Philip Taylor has argued that once war breaks out, there are two types of 'war' that have to be managed by national governments and the armed forces.[14] The first is the 'real war' in which combatants may perish and the second is the 'media war' whereby the grim realities of conflict are reported and represented to a distant and non-participating audience. As Taylor contends:

> Real war is about sounds, sight, smell, touch and taste of the nasty, brutal business of killing people … Media war, however, is literally a mediated event which draws on that reality but which, in and of itself, is confined to merely an audio-visual – and therefore inherently desensitizing – representation of it.[15]

When the decision was taken to send a task force to the South Atlantic, there was considerable confusion over the role of the media in the event of conflict. It should be recalled that there were many political and military figures in Britain and the USA who believed that war could be averted and that the length of sailing time [three weeks] to the South Atlantic provided further opportunities for conflict resolution. Despite Mrs Thatcher's personal resolution, the American Secretary of State, Alexander Haig was to be embarked on a hectic round of shuttle diplomacy in an attempt to prevent the outbreak of conflict. However, given the political stakes on both sides, it was always highly unlikely that Argentina would withdraw from the Falklands without some form of recognition of their sovereignty.

Notwithstanding those American endeavours, the despatch of the task force in early April meant that the question of media reporting and the release of information to the public had to be addressed forthwith. As Bernard Ingham, the then press officer for the Prime Minister recalled, there was considerable hostility from the Royal Navy for any journalists to accompany the task force.[16] Unlike the Army with their extensive experience of media reporting in Northern Ireland, the Royal Navy [sometimes called the silent service] unaccustomed to the media ignited a fracas between Whitehall, the armed forces and media organisations to secure the presence of journalists during a military campaign.[17] It was eventually agreed that journalists should be present in order to record events not only to prevent a public row with the domestic media but also to maintain public support in the event of conflict.

Agreeing the final number of accompanying journalists had been the source of considerable argument as the Ministry of Defence (MOD) initially proposed just one representative from four national newspapers. John le Page [or possibly even his wife], the then Director of the Newspapers Publishers Association, carried out a 'lucky dip' and the four lucky winners were the *Daily Mirror*, the *Daily Express*, the *Daily Telegraph* and the *Daily Mail*. After further intense negotiations involving Bernard Ingham a total of 29 all-British party of journalists including 2 photographers representing a range of national and regional newspapers and media organisations such as the BBC, ITN and the Press Association were approved. Alarmed by the potential of the media to interfere with a military campaign, task force commanders were reluctant to accommodate the working needs of journalists which led to complaints that the lack of communication facilities hindered the despatch of copy from the South Atlantic. Throughout the Falklands crisis, the media accused the military of using 'technical' excuses in order to prevent the transmission of visual and written material from the battlefront to London and elsewhere in the UK. But the journalists were not alone. The Ministry of Defence also suffered its own information delays and remained highly dependent on a borrowed American satellite for any kind of direct communication linkage with the task force.

With no means of direct transmission of material from the Falklands, films had to be transferred to Ascension Island and then flown to Britain. Delays and accusations of interference proved a frustrating experience for journalists eager to despatch copy to news managers. The average gap between filming and transmission was 17 days, a substantial time lapse in the modern world of media news networks.

While technical constraints and geographical distance typified the constraints of reporting the Falklands crisis, the MOD choreographed the news agenda. Working on the assumption that the public 'right to know' has to be balanced against a government's responsibility to handle a conflict, most analysts have argued that the Thatcher government pursued a policy of considerable media control. According to the academic and journalist Peter Hennessy, the Prime Minister received advice from World War Two veterans such as Sir Frank Cooper, the Permanent Secretary of the Ministry of Defence and the former Prime Minister Harold Macmillan who had handled the government's media response to the 1956 Suez Crisis.[18] The specially created 'war cabinet' [without the presence of the Treasury] had to negotiate two major restrictions: formal censorship and associated controls imposed by the Ministry of Defence. These formal controls involved MOD media officers actively intervening in London and the South Atlantic to restrict news coverage of particular events. Led by the acting head of public relations, Ian McDonald, who was not a professional public relations officer, the MOD sought to restrict the flow of information by using short and formal statements in combination with a D notice system of voluntary restraint. His slow and rather halting style of delivery was designed to ensure that clearly understandable accounts of the task force were presented for the domestic and international media. Until his replacement by a professional news officer, Neville Taylor, lobby briefings and progress reports from Sir Frank Cooper supplemented McDonald's recorded briefings of the task force's progress.

Appropriately for a country with a highly developed culture of official secrecy, 'operational security' became a catch-all term to protect a range of ills from incompetent military planning, misinformation, lack of planning, inter-service rivalry and poor organisation. The second area concerned the practices relating to self-censorship by media managers in the name of 'good taste' and public opinion. The latter proved particularly significant as during the crisis and subsequent conflict, sections of the media found themselves under intense criticism not only for 'unpatriotic' behaviour but also for excessive jingoism such as the sinking of the *Belgrano*.

In terms of formal censorship and controls imposed by the MOD, examples abound of deliberately restricted or hindered media reporting in the build-up and subsequent confrontation. In the absence of any clear policy relating to media-political relations bar a 1977 Army paper on information policy, most journalists concur that the handling of the crisis was at times crass and ill informed. Despite these criticisms, it was clear that Sir Frank Cooper of the Ministry of Defence was instrumental in drawing on-the-spot guidelines for the media, which requested no commentary be voiced on operational plans, military capability, communications and military tactics and possible responses by the Argentine forces. These arrangements were often unsatisfactory and the curtailment of the off-the-record briefings in late April 1982 as the prospect for a diplomatic resolution began to recede, the MOD decided that these briefings could jeopardise military security and thus they were suddenly ended.

The MOD also began to withdraw accredited contact with journalists with the effect of denying access to additional information on the task force. As the BBC journalist, Peter Snow recalled, 'And there was a sort of barrier building up between the press and the Ministry of Defence which was really hurting both sides'.[19] While the decision was reversed in late May 1982, evidence accumulated that the MOD was engaged in a deliberate policy of misinformation, which delayed release of details relating to British losses and casualties. One such example concerned the landing of the task force at San Carlos when Sir Frank Cooper did use off-the-record briefings to inform the media that there would be no 'D-Day' style landings on the Falklands. Another concerned events surrounding the despatch of the nuclear submarine HMS *Superb* in April 1982 when the media were given the impression that the vessel was sailing from Gibraltar to the Falklands when in fact it had sailed back from the South Atlantic.

On the battlefront too access was constrained and the journalists often found themselves highly isolated from the military and the MOD press officials accompanying the party. After the sinking of the Argentine warship *Belgrano*, the chances of a peaceful negotiation appeared to recede still further as the Argentine junta rejected the Peruvian peace proposals.[20] Instead, the conflict intensified and the loss of HMS *Sheffield* two days later shocked British public opinion and brought home the grim realities of conflict. It was the first time the Royal Navy had lost a ship in battle conditions since the Second World War. Sobered by events, concern mounted that press reporting of any subsequent confrontations should not impede the security needs of the task force. However, when the officers in charge of HMS *Hermes* insisted that the media contingent remained on board for 10 days after the landing in San Carlos, East Falkland, accusations abounded that the military were actively hindering war correspondents by limiting access if they thought 'operational security' was being compromised.[21] However, this type of constraint could be applied in a crude fashion if it was felt that either morale was threatened or military detail compromised. Patrick Bishop, who worked for the *Observer* provided one example of how military censors prevented copy from being despatched on the grounds of so-called 'inaccuracies':

On the day the landing ship, *Sir Galahad* was sunk we interviewed many of the survivors whose accounts made it plain that the disaster was at least partly due to bad planning and unnecessary risk-taking by the Task Force commanders. I submitted an article to the censors on board HMS *Fearless* quoting the survivors extensively but taking care not to highlight the critical elements of their stories in the hope that these would not be picked up once the despatch reached the *Observer*. Returning to the ship four days later I checked with the minder to make sure the article had been sent. He had decided against letting that one go, he replied. There had been some 'inaccuracies' which he felt I would have liked to correct for myself before the piece was transmitted. The inaccuracies were miniscule and the piece was now hopelessly out of date.[22]

This policy was reversed when images or stories judged to be 'supportive' were transmitted to London with alacrity such as the now famous picture by the *Daily Express* photographer Tom Smith of a soldier accepting a cup of tea from a Falkland Island family. Published by the *Sunday Mirror* on 23rd May under the banner headline of 'Cuppa for a Brave Para', it offered readers a reassuring image of the progress of the campaign. As Caroline Brothers has astutely noted:

The photograph was a quintessential image of Britishness. The custom of tea drinking was projected as a hallmark of English culture, while the symbolic picket fence signalled ownership and domestication of this far-flung corner of empire, legitimising the campaign to re-establish sovereignty over it. The smiles of the village women and children expressed gratitude for a job well done, fitting effortlessly into the up-beat narrative of a conflict whose less pleasant aspects had been conscientiously expunged.[23]

Smith's comforting image appeared only two days after the task force had landed at San Carlos whereas Martin Cleaver's spectacular photograph of HMS *Antelope's* explosion was delayed for three weeks because it was judged to be bad for morale.[24] Moreover, journalists were not always treated equally and some such as Max Hastings of the *Standard* appeared to receive favourable treatment when it came to covering the battle scenes in the Falklands. Hastings was famously the first journalist to walk into Stanley and was able to get his report away of the re-capture of the Falklands because a helicopter organised by the army was able to whisk him away to a ship with transmitting facilities.[25]

In the prevailing context of delays and corresponding visual vacuum, the domestic reporting of the Falklands crisis assumed considerable importance given Prime Minister Thatcher's deployment of a political discourse littered with references to 'our boys' and patriotic fervour. Most of the British media with the exception of the BBC, the *Daily Mirror*, the *Guardian* and the *Financial Times* were actively sympathetic to the despatch of the task force and the eventual need for armed confrontation. Punctuated by human interest stories, the tabloid newspapers such as the *Sun* [who were affected by an industrial strike at the time] elicited public support for the task force by publishing accounts which demonstrated that their readers together with the help of topless models were fully behind the war effort. Infamous headlines by the *Sun* such as 'Up your Junta' and 'Gotcha' while part of war rhetoric, ignored the deadly consequences of conflict. In the name of good taste and mindful of the emotionally sensitive state of relatives of the task force, large sections of the print media willingly succumbed to government urgings avoid sensationalising the actual conflict and the possibilities of British casualties.

Broadcasters such as the BBC, already accused of bias during the coverage of the 1981 Brixton riots, found themselves under intense political criticism for their coverage of the conflict. In one notorious example, involving a *Panorama* broadcast of 10th May 1982 the BBC were charged with bias and unpatriotic behaviour by some Conservative MPs for daring to either consider the legitimacy of the war campaign or publicly support the BBC. Despite the criticism, the BBC developed new policies of self-censorship and examples abounded of journalists and media managers declining to publish stories judged to be harmful to the military campaign. The BBC's decision not to publish details of the armed forces' landing at San Carlos was taken in response to a MOD request that the media exercise restraint in order to prevent the Argentines from gaining valuable military information. As the BBC statement later recorded, 'Speculation about future operations was avoided except in the broadest terms of describing British options. Studio analysis tended to confine itself to comment on the day's press statement, coupled with whatever could be gleaned from Argentine communiqués. Less information was broadcast than was available from foreign sources'.[26] Questions of military security and matters of taste and media organisations had to juggle difficult decision concerning whether to broadcast pictures of British casualties such as those sustained at Bluff Cove where landing ships at anchor were attacked by Argentine aircraft. While ITN declined to broadcast, the BBC decided to show a clip of a solider being carried away from the battle with a severed leg that had been blown off. Full pictures of the solider were not, however, shown by the BBC until several weeks after the campaign. Peter Woon, the then editor of BBC TV News argued that unlike other parts of the world, British casualties were distinct:

> We edit for exactly the same reasons of taste and not lingering, but you do not have to consider in Beirut the impact on relatives and friends and all that: it is not their sons and daughters in Beirut.[27]

If the BBC or other had broadcast scenes of British casualties then they would have been subjected to considerable outpourings of anger from the relatives, local and national newspapers and politicians.

The control of visual information during the Falklands crisis was due to an extraordinary combination of factors ranging from technical and human considerations to active government intervention to restrain the flow of information. More disturbingly, perhaps, for a democratic culture was the media's self-imposed form of censorship, which ensured that no pictures of British defence facilities and or casualties were shown to domestic viewers even if some may have been relatives of the dead and or injured. As a consequence, newspapers such as *The Scotsman* contended that the reason for was to reassure public opinion that the conflict was relatively blood-free. However, despite the myriad of restrictions and delays facing journalists it would be wrong to conclude that expressions of dissent during April-June 1982 were expunged from public debate. There is no simple correlation between public support for a conflict such as the Falklands and the absence of any visual evidence of human loss. Most viewers are intelligent enough to realise that war carries heavy risks of casualties.

The Fantastical Falklands and a Culture of Dissent

The representations of place are never politically innocent. Notions of geography, identity and territory are critical in understanding not only nationalist politics but also the bloody struggles they provoked. When the news broke on the invasion of the Falklands in April 1982, asides and jokes regarding the geographical location of these remote islands accompanied expressions of disbelief. A far-flung corner of the empire had been invaded and a British policy since 1968 of attempting to persuade the Falkland Islanders to transfer their allegiance to Argentina was exposed as bankrupt. The resulting conflict with Argentina seemed to confirm conventional international relations theory that states will fight one another over territory and the control of resources but these disputed islands were also imbued with considerable amounts of historical fantasy and national mythologies. Complex histories and realities were overwhelmed and effaced by historical analogies to World War II, which elevated the Falklands from their historical and geographical co-ordinates. In the intense atmosphere of the first Saturday sitting of Parliament since the 1956 Suez Crisis, the Prime Minister established this particular scene:

> The people of the Falklands like the people of the United Kingdom are an island race. Their way of life is British, their allegiance is to the crown. They are few in number [sic], but they have the right to live in peace, and to choose their way of life and their allegiance.[28]

Mrs Thatcher was not alone in her expression of outrage, the Labour shadow cabinet led by Michael Foot and John Silkin, also contended that the Falklands deserved the protection of the UK despite unsuccessful attempts of both Labour and Conservative governments to dispose of the islands. As Michael Foot contended on 3rd April 1982, 'there is a longer term interest to ensure that foul and brutal aggression does not succeed in the world. If it does there will be a danger not merely to the Falkland Islands, but to the people all over this dangerous planet'.[29] It was argued that the Falklands had been brutalised by a vicious regime hell-bent on spatial expansionism and the domination of place. Apart from the collective fate of the Falkland Islanders, there were important principles of international law relating to the illegal invasion of territory, which had to be protected. For a place that was virtually unacknowledged during the Cold War, the Falklands suddenly became hugely controversial in the midst of Cold War rhetoric and the Soviet Union as an 'evil empire'. Mrs Thatcher, a child during the Second World War, now invoked the dangers of 'appeasing' dictators and warned that the Falklands question was the greatest foreign policy priority facing the UK. As the Prime Minister informed the House of Commons on 8th April 1982, 'Throughout the Western world and beyond there is a realisation that if this dictator succeeds in unprovoked aggression, other dictators will succeed elsewhere. We are fighting a battle against that type of aggression, and once again it is Britain that is fighting it'.[30]

Despite the feverish atmosphere of the House of Commons in the first days of the Falklands campaign, dissenting parliamentarians such as Tony Benn were prepared to question the legitimacy of outrage. It was noted that Britain had expressed a willingness to hand-over the Falklands and moreover, if there was concern over the intentions of the Argentine regime, then why had British firms continued to export weapons to Buenos Aires? To compound matters still further the 1981 Nationality Act ending denied the Falkland Islanders the automatic right to British citizenship. Sections of the British media were initially highly sceptical of the government's claims regarding the symbolic and political importance of the Falklands. Journalists questioned the motives of Prime Minister Thatcher and her intense suspicion of elements of Whitehall particularly those who dealt with 'foreigners'. As Peter Jenkins of the *Guardian* noted:

> By what weird calculus was it reckoned that the fate of all the free peoples hinge upon the fate of 1800 islanders and their 600,000 sheep? This crisis has brought to the surface every harboured grievance and fantasy. The Foreign Office have become a nest of traitors; the navy cuts, Trident, the common market – they were to blame. Not only are we able to defend our own citizens around the world but we are in the process withdrawing their full citizenship rights. Under the Nationality Act it is improbable that Don Pacifico would have qualified as a British citizen. The tin-pot dictator provides the chance to avenge the loss of empire, the true humiliation of Suez and the long slide in power and influence.[31]

For most on the political left, already angered by the Prime Minister's assault on public services and trade unions, the Falklands campaign became a turning point in their hostility towards the neo-right and their expressions of aggressive nationalism. Accordingly as Kevin Foster has argued, 'the Falklands had been transformed [by the political right], by a process of literary and cultural association, into the 'Falklands' ... a rallying point for national regeneration'.[32]

It is also important to recall that scepticism relating to the Falklands campaign was not simply the product of left-wing intellectuals and high-profile dissidents such as Tony Benn. Public opinion was generally supportive to the government but not overwhelmingly so. In April 1982, polls indicated that 70% of people questioned thought that islands should be recovered but were circumspect as to initiating a war over the ownership of the Falklands.[33] If one takes into account some of the published letters by readers to national newspapers, the public was not uncritically accepting government pronouncements on the handling of the crisis. Contrary to some of the literary critics such as Foster, the transformation of the Falklands into a national crusade was not assured and official restrictions on media reporting support the notion that political leaders agonised over whether public opinion could be relied upon in the event of heavy losses. World War Two veterans and members of the War Cabinet, such as Willie Whitelaw and Francis Pym, were said to be particularly anxious about the potential human costs of military options.

Dissidents of the conflict also filled the visual and political vacuum during the weeks leading up conflict in the Falklands with their critiques of the crisis.[34] The cartoonist Steve Bell of the *Guardian,* in one strip, showed a naval officer rallying the task force with the cry 'You and these hand-picked dogs will attack the islands at dawn and liberate 50,000 sheep'. Rather than representing the Falklands' rural life as a reassuring symbol of British identity, the bleak landscape and over-abundance of sheep became a source of ridicule. The sheer number of sheep compared to the declining human population on the Falklands added to the air of unreality and fantasy. Interestingly, his *If...* strip cartoons combine a stinging critique of the domestic consequences of Thatcher's economic programme with a persistent interrogation of the British justification for the despatch of the task force. His cartoons of the conflict appeared in the second week of the invasion and concentrated on developing a dialogue between two naval personnel, Jack Middletar and Kipling, sailing on board the nuclear punt HMS *Incredible*.[35] Middletar was reminiscent of real-life Falklands veterans such as the late naval officer David Tinker whose posthumous letters revealed his dissent, 'we were going to leave [the Falkland Islands] undefended in April, and deprive its residents of British citizenship in October. And to recapture it, having built up their [i.e. Argentina's] forces with western arms'.[36]

Bell's cartoons question not only the legitimacy of the 26,000 strong task force but also the media's response to the representation of the task force and the distant place they were being asked to defend. Once Unites States and United Nations-sponsored diplomacy failed these representational issues intensified as the Thatcher government sought on occasions to encourage and at other times to restrain the media from publishing critical stories and images which might destabilise public opinion. When Steve Bell attempted to publish his cartoon of the sinking of HMS *Sheffield* in mid-May 1982, it was refused on the grounds of 'good taste'. His sense of the absurd came to the fore once the task force landed in the Falklands and the armed forces rather than being 'our boys' are renamed as the Special Iron Lady Service for the duration of the conflict.

In May 1982, as the fighting intensified, an ITN poll suggested that 55 per cent of respondents agreed that the Falkland Islands were worth the loss of more British lives as opposed to 38 per cent who disagreed with the proposition.[37] Given the lack of overwhelming public support, government and military restrictions on material from the battlefront were deemed extremely important in maintaining the Falklands as a place worthy of recovery. Tom Smith's photograph of the soldier receiving a welcome cup of tea after the San Carlos landing coincided with protests in London against the war. Mainstream broadcasters were eager to stem opposition to the task force and ITN interviewed Tony Benn asked about the 'appropriateness' of a peace march in the aftermath of the San Carlos landings and resultant casualties. In contrast, an event celebrating the war campaign with a public outburst of patriotic songs at Pier Head in Liverpool on 12th May 1982 received lavish coverage by the BBC and ITN.[38] Critics of the conflict including Steve Bell contended that the government was being assisted by section of the media through their jingoistic reporting which cultivated childish stereotypes and imperial fantasies of a 'Great Britain'. In the absence of television pictures of the bloody realities of conflict, these representations of a 'good war' were politically resilient in the wake of reporting restrictions imposed on the journalists in the field and in London. When the mainstream media attempted to portray the crisis in more critical terms, Mrs Thatcher was swift to denounce their dissent. As she told Parliament in May 1982, 'I understand that there are occasions when some commentators will say that the Argentines did something and then the 'British' did something. I can only say that if this is so it gives great offence and causes great emotion to many people'.[39]

The continued exercise of self-censorship by media managers called into question the critical independence of the journalists at a time of war. In the absence of regular visual material regardless of technical or political reasons, effectiveness and integrity of journalists especially in a context where professional careers may depend upon maintaining good working relations with government departments. Arguments relating to 'good taste' can be particularly invidious as government ministers and civil servants attached to the Ministry of Defence implored editors not to report military disasters such as the loss of helicopters over South Georgia in April 1982 and to withhold pictures of British fatalities. In different media-reporting circumstances and if casualties had mounted sharply, the government might have been forced to confront more openly the rationale and justification for the military response to the Falklands invasion. Luck played a major part in this conflict and many of the British soldiers owe their lives to unexploded Argentine bombs. In the absence of other sources of information especially in such a remote place with no freelance or overseas reporters, the armed forces' control of information from the battlefront was critical in shaping the availability of visual material.

After the cessation of the conflict in June 1982, more critical accounts of the campaign inevitably began to emerge from the writings of journalists and soldiers. While some were hostile of government censorship, others focussed on the cultural and geographical conditions of the Falkland Islands. Due to a general lack of knowledge, their transformation in political discourse helped to erode the great distances between the Falklands and the UK. When *The Times* proclaimed that 'We are all Falkland Islanders now' in April 1982, it consolidated a government argument that we had an obligation to defend the rights of a distant British community, a mythical Ambridge in need of rescue.[40] David Tinker's letters published after his death on HMS *Coventry* revealed his ambivalence towards events and 'all this killing going on over a flag for a rock with a village population'.[41] Simon Weston, who sustained horrific burns during the Falklands conflict, argued that the Falklands were 'empty, bleak, desolate and inhospitable … I never saw a single tree'.[42] While the supporters of war attempted to portray the Falklands as a quasi-Ambridge, the visiting soldiers and journalists began to challenge the kinship of this 'island race' in the bleak and unforgiving South Atlantic environment. Many of the first hand accounts of the fighting indicate how those images of place and the local inhabitants failed to live up to their expectations. In one immortal exchange, Des King the then manager of the Upland Goose Hotel barked at some members of the Parachute Regiment, 'First, the fucking Argies now you lot. When are you going to clear off and leave us in peace'.[43]

To the critics of the war, media restrictions in combination with the lack of effective dissent helped to maintain the claims of the British government that the Falklands was worth dying for. The censorship of visual images from the battlefront spared watching audiences the horrors of war and arguably the bleak qualities of the Falklands landscape.[44] As Walter Little has concluded, 'Why Argentina should want the Falklands at all is a bit of mystery to some British observers. After all, Argentina has more land than it knows what to do with and the Falklands, by common consent, are hardly an attractive piece of real estate'.[45]

'Lessons' from the 1982 Falklands Conflict

For British audiences, the Falklands conflict was dominated by radio rather than television reports. At a time of Cold War tension and intercontinental missile technology, it was striking to see a traditional territorial conflict unfolding over the Falklands theatre. After the conflict, Mrs Thatcher reflected on the purpose of the conflict and argued that the task force would not have 'risked their lives in any way to have a United Nations trusteeship. They risked their lives to defend British sovereign territory, the British way of life, and the right of British people to determine their own future'.[46] For many on the political right, even twenty years after the event, the 1982 Falklands conflict continues to embody the determination of the British people to restore the wounded pride of the British nation. The official experiences from the South Atlantic helped to guide diplomacy and war rhetoric in the aftermath of the Iraqi invasion of Kuwait. As Mrs Thatcher reminded her readers, 'As so often over these months, I found myself reliving in an only slightly different form my experiences of the build up for the Falklands. No matter how little chance there is of negotiation succeeding, the case is always made for yet another piece of last ditch diplomacy'.[47] Regardless of whether Kuwait was an ex-colony or a remaining element in Britain's declining imperial portfolio, the lesson of the 'Falklands' was that invaders have to be stopped. In political discourse, the 'Falklands' has become a symbol of British determination even though some places were deemed worthier of intervention and decisiveness than places where British interests are less obvious such as East Timor which was illegally invaded by Indonesia in 1975.

In the aftermath of the Falklands crisis, the House of Commons Defence Committee concluded that there had been a greater level of censorship then could be reasonably justified under the name of 'operational security'. Given the nature of the conflict, journalists attached to the task force were dependent on the military for transport to and from the conflict zone as well as communication facilities. Journalists were also very conscious of the fact that their close proximity to the British troops played a part in ensuring a collective loyalty to one another. When news managers in London and elsewhere resorted to using Argentine material in the absence of British footage, they were accused of unpatriotic behaviour. The military defended these restrictions and delays used during the Falklands campaign and future military planners advocate it as a case of good practice in terms of media-military management. As with the Gulf War in the early 1990s, military figures such as Chief of Defence Staff, Sir Terence Lewin defended the charges of misleading the media and public opinion:

I do not see it as deceiving the press or the public; I see it as deceiving the enemy. What I am trying to do is to win. Anything I can do to help me win is fair as far as I'm concerned, and I would have thought that that was what the Government and the public and the media would want, too, provided the outcome was the one we were all after.[48]

This well-versed argument relies on the basic assumption that all interested parties can agree on the identity of the 'enemy' and the references to 'we'. While it is obvious that the enemy was Argentina, Mrs Thatcher's wartime rhetoric was also hostile towards dissenters such as anti-war protesters, the BBC, the political left and trade unionists. In the absence of wider wartime coverage, the role of journalists in deliberately or accidentally participating in military deception campaigns becomes all the more significant. The 1991 Gulf War campaign once again demonstrated the complicity of journalists in this awkward equation with the military, as stories of a sea-borne assault by the Allied forces against Iraqi forces were faithfully reported despite the fact that no such plans were intended.

The final 'lesson' from the Falklands crisis is that British imperialism is not dead despite a post-war period dominated by post-colonial change. On reflection, perhaps a majority of the public wanted to hear, read and see stories about a victorious Britain instead of the jibes relating to a country hit by industrial decline, mass unemployment and urban unrest. 'The sick man of Europe' had had the 'Great' put back into 'Great Britain' and perhaps the Falklands was an enjoyable fantasy which censorship and reporting restriction perpetuated in terms of the political inconsistencies of the campaign and the pictorial absence of British casualties. One hundred years before the Falklands crisis, Britain completed an imperial project as Antarctica was incorporated into the imperial map. Unlike other parts of the British Empire, signs of post-colonial resistance were understandably rare in the stormy seas and polar wastelands of the far south. Until the Argentine invasion in April 1982, British imperialism prevailed. Victory in the Falklands transformed the Conservative government. As the Falklands question and the IRA's determination to strike at the 'heart of empire' in April 1992 illustrate some colonial questions remain dangerously persistent.[49]

NOTES

1. B. Ingham, *Kill the Messenger* (London, Harper Collins, 1992), p. 283.
2. Colonel Robert O'Brien, the then Pentagon Deputy Director of Defence Information talking to CBS in the aftermath of the 1983 US invasion of Grenada. Quoted in C. Brothers, *War and Photography* (London, Routledge, 1997), p. 206.
3. Quoted in C. Brothers *War and Photography* (London, Routledge, 1997), p. 206.
4. Brian Hanrahan's famous phrase 'I counted them all out and I counted them all back' when commenting on the return of British Harrier jets was highly evocative at a time when the supply of television pictures was meagre.
5. Quoted in S. Carruthers, *The Media at War* (London, Macmillan, 2000), p. 121.
6. See the analysis in R. Harris *Gotcha!, The Media, the government and the Falklands crisis* (London, Unwin 1983).
7. P. Knightley, 'Managing the media in wartime' cited in *Index on Censorship* Volume 11 number 6 (1982), p. 7.
8. See P. Beck, *The Falkland Islands as an International Problem* (London, Routledge, 1988), for relevant details leading up to the Falkland crisis.
9. On the role of the Falklands lobby see C. Ellerby, *'British interests in the Falkland Islands: Economic development, the Falklands lobby and the sovereignty dispute 1945-1989'* (Unpublished D.Phil. University of Oxford 1990).
10. K. Dodds, 'Geopolitics and the geographical imagination of Argentina' in K. Dodds and D. Atkinson (eds), *Geopolitical Traditions: A Century of Geopolitical Thought* (London, Routledge, 2000), pp. 150-184.
11. L. Freedman and V. Gamba-Stonehouse, *The Signals of War* (London, Faber and Faber, 1990), p. 6.
12. There has been some debate within Whitehall on the future of British Antarctic Survey and whether a base would be retained in South Georgia given existing funding pressures and that scientific priorities lay within the Antarctic Treaty region. See R. Headland, *The Island of South Georgia* (Cambridge, Cambridge University Press, 1984).
13. On the significance of Sir Henry Leach and his belief in British naval capabilities see M. Hastings and S. Jenkins, *The Battle for the Falklands* (London, Michael Joseph, 1983).

14. Philip M. Taylor, 'War and the media' Lecture presented to a conference on media-military relations at the Royal Military Academy at Sandhurst in 1995. Accessed on www.leeds.ac.uk/ics/arts-pt2.htm [16th February 2001].

15. Ibid., p. 1.

16. B. Ingham, *Kill the Messenger* (London, Harper Collins, 1992), pp. 284-285. For a senior military view of the Royal Navy and its attitude towards the media, see J. Moore, 'The Falklands War: a commander's view of the defence/military interface' in P. Young (ed.), *Defence and the Media in the Time of Limited Wars* (London, Frank Cass, 1992), pp. 142-154. See also the review of the Falklands campaign by M. Hudson and J. Stainer, *War and the Media* (Stroud, Sutton Publishing, 1997).

17. The Royal Navy had not taken any journalists on board their ships during the height of the so-called Cod War with Iceland in the 1970s. As a consequence, as British journalists recorded, the Icelandic embassy in London was extremely effective in taking advantage of the visual vacuum by releasing their own visual material of the struggle between rival naval and fishing vessels in the North Atlantic. See D. Morrison and H Tumber, *Journalists at War* (London, Sage, 1988), p. 192.

18. P. Hennessy, *The Prime Minister: The Office and its Holders Since 1945* (London, Allen Lane, 2000).

19. Quoted in D. Morrison and H. Tumber, *Journalists at War* (London, Sage, 1988), p. 201.

20. For more details on the sinking of the Belgrano see A. Gavshon and D. Rice, *The Sinking of the Belgrano* (London, Secker and Warburg, 1984), and C. Ponting, *The Right to Know* (London, Sphere Books, 1985). The Labour MP Tam Dalyell campaigned in the House of Commons for years in an attempt to force the British government to publicly account for its decision to sink the ship while it was heading towards its home port in Argentina.

21. See the commentary in S. Carruthers, *The Media at War* (London, Macmillan, 2000).

22. P. Bishop, 'Reporting the Falklands' *Index on Censorship*, Volume 11, Number 6, (1982): p. 7.

23. C. Brothers, *War and Photography* (London, Routledge, 1997), p. 208.

24. See P. Young and P. Jesser, *The Media and the Military* (London, Macmillan, 1997).

25. See his recent reflection on the campaign in M. Hastings, *Going to the Wars* (London, Pan Books, 2000). Resentment at his favourable treatment led to the immortal utterance from another journalist that 'This was neither the time nor the place to kill Max Hastings'. Other commentators have argued that Hastings was instrumental in leading the 'flag waving charge' see B. Cummings, *War and Television* (London, Verso, 1992), p. 100.

26. Quoted in D. Morrison and H. Tumber, *Journalists at War* (London, Sage, 1988), pp. 221-222.

27. Ibid., p. 224.

28. *The Falklands Campaign: A Digest of Debates in the House of Commons between 2 April and 15 June 1982* (London, HMSO, 1982), p. 5.

29. Ibid., p. 7.

30. Ibid., p. 14.

31. P. Jenkins 'Taking leave of our sense' *The Guardian* 6th April 1982. There is a longer history of scepticism towards the Falkland Islands and the best known is Samuel Johnson's 'Thoughts on the late transactions respecting Falkland's islands' in D. Greene (ed.), *The Yale Edition of the Works of Samuel Johnson* (New Haven, Yale University Press, 1963).

32. K. Foster, 'Signifying the wasteland: selling the Falklands' *War, Literature and the Arts* 3 (1991): pp. 35-55. The quote is taken from p. 42.

33. Quoted in J. Laffin, *Fight for the Falklands* (New York, St Martin's Press, 1982), p. 27.

34. See my earlier work on Steve Bell in K. Dodds, 'The 1982 Falklands War and a critical geopolitical eye: Steve Bell and the If...cartoons', *Political Geography* 15 (1996): pp. 571-592. On the importance of cartoons as a popular geopolitical source see K. Dodds, *Geopolitics in a Changing World* (Harlow, Pearson Education, 2000).

35. The central character, Kipling was based on the figure of the popular gallant sailor Jack Tar who emerged as a proletarian hero in early 19th century theatre. He is understood not only as a symbol of naval power and fair play but also a figure whose liberal conscience causes nothing but trouble for the authorities. Kipling's constant probing of Thatcher's diplomatic agenda raised troubling issues over the legitimacy of the task force and possible conflict. Captain Middletar was based on a parody of a Captain Dan-Dare like figure – squared jaw, fate on his side and an unstinting loyalty to his superiors. As the crisis unfolded, Bell represented a strong element of the political left which despised her gunboat diplomacy and the satirical adventures of HMS *Incredible* and HMS *Amazing* was indicative.

36. H. Tinker, *A Message from the Falklands: The Life and Death of David Tinker, Lieut. RN. From his Letters and Poems* (London, Junction Books, 1982), p. 16.

37. Quoted in Glasgow University Media Group, *Industry, Economy, War and Politics* (London, Routledge, 1995), pp. 142-143.

38. Ibid, p. 135.

39. *The Falklands Campaign: A Digest of Debates in the House of Commons between 2 April and 15 June 1982* (London, HMSO, 1982), p. 112.

40. *The Times* 'We are all Falkland Islanders now' 5th April 1982. I have explored the significance of this particular implicit moral and geographical claim in K. Dodds, 'Enframing the Falklands: identity, landscape and the 1982 South Atlantic War' *Environment and Planning D: Society and Space* 16 (1998): 733-756. On the transformation of the Falklands into a quasi-Ambridge see A. Barnett, *Iron Britannia* (London, Allison, 1982).

41. H. Tinker, *A Message from the Falklands: The Life and Death of David Tinker, Lieut. RN. From his Letters and Poems* (London, Junction Books, 1982), pp. 180 and 190.

42. S. Weston, *Walking Tall: An Autobiography* (London, Bloomsbury, 1989), pp. 129-131.

43. Quoted in R. McGowan and J. Hands, *Don't Cry for me, Sergeant Major* (London, MacDonald, 1983), pp. 273-274.

44. See D. Mercer, G. Mungham and K. Williams, *The Fog of War: The Media on the Battlefield* (London, Heinemann, 1987).

45. W. Little, 'The Falklands affair: a review of the literature' *Political Studies* 32 (1984): pp. 296-310. The quote is taken from p. 302.

46. Quoted in *Hansard*, House of Commons 15 June 1982 col. 734.

47. M. Thatcher 'No time to go wobbly on Saddam' *Sunday Times* 31st October 1993.

48. Quoted in P. Taylor 'War and the media' *op cit*.

49. I would like to thank Professor Colin Seymour-Ure for his detailed comments on this chapter and to David Welch, Mark Connelly and all the participants at the War and Media conference. I also had the benefit of speaking at a one-day seminar on 'Narrating Modern Conflict' at the University of Wales, Swansea and thank the participants for their comments as well. The responsibility for the analysis lies with the author, however.

Chapter Fifteen
MISSING IN AUTHENTICITY? MEDIA WAR IN THE DIGITAL AGE
Susan L. Carruthers

Virtual Waugh

In 1938, before setting sail to report an obscure African war, a gauche young British correspondent was offered the following advice by his paper's proprietor:

> What the British public wants first, last, and all the time is News. Remember that the Patriots are in the right and are going to win. *The Beast* stands by them four-square. But they must win quickly. The British public has no interest in a war which drags on indecisively. A few sharp victories, some conspicuous acts of personal bravery on the Patriot side and a colourful entry into the capital. That is *The Beast* policy for the war.[1]

The recipient of this sage counsel was, of course, Evelyn Waugh's masterful comic creation, William Boot. While *Scoop*'s hapless hero is best remembered for his equivocal attempts to feign agreement with his patron's wilder requests ("Up to a point, Lord Copper"), Boot scarcely found anything pass-remarkable in this particular injunction. Indeed, decades later Lord Copper's warning about the limits of public interest in distant conflicts continues to strike a resonant chord. Waugh's fictive contest in Ishmaelia concerns 'warring tribes' of whom attenuated audiences know little. Public attention, patience and empathy being in short supply, editors must supply a black-and-white narrative of villains and heroes ('Patriots' versus 'Traitors'), and – crucially – a quick victory by the forces of virtue. Interest is sparked and illuminated as though by a firework display. Exclamations over the colourful explosions last only as long as the novelty of vicarious alignment with the self-evidently virtuous Patriots, the spectacle afforded by their 'conspicuous acts of bravery', and the pageantry of victory. In short, decades before it became fashionable to talk of 'spectator sport war', Waugh's war was already 'virtual' – in much the same way as was NATO's campaign over Kosovo in Michael Ignatieff's description:

> For the citizens of NATO countries… the war was virtual. They were mobilized, not as combatants but as spectators. The war was a spectacle: it aroused emotions in the intense but shallow way that sports do. The events in question were remote from their essential concerns as a football game, and even though the game was in deadly earnest, the deaths were mostly hidden, and above all, they were someone else's.[2]

Varieties of virtuality

Info-war; cyber-war; net-war; anti-war; virtual war; spectator-sport war; humanitarian war; zero-casualty war; post-modern war…[3] War-waging and phrase-making both proliferated over the 1990s as commentators from a variety of disciplines and vantage-points attempted to capture the altered character of contemporary conflict. Some analyses derive from the 'hyper-real' Gulf War of 1991, while others extrapolate from the 'interventions' in Somalia and Former Yugoslavia, particularly NATO's Kosovo campaign of 1999, to draw conclusions about the emergence of 'humane warfare' in the post-cold war era. Some accentuate the deterritorialization of military strategy as it shifts from attrition of enemy materiel and morale to degradation of computerized infrastructure. Others foreground the altered political and social contexts in which western states resort to force, highlighting the limitations policy-makers impose (or which casualty-shy publics compel) on the selection of targets in increasingly asymmetric contests. What they share is a sense that the 'Revolution in Military Affairs' – epitomized by the precision guidance of missiles and of public perceptions alike – has transformed digital age war into a phenomenon radically unlike war past.

For all their newness, at least some of these coinages already exhibit signs of depreciation in the aftermath of September 2001. Can one convincingly argue, for example, that 'western publics' supportive of the 'war on terror' are as loathe to inflict casualties as to incur them? In the wake of 9-11, would Ignatieff still maintain (as he did in 2000) that the United States is a 'post-heroic' society, no longer wedded to warrior models of masculinity?[4] The attacks of September 11, 2001 exposed the inadequate foundations of the Twin Towers and at least some contemporary analysis alike, had these not been sufficiently apparent before. This chapter examines various of the virtualization hypotheses, proposing that for all the futurity of their orientation, many critiques of virtual war lapse into a nostalgic conception of war past in order to fulfil authorial prophesies of a present and future floating free from historic bearings. While claiming to offer an account of the distinctive contours of contemporary conflict, they more often mystify the nature of the experiential and epistemological break that supposedly severs new war from its antecedents.

Convergence and collapse mark many of the processes unfurled under the banner of virtuality. How we fight; who we fight; why we fight; and how we imagine we *will* fight are all couched in a paradox-laden vocabulary of shrinkage and simulation, attenuation and atrophy. The how and the why of contemporary war are, for Ignatieff and other liberal commentators, inextricably linked – their interlinkage constituting a disturbing double-bind. Post-cold war conflicts have been waged not to secure vital national interests—as during two total wars which posed a clear and present danger to state sovereignty—but on behalf of humanitarian objectives: to alleviate hunger and interdict human rights abuses. The altruistic ends for which violence is mobilized demand that force itself appear 'humane': restricted in its intensity and targeting in such a way as to minimize the oxymoronic character of 'humanitarian warfare'. 'Western societies', announces Christopher Coker, 'can now only fight wars which minimise human suffering, that of their enemies' as well as their own'.[5]

However, the desire to bring bombing into alignment with humanitarianism is not the only determinant of these deployments (at least in some critics' eyes). Because altruistic objectives command only superficial support among distant publics in post-military societies, strategy is also predicated on a self-interested desire to preserve service personnel safety while jeopardizing others' lives, all in the name of universal humanism. This asymmetric valuation of 'our' lives as more precious than 'theirs' is encouraged – but then obfuscated – by the promotional packaging of such interventions as a new form of war in which *no one* need get hurt.[6] In James Der Derian's analysis, virtuality and virtuosity present themselves as felicitous bedfellows: war which announces the virtue of its own intentions ('bombing barbarians' to 'save strangers' in danger) simultaneously lays claim to life-preserving precision in its technical delivery.[7] 'Cleanliness' and justness go hand-in-hand. But antiseptic techno-war is only bloodless in the eyes of distant beholders, not for the bodies in its path, as events in Kosovo in 1999 made all too clear. With sorties flown at an untouchable 15,000 feet, NATO ensured the immunity of its service personnel from retaliatory strikes. Meanwhile, Serbian abuses against Kosovars – which bombing purported to halt – proceeded apace, enabled by the turmoil into which NATO actions had plunged Kosovo, and unchecked because of western governments' reluctance to deploy ground forces whose safety could scarcely be guaranteed.

Kosovo is thus emblematic of wars rendered virtual, in part, through their lopsidedness: one party possessing both the technical capacity and moral audacity to engage in violent coercion without endangering itself in the process.[8] But Kosovo has also been interpreted as indicative of virtualizing trends in other ways too. In its extensive image-management - the ubiquity of NATO's spinner-in-chief Jamie Shea - Kosovo underlined the military's growing concern with 'information control' extending from the localized battlefield to the dispersed terrain of popular perceptions. Picking up where the 1991 Gulf War left off, the Kosovo campaign saw extensive efforts on the part of NATO image-managers to insist that new missile systems can actually *realise* the aspiration of casualty-free war on both sides. Civilian fatalities were repeatedly described as the result of either faulty human intelligence or of Milosevic's dastardly – cynically placing people in harm's way in order to expose NATO's self-proclaimed scrupulosity over 'collateral damage' as sham.[9]

To those who had prophesied a dematerializing shift in the locus of war, Kosovo also afforded suggestive evidence that the battlefield of the future will be more ethereal than physical. Hailed as the first 'internet-war', Kosovo attracted much media discussion of Serbian hackers' efforts to disrupt NATO's command and control systems, to corrupt its website and jam its email traffic, accompanied by suggestions that a superior NATO strategy, rather than bombing Belgrade's infrastructure, would have been the electronic depletion of Milosevic's bank account.[10] Certainly Kosovo was a conflict during which both parties made copious use of the internet to promote their own account of the rights and wrongs of NATO's intervention; of the sovereign status of Kosovo and the character of the Kosovo Liberation Army. Belgrade also made an attempt to use its website to deter NATO publics from entertaining thoughts of a ground campaign, prominently displaying photos of cowering soldiers to illustrate the point that 'NATO soldiers would face hell in Kosovo' – though it is less certain whether distant civilians either needed or noticed such warnings.

Missing in Authenticity

Commentators on contemporary conflict diverge on a number of key propositions – primarily the character of post-cold war humanitarianism (if that is indeed the animating impulse behind recent 'interventions'), and its consequences for military strategy. What unites many critics, however, is an insistence that war, for both those fighting and viewing it, has become 'less real'. The very notion of *virtual* war implies its antithesis: *real* war, in which everything now masked, obfuscated, distanced and dissimulated was formerly palpable, recognized, enunciated and knowable – whether the interests served by war, or the fact of death and injury as militarised conflict's inevitable concomitants. However implicit or latent the comparison, discussions of vituality invariably conjure more authentic antecedents, tinged with regret at their passing.

Authenticity has apparently gone AWOL as further distinctions fold: between training and combat; war and game; man and machine; sighting and viewing; soldier and spectator. Der Derian, for example, makes much of the elision between exercises (both virtual generations and more corporeal forms of 'gaming') and live engagements conducted by satellite-positioned personnel for whom digitally-scoped targets are as 'unreal' as those fabricated in training simulations. Moreover, the ways in which future conflicts are envisaged by the US military – story-boarded and graphically generated with the assistance of Disney 'imagineers' – does more than draw attention to the way in which war's mediated projection now preoccupies strategists. The creative energy, not to mention commercial costs, invested in imagining war conjures the phantasm into existence: 'actual' conflicts are not only bound to follow such exhaustive preparations but to follow their script.[11] For Der Derian, the spectacularization of war reaches its apogee in this collusive collision between entertainment corporations and the military-industrial complex, or what he calls MIMENET (the military-industrial-media-entertainment network).[12]

More than a function of confusion between war-gaming and war-waging, processes of disembodiment are generated by new technologies simultaneously placing greater physical distance between soldier and target, while fixing the latter in higher definition. The post-ocular 'cyborg soldier' – man melded with machine – perceives his own location on the battlefield, along with targets of destruction, through his helmet-mounted digital video camera.[13] As Der Derian laments, the objects of violence at once sharpen and blur. No longer recognizably human, 'electronically signified "targets of opportunity"' are more easily dispatched – twice over. Precision guidance enables 'cleaner' targeting, with smart weapons simultaneously allowing clearer consciences.[14] The most worrisome dimension of virtual war, for many commentators, is thus soldiers' growing attenuation from the business of inflicting bodily harm. What attaches proper substance to war is soldiers' dual awareness of threat and danger: an appreciation of both risks run and damage delivered. *Real* war requires the

democratisation of danger – dispersed among combatants on both sides. Ignatieff
reaches this conclusion when a pilot involved in the Kosovo campaign mused on
the impunity with which NATO had flown over Yugoslav airspace: "Having
somebody shoot at me... makes me feel like I'm at war". Hence Ignatieff's
assertion that 'war without death – to our side – is war that ceases to be fully real
to us: virtual war'.[15]

Virtual war's critics exhibit particular concern over the attendant
atrophy of *moral* sense. Soldiers immune from the prospect of injury themselves,
who no longer see what they destroy, suffer a diminished capacity to attach
appropriate meaning to their actions. Death has been divorced from destruction.
Targets are neither announced nor perceived as human. That attacks on
'infrastructure' have real human costs goes unrecognised because the moment for
reckoning the consequences is so deferred – registering dimly as 'higher rates of
infant mortality, untreatable diseases, and malnutrition' at a date sufficiently
distant from the moment of impact that 'humane' bombing can invisibly slip
from the chain of cause and effect.[16]

Since 'the way we fight and report wars' has converged 'onto a single
screen of electronic representation', the de-realizing properties of virtual war suck
viewers into an ethical void too. How, then, do we establish the materiality of
virtual war? Is it possible to reinvest wars fought and represented as risk- and
consequence-free with solidity? How can we recover what's *actual* in virtual war
when computer-generated graphics blend indistinguishably with nosecone
footage bringing us the missile's eye view of war, both images appearing as real or
unreal as one another? Weapons of destruction may now allow us to witness their
implosion, but do they facilitate or circumvent an understanding of the flesh-and-
blood consequences? Many commentators fear a suspension of belief in war's
fatal destructiveness. Hence Margot Norris writes of the 1991 Gulf War's best-
remembered press briefing:

> the miniaturized and abstracted dots and lines inside the cross hairs...
> made Schwarzkopf's "luckiest man in Iraq", the tiny vehicle just safely
> crossing the exploding bridge, a Pac-man. Schwarzkopf's video of an
> actual bombing and an actual potential killing cannot be distinguished as
> a representation with a "real" or actual reference from a simulacrum or
> pure model of the same event.[17]

Der Derian similarly doubts that we can tease apart 'the reality and the
virtuality of war': 'television wars and video war games blur together', not just in
the Gulf or Kosovo, but when teenagers 'confuse the video game Doom for the
highschool classroom'.[18]

The indeterminacy of artifice and life traps virtual war's combatants and
spectators alike, floating as free from ethical encumbrance as one another.
Civilians are repeatedly told that they enjoy a more immediate and intimate
visioning of war than ever before. But as many critics have averred, media
coverage of conflicts since the Gulf War provides only the illusion of completion,
substituting a profusion of images – and the promise of instantaneousness – for
context and meaning. Whether virtual or not, war's mediated representation is
certainly *partial,* in both senses of that term (as the scathing coinage, 'Pentavision',
for US television coverage of the Gulf War implies).[19] Above all else, it is the
dead body that has gone missing in contemporary war – a retreat from palpability
that results as much from wilful deliberation as a more diffuse technological

determinism. [20] In other words, human casualties were not simply 'disappeared' by the virtualizing revolution in military affairs, they have been deliberately excised by militaries unshakeably wedded to the axiom that television war precludes victory – unless battlefield images are rigidly rationed. This most stubborn lesson extracted from Vietnam (despite insufficient evidence that television imagery did in fact corrode public support for the war to the point of unsustainability) continues to fuel the Pentagon's preoccupation with creating a hermetically sealed 'information environment' wherever US forces are engaged. [21]

Led by the United States, western militaries – eager to forestall 'another Vietnam' – have refined their strategies for virtualizing the representation of war. Believing that Vietnam was lost to communism by television's surfeit of graphic reportage, strategists have determined to reconfigure popular perceptions of war. No more atrocities; no more body-bags; no more bodies. Without evidence of injured flesh, the resort to war will be more readily sanctioned as its consequences are only dimly understood or disowned altogether:

Necrology, or knowledge of the dead, is... central to the phenomenology of war. Censorship that conceals the body, like that imposed by the Pentagon during the Persian Gulf War, makes war *both more and less real* to the public at home – making it seem more like a "real" war than the military adventurism or packaged media event it was, yet less historically significant, less humanly meaningful, and therefore less politically consequential than other wars. [22]

Civilian publics may thus be engaged by the spectacle – mobilized by the rhetoric and symbolism of war as communal endeavour – but their participation is (and only needs to be) shallow. Death-free war thus slides into 'spectator-sport', in which nothing very meaningful, or very 'real', seems to be at stake for all that crowds might enthusiastically cheer their own team on to victory. The ends served by organized violence are obfuscated: material interests masked by assertions of disinterested benevolence. [23] Real people don't seem to get hurt, and no one appears to be the enemy. Indeed, the whole concept of 'enmity' in virtual/virtuous war has become anachronistic, several commentators claiming, along with NATO's Wesley Clark, that in a 'period when there is an increased effort of universalism, [we] see people as people, not as the "enemy"'. [24] Humane war is too concerned with preserving life – or with the *appearance* of life-preservation – for any national group to be assigned enemy status. Bloodless war is correspondingly passionless war, in which enmities shrink to the size of a single, readily caricatured, figurehead: the sole, demonic figure of Saddam or 'Slobbo' against whom a manufactured animus is directed. [25] Hence Jamie Shea's insistence on 5 April 1999, even as NATO planes bombed Belgrade, that 'We're not at war with anybody, and certainly not with the people of Yugoslavia'. [26]

In quite distinct ways, then, virtual war confounds the ability to arbitrate what's 'really real'. But on the *implications* of this unknowability, virtual wars' critics diverge. For some, the problem is how to recover an appreciation of 'the real' when technology allied to, and harnessed by, the purposes of military dissimulation increasingly frustrates civilians' capacity to do so. Behind the blizzard of signs, symbols and spin, lurks the 'real war' – shrouded in a smokescreen of military-manufactured dry ice masquerading as the 'fog of war'. While such critics might invoke a language of 'post-modern' war, they cling to a thoroughly modern schism between the actual and the simulated, as seen for example in Douglas Kellner's account of the Gulf War:

It was postmodern in that… it was experienced by most of the world in real time and hyperreal media space as a political spectacle, as a carefully manufactured attempt to mobilize consent to US policy, in which distinction between truth and reality seemed to blur, and image and spectacle prevailed.[27]

For others, on the contrary, what makes contemporary conflict distinctively post-modern is precisely that we've outgrown modern illusions that the 'real' is ultimately out there—behind or beyond the simulation—waiting for the masks to be stripped away, for the representation to give way to the real. In post-modern interpretations of post-modern war, the contention is not that 'truth' has been pixiliated into non-existence, signs severed from real-world referents, but that the notion of 'unmediated reality' is exposed as the artifice it always was.[28] To endorse this position is not to deny that virtual wars inflict actual bodily harm—a charge commonly levelled at Baudrillard by those misreading, or reading only the title of, his (in)famous assertions that 'The Gulf War did Not Take Place'.[29] Rather it requires that we consider simulacra 'in all their positivity', not simply regarding the spectacle as foil for a parallel 'real war', conducted imperceptibly to all but its casualties.[30]

When was *real* war?

Since very few are prepared to make this conceptual leap, the post-modern variant remains considerably less common than its various liberal counterparts. More frequently, a good deal of nostalgia – and epistemological angst – surrounds the discussion of virtuality. Like many treatises on the social and ethical consequences of new technology, they cast ahead to a transformed future while hankering for a lost age of authenticity. In particular, many authors yearn for a restitution of the dead or injured body to popular (and soldierly) conceptions of war. But this concern with authentic war experience begs a number of questions. What does it *mean* for war to seem 'real' to its participants or spectators? Is war really 'less real' than it used to be? When *was* war properly knowable, and sufficiently corporeal? Is it possible that the experience of war always contains elements of the 'virtual' – or at any rate, up to a point?

Fears about the emergence of the cyborg soldier, whose sighting equipment does the 'seeing' on his behalf, betray a decidedly modern ocular-centrism whereby sight is privileged as epistemological master-sense. We know war by apprehending it for ourselves. If to see is to believe then it follows that what cannot be seen through human eyes cannot be fully trusted. Since this sensory confirmation of war's 'reality' alone enables appropriate ethical engagement with the business of killing, the substitution of mechanical 'eyes' has particularly worrisome implications for many commentators. But there is surely much to this logic – and its implicit invocation of a past in which war really *was* properly perceptible – that might be questioned.

Leaving aside, temporarily, the question of whether 'materiality' and morality are symbiotically conjoined when war is witnessed close-up, processes of attenuation have a long lineage. Various 'distancing effects' imputed to virtual war are not peculiar to the digital age. It is certainly not uncommon for airmen to express detachment from their targets. In February 1942 the *New York Times* carried an item about the shooting down of a German pilot after a bombing sortie over Leningrad. Wandering disoriented around the city's streets, he took no evasive action and was quickly captured: 'he had never thought of Leningrad as a real place but only as a target on a map'.[31] This vignette resonates with pilots involved in the Gulf War and Kosovo resorting to 'video-game' vernacular in describing their bombing missions.

Is this attenuation from the targets of violence, then, a distinctive function of airpower – if not of new 'virtual' technologies? Arguably not, since a recurrent theme in soldiers' accounts of twentieth-century war is precisely this sensation of disembodiment; of dislocation from immediate physical surroundings. Repeatedly, veterans capture this sense of estrangement and unreality by writing that combat appeared to them as something distantly observed on-screen. Retrospectively trying to fix the inchoate sensations of battle, they conjure others' – but also their own – participation in war as something caught on camera, and seen only in projection. This phenomenon dates as far back as the origins of commercial cinema itself, a development narrowly preceding World War One, as attested by a British soldier's attempts to convey his experiences at Gommecourt: 'The other men were like figures on a cinematograph screen – an old film that flickered violently – everybody in a desperate hurry'.[32]

The trope came of age in Vietnam, however. Film historian, Thomas Doherty points out that 'virtually all Vietnam war memoirs preconceive war in Hollywood terms and continue to mediate the combat experience in those same terms'.[33] Many veterans duly explain their initial enthusiastic participation with reference to Hollywood—a glut of John Wayne movies consumed in youth. In-country, however, they reach a Damascene awareness that, for all their attempts to act out pre-scripted notions of soldierly heroism, the plot in which they play bit-parts confounds generic conventions. "I *hate* this movie", a disenchanted grunt tells Michael Herr in *Dispatches*.[34] But to *hate* the movie is not the same as insisting that the war is not a movie at all. Accordingly, Michael Clark proposes that 'writing about Vietnam usually lacks the counterbalance of what might be called epiphany or moments of illumination in which a heightened sense of the real war supplants romantic fantasy'.[35] No wonder, then, that for some critics Vietnam properly merits the appellation first 'post-modern' war—at least in part because first-hand accounts repeatedly elide participation with spectatorship. Clark offers one particularly telling example of the passive grunt's eye-view:

> I was a grunt radioman, so I used to hang back with the CO and keep squad together. I got to watch the whole war with my eyes. I loved to just sit in the ditch and watch people die. As bad as that sounds, I just liked to watch no matter what happened, sitting back with my home-made cup of hot chocolate. It was like a big movie.[36]

Taking part in combat offers no automatic corrective—no guaranteed restoration of 'reality' to first-hand experience. In Herr's *Dispatches* seeing and knowing are radically discontinuous activities. In part, the untrustworthiness of vision is a product of night having been 'the war's truest medium', when operations proceeded under cover of darkness, shielded from the eyes of the television cameras.[37]

But the phantasmic properties of war don't derive solely from the shrouding of much combat in darkness. Night might obstruct vision, but drugs further tamper with the grunts' ability to make non-hallucinatory sense of what their eyes see. Cognition, after all, is a function of mental filtration not just ocular perception.

So when *did* war seem real to its participants? If we're looking for decisive 'breaks' in the history of warfare – trying to locate the onset of depersonalisation – then we may need to retreat further back than Vietnam; further than the advent of airpower. We could, for example, make a case that the arrival of artillery (fired 'indirectly', with gunners placing their fire on impersonal map co-ordinates) constitutes the decisive moment when the business of killing lost its 'reality'. Or do we step further back, to the arrival of rifled firearms and cannon? Or yet further, to the development of organized warfare—when the clash of men in formations replaced the personal combat of warriors? But before the search for missing authenticity vanishes into pre-history, we should surely probe the assumption that distanced, 'mechanical' warfare necessarily involves greater emotional dissociation, and hence ethical disengagement, than warfare conducted at extremely close quarters.

Much commentary on virtual war is underpinned by a concern with the conditions under which organized violence (killing, to put it at its bluntest) becomes possible. Without directly engaging scholarly debates on precisely this question, the nostalgic thrust of virtual war-talk valorizes an older, more authentic way of war – when the ethical consequences of killing were inescapable; when fighting was bloody and personal. By implication, a tangible, visceral confrontation with the fact of death-in-war made the resort to violence less conscionable. But is the insinuation warranted? One might counter that the most significant processes in warfare's 'depersonalization' – those that make killing possible – owe more to psychology than technology. Some military historians and sociologists conceive these distancing mechanisms as largely a function of racist ideology, often deliberately heightened through motivational propaganda to which recruits are intensively exposed. Officially sanctioned hatred thus overrides humans' innate disinclination for harming others by persuading them that their enemies are not, in fact, fellow humans at all.[38] Others attach greater weight to the structure of combat itself, which channels latent human energies for collective, organized violence in ways that owe very little to soldiers' self-conscious (or sub-conscious) beliefs and attitudes.[39]

Whichever analysis one finds more persuasive, for evidence that confronting an enemy up close does not necessarily occasion a moment of ethical awareness, one need cast no further back than events in Rwanda in 1994. There, genocide was enacted by men wielding pangas. *Interahamwe* death squads slashed, chopped and maimed their victims in situations as brutally intimate as it's possible to conceive.[40] Their deaths might appropriately serve not only as a warning against the romanticization of pre-mechanical warfare but also as a reminder that virtualizing technologies have not, in many places, replaced much more old-fashioned modes of killing.

Screening out the body

If war has long presented itself as an intensely physical yet simultaneously disembodied phenomenon for its participants, what of those watching – civilian publics now regularly conceived as spectators, only thinly and superficially immersed in the media spectacle of distant conflict? Here again, the Cassandras of virtual war invoke a 'golden age' of corporeal substantiality, along with a further cluster of assumptions. First, that 'total war' (virtual war's starkest antithesis) engaged whole populations in meaningful participation, and was correspondingly experienced by these fully mobilized, engaged citizens as a three-dimensional struggle in which life-or-death issues, and life and death themselves – individual and national – was incontrovertibly at stake. By contrast, Ignatieff laments that: 'We now wage wars and few notice or care. War no longer demands the type of physical involvement or moral attention it required over the past two centuries': 'War thus becomes virtual, not simply because it appears to take place on the screen but because it enlists societies only in virtual ways.'[41] A second hypothesis stems from Vietnam, from which many commentators derive the conclusion (along with the Pentagon) that when civilians *see* war they place limits on its abuses, and may even withdraw support for its political objectives altogether: 'Wars whose consequences are visible are unsustainable in the long term'.[42]

A different historical perspective suggests correctives to all of these propositions. While 'spectator sport war' reifies total war as the paradigm lost, most military engagements waged by western industrial powers over the past two centuries bear much closer resemblance to recent campaigns in Kosovo, Somalia or the Gulf than to the twentieth-century's two all-consuming cataclysms. Imperial warfare struck many of its more critical observers as spectacular in precisely the same ways as *fin de siècle* virtual war. Aerial 'policing' (practised intensively by the British during the Arab Rebellion and by Mussolini's Italy in Abyssinia) similarly married the logistics of sighting to those of cinematic representation, and was every bit as asymmetric in terms of the impunity with which self-proclaimed forces of civilization could bomb barbarians without placing themselves in danger.[43]

But if imperial wars all too readily appeared as distant pyrotechnical theatre, 'total war' did not invariably impress itself on its civilian spectator-participants as a fully 'real' phenomenon either. Long before war proclaimed itself (at least putatively) 'casualty free', combat footage and photography were generally required to obscure bodily suffering, whether by outright avoidance or aestheticization. In World War Two, it was only late in 1943 that US censors decided to allow limited publication of photographs of injured service personnel, if suitably and artfully composed.[44] Official parsimony with images of suffering was by no means solely an American strategy. The British trade journal, *Newspaper World*, lamented as late as April 1945 that the War Office 'seems to pursue the policy that no British soldier is killed in this war and that it is all a nice neat little affair' – a feature of the wartime newsreels variously lambasted by some cinema-goers and welcomed by others who (like their counterparts in more recent conflicts) have insisted that civilians *know* people die in war without actually wanting or needing to see material evidence.[45]

To suggest that the vanishing body was a distinctive innovation of the Gulf War obscures the degree to which injured flesh and human corpses have invariably been casualties of war's mediated representation in the twentieth century. Indeed, to imagine that the body hitherto loomed large in popular consciousness of war may rest on a somewhat selective memory: of Vietnam as 'a war about the human body'.[46] With hindsight certainly iconic images of 'flag-draped caskets, of massacres, atrocities and mass burials', of immolated monks, and of a single naked Vietnamese girl, running from a napalm attack, continue to structure perceptions of that war.[47] Yet these stark markers of atrocity do not, in fact, typify the visual register of Vietnam – at least as it appeared nightly on US network television news. Despite widespread post-war insistence that television reportage not only was exceptionally bloody but even 'lost the war', the networks were, pictorially, far from graphic in most of their coverage and, politically, 'lopsidedly favourable' to the war effort until political consensus on Capitol Hill itself fractured.[48]

Vietnam was lost neither by nor on television. Much coverage, at least until the Tet offensive of 1968, was mute – in criticism and 'realism' alike. Networks calibrated their reportage closely to prevailing opinion in Washington, espousing a somewhat more challenging position only after elite opinion took an oppositional turn: a development that post-dated polling evidence of a decline in popular support for the war. Far from television catalysing anti-war sentiment, research points to a stronger correlation between watching network news and *supporting* the military.[49] Such findings hardly reflect how Vietnam as 'media war' has passed into historical memory, and the conclusions drawn from equating television war with military defeat. Thus British broadcaster, Robin Day, famously mused that, since 'blood looks very red on the colour television screen', it might prove impossible for 'a democracy which has uninhibited television coverage in every home… ever [to] be able to fight a war, however just'.[50] Similar forebodings have clearly animated both British and American attempts to ensure that future wars did not – and will not – receive 'uninhibited' coverage, just as they colour Ignatieff's fear that (despite his commitment to full-bodied, full-blooded humanitarian war) television is inimical to wars both good and bad, actual or virtual. But one could make quite the opposite argument, as Michael Arlen did in 1982, when staking a claim for Vietnam as first 'living room war':

> I can't say I completely agree with people who think that when battle scenes are brought into the living the hazards of war are necessarily made "real" to the civilian audience. It seems to me that by the same process they are also made less "real"—diminished, in part, by the physical size of the television screen, which, for all the industry's advances, still shows a picture of men three inches tall shooting at other men three inches tall, trivialized, or at least tamed, by the enveloping cozy alarums of the household.[51]

In this view, Vietnam, 'the living room war', bears a decided resemblance to the Gulf war, as first made-for-television spectacle – only lacking the snazzy packaging, the graphics, the nosecone footage.

So what, then, is distinctively new in accounts of virtual war? If not the synergy between Hollywood and the military, nor the body's disappearance, then perhaps the viewer's inability to adjudicate images' authenticity in an age when we know all too well that the camera (along with political elites) can lie, and frequently does? Decrying the tendency of 'information networks [to] collapse representational distinctions between fact and fiction', Der Derian, Ignatieff et al seem to bemoan a central facet of modernity itself: that we experience the world through representation, suspecting that a flesh-and-blood 'real' must duly lie behind or beneath the representational screen, but perpetually bemused as to where precisely the demarcation lies.[52]

To rue this retreat of 'reality' in a vertiginous hall of mirrors has long been a staple of commentaries on technology's double-edged social transformations. Irrespective of their co-ordinates on a left/right political axis – from Lasswellian technocrats to Frankfurt School pessimists – mass media critics have decried the paradoxical properties of media that amalgamate individuals into passive, homogenized 'masses' while leaving them stranded and stupefied as isolated readers, listeners, or viewers. It required no Francophone vocabulary of hyperreality or simulacra for Walter Lippmann to warn in *The Phantom Public*

(1925) that media-consuming masses inhabited 'pseudo environments' – bemused as to what was 'real', incapable of vigorous participation in deliberative democracy, as mutely incomprehending as 'a deaf spectator in the back row'. With fewer meaningful face-to-face interactions, and a shrivelled public sphere as individuals sought community through radio-listenership or newspaper-perusal, Lippmann gloomily concluded that mass man 'lives in a world he cannot see, does not understand and is unable to direct'.[53]

Similarly bleak conclusions about our ability as mass-mediated citizens to access 'the real' mark much recent commentary. 'Truth is always a casualty in war', opines Ignatieff, 'but in virtual war, the media creates the illusion that what we are seeing is true. In reality, nothing is what it seems'.[54] Assertions of consumer-citizens' thralldom to war as televisual spectacle come easily to critics of virtual war. But it is considerably harder to demonstrate that the 'masses' do indeed devour media war in a state of pre-ironic grace. Might it not be possible that the increasingly obvious stage-management and promotional packaging of media war draws attention to the slippery ontological status of the simulation? Perhaps the fundamental issue – for those sceptical of the ways in which 'humane war' is conducted or the ends it serves (or both) – is less that untrustworthy channels of vision are so widely trusted but that channels for dissent are so narrow, or that the impulse to protest the militarization of foreign politics is currently so fragile. Unlike much else about seemingly virtual war, these political and cultural phenomena, while clearly interrelated, ought not to be conflated. To ponder the demise of dissent requires a separate story.

NOTES

1. Evelyn Waugh, *Scoop* (Harmondsworth: Penguin, 1943), p.42.
2. Michael Ignatieff, *Virtual War: Kosovo and Beyond* (London: Chatto and Windus), pp.3-4.
3. The literature is sizeable and growing. For representative examples, see: Heidi and Alvin Toffler, *War and Anti-War: Survival at the Dawn of the Twenty-First Century* (Boston: Little, Brown, 1993); James Der Derian, *Antidiplomacy: Spies, Terror, Speed and War* (Cambridge: Blackwell, 1992) and *Virtuous War: Mapping the Military-Industrial-Media-Entertainment Network* (Boulder: Westview Press, 2001); Colin McInnes, *Spectator-Sport War: the West and Contemporary Conflict* (Boulder: Lynne Rienner, 2002); Christopher Coker, *Humane Warfare* (London: Routledge, 2001); Chris Hables Grey, *Postmodern War: the New Politics of Conflict* (London: Routledge, 1997); Michael Bibby (ed.), *The Vietnam War and Postmodernity* (Boston: University of Massachusetts Press, 1999).
4. Ignatieff, *Virtual War*, pp.187-88
5. Coker, *Humane Warfare*, p.2.
6. Critics diverge over the degree to which western publics really are as scrupulous over the loss of 'others'' lives as of their own. McInnes, in *Spectator-Sport War*, suggests as much, but others (including Ignatieff) are less persuaded that humanitarian cosmopolitanism extends so far.
7. Der Derian, *Virtuous War*, p.xv.
8. Ignatieff, *Virtual War*, pp.161-64.
9. On Kosovo see Philip Hammond & Edward S. Herman (eds), *Degraded Capability: the Media and the Kosovo Crisis* (London: Pluto Press, 2000); Philip Knightley, *The First Casualty: the War Correspondent as Hero and Myth-Maker from the Crimea to Kosovo* (London: Prion Books, 2000), pp.501-26.

10. Goran Gocic, 'Symbolic Warfare: Nato versus the Serbian Media', in Hammond & Herman, op cit, pp.88-93.

11. This is precisely the phenomenon that Baudrillard's notion of hyperreality attempts to capture: 'The territory no longer precedes the map, nor survives it. Henceforth, it is the map that precedes the territory—precession of simulacra—it is the map that engenders the territory'; *Selected Writings*, ed. Mark Poster (Stanford: Stanford University Press, 1988). p.166.

12. Der Derian, *passim*. The centrality of gaming as war-waging's precursor is underscored by the high profile accorded to the US military exercise, 'Internal Look', staged in December 2002; *New York Times*, 1 December 2002, A1, A30.

13. On the emergence of the cyborg soldier, see Gray, *Postmodern War*, pp.195-211.

14. Der Derian, *Virtuous War*, p.120.

15. Ignatieff, *Virtual War*, p.5.

16. Der Derian, *Virtuous War*, p.147. Indeed, as both Der Derian and Ignatieff point out, 'infrastructural' targets collapse the civil-military divide, since much of a state's communications network—whether roads, bridges, radio transmitters or broadcasting stations—have dual purposes; ibid, p.147, and Ignatieff, *Virtual War*, p.170

17. Margot Norris, 'Only the Guns have Eyes: Military Censorship and the Body Count' in Susan Jeffords and Lauren Rabinovitz (eds), *Seeing through the Media: the Persian Gulf War* (New Brunswick: Rutgers University Press, 1994), pp.291-92.

18. Der Derian, p.11.

19. For critiques of the Gulf War see Douglas Kellner, *The Persian Gulf TV War* (Boulder: Westview Press) and Bruce Cumings, *War and Television* (London: Verso, 1992).

20. For an extended discussion of this phenomenon with particular reference to the Gulf War, see John Taylor, *Body Horror: Photojournalism, Catastrophe and War* (Manchester: Manchester University Press, 1991).

21. See Daniel Hallin, *The 'Uncensored War': The Media and Vietnam* (New York: Oxford University Press, 1989) and Susan Carruthers, *The Media at War: Communication and Conflict in the Twentieth Century* (Houndmills: Palgrave, 2000), pp.108-96.

22. Norris in Jeffords & Rabinovitz, op cit, pp.285-86.

23. Ignatieff, *Virtual War*, p.189.

24. Cited by Der Derian, *Virtuous War*, p.196.

25. See Ignatieff and McInnes, passim, and Coker, *Humane Warfare*, chapter 4, 'War without Hatred'.

26. Cited by Seth Ackerman & Jim Naureckas, 'Following Washington's Script: the United States Media and Kosovo', in Hammond & Herman (eds), op cit, p.105.

27. Douglas Kellner, 'From Vietnam to the Gulf: Postmodern Wars?', in Bibby (ed.), op cit, p.218. See also Cumings on the Gulf War as the 'first television war'.

28. Few writers adopt this position. Even those whose names are most frequently conjured in connection with 'postmodern war'—especially Jean Baudrillard—stop short of proposing that there is no 'real' war with which

the virtual might be contrasted. For a more whole-hearted endorsement of an anti-nostalgic postmodernism, see McKenzie Wark, *Virtual Geography: Living with Global Media Events* (Bloomington: Indiana University Press, 1994).

29. Baudrillard's assertions that the Gulf War would not take place—and subsequently had not—were published in *Liberation* on 4 January and 29 March 1991. The apparent irresponsibility of this position has been widely attacked by critics on both the left and write. For a sustained assault from a leftist critical theory position, see Christopher Norris, *Uncritical Theory: Postmodernism, Intellectuals and the Gulf War* (London: Lawrence and Wishart, 1992).

30. McKenzie Wark, 'Line Up, Line Up. It's a Shooting Party', *The Australian*, 2 August 1995; at http://www.dmc.mq.edu.au/mwark/warchive/cv/columns/cv-oz-baudrillard.html.

31. *New York Times*, 26 February 1942, cited in Siegfried Kracauer, *From Caligari to Hitler: A Psychological History of the German Film* (Princeton: Princeton University Press, 1947), p.296.

32. Modris Eksteins, *Rites of Spring: the Great War and the Birth of the Modern Age* (London: Black Swan, 1980), p.302.

33. Thomas Doherty, 'Witness to War: Oliver Stone, Ron Kovic, and *Born on the Fourth of July*' in Michael Anderegg (ed.), *Inventing Vietnam: The War in Film and Television* (Philadelphia: Temple University Press, 1991), p.255.

34. Michael Herr, *Dispatches* (London: Picador, 1979). p.153.

35. Michael P. Clark, 'The Work of War after the Age of Mechanical Reproduction', in Bibby (ed), p.18.

36. Mark Baker, *Nam: the Vietnam War in the Words of the Men and Women who Fought There* (NY: William Morrow, 1991), p.93, cited by Clark, op cit, p.20.

37. Herr, *Dispatches*, p.40.

38. One could, of course, take further issue with the core proposition that killing is such an intrinsically distasteful activity to humans that its wartime commission requires any particularly elaborate explanation at all. That killing might be experienced as pleasurable to men at war is, succinctly stated, the argument made by Joanna Bourke in *An Intimate History of Killing: Face-to-Face Killing in Twentieth-Century Warfare* (London: Granta, 1999).

39. The debate over combat motivation has been particularly intense with regard to explaining the actions of the German *Wehrmacht* during World War II: whether Hitler's troops were convinced Nazis or enmeshed in military organizations and activities which structured their participation in killing, irrespective of their adherence, or otherwise, to Nazi ideology. This debate is played out between Omer Bartov in, *Hitler's Army: Soldiers, Nazis and War in the Third Reich* (New York: Oxford University Press, 1992) and Christopher Browning, *Ordinary Men: Reserve Police Battalion 101 and the Final Solution in Poland* (New York: Harper Perennial, 1993).

40. Philip Gourevitch, *We Wish to Inform You that Tomorrow We Will Be Killed With Our Families: Stories from Rwanda* (New York: Picador, 1999). For a critique of the view that 'ethnic hatred'—galvanized and officially sanctioned by preparatory radio propaganda—inspired this orgy of bloodletting, see John Mueller, 'The Banality of "Ethnic War"', *International Security*, 25, i (Summer 2000), pp.42-70. Here he argues that violence resulted from 'a situation in

which common, opportunistic, sadistic, and often distinctly non-ideological marauders were recruited and permitted free rein by political authorities'.

41. Ignatieff, *Virtual War*, p.184 and p.191.

42. Ibid, p.187.

43. For Walter Benjamin, the spectacle of war in Abyssinia represented the culmination—and inevitable terminus—of Fascism's aestheticization of politics, in which war supplied 'the artistic gratification of a sense of perception that has been changed by technology'; 'The Work of Art in the Age of Mechanical Reproduction', reprinted in *Illuminations* (London: Fontana, 1992), p.235.

44. For a history of the shift from a totally restrictive to a somewhat less parsimonious approach towards censorship (based on an equally strategic calculation that greater realism would jolt American civilians out of putative complacence), see George Roeder, *The Censored War: American Visual Experience of World War Two* (New Haven: Yale University Press, 1993).

45. *Newspaper World* cited by Barbie Zelizer, *Remembering to Forget: Holocaust Memory through the Camera's Eye* (Chicago: University of Chicago Press, 1998), p.38. For civilian responses to wartime British newsreels' bloodlessness, see the Mass-Observation reports compiled by Jeffrey Richards & Dorothy Sheridan, *Mass-Observation at the Movies* (London: Routledge and Kegan Paul, 1987). On more recent civilian disinclination to see casualties of war given more graphic televisual treatment, see the post-Gulf War focus group findings of David Morrison, *Television and the Gulf War* (London: John Libbey, 1992).

46. WJT Mitchell, *Picture Theory: Essays on Verbal and Visual Representation* (Chicago: University of Chicago Press, 1994), p.401.

47. Ibid, p.401.

48. The classic statement of the conventional wisdom that the war was lost by the corrosive power of televisual imagery is Robert Elegant's 'How to Lose a War', *Encounter*, 57, ii (1981), pp.73-89. The 'revisionist' case is vigorously sustained by Hallin in *The Uncensored War*.

49. Richard Hofstetter & David Moore, 'Watching TV News and Supporting the Military: A Surprising Impact of the News Media', *Armed Forces and Society*, 5, ii (Feb. 1979), pp.261-69; and Daniel Hallin, 'The Media, the war in Vietnam, and political support: A critique of the thesis of an oppositional media', in Hallin, *We Keep the Media On Top of the World: Television Journalism and the Public Sphere* (London: Routledge, 1994), pp.40-57.

50. Cited in Alan Hooper, *The Military and the Media* (Aldershot: Gower, 1982), p.116.

51. Michael Arlen, *The Living Room War* (New York: Penguin, 1982), p.8.

52. This facet of modernity is particularly well illuminated by Timothy Mitchell in *Colonising Egypt* (Berkeley: University of California Press, 1991).

53. Walter Lippmann, *The Phantom Public* (New York: Harcourt, Brace, 1925). For further examples of early critics of the 'virtualization' of the public sphere in an age of mass circulation newspapers and telegraphy, see Stuart Ewen, *PR! A Social History of Spin* (New York: Basic Books, 1996), chapter 4.

54. Ignatieff, *Virtual War*, p.196.

Chapter Sixteen
THE FOURTH ARM AND THE FOURTH ESTATE: PSYCHOLOGICAL OPERATIONS AND THE MEDIA

Philip M. Taylor

Beyond the world of its practitioners, the conduct of psychological operations (or PSYOPS) is shrouded in suspicion, myth and confusion.[1] As the successor to what many people still describe as psychological warfare (PSYWAR), there is a popular tendency to associate it somehow with brainwashing, dirty tricks, deception, devious war fighting, 'psy-cops' and that other nasty 'P' word: propaganda.[2] In fact, today, it falls within a wider military doctrine known as Information Operations (IO). Given that PSYOPS have in many respects become, as we shall see, the military equivalent of marketing or advertising campaigns, there is an interesting question to answer as to why such professional military communicators have singularly failed to dispel the misconceptions that surround their work.[3] Perhaps it is because PSYOPS tend to be conducted by Special Forces or from within Intelligence Corps - themselves the subject of considerable popular mythology - or that many military establishments sustain policies of not discussing in any detail what such forces actually do in operations. Western democratic politicians are notoriously nervous about admitting that their soldiers are undertaking anything that could be remotely likened to the propaganda of past adversaries like Nazi Germany or the Soviet Union. Yet this policy of official secrecy serves to create an information vacuum that is filled by all sorts of speculation, guesswork and misinformation. This chapter aims to go some way towards rectifying this situation.

Know Your History

The morale of troops has always been an important factor in determining victory or defeat on the battlefield. Although warfare is as old as human history, ancient military strategists such as Sun Szu understood that 'to subdue an enemy without fighting is the acme of skill', while more modern commanders such as Napoleon inherently understood that 'there are but two powers in the world, the sword and the mind.[4] In the long run the sword will always be beaten by the mind'.[5] But it was the 20th century fusion of warfare, modern communications and the new discipline of psychology which saw the practice of psychological warfare, as both an art and a science, come into its own. It was the British during the First World War who first pioneered the craft, even though it was the Germans who initially experimented with the dropping of leaflets over Allied lines in 1914. By the end of the war, the British had developed a fully blown 'Department of Propaganda in Enemy Countries' situated at Crewe House under the supervision of Fleet Street newspaper proprietor, Lord Northcliffe.[6] At the same time, a separate Ministry of Information under fellow Press Baron Lord Beaverbrook was created to conduct propaganda in allied and neutral countries. This separation of duties, seemingly determined by foreign target audiences, owed more in fact to political infighting within Whitehall than to any fully thought through organisational approach.[7]

Thus began the genesis of an uneasy relationship between psychological warfare – or political warfare, as the British preferred to call it at that time – and the modern mass media. Northcliffe, as owner of *The Daily Mail* and *The Times*, and Beaverbrook, as owner of *The Daily Express*, were emerging as key players within a rapidly changing British political scene at the end of the war. It was felt that they, as pioneers in the new world of publicity, understood the mind of the 'common man' much better than the mandarins of Whitehall whose 'secret diplomacy' was widely believed to have helped cause the war. Thanks to the 1918 Representation of the People Act, which trebled the size of the British electorate (including the first over 30 year old female voters), the idea that politicians would henceforth need to communicate effectively with their constituents in a consistent and systematic way gave rise between the wars to political communications as a fact of modern democratic life.[8] The dangers of not taking public opinion into account were apparent for all to see from the experience of the Bolshevik Revolution which saw the execution of the Tsar and his family and took Russia out of the war in 1917. In international affairs, President Wilson spoke of 'open covenants, openly arrived at'. Beaverbrook and Northcliffe wanted their wartime departments to continue into the peace but this was a bridge too far for politicians who were still coming to terms with their new-found relationship with what Neville Chamberlain called 'an immense mass of ignorant voters, of both sexes, whose intelligence is low and who have no power of weighing evidence'.[9] In short, it would have made the press far too powerful and the wartime propaganda machine was rapidly closed down, leaving only a remnant in the Foreign Office.[10] It took another decade for Downing Street to establish a Press Office in 1930, two years after the introduction of a genuine universal franchise.[11]

In the meantime, the British wartime experience was attracting the interest of a wide range of people, from American academics such as Harold Lasswell to budding German dictators such as Adolf Hitler. Lasswell wrote the first academic study of propaganda about the British wartime experiment in 1927, while in *Mein Kampf* Hitler set out his blueprint for modern propaganda usage based on observation largely of British wartime adeptness at the new 'weapon'.[12] In Britain itself, however, there was an acute sense of embarrassment at the praise being lavished upon the success of their ability to either 'dupe' the United States into involvement on the Allied side in 1917 or, as General Ludendorf claimed, to 'hypnotise' the soldiers of the German Army 'like a rabbit is by a snake'.[13] The culmination of this discomfiture came in 1928 with the publication of Lord Ponsonby's best-selling paperback, *Falsehood in Wartime*, which irreparably sealed the popular notion that propaganda, including political warfare, was in the business of telling lies.[14]

At the same time, it drove the practice of psychological warfare into the shadows of the intelligence community. During the Great War, despite the creation of Crewe House, military intelligence had retained its role in *distributing* material produced by the civilian agencies in combat zones. The relevant section, MI7b, has rarely received the recognition it deserved for dropping millions of leaflets of enemy lines on the western and southern fronts.[15] It had originally been responsible to producing the PSYWAR messages as well, but it became common wisdom in the Lloyd George government from late 1916 onwards that the military prosecution of the war was no longer best left solely to the generals. Even so, when the political appointment of Northcliffe resulted in the formation of Crewe House, the military insisted that it retain control of distribution in combat theatres. Because, just prior to this, the Germans had captured two Royal Flying Corps pilots and threatened to execute them for distributing leaflets in defiance of existing military-legal conventions, it was decided that all future leaflet-dropping on the western front should be done mainly by balloon. Although this limited the capacity of the Allies to reach German civilian populations (because the western front was mainly in France and the low countries), it tended to reinforce the notion of psychological warfare as being mainly a new arm of combat operations. The tendency thereafter to see this new weapon as a tactical tool in support of military operations – as a 'fourth fighting arm' - has largely prevailed ever since.[16]

So also has the degree of tension between civilian and military practitioners. The British experience was echoed by the Americans when they entered the war in 1917. Two journalists, Herber Blankenhorn and Walter Lippmann, who were commissioned to work with the Military Intelligence Branch of the American General Staff, frequently ruffled the feathers of the military authorities waging psychological warfare in theatre.[17] The culture of military secrecy seemed incompatible with the imperative to communicate openly with enemy forces. But for all the tension and the muddling through, both the British and Americans learned one of the fundamental axioms of successful psychological warfare: that to deliberately lie was counter-productive. This does not mean that the 'whole truth' was told. Nor does it mean that military deception was suddenly eschewed as an essential feature of warfare. But it was realised that a lie would, sooner or later, be discovered and, when that happened, the credibility of any material emanating subsequently from the same source would be jeopardised in any future operation. In the words of one later PSYOPS veteran:

> This is the heart of the matter, then. Friendly psychological warfare [sic] dissemination must be steeped in – must be cloaked in, must give off, must read, sound, look, smell, must fairly reek – credibility.[18]

Allied leaflets in the Great War included *Le Courier de l'Air*, an air-dropped newspaper containing information denied to the occupied French population and frequently read by the German troops. Leaflets were dropped containing maps showing the way home, or instructions on how to surrender. A constant theme was the humane treatment that prisoners of war could expect from the Allies, using photographs of smiling prisoners and facsimile letters written by detainees describing their creature comforts in captivity. Leaflets attempting to drive a wedge between soldiers in the field and their commanders, especially their political leadership, proved particularly effective on the southern front and played a significant part in the break-up of the Austroa-Hungarian empire and its departure from the war.[19] The degree on the other hand to which the Allied PSYWAR effort contributed towards Germany's demise, for all the claims made by Ludendorff and Hitler, remains open to question, not least because balloon distribution of material to the German heartland was at best limited.[20]

There are several good reasons for placing so much emphasis on the Great War experiment. One is that much 'best practice' was learned in the conflict, including the importance of what may termed 'factual truths'. Equally, one of the most fundamental mistakes that could ever have been made occurred when the propagandists began issuing messages which ran ahead of policy. These were proclamations from Crewe House, both implicit and explicit, that if the subject nationalities of central, eastern and south-eastern Europe rose up and overthrew their political/imperial leaderships they would be rewarded by national self-determination and a return to 'the community of civilised nations'. Although Allied policy, especially through American President Wilson's Fourteen Points, had made vague promises in this direction of 'national self-determination', the propagandists seemed to go much further by offering the rewards of revolution than the politicians were prepared to commit to. Propaganda promises thus became policy imperatives at the post-war Peace Conferences, while the formation of vulnerable new states like Hungary, Poland, Czechoslovakia, Romania and Yugoslavia were to be a precipitate cause of a Second World War less than a generation later. This was to be a fundamental 'lesson not learned' in subsequent conflicts right down to the Persian Gulf War of 1991.

While the maturing western democracies tried to eschew the use of psychological warfare in the 20-year peace that followed the Great War, the emerging dictatorships were drawing upon the wartime experiment to place propaganda as a central function of their state machineries. Exploiting new technologies, in the 1920s the Soviets build the most powerful radio transmitter in the world - Radio Moscow - to spread their internationalist ideology that 'workers of the world unite'.[21] Thus began an ideological struggle between democracy and its challengers, including Fascist Italy and later Nazi Germany. These revisionist regimes not only regarded propaganda as an alternative to consensus for seizing and securing power at home, but they also saw it as a weapon for extending their influence abroad. As radio grew in popularity, and as radio transmissions transcended physical boundaries as well as class, creed, nationality and literacy, it became a strategic vehicle for attacking the democracies inside those democracies. Traditional notions that states did not interfere with the internal affairs of other states crumbled thanks to the fusion of ideology and communications technology. Having pioneered the use of propaganda and psychological warfare between 1914 and 1918, however, the British now found themselves on the defensive in what was essentially a strategic ideological conflict and a precursor of the Cold War.

The inter-war ideological conflict saw some rudimentary British psychological warfare activities conducted in the realm of the secret services. Because the official files remain largely closed, we still know very little about this activity but during the Munich Crisis of September 1938, when Europe went to the brink of war over Czechoslovakia, the British did get involved in a remarkable 'black' operation. Black or covert propaganda purports to emanate from a source other than the true one. This operation secretly used Radio Luxembourg to beam into Nazi Germany the British government's position over the crisis – technically a violation of an international agreement brokered by the League of Nations in 1936 to prevent the use of radio for 'propaganda' purposes. More honoured in the breach by the dictators, the very fact that the British should effectively launch an appeal directly to the German people rather than through their government could be said to be the final nail in the coffin for the principle held by democracies yet long betrayed by the new dictatorships that nation-states should not interfere with the internal affairs of other countries.[22]

In a sense, they had already conceded this point several months earlier in 1938 when the British government asked the BBC to begin broadcasting in foreign languages for the first time. The genesis of the World Service began with broadcasts in Arabic to counter the Italian anti-British propaganda transmitted by Radio Bari into the Middle East, and was followed by the Spanish and Portuguese service for Latin America. The Munich crisis saw the service extended to European languages. These were what would be called 'white' or overt propaganda – although it was always denied that this was propaganda. Rather these were news-based 'information services' transmitted by a supposedly independent news organisation with a reputation for credibility, and hence not really propaganda at all. It was rarely appreciated abroad that the BBC foreign language broadcasts were paid for by the Foreign Office. Although no great secret was made of this, a case could be made that these were 'grey' forms of psychological warfare.[23] Yet what is really significant here is that decisions were being made by governments to speak directly to foreign peoples using their own government-controlled or quasi-independent media of communications. In democracies, the free media remained an important channel of communicating politics to domestic audiences. Foreign governments may have scrutinised national media, whether free or government-controlled, for clues concerning the state of public (i.e. media) opinion in a given country, or concerning the thinking of government in state-controlled media societies, but they also recognised that they themselves now needed to get into the business of international communication. The age of what we now call 'public diplomacy' had arrived.

Know Your Enemy

Although, during the Great War, it had taken several years for the British to build up to a concerted psychological warfare effort, the next time would be different. Indeed, the opening night of the Second World War saw RAF bombers pepper Germany with 'paper bullets'. However, the Air Ministry remained highly reluctant to risk its aircraft and crews for dropping what the Americans would later call 'bullshit bombs'. The leaflets reassured the German people that Britain had not declared war on them, but rather on their Nazi leadership. This theme, so beloved of PSYOPS today, was soon to be abandoned, especially after the declaration of Unconditional Surrender by the Allies in 1942. From a PSYWAR point of view, this was arguably the single biggest policy mistake of the entire war. The policy, by insisting on complete surrender of the Axis Powers and by promising no negotiated armistice and peace treaty (as in 1918), deprived PSYWAR of key themes, such as 'rise up against your government and you can return to the community of nations' (as in 1918) or even 'surrender or die' messages since surrender might now result in war crimes prosecution.

Conceptually, this situation was the exact opposite of World War One. Now the policy had run ahead of the propaganda imperatives. Nazi propaganda minister Joseph Goebbels was delighted. In a stroke, the policy of Unconditional Surrender had linked the destiny of the German people to the fate of the Nazi Party after the war in a way that none of his own domestic propaganda had been able to achieve. It enabled the Nazis to promote their own themes such as 'Victory or Death' and to urge fighting to the bitter end because the consequences in defeat would be dire.

The German army and people did indeed fight to the bitter end. But in the opening months of the war, such a likelihood seemed remote to say the least. As German armed forces blitzkrieged their way through Poland and then Western Europe, the axiom that successful propaganda loves a winner was plain for all to see. It was the British who were on the defensive, both militarily and psychologically, as they stood alone in their 'finest hour'. After Dunkirk, propaganda and psychological warfare were amongst the limited offensive options that remained open to the British. In this respect, they held one trump card: the BBC. Within a generation of its foundation in the 1920s, the BBC had become a 'national institution'. Within the six years of the Second World War, it was about to become an international institution with a reputation for credibility worldwide matched by no other broadcaster.

The BBC was left in charge of Britain's 'white' radio propaganda working relatively independently of Ministry of Information (MoI) control. Not that it was called propaganda; that was something the enemy engaged in. 'We' told 'the truth'. Or, as the MoI put it, 'to tell the truth, nothing but the truth – and, *as near as possible*, the whole truth'. When the BBC began extending its remit to broadcasting in the foreign languages of nations under Nazi control, this principle was applied rigorously – and it greatly aided the development of the institution's credibility as the most reliable of international broadcasters. The Nazis were so frightened of this alternate view of the war that they banned the listening of foreign broadcasts, punishable by death. There were to be no hypnotised rabbits this time.

This presented the British with a formidable challenge from the psychological warfare point of view. Although, of course, many people in occupied Europe did listen to the BBC, the latter valued its reputation for credibility created by its *news*-based approach. In the Political Warfare Executive (PWE) there was a need to generate *views* in support of the Churchill-inspired mission 'to set Europe ablaze' with rumours (or 'sibs'), espionage and insurrection. Once again, the government looked to the worlds of the media and academia for creative people who could provide innovative ideas for how best to achieve this.[24] It was Sefton Delmer, former Berlin correspondent for *The Daily Express,* who came up with the idea of PWE using 'black' radio transmissions to subvert Nazi control. Using the codename 'Research Unit', Delmer established several black or covert radio stations, including Soldatensender Calais and GS1 (or Gustaf Seigfreid Eins, an apparent German dissident in fact played by Delmer himself). The point of these transmissions was that ordinary law-abiding German citizens could come across these stations on their radio sets without realising that they were emanating from Britain. The aim was simple: to sow seeds of doubt about the possible existence of internal German opposition to the Nazis. But this was a highly secret operation. Amongst the German armed forces – always recognised as a tough psychological nut to crack made even tougher by the policy of Unconditional Surrender – the aim of white allied broadcasts and leaflets was more 'informational' than propaganda designed to provoke desertion, defection, surrender or insurrection. Once again, however, credibility was essential and we should now begin to start thinking conceptually less in terms of 'the truth' but rather in terms of 'credible truths'. When for example in 1943, the Americans dropped a leaflet over German forces in Italy stating that, in the event of surrender, German PoWs would be treated well, including a breakfast of bacon and eggs - which was true - the German soldiers simply refused to believe it.

Techniques of political and military persuasion tend to reflect the political and philosophical values of the society which practices them. Allied (or at least Anglo-American) propaganda had several characteristics that made it different from the type of propaganda being conducted by Britain's enemies. These included the notion of 'credible truths' in accordance with the Anglo-American 'Strategy of Truth'. This does not mean the whole truth was told. Censorship was an essential component of this but news was censored at source prior to distribution to the media in case enemy agents (a 'fifth column' – in fact non-existent in Britain) were scouring the media for useful intelligence. British propaganda was based on the importance of censoring news (for operational security and morale) rather than views. British 'political warfare' conducted by the PWE set the standard for the approach adopted by the Psychological Warfare Department of the Supreme Headquarters of Allied Command in Europe once the Americans entered the war. This was also a combined civilian and military effort, essential for any campaign targeting soldiers *and* civilians. The American Air Force dedicated an entire squadron to leaflet dropping, while the advent of radio also embraced civilians within enemy and enemy-occupied countries as a key target audience.

PWE was a combined civilian-military unit. It emerged from the shadows of the secret intelligence services from late 1938 onwards until it was formed in this manifestation alongside the Special Operations Executive (SOE) in 1941. It was riddled with tensions and personality clashes and enjoyed strained relations with the BBC whose journalists tried to keep their distance from the black activity in order to preserve their own credibility as 'purveyors of truth'. Whereas in the Great War, there was no real conceptual understanding of the differences between black, white or even grey propaganda (where the source is indicated neither one way nor the other), the more sophisticated practitioners of World War Two recognised that, in a war against Fascism and Nazism, every single weapon would be required if democracy was to survive and then prevail. However, over the past 30 years, as the wartime record of codebreaking and intelligence has become clearer, historians have concluded that the ability to break the German 'Enigma' codes probably knocked around two years off the war. They can make no similar claims for propaganda and psychological warfare. Perhaps this was down to the policy of Unconditional Surrender. Perhaps it was due to the effectiveness of Nazi domestic propaganda and the allies' inability to break German military and civilian morale, although this was not for want of trying. Over 1.5 billion leaflets were dropped by the allies between 1939 and 1945. Ingenious techniques involving deception were tried and tested for the first time, including Operation Fortitude which fooled the Germans about the actual location of the D-Day Landings. But regardless of the overall allied psychological warfare record, it is important to emphasise that this was a 'Total War' in which the gap between the military and civilian fronts narrowed substantially. Because of the advent of the bomber, civilians were in the front line now too.[25] And because, for the British at least, the war lasted for almost six years, 'Total Propaganda' was the order of the day.

The Cold War and Strategic Propaganda

As with the aftermath of the Great War, the British again chose to dismantle their wartime propaganda machinery. This time, however, some of it survived in the form of the Central Office of Information to conduct government 'publicity' campaigns relating to such issues as public health and road safety - recognition of the permanent need for government to explain itself in peacetime to the citizens who elected it. But Britain's wider position in the world was in decline, epitomised in the 1940s, 1950s and 1960s by the 'retreat from Empire'. Two superpowers had emerged from the war in the shape of the USA and the Soviet Union. As Britain lost its Empire and struggled to find a new role in world, or European, affairs, the outbreak of the Cold War from around 1947 onwards meant that the ideological struggle between two conflicting ways of life involved a global propaganda struggle for hearts and minds – and one in which the British took a back seat.

They did contribute in what was often a covert struggle, conducted partly through the media, in the form of the secret Information Research Department of the Foreign Office.[26] But in what was essentially a worldwide strategic psychological warfare campaign that was to last for another 40 years, the British involvement was minor by comparison to the efforts of the CIA and KGB. On an overt level, the Americans established the United States Information Agency (USIA) to counter the 'disinformation' campaigns of the numerous Soviet propaganda agencies attempting to bring the newly independent countries of the 'Third World' under Soviet influence. Indeed, it was in those former British colonies where independence movements resorted to armed guerrilla warfare that the British military relearned the importance of psychological warfare on a tactical level. Having encouraged numerous peoples to rise up and overthrow their 'oppressive rulers', they now found themselves cast in the role of imperial overlords and the very targets of psychological and guerrilla warfare techniques which they had pioneered. In Malaya, in Aden, Cyprus, Kenya and in the Suez Crisis, the British resorted to leaflet drops and broadcasting to tell their side of 'the truth'. The most famous exponent of PSYWAR in Low Intensity Conflicts was General Templar whose experience in Malaya was drawn upon by the Americans in the early 1960s as they increased their involvement in Vietnam.[27]

By that time, the separation of white 'propaganda' conducted by civilian diplomatic and strategic agencies such as the USIA, covert propaganda conducted by the intelligence agencies and overt psychological warfare at the tactical level conducted by the military had been institutionalised. Co-ordination between the various agencies had become an essential necessity, although it didn't always happen in practice. The explosion of propaganda in what was now being termed 'the information age' had become a fact of life. 'We' still told 'the truth' while 'the enemy' still told lies, but the prominence of 'propaganda' only really became apparent to the general public in times of limited war, such as the Falklands Conflict of 1982. By that time, however, British PSYWAR capability had shrunk so low that even though a single leaflet was produced for the Argentinean forces, there was no means of disseminating it.

The Gulf War of 1991

Partly because of the American defeat in Vietnam, military psychological warfare had also entered a period of decline and discredit in the United States. It was Ronald Reagan, the President known as the 'Great Communicator', who revitalised American PSYOPS in the 1980s.   At the strategic level, communications was used as means of flooding the Soviet bloc with western truths, especially after the arrival of satellite television and the arrival of New Communications Technologies such as the videocassette and the fax machine (and later the mobile phone). The extent to which revitalised public diplomacy programmes helped to end the Cold War remains a matter of much debate, but it is hard to imagine the fall of the Berlin Wall and the downfall of dictators like Nicolai Caeuşescu without them.

At the tactical level, the first indication of the value of a revitalised military PSYOPS campaign came with the 1989 Panama episode. President Reagan had authorised a Department of Defence Master Plan which provided the basis for an enlarged 4th Psychological Operations Group (4POG) operating out of Fort Bragg. Then, following Iraq's invasion of Kuwait in August 1990, President Bush was persuaded to incorporate PSYOP planning as an integral part of Operation Desert Storm. Although the British contribution (Operation Granby) constituted only 5 per cent of the overall war effort, and indeed there was only one full-time British PSYOP officer at that time, the success of the American PSYOP campaign in the Gulf was to signal a new era for what was now being termed 'a combat force multiplier'. 69,000 Iraqis surrendered or deserted – many more than were actually killed – and at a relatively small cost to the overall war effort. 29 million leaflets were dropped over Iraqi lines, supplemented by radio messages transmitted both from ground-based transmitters and from an airborne PSYOPS platform known as 'Volant Solo' – a converted EC130 aircraft containing a full spectrum capability for radio (and television) broadcasts. Tactical loudspeaker teams also accompanied coalition forces blasting out messages to 'surrender or die' with instructions on how to do this safely. The largely conscript Iraqi army proved highly susceptible to any suggestions for getting out of the combat theatre safely, and the coalition knew that they were hardly likely to desert and go back home as 'traitors'. The resultant lines of surrendering Iraqi troops clutching 'safe conduct' leaflets presented the coalition with its biggest logistical prisoner-of-war accommodation problem since the end of World War Two. But, in the process, PSYOP on the battlefield had come of age.

Operations Other Than War

The post Gulf War era witnessed a series of international crises – in Bosnia, Somalia, Rwanda, Haiti, Kosovo and East Timor – which all saw PSYOPS deployed in support of these military 'operations other than war'. The clumsiness of this phrase reflected a recognition that there was now a 'New

World Order' (some would say 'disorder') where new ways of thinking were required to address what many saw as a Revolution in Military Affairs (RMA) prompted by the first so-called 'information war' in the Gulf. Advances in technologies, especially in communications, drove this revolution, together with new rules of operation in world affairs. PSYOPS were seen as a genuinely useful tool in support of these operations, although the products – and even the philosophy behind them – were very different from the use of 'traditional' psychological warfare.

As the 1990s unfolded, the changing nature of international crises – from inter-state to intra-state conflicts – saw a series of military interventions on the part of the American-led international community which placed more emphasis on the ability of troops to communicate with local populations rather than to fight battles with them. The complexity of these crises also required greater attention to the international media corps that invariably followed the military deployments. Three distinct, but increasingly overlapping, military communications disciplines began to emerge in the form of PSYOPS, Civil-Military Affairs (CMA) and Public Affairs (PA). PSYOPS was now being defined in a number of slightly different ways by different military organisations, but the US definition from 1996 was as good as any: 'operations planned to convey selected information and indicators to foreign audiences to influence their emotions, motives, objective reasoning, and ultimately the behaviour of foreign governments, organizations, groups and individuals'.[28] Examples of this ranged from leaflets dropped in Somalia informing people to keep off the roads while humanitarian convoys passed through the area to broadcasts from Volant (now Commando) Solo of speeches by President Aristide as part of Operation Restore Democracy in Haiti. Civil-Military Affairs usually took over when PSYOPS had completed its short-term operational role and constituted what critics would term as 'nation-building' once the immediate humanitarian or other crisis had passed. This forms a large part of the communications effort on the ground in post Dayton Bosnia. Public Affairs, known as Public Information in NATO and Media Operations in the UK, is primarily responsible for dealing with the media. Many soldiers working in this branch maintain vehemently that they are in the information business, and not in the business of influencing people. While there is much to debate here, the attempt to distance themselves from other 'influence operations' reveals the degree to which tension between civilian journalists and military communicators has, if anything, worsened since the British and the Americans abandoned conscription more than a generation ago.

The subtle internal differences between PSYOP, CMA and PA are frequently lost on the media which tends to see 'the military' as one monolithic entity – and one, when it gets into the business of communications, which is trying to 'propagandise'. A general decline in the overall number of specialised defence and foreign correspondents since the end of the Cold War, together with the declining number of journalists with some actual military experience, has not helped mutual understanding. Nor has increasingly complex and emerging military doctrinal thinking, especially in the area of 'Information Operations' (IO). This is an umbrella term for all forms of military communications - both offensive and defensive - in the Information Age. The increasing dependence of the military upon technology has also increased its vulnerability to what has been described as 'an electronic Pearl Harbour'. But this also brings new opportunities for helping to shape the information 'space' in order to reduce casualties, on all sides, in dangerous environments. In the early 1990s, the emphasis in this thinking was more on systems – computer and electronic networks – than on people. But since 19 hijackers flew civilian aircraft into the World Trade Centre and the Pentagon on 11th September 2001, there has been a discernible shift back on to people in what is now being termed 'Perception Management'.[29]

Perception Management is an ugly phrase, the latest in a long line of euphemisms devised by western democracies to detract from them being in the business of propaganda. This propaganda is invariably overt and falls within tried and tested techniques developed during the course of the twentieth century. It is based upon western value systems which place great emphasis on truth-telling and avoiding deliberate lies. But, as we have seen, such terminology is not very sophisticated when we are discussing propaganda. Yet it helps to explain the media's misunderstanding of the most celebrated propaganda scandal of most recent times. This was when, as part of its declared 'war' on terrorism, the Pentagon announced in early 2002 that it had established an Office of Strategic Influence (OSI) to conduct a global campaign for hearts and minds to portray the United States as a 'force for good in the world'. The problem arose when it was also admitted that deception would be part of the OSI's remit. The media immediately assumed that the Pentagon was going to use it as a vehicle for deception, when this would not only have belied all the lessons learned from earlier conflicts but it also displayed considerable misunderstanding of the doctrinal distinctions between deception as an ancient weapon of war and other forms of influence operations. Not did the Pentagon, itself engaged in a turf war about this issue with the State Department, explain this clearly. The OSI debacle once again revealed the gap which had opened up between the military and the media in terms of the one being unable to explain itself properly to a suspicious media corps only too able and willing to believe the worst.

Despite surviving political nervousness about the 'P' word – hence the British change of name in 1999 from 15 (UK) Psychological Operations Group to 15 (UK) Information Support Group – psychological operations today have moved a long way from the 'dirty tricks' image of the past.

They are still about changing or reinforcing human perceptions, but now they are more about not just helping the mission but also about helping the people the mission is there to assist. Today, this is more about peace support than traditional war fighting – although PSYOPS is still required for that, as evidenced by the 103 million leaflets dropped over the Serbs during the 1999 Kosovo conflict or the 80 million leaflets dropped in Afghanistan in 2001-02. As combat tools, leaflets and broadcasts enable military forces to communicate with their adversaries. Few journalists have any problems with that. But they do have a problem with being used indirectly as a medium through which PSYOP messages are disseminated. This was why the Office of Strategic Influence aroused so much suspicion. That it was handled so badly by the Pentagon suggests that a great deal still needs to be learned about dealing with the media. Gone are the days when media moguls were recruited by governments to conduct this type of activity. The rise of professional military communicators has ironically created a situation whereby the media have become part of the problem, not the solution.

NOTES

1. PSYOP tends to be the acronym preferred by the American military, although European armed forces prefer PSYOPS when they are not calling it something else, such as Operational Information (OPINFO), the preferred German term, or Information Support, the preferred euphemism of choice by the UK military at time of writing.

2. For example, in the 1999 Hollywood movie, *The General's Daughter*, which features a PSYOP group in which a murder takes place, John Travolta asks what PSYOPS are, to which comes the reply: 'we fuck with people's minds', thus perpetuating the popular view. The phrase 'psy-cops' was used by a journalist questioning me in the first days of Operation Enduring Freedom in October 2001.

3. There are some websites which attempt to do this, most notably www.psywarrior.com maintained by a veteran. These are, however, in a minority when compared to sites that portray PSYOP in a negative light.

4. Sun Szu, *The Art of War*, Translated and with an introduction by Samuel B. Griffith (Oxford, Clarendon Press, 1963

5. Napoleon said that 'four hostile newspapers are more to be feared than a thousand bayonets'. See Paul Johnson, *Napoleon* (London, Viking Press, 2002)

6. Sir Campbell Stuart, *Secrets of Crewe House* (London, Hodder & Stoughton, 1920)

7. See chapters 1-3 of Philip M. Taylor, *British Propaganda in the 20th Century: Selling Democracy* (Edinburgh, Edinburgh University Press, 1999).

8. T. J. Hollins, 'The Presentation of Politics: the place of party publicity, broadcasting and film in British Politics, 1918-39', University of Leeds PhD thesis, 1981.

9. K. Feiling, *The Life of Neville Chamberlain* (London, 1946) p. 110.

10. Philip M. Taylor, *The Projection of Britain: British Overseas Publicity and Propaganda, 1919-39* (Cambridge, Cambridge University Press, 1981).

11. By which I mean all voters, male and female, over the age of 21.

12. H. Lasswell, *Propaganda Technique in World War* One (London, MIT Press, 1971 reprint) A. Hitler, *Mein Kampf* with an introduction by D.C. Watt (London, Hutchinson, 1969). The best example of the former is H.C. Peterson, *Propaganda for War: the Campaign for American Neutrality, 1914-17* (New York, Kennikat, 1939) while the rabbit and the snake analogy was used by General Ludendorff in his memoirs published in 1919.

13. Arthur Ponsonby, *Falsehood in Wartime* (London, 1928).

14. For a History of the work of MI7, see Public Records Office (PRO), INF 4/1B

15. In more recent times, I have heard PSYOP referred to as a 'fifth' fighting arm, after the army, navy, air force and outer space.

16. H. Blankenhorn, *Adventures in Propaganda: Letters from an Intelligence Officer in France* (Boston, 1919).

17. Paul A. Linebarger, *Psychological Warfare* (New York, 1954) p. 223.

18. H. Blankenhorn, *Adventures in Propaganda: Letters from an Intelligence Officer in France* (Boston, 1919).

19. Mark Cornwall, *The Undermining of Austria Hungary: the Battle for Hearts and Minds* (London, Palgrave, 2000).

20. See Michael Balfour, *Propaganda in War 1939-45* (London, Routledge & Kegan Paul, 1979).
21. See Julian Hale, *Radio Power: Propaganda and International Broadcasting* (Philadelphia, Temple University Press, 1975).
22. N. Pronay and Philip M. Taylor, '"An Improper Use of Broadcasting...." The British Government and clandestine radio operations against Germany during the Munich Crisis and after', *Journal of Contemporary History*, 19 (1984) pp. 357-84.
23. Grey propaganda does not designate its source and deliberately leaves it ambiguous.
24. From the Latin *sibilare* or whispers.
25. N.C.F. Weekes and Philip M. Taylor, 'Breaking the German Will to Resist, 1944-45: allied efforts to end World War Two by non-military means', *Historical Journal of Film, Radio and Television*, Vol. 18 (1998) No. 1, pp. 5-48.
26. See Paul Lashmar and James Oliver, *Britain's Secret Propaganda War, 1948-1977* (Gloucestershire, Sutton Publishing Group, 1988).
27. Susan Carruthers, *Winning Hearts and Minds: British Governments, the Media and Colonial Counter-Insurgency, 1944-60* (London, Mansell, 1995).
28. Taken from Joint Publication 3-53, 'Doctrine for Psychological Operations', 10 July 1996. In author's possession, but widely available on the world wide web. The British definition is 'planned, culturally sensitive, truthful and attributable activities directed at approved target audiences within the Joint Operational Area in order to achieve political and military objectives by influencing attitudes and behaviour'.
29. See the special issue of *The Journal of Information Warfare*, Vol. 1, No. 3 (2002).

Chapter Seventeen
LEARNING THE LESSONS OF THE 20TH CENTURY: THE EVOLUTION IN BRITISH MILITARY ATTITUDE TO THE MEDIA ON OPERATIONS AND IN WAR

Lt Col Angus Taverner

Traditionally, the relationship between the military and the media has never been easy. Mutual suspicion and seemingly irreconcilable objectives have proved fertile ground, not only for academic study but for fiction, drama and a host of autobiographical tales. In short, the perception persists that 'truth is always the first casualty of war' and that the military remains determined to frustrate the media; preventing them from delivering the 'first draft of history'.

This perception has developed over time; rooted in the deliberate and willing deceptions of World War II and fanned by the wave of adverse media reflection in the wake of the Falklands War. In this paper, I hope to show that the relationship between the military and the media has evolved, and continues to develop, along a positive path. Indeed, I suggest that the British military, including the Ministry of Defence, has heeded the criticism directed at it over the years so that a more understanding and balanced relationship has started to emerge.

Although this paper is titled: 'Learning the lessons of the 20th Century', it will concentrate mainly on the evolution, some might argue revolution, of the military-media relationship over the past 20 years. The 1982 Falklands War marks the start of this period and it continues to punctuate the history of the media at war as an unsatisfactory benchmark from which both sides took stock and determined to do better 'next time'.

The literature spawned by this post-colonial conflict is multifarious: a process that continues to this day. Most of it perpetuates the view that the military-media relationship is destined to be forever adversarial and antagonistic. In 2002, writing a new Forward to his original 1984 account, 'Falklands Commando'[1], soldier turned journalist Hugh McManners comments: ' ...without an enormous (and depressingly unlikely) change of attitude, culture and perception by the MOD's media organisation, the battle for [the] all-important public opinion mandate will become increasingly more difficult for military commanders to win.'

Many of the 30 journalists who accompanied the Task Force to the South Atlantic seized on the unique opportunity to provide personal, eye-witness accounts of their experiences. In some cases, these were used to vent individual frustrations at the restrictions under which they had endured – many of which had little to do with 'the minders' and the censors' pencil - and more to do with their inability to get stories out, to broadcast from the theatre of operation and the often atrocious conditions in which they had been forced to live. Moreover, as many of these reporters are still working, their perceptions of this conflict, 20 years on, continue to be aired.

In London, the daily briefings by Ian McDonald, the MOD's acting Chief of Public Relations and principal Spokesman, created a similar atmosphere of frustration amongst the press and broadcasters. The perception of obfuscation and evasion was subsequently fuelled by Robert Harris's account of the Falklands media involvement: 'Gotcha!'[2]. In his concluding comments, Harris summed up: 'The instinctive secrecy of the military and the Civil Service; the prostitution and hysteria of sections of the press; the lies, the misinformation, the manipulation of public opinion by the authorities; the political intimidation of the broadcasters; the ready connivance of the media at their own distortion... All these occur as much in normal peace time Britain as in war.'

With the benefit of 20 years' hindsight, personally I do not believe that the military-media relationship was as poisonous as it has been portrayed. Some journalists enjoyed considerable success in garnering a string of exclusive stories and, for many of them, it was a pivotal point in subsequently successful careers. However, this is not the place for a detailed analysis of the Falklands media campaign and the fact remains – in the military mind as well in the wider perception – that 1982 provided lessons which had to be learned and acted on.

Within the MOD, the post-operation review highlighted the shortcomings of its media relations, both in London and in the South Atlantic, and took steps to overcome these. Notably, General Sir Hugh Beech conducted an internal inquiry on the perceived shortcomings of the MOD's media operation. This ultimately led to the negotiation and agreement of the so-called 'Green Book': 'Working Arrangements with the Media in times of Emergency, Tension and Conflict or War'[3], which is still in use today.

In this paper, I want to provide a military perspective, particularly as it pertains today. And I will set out the fundamental tenets of the military-media relationship, outlining the reasons why the military has to work with the media and the ways the military (which includes MOD for the purposes of this paper) has developed to conduct this, sometimes fractious, relationship.

Factors I would suggest that there are three broad strands that have led to current military thinking on how business should be conducted with the media. First, the military understands that the media is the prism through which the wider public, both at home and abroad, forms its opinions about strategic security and national defence. In the UK today, less than 7% of the population has any direct experience (either personally or through immediate family) of life in uniform. Unlike health or transport or law and order, individuals have little personal basis on which to form a view. Accordingly, as with international relations, public perception of defence is largely shaped by the way it is reported in the media.

It is perhaps the case that, over the last decade particularly, military commanders have re-discovered an old truth: public support is a vital ingredient in the successful prosecution of a military campaign. Witness an address in 1948, when General Dwight D. Eisenhower proclaimed that: 'Fundamentally, public opinion wins wars.' One hundred and fifty years earlier, Napoleon is similarly claimed to have commented that: 'Four hostile newspapers are more to be feared than a thousand bayonets.' The fight for the high ground of public opinion is certainly not new.

The second driver is the media themselves: their changing approach, their reach and their increasing rapidity of response: Nik Gowing's 'tyranny of time'[4]. As such the media is now a major factor in every operation and prudent military commanders have to vector media coverage into their plans for battle.

The third factor, and probably the most open to misunderstanding, is the military's involvement with the media in relation to the desire to influence adversaries – so-called Information Operations. Here it is easy to level charges of manipulation, dissimulation and propaganda. I hope to show that this is firmly not the case.

Public Support

Prevailing British Defence Doctrine emphasises 'the manoeuvrist approach'[5], not attrition, as the underlying principle for the conduct of modern military operations. This emphasises that: 'shattering the enemy's overall cohesion and will to fight, rather than his materiel, is paramount.' It applies not only to physical manoeuvre in the three dimensions of 'the battlespace' but also implies a state of mind; a way of thinking. As Sir Basil Liddell Hart commented in 1944: 'The real target in war is the mind of the enemy commander, not the body of his troops.' At all times, a military commander aims to maintain 'freedom of manoeuvre' while simultaneously denying it to his adversary.

Ultimately within the UK, military operations are mounted and conducted at the behest of governments. Politicians are susceptible (and democratically accountable) to public attitudes and opinion. The corollary to this is that ministers decide when, and often how, operations should be mounted within certain limitations – manifested in so-called 'Rules of Engagement'. Classically, during the 1999 Kosovo campaign, concern at the potential risk posed by Serbian Anti-Aircraft Artillery, led the Blair government to restrict the RAF offensive air campaign to no lower than 15,000 feet – operations that, tactically, could be done from much lower altitudes. During the Falklands conflict, the main focus of British operations was restricted to the seas around the islands themselves and South Georgia – when military decision-making by itself clearly suggested interdiction of the Argentine air force on the South American mainland. At the end of the Gulf War, operations were famously halted as news reports made clear the extent of the Iraqi casualties on the Basra road. Again, it can be argued that the military option would have continued to pursue the rout.

Each of these decisions was made because of wider political concerns as to what would be publicly acceptable and what would not. In the case of the

Falklands, the ensuing debate over the decision to attack the Argentine cruiser, 'General Belgrano', demonstrates the difficulties that democratic governments have to confront in coming to such decisions.

Throughout the decades of the Cold War, it seems that the UK, as part of NATO, was locked in a wider campaign of national survival – a struggle in which public support was assumed, notwithstanding pressure groups such as CND. In today's geo-strategic climate, it may be argued that the UK conducts military operations as a matter of 'choice' rather than as a matter of national necessity. They are an instrument of international political engagement. In electing to intervene in Sierra Leone, the British government did so in pursuit of 'an ethical foreign policy' and a national desire for natural justice. There was no threat to British national security involved and only marginal British interest in terms of national influence. I suggest therefore that wars of national survival imply and assume public support – the very way of life of the nation is at stake. When no such overwhelming threat is present, public support has to be earned and then sustained, both in the objectives of the campaign and the manner in which it is conducted, which must be seen as just and proportionate. In a, perhaps facile, hypothetical example: as a response to the 2001 Al-Qaida attack on New York's World Trade Centre, it would have been disproportionate for the US to have launched a nuclear strike against terrorist training bases in Afghanistan. As likely as not, this would have ceded worldwide support for the US in the wake of the tragedy to the Taliban regime – and possibly to Al-Qaida.

These examples demonstrate that the military's desire for an unfettered hand will always be tempered by the political thermometer in the body of public understanding. That public understanding and thus support is largely gained through the media, it is therefore unsurprising that the military at all levels now recognise that positive engagement with the media is an essential ingredient of modern war-fighting. As the last Chief of Defence Staff, General Sir Charles (now Lord) Guthrie put it: 'I think we in the military must do more to help the public understand defence and to get the right message across.' He went on, 'All we are attempting to do is communicate, and to get our story into the media in an accurate and favourable manner. Proactive Media Operations are [an] integral part of the New British Way of Warfare.' [6].

In addition to the freedom of action that flows from public support, a second and arguably as significant a factor, is the affect of public support on the morale of fighting forces. On any operation, soldiers, airmen and sailors become avid news watchers, listeners and readers. Their families at home try to catch every bulletin of news while their colleagues left behind, both civilian and military, are affected by the news from the operational theatre. Positive reporting implying success inevitably buoys up morale. Negative coverage, particularly over a sustained period, is likely to have the opposite effect. I am aware of the academic arguments that now challenge the widely held view that the Vietnam War was lost on the TV screens of continental USA. However, I think it is absolutely the case that the constant barrage of negative reporting of operations in Indo-China led the people of the US to question whether the fighting and loss of life was worthwhile. By 1971, President Nixon was campaigning on a promise to 'bring our boys home' and, in Vietnam, it led to a further loss of US morale, an unwillingness to take risks, loss of confidence and a growing acceptance that US forces were involved in a cause that might not worth fighting for.

By contrast, the positive reporting of the US-led coalition to expel Iraqi forces from Kuwait sustained morale at the highest levels throughout Operation DESERT STORM. It also restored the US military's belief in itself and, I would argue, set the pattern of the continuing level of US engagement around the world ever since.

Broad public support brings other benefits. At a strategic level, it helps to shore up complicated and extended alliances or coalitions. During the Kosovo operation, a number of NATO members were a little daunted by the US-led action. After all, Hungary, Serbia's close neighbour, had only been a NATO-member nation for nine days when the first air attacks were launched. The sympathies amongst some sectors of the Greek population were aligned more closely with those of their Serbian cousins than those of the Kosovars. These inevitable fissures in any alliance need widespread international support to buttress governments that need to make hard choices – particularly when these may run counter to the wishes of sections of their own populations.

From a longer-term perspective there are further reasons why the military has to be positive in its dealings with the media. While the UK does not have a written constitution, it is generally held that the armed forces must demonstrate their democratic accountability to the tax-paying British public. This may seem a slightly academic point but, for the Armed Services themselves, it is important that their activities, their training and operations should be subjected to public scrutiny. While the Services may not always like the way they are portrayed in the media, it is understood that long-held perceptions take time to change and this requires continuous engagement – in this respect the Services are no different to any other organisation with a public profile. Military operations are clearly the most newsworthy activity which the Services undertake, and therefore the need to engage the often feverish media interest and speculation becomes part of wider, ongoing corporate communications activities.

It is also acknowledged that the MOD has to show that it provides value for money and that it is engaged in a continuing tussle for resources with other government departments. It is rare today to find politicians who have any direct experience of military service and therefore the MOD cannot assume first hand experience when making the case for public expenditure in the defence arena. Public support for defence makes the arguments easier to justify.

Money is not the only resource the Services need. The Armed Forces also need people – and lots of them every year. Annually, the Army alone has to recruit 15,000 people to maintain its manned strength. Again, public support plays a major part in the success of this. The jobs available must look attractive to young men and women. Parents have to be reassured that the Services are a responsible employer. Perhaps most importantly, potential recruits, many with no previous contact with Service life, need to perceive a time in uniform as a positive step to take. This is subject to peer pressure, personal challenge and a range of wider influences.

Finally, it may seem obvious but many of the peace support operations in which the UK has become involved since 1991 are the direct result of media reporting. Journalists working in Kosovo, East Timor and Sierra Leone have awakened the public conscience that have led to demands that 'something must be done.' The something is often to mount a military operation, either to alleviate human suffering directly, as in the case of the 1999 Mozambique floods, or more frequently, to change the political conditions which led to the disaster:

so-called 'regime change'. Examples include: Kosovo and the wider Balkans, and currently Afghanistan. Having created the public demand for intervention, the intervenors (the military) normally mount operations on a tidal wave of public support. Commanders now accept that the media are a major factor in maintaining that support.

In, summary, public support is a key element, perhaps more than ever before, in the conduct of most modern military operations. Even when operations are covert, it is important that it is understood that these are carried out within the context of wider popular approval. Today, it is difficult to conceive of any British military involvement where public support is not important. To achieve that, a positive and proactive approach to dealing with media interest is essential.

The Media Challenge

Much of the argument and vented frustration that emerged in the wake of the Falklands conflict focused on the military's seeming unwillingness to give priority to the transmission of correspondents' copy back to the UK. At the time technology with global reach was still in its infancy and, of course, there was considerable suspicion that the Task Force commanders were deliberately trying to manipulate the media's output by limiting or even denying access to military communication systems. This, and the widely criticised attempts to over-censor material, led to many of the purported disputes between the military and the media – subsequently portrayed as a culture clash of epic proportion.

Of course there was more than a measure of truth, as well as wise hindsight, in the post-conflict analysis and, it would probably be fair to say that in the heat of most military operations, military commanders (and indeed Service personnel) would prefer the media to be elsewhere. In the starkly pressured environment of battle, the media creates a further circle of stress and uncertainty. However, I believe that today, military commanders understand, albeit sometimes reluctantly, that positive involvement with the media can bring as many benefits as potential problems. They also recognise a new factor: that the media is almost certainly going to be there. Therefore, as with terrain, weather and civilian populations, they will have to be factored into the military plan. The Americans describe this pithily as: 'The media are like rain, so go out and get wet.'

The media's exploitation of modern technology now ensures that they can report from almost anywhere on the earth's surface. And they can do so using equipment that is readily carried in a backpack. With the accelerating march of digital and satellite capability, combined with miniaturisation, the military has to accept that soon the media will have the roving capability to report live from a battlefield. So called 'real-time reporting' will introduce further pressure – particularly when the military is trying to conceal its intentions from an enemy.

So the second set of drivers that have led the military to a more accommodating and positive attitude towards the media is that journalists today cannot be 'controlled' through limitations on access to the military communication infrastructure. Correspondents no longer need this. In many places a humble mobile telephone will suffice. If not, either an Inmarsat transceiver or a satellite based 'Worldphone' will provide all the communications required. With an Inmarsat in a holdall, a newspaper photographer is only 9 minutes away from his Picture Desk anywhere in the world. Moreover, the TV satellite real-time uplink capability that required an ISO container to move in 1991, today weighs less than 750 kilogrammes. I confidently predict that this capability may soon be fitted into a carry-on flight case. In short, technology has unshackled the media and the military has accepted that engagement is the only option; avoidance and control only leading to antagonism and consequent negative coverage.

Not only has technology provided the media with reach but it has enabled the media to make a truly global impact. Broadcasters and newspapers around the world no longer have to wait for pictures. This morning a bomb kills and maims 250 people on the other side of the world, an hour later the BBC or CNN are broadcasting from the scene of the atrocity. Many theorists have argued over the wider impact of this in terms of the depth of analysis, the potential distortion of facts and the unevenness of coverage it may induce. However, for the military it has introduced a new factor: what the military has termed 'The Strategic Corporal' – more prosaically, the potential strategic impact of events at the lowest levels of fighting.

Government ministers and politicians generally have been forced to deal with the effects of a new media that can report near instantaneously from almost anywhere in the world – and moreover a media that demands a similarly rapid response. This leads politicians to become more interested in what is happening at the lowest levels of military activity – not just because they can but often because they have to. Accordingly, a minor military incident can suddenly attract Prime Ministerial attention. Again, this has led the military to the need to deal with the media in a theatre of operations – both to explain breaking news and to engender a wider spirit of trust and confidence in both camps. It has also led them to accelerate the passage of information from the frontline to the most senior decision-making levels.

The Information Campaign

Perhaps more than ever before, modern military campaigns are struggles of information and perception. The Tofflers' analysis[7] of the move to information based warfare, which sees information itself becoming the target, has been much picked over in recent times. War-fighting has always contained some measure of this element; historian Richard Holmes recently commented: 'A battle is not lost until the defeated side believes it has lost.' The so-called Revolution in Military Affairs (RMA) emphasises particularly the importance of information and the need to achieve 'knowledge superiority'. Part of this is to achieve 'situational awareness' so that military commanders can make timely and as near perfectly informed decisions as computerised technology enables. But it is also very much in the business of influencing the adversary: to persuade him of one's intent and to influence his courses of action.

This growing area of military endeavour is called 'Information Operations'[8]. Current British doctrine recognises that it is important that military dealings with the media, so-called 'Media Operations'[9] should never be open to charges of duplicity or deception. Accordingly, Media Operations are not directed under the umbrella of Information Operations but it would be patently foolish if they were in any way inconsistent or counter-productive. For this reason, the two areas of activity are co-ordinated as part of a wider Information Campaign – a pan-Government, maybe pan-Alliance, activity aimed at emphasising the rectitude of military action and, as likely as not, highlighting the wrongness of the opposing position.

Arguably, both sides of the relationship now accept that information has potency which can be harnessed to the benefit of the military campaign. Reflecting on the Kosovo operation, Prime Minister Tony Blair's then Spokesman, Alastair Campbell, observed: 'Getting the message through that our cause was just, that our demands were absolute, that we were not going away until they were met; that was about words and pictures, not just bombs and aeroplanes.'[10] On a similar theme, writing nearly three years later in the MOD's in-house newspaper, 'Focus', *The Times* Defence Editor, Michael Evans, noted: 'Every operational commander today knows that in all campaigns and peacekeeping missions, the use of information as a weapon can sometimes have as much impact on the enemy as the firing of a gun, and the media, wittingly or unwittingly, play a role in this psychological game.'[11]

The Information Campaign plays a particularly important role in crisis management. If declarations of intent and diplomatic pressure are correctly presented, in part, through media coverage, then this becomes a recognised tool in reducing tension. An example of this is the continuing diplomatic and international pressure on both India and Pakistan to deter those two countries from embarking on all-out war over Kashmir. As the most important influence on public support, and a trusted communication medium, the media plays an increasingly important role in the process. Moreover, if deterrence fails, it remains the open channel through which adversaries can, indirectly, continue to communicate – and do so instantly. It would be wrong to assume from this that the military will use the media as an unwitting partner. Rather, it is recognition that the media are powerful, influential and, in many ways, a trusted intermediary – an honest broker.

UK Media Operations Doctrine

There are, as I hope I have outlined, a broad swathe of reasons why the British military have heeded the lessons of the past and now accept that dealing positively with the media, whether in the UK or around the world, reaps rewards beyond any perceived advantages of hiding behind a cloak of secrecy.

This has required the military establishment to accept a number of fundamental truths. First, the military has no control of the media. They are not 'under command', nor do they obey orders. Unless they have agreed otherwise, their only control comes from the news editors for whom they work. Residual concepts of maintaining control through access to military facilities, particularly communications, are outmoded.

As mentioned earlier, the military have also come to accept that the media are a fact of modern operations – they will almost certainly 'be there' and therefore they have become a factor that has to considered in all military planning. By the time the British-led ground force crossed the Macedonian border into Kosovo in 1999, it is estimated that some 3,574 correspondents had been registered (not accredited) by NATO. In military terms, this represented half a Brigade – a physical presence that was hard to ignore.

It is also now accepted that bad news rarely improves over time. Given the uncertain nature of almost all military operations, there is every likelihood that operations will not run as planned, errors will be made and, sadly, casualties will occur. It is therefore understood that it is better to break adverse news early than to try and cover things up. When information is not forthcoming, speculation will often take its place. This can be just as damaging, if not more so. The military has recognised that the media, like nature, abhors a vacuum. It is better that stories should be released as fully and swiftly as the situation allows than to stay silent and hope that events will move on.

The principles under which the MOD and the military now deal with the media are clearly articulated and taught both at Staff Colleges and on tailored training courses designed to equip selected officers with the knowledge and skills to provide a positive interface with the media.

Truth is the most important of these principles. The temptation to deceive, evade or even lie is, on occasions, very powerful. This has to be resisted. Any short-term gain will be swiftly overtaken by the longer term disadvantages of loss of integrity, damaged relationships and, as likely as not, hostile media coverage.

The military has also recognised that personal and organisational credibility is vital in building and sustaining positive relationships with the media. It may seem to be a statement of the obvious, but the British military quietly acknowledge that, while on the one hand their image may be a little staid and authoritarian, on the other there is a perception that they are honest, loyal, trustworthy and professional to their core. Accordingly, when a military spokesman goes 'on the record' the media, rightly, assume that they are dealing with an individual who is speaking from a background of knowledge and experience. He or she must be someone they can trust. Moreover, they expect that individual to be consistent and reliable. In dealing with correspondents, it is essential that the military remembers this – no side-deals, no favouritism; instead balanced and honest comment rooted in absolute fact.

Sometimes this in itself causes problems as facts have to be checked and verified. Frequently this takes time but doctrine directs that military staff should always work to the principle of: maximum disclosure with minimum delay. If all the information cannot be released immediately, it is recognised that it is better to give what is known than to hold back until the full story has been checked.

The major stumbling block along this apparently virtuous road is the factor of so-called 'operational security'. In training and educating Service personnel to have an awareness of the media and how to behave when they encounter a journalist, the primary concern that is always raised is how to 'prevent' the media from disclosing plans to the adversary. This remains a legitimate concern. After all servicemen and women's lives are at risk. And it is not even the case that the media will always disclose information deliberately – it may be done wholly unwittingly.

Again experience has shown that trusted relationships between military and media allow limited disclosure without compromising secret plans. This will always remain a matter of fine judgement but there are correspondents who are trusted and those who are less so. The key is that, while the media has the right to be informed, it does not have the absolute right to be informed on every aspect of an operation. Most journalists understand this and it is on this basis that operational security can be maintained.

Current British military doctrine finally focuses on preparation. I have mentioned the importance of relationships founded on mutual trust and I have also commented on the need for a positive approach when dealing with the media. This does not just happen and it is important that the military continues to recognise the need for continuous dialogue that builds confidence and nurtures relationships, particularly when events conspire to make this difficult. There will always be a temptation to withdraw behind a wall of officialdom, to decline to comment on plans that have gone awry or simply avoid the media altogether but it is particularly at these moments that greater efforts have to be made maintain engagement. In the past, the easier path has, all too often, been taken and the perception of secrecy and avoidance has been fostered and persists.

Working with the Media

In practical terms, the military now understands that its dealings with the media must be founded on respect and recognition of the role they carry out. What defence journalist, Robert Fox, has termed 'The Bargain'. This strives to balance the media's need to report with the military's requirement to conduct operations effectively and decisively while limiting the risk to their own side as far as possible. As I hope I have made clear, in carrying out its mission, the military remains accountable to the court of public opinion and therefore, not only does it have to be effective but it must be seen to be doing so in a manner that remains publicly acceptable – a just cause and a proportionate response.

To make this relationship work, to strike Fox's 'bargain', the military recognise that the media require assistance. First, they need information – a continuing stream of facts and figures to provide the framework for the stories being written and broadcast. Secondly, successful journalists need access: to commanders, to picture opportunities, to fighting elements and to the battle area. Many will seek this on an exclusive basis and judging when to allow this, when to 'pool' the opportunity and when to make it widely available, is one of the enduring dilemmas for military media operations' staff.

Both TV and stills photographers need opportunities to capture exciting imagery and action. It may seem obvious, but too often the media have been invited to a military 'facility' only to witness static equipment devoid of service personnel, or cameramen and photographers who are corralled in the 'wrong place' while the action passes them by. The military now recognise that successful coverage is predicated on exciting visual imagery. This means the media need action: in-flight, at sea or tracking through the mountains of Afghanistan. Finally, while I have emphasised how far technological development has freed correspondents from dependency on the military, it remains the case that they normally welcome a measure of support: some shelter for the night, food, fresh water and perhaps a shower.

This cannot be, however, a wholly one-way street. The bargain implies responsibilities on the part of the media as well. In particular, it demands respect for the basis on which access and information is given. It recognises the military necessity of preserving operational security, especially concerning future plans, and it implies respect for the young servicemen and women who are being asked to do a tough and dangerous job in often arduous and nerve-racking conditions.

At the start of this paper I commented that the military are still learning the lessons of the 20th century, and particularly of the past two decades. It is clear that important lessons have been acknowledged and that, as General Sir Charles Guthrie was eager to emphasise, proactive media relations are not only unavoidable but should be positively beneficial.

In some ways, this is a relationship in which the MOD and Armed Services should never ultimately prevail. Rightly, the media should retain a healthy scepticism. If the military's media relations become too sophisticated, accusations will be levelled of 'spin' or manipulation. However, in the pursuit of balance and objectivity, I also believe that the media must be wary of being misled by an adversary's propaganda. The evidence of one's own eyes may not be all that it seems.

If I have given the impression that the military is now looking to 'use' the media, either knowingly or unknowingly, as part of a wider Information War, then I have misled you. Positive media relations are not about propaganda or even psychological operations, although the areas confusingly overlap and therefore need to be properly managed. Rather, they are concerned with the enduring requirements of maintaining support for military action carried out on the public's behalf and about sustaining the morale of the individuals involved, both directly and indirectly, in conducting those operations.

Technology may have freed the media from the physical constraints under which correspondents used to labour. But it has also introduced new tyrannies: the need to service 24-hour rolling news channels and editorial interference from afar. The media continues to evolve as indeed does the military. I only hope that as the military finally learns to open up to a media that reports honestly and with integrity, the media does not succumb to commercial pressure that sees coverage increasingly as a form of entertainment, sensationalising serious issues, to the detriment of public understanding.

NOTES

1. H. McManners, *Falklands Commando* (London: HarperCollins*Publishers*, Rev Ed 2002), p.17.
2. R. Harris, *The Media Trilogy – Gotcha!* (London: Faber and Faber, 1994), pp. 185-186.
3. UK MOD, *Working Arrangements with the Media in Times of Emergency, Tension and Conflict or War (The 'Green Book'), (Notes for MOD Personnel, editors and correspondents)* (London: MOD Director News, 2001 latest revise).
4. N Gowing, *Real Time Television Coverage Of Armed Conflicts and Diplomatic Crises: Does It Pressure Or Distort Foreign Policy Decisions?* (Harvard University, John F Kennedy School, 1994).
5. UK MOD, *British Defence Doctrine*, 2nd Edn, October 2001.
6. General Sir Charles Guthrie, Chief of Defence Staff, *The Liddell Hart Lecture* – King's College, London, 12 February 2001.
7. G. and H. Toffler, *War and Anti-War*. (Boston, Toronto, New York, London: Little Brown and Company, 1993).
8. NATO Doctrine defines 'Information Operations': 'Actions taken to influence decision makers in support of political and military objectives by affecting others' information, information-based processes, command and control systems, and command and information systems while exploiting and protecting one's own information and/or Information Systems.'
9. NATO Doctrine defines 'Media Operations': 'That line of activity developed to ensure timely, accurate, and effective provision of Public Information and implementation of Public Relations policy within the operational environment, whilst maintaining Operational Security.'
10. Campbell, Lecture to the Royal United Services Institute for Defence Studies, 1999.
11. M Evans, MOD 'Focus', July 2002.

Chapter Eighteen
STRADDLING THE DIVIDE – SPINNING FOR BOTH SIDES
Mark Laity

...a cannon shot could not be fired in Europe without all the cabinets having some interest in the occurrence. A new Alexander must therefore try the use of a good pen as well as his good sword...[1]

Clausewitz may be better known for declaring moderation in war an absurdity, or war a continuation of politics by other means, but his wide-ranging historical analysis also took in a touch of what today would be called public diplomacy. It was clear long before the 21st century that a soldier cannot live by the sword alone. What has increased though, indeed exponentially increased, is the importance of the soldier having presentational skills, or access to them. In an uncertain age of highly conditional half-victories, harnessing the power of the media is now a prime factor in who wins. The media is, in other words, a weapon – and a very potent one. Of course, as other essays in this volume make clear, to some degree it always has been, but it is the scale to which this can happen which is new. Philip Bobbit, in his influential 'The Shield of Achilles', goes as far as saying, 'In the market-state, the media have begun to act in direct competition with the government of the day.'[2]

It is a reflection of many features of modern society. Some are technological, such as 24-hour news and cheap global communications; others are societal, such as the death of deference and distrust of governments; some reflect modern foreign policy, such as the seeming lack of existential threats and an aversion to casualties; while others seem almost petty such as 'star' journalism and an addiction to bad news.

There are more, and together they add up to making life increasingly tough for the military – Bobbit remarks that the 'media are well situated to succeed in this competition' between government and media. It's their dawning awareness of this that has made media handling something of a growth industry for Western militaries, but for all this they mostly regard the media as more problem than opportunity.[3] It may be a weapon, but they feel it is more often one they have to combat rather than use. I can recall one frustrated British officer telling me in Macedonia in 2001, 'The only way we'll make them happy is if we cock it up.'

For its part, the media understandably object to the idea of anyone else using them as a weapon, but it is a reality they cannot escape. Michael Ignatieff, writing in the wake of Kosovo, commented, 'When war becomes a spectator sport, the media becomes the decisive theatre of operations. ...it also transforms journalists from observers into protagonists, and makes the media much more than mediators.'[4] The consequences of this are not something the media have really faced up to. Journalists enjoy – and why not? – their fame and relish making waves, but they have to rise to the challenge of handling the power that has been thrust upon them.

Unsurprisingly both sides on the military/media divide often feel they get the dirty end of the stick, but where lies the balance of power? I hold an unusual position having been reasonably prominent on both sides of this divide, when after 11 years as BBC Defence Correspondent I moved in 2000 to become a policy adviser to the NATO Secretary General and Deputy Spokesman for the alliance. Having been both hunter and hunted, I can tell the difference, and life was far more comfortable hunting with the media pack!

Of course even to talk of 'us and them' is both a presumption that there is a straightforward divide, and an assumption that there is just one 'us' and one 'them'. The truth, as ever, is more complex, but anyone who has sat on the inside can testify to the extraordinary preoccupation with what the media says and does, and how to respond.

Smart Words v Smart Bombs

One core reason for this is that in an era when total war is an increasingly distant memory the media has become a prime weapon in what the military fashionably call asymmetric warfare. In the age of one superpower and Western military dominance, for any group or country to fight the West on its own terms is to invite easy defeat, (ask Iraq) so in the face of conventional firepower the weaker party uses different weaponry. This 'asymmetric warfare' could be terrorism, guerrilla warfare – or information warfare. Indeed it can be argued terrorism is itself a particularly nasty form of information warfare. For Osama bin Laden the actual death toll on September 11 was incidental to his real purpose of terrorising everyone else. He was not so much trying to kill 3,000 people as to scare 3 billion others who had a grandstand view. Asymmetric warfare is surely going to be the dominant form of conflict in the modern era, simply because of the lack of enemies capable of contemplating a conventional war against the West. This means the media will be in the frontline not just as reporters, but as unwilling participants through being a weapon of choice for the militarily weaker side in particular.

There is nothing new in the aggressive use of propaganda against your enemy; whether it is Lord Haw-Haw or leaflet drops on Iraqi soldiers, but what is different is the primacy of the use of media as a weapon. Kosovo is an obvious recent example. Milosevic knew his only hope of victory was not to defeat

NATO in battle, but for the alliance to simply have to stop fighting because it lacked the public support to continue. In hindsight victory usually carries an air of inevitability, but it certainly did not look like that at the time, and the Milosevic regime's exploitation of the media gave NATO many of its toughest problems.

Indeed, although no two conflicts are ever identical, Kosovo illustrates many of the common features of today's wars that makes media handling so central to its successful conduct. NATO entered into the conflict reluctantly, with only soft public support and doubts remaining amongst many governments. The cause itself, although morally strong, was not central to most nations' interests. Unrealistic expectations of a short war and the impact of heavily constrained airpower combined with initially ill-defined war aims to add to doubts and uncertainties. In such circumstances, as the conflict dragged on with no end in sight, NATO's ability to stay the course was questionable.

The impact of the media in such circumstances was critical, and as the campaign progressed Milosevic grew more adept at exploiting the Western media. For instance, the movements of Belgrade-based journalists were usually heavily restricted, but whenever a bomb missed its target and killed civilians, coaches were laid on to view the carnage. It was simple but effective. The reports and images had an emotional punch, while simultaneously questioning the competence of NATO and whether it was achieving its aims. Doubts were also cast on the morality of a conflict, started to defend the innocent, which was instead killing some of them.

Much of the Kosovo air campaign reporting became about a small number of bombs that missed with tragic consequences, than a far larger number that hit – and of course in a fight between powerful images and words there can be only one winner. It diverted attention from what Milosevic was doing to what NATO was doing, and damaged the alliance's credibility.

In effect Milosevic, unable to counter NATO's bombs with his own, used NATO's misaimed bombs against it as a kind of information bomb. He also demonstrated how vulnerable the West is to such asymmetric warfare. Able to control his own media, he took advantage of the freedom of the press in his enemies' countries. Ignatieff says journalists were exploited by both sides, but comments, 'Western journalists in Belgrade were faced with difficult choices: if they went on Serb-organised tours of NATO attack sites and reported what was presented to them as true, they risked being seen as dupes of the Serbian regime; if they refused, they risked deportation, or what was worse, losing the pictures to their competitors.'[5] In the end Milosevic's strategy did not work, but the media battle was both critical and close-run.

My point is not to revisit the still sensitive debate within the media about who was right or wrong in their reporting of Kosovo, but to emphasise that Milosevic needed the media as an offensive weapon in a way NATO did not. While NATO needed to maintain public support to continue its bombing campaign, for Milosevic the media was the weapon. In this context I still find it odd that the bulk of the post-Kosovo internal media debate was about how to respond to NATO's media handling, not Milosevic's.

It is certainly an open question whether NATO would have won if Milosevic had not handed his enemy an early propaganda gift by so openly and brutally driving hundreds of thousands of Kosovars into Albania and Macedonia. Without that clear evidence (emotive and visual not statistical) of Milosevic's evil could NATO have withstood the later media setbacks? It is certainly an intriguing 'what if?', and I have no doubt if the might of the US and NATO had been defeated by Serbia the prime cause would have been losing the media war.

The West's vulnerability to this form of asymmetric warfare was further demonstrated in the US-led campaign in Afghanistan in autumn 2002. Again al-Qaeda and the Taleban's only hope was to undermine the coalition that was backing the US, and despite their disdain for the West both al-Qaeda and the Taleban soon worked out what suited them best in media terms. To that end a key media weapon was again stray bombs and missiles killing civilians, raising once more the issues of competence, prospects of success, and the morality of killing civilians in a campaign based on morality. The abrupt collapse of the Taleban, producing a much shorter conflict than in Kosovo, meant the true impact of this coverage will never be known. Nevertheless the trend of reporting had already forced the US and UK into a radical revision of their media strategy amid worries that the battle for hearts and minds was being lost. This was not so much in their home constituencies, but in other important countries and regions where support had always been more equivocal.

In all the conflicts or crises I have covered, whether as reporter or spokesman, one feature has usually stood out; there has often been a huge disparity of power between the combatants, but the stronger has mostly had great difficulty in making this power count. Pure strength is no longer enough. The reasons vary, for instance increasing legal restraints, but the inability for the strong to make their military power count is why other factors, such as the media, have become relatively more important as a factor in warfare. In the media's case of course, its role as both witness and self-appointed judge can be one of the reasons inhibiting the full use of military power.

This can of course cut both ways. The presence of the media probably restrained Milosevic from pounding Sarajevo into submission, but Bobbitt talking about precision bombing campaigns of the type seen in Kosovo, remarks, 'such bombing campaigns require patience – which the publics of market-states, fed as they are by hyperbolic media and sensitised to the suffering of civilians who are harmed by the bombing, will seldom tolerate – and modest goals.'[6]

Reluctant Warriors and Uncertain Causes

During the 1991 Gulf War I was the BBC's Saudi-based Defence Correspondent, and the point at which it became truly clear for me that the game was really changing was the media and public reaction to the aerial destruction of the retreating Iraqi forces on the Mitla Ridge, as they fled up the Basra Road from Kuwait City. In military terms it was a 'no-brainer'. No-one had surrendered, retreating forces could re-group to fight again, so coalition aircraft bombed the head of the convoy to stop them going north, then the tail to stop them going south, and then worked their way up and down the now static convoy. The effect was devastating and horrible to see, (although post-war analysis showed the deaths were in the low hundreds not the thousands guessed at then) but militarily it was what you were meant to do – catch the enemy at a disadvantage and kill, wound or capture them.

It certainly did not surprise me. It was what the RAF had done to the Germans at Falaise in 1944, and to the Turks in Palestine in 1918, and regarded then and since as classic demonstrations of airpower. Not this time – I had missed the zeitgeist. It was reported in tones of shock, horror, and disapproval, amidst allegations of massacres. It certainly played a part in bringing the war to an early close, and General Colin Powell recalls telling General Schwarzkopf, 'The television coverage, I added was starting to make it look as if we were engaged in slaughter for slaughter's sake...' We don't want to be seen as killing for the sake of killing, Mr President,' I said.'[7]

Even more striking for me was the impact of a single photograph showing the hideously burnt head of an Iraqi soldier poking out of the driver's hatch of an armoured vehicle. It was a shocking picture, and many used it to challenge the morality of the allied campaign. Now of course it was by no means the first photograph to be used in this way, but what was different was that this was not a naked, napalm-scarred girl running down a road, or a prisoner being illegally executed, but an enemy soldier, a combatant, lawfully killed in action. Killing the enemy had become debatable.

It was in the Gulf conflict that the act of killing *too many* enemy soldiers in combat became an issue. There were even suggestions that it made a difference that the Iraqi army was largely conscripts, while attacking retreating forces was a little unfair. In effect you should win without killing too many of the enemy. It illustrates a changing world, which has tended strongly towards increasing inhibitions on the use of force, and therefore ever-greater debate on whether those limits have been breached, should be further tightened, or whether force is even justified in the first place. The media of course is at the heart of such debates, both as conduit and participant.

This itself reflects the lack of existential threats to the Western nations in particular. Wars of national survival make debate irrelevant in the struggle to live, while total conflict tends towards extremes, which leaves little room for discussion in the centre. However we are in the era of 'Wars of Choice', and so whether we fight and how we fight becomes literally and metaphorically debatable. Even suggestions a dangerous threat exists, for instance from terrorism, are a 'hard sell' without the evidence of battleships sinking in harbours, tanks rumbling over frontiers, and continuing military assaults.

As already indicated, limited conflict also usually results in limited means of waging war. The basic military aim of hitting the enemy 'fastest with the mostest' is rarely an option, often leaving the stronger party in the uncomfortable position of being accused of being a bully without actually being able to act like one by using all its power. A colleague refers to this as the 'gentle giant syndrome'. It is not the purpose of my contribution to itemise all the restrictions, but it is important to understand how many there are because they all have an impact on the military/media relationship.

For instance, even the weapons used can become a potent source of dispute, as with Depleted Uranium and Cluster Bombs, and sometimes an opponent can play on this. In the Kosovo conflict the Serbs blamed Cluster Bombs for incidents where less controversial weapons had in fact been used. The aims of current conflicts or peace support operations also add tension to the military/media relationship because limited operations tend to have limited aims. These can be hard to explain, or sometimes, as with UNPROFOR in Bosnia, hard to justify. The mandates and rules of engagement for such operations can be very restrictive and technical, leaving the military vulnerable to media accusations for either exceeding their mandate, or leaving innocents to suffer because they stick to them.

Coalition crisis management, and the friction that goes with war by committee, is obviously also an exercise in the lowest common denominator, for media spokesman as well as commanders. I can speak with feeling about the practical problems of navigating the rocks and shoals of sometimes contradictory national sensitivities. Victory may ultimately be the best answer to criticism, but in today's limited and conditional conflicts even victory itself can be hard to define. The liberation of Kuwait may have been the aim of the allies in 1991, but pretty soon much of the media were more focused on the fact Saddam has not lost his hold on power, which in 1991 at least was at best a hope not a war aim. Once upon a time it may have been a case of 'To the victor the spoils', but now it is often, 'To the victor the problems' as they get involved with post-conflict nation building.

Changes in society have also had a massive impact, almost totally in favour of the media. Such is the degree to which it is now accepted that it is easy to forget how strong the tide towards openness on military affairs is flowing. The degree this has reached is demonstrated by the protests from the US media about the fact it did not accompany Special Forces on their behind the lines airborne raid in Afghanistan in autumn 2001. Even more, secrecy has to be justified, and although the need for operational security is not challenged in principle much of the media feels it is the best judge of whether something should be secret.

Society itself has become less deferential to those in power, and is also often distrustful of the establishment. When, as spokesman, defending NATO against claims that Depleted Uranium was causing ill health in the Balkans I often felt NATO was unfairly paying the price for a whole series of health disasters such as BSE, and dioxin in food, where government had certainly not shone.

Even more than this is the growing unacceptability of war to European public opinion in particular. Almost sixty years of peace and the end of the Cold War has made the experience of conflict remote and increasingly distasteful. Obviously the experience of many other parts of the world, both in terms of democracy and the recent experience of war, leaves them in a very different situation, but I am focussing here on the areas I know best. So in Europe justifying going to war, and then the methods used to conduct it, although not impossible, is certainly increasingly hard.

Britain, like France, has an imperial past that means there is still something of a habit of intervention, including acceptance of conflict in faraway places, but the history of most other European nations is very different. Direct defence of home territory is one thing, but power projection is quite another. Along with this is an aversion to casualties also related to the limited nature of such conflicts – if it is of strictly limited national interest then the national involvement and casualties must be similarly limited. Ignatieff further notes, 'Kosovo made it obvious that wars waged in the name of values invariably turn out to be more controversial than wars waged for interests.'[8]

Clausewitz in his historical survey *On War* referred to conflict in the eighteenth century, which he called the Age of Professionals, as a 'restricted, shrivelled up form of war', concluding, 'in all these cases in which the impulse given by interest is slight, and the principle of hostility feeble...in short where no powerful motives press and drive, cabinets will not risk much in the game; hence this tame mode of carrying on war, in which the hostile spirit of real war is laid in irons.'[9] I find it a striking parallel, and although some may argue today's conflicts are not 'tame', it is of course all relative, and compared to even relatively recent history the levels of violence are far lower, weapons far more accurate, and the restraints on their use far higher.

The modern military spokesman is more likely to be part of a so-called Peace Support Operation than a war, and defending the use of any force at all, the raison d'être of the military, can be an issue. In essence explaining the conduct of military operations is hard when faced with a public that is increasingly unsympathetic to the use of force, and also, as experience of war fades away, ignorant. I mean this literally not pejoratively, and of course, in the case of war, ignorance is bliss! It was also, I believe, Trotsky who said, 'You may not be interested in war, but war is interested in you.' This is where the journalist comes in.

Jaw Jaw about War War

For most journalists being a war reporter remains far and away the most glamorous and sought after branch of their craft, second only to being a presenter on a major news bulletin in getting recognition in a trade where fame is a considerable spur. Like ambitious officers, having what the military used to call 'a good war' is good for your career. As with so much journalism other peoples' bad news is their good news – including of course, once upon a time, mine. I only state this because one should always bear this in mind with regard to journalists (there are mercifully few, although sometimes sadly prominent) whose stock in trade is moral posturing and outrage as they hop from war to war.

Many of the features of modern journalism itself seem also designed to add stress to the media/military relationship, even allowing for the fact most journalists and spokesmen know they need a good professional working relationship. Not least is the fact many journalists share the ignorance of the public about warfare. The best journalists have formidable experience of conflict, and compared to many I only dabbled in the shallow end of frontline reporting, and I am still in awe of the tactical instincts and knowledge of some I met. However even some of these could be narrowly focussed, with a formidable nose for a story on the frontline, but not knowing why a Jaguar fighter-bomber could not drop its bombs in bad weather, and having more feel for the squaddie's tactical problems than the general's strategic issues. This would not matter as long as the strategic issues are not dismissed as irrelevant to 'what's really going on', or knowledge of technology seen as mere 'toys for boys', but some, if not the best, do exactly this, often as part of a more emotional form of journalism.

Even then this lack of breadth would not matter if it were not for the dominance given to the frontline reporter, especially on TV and radio, where the tone of the whole coverage is set by the report closest to what is often known as the 'bang-bang'. The wrap-up 2-way, covering the global waterfront is often with a reporter whose inevitable ignorance about events beyond his small section of the frontline is hidden by being fed the latest agency reports. In a similar way the reporter super-glued to a live camera position for regular 2-ways is similarly reliant on second-hand information, giving the whole process an appearance of authenticity that is more apparent than real.

War reporting is also a growth industry, and the knowledge of some cannot disguise the ignorance of many others when any big crisis means the arrival of hundreds or even thousands of journalists of varying knowledge and ability, not the scores of a previous era. Knowing relatively little, and with little time to learn, many simply follow the media pack, which means once the tone of the coverage has been set it is hard to shift regardless of events. For all the sheer numbers of journalists, the reporters and organisations that set that tone is often very small, frequently divided between those respected by the journalist in the field, and the often quite different individuals read by editors and producers in London!

The modern media pack is also highly international, both in terms of multi-nationality and outlook. Traditional war reporting always had a strong element of sticking to 'your' side, and while national fellow feeling still crosses the military/media divide it has been weakened in today's uncertain conflicts. After all, as previously indicated, the issues are rarely of national survival, but ones of debatable policy, so journalists do not feel disloyal when they are disagreeing with a government policy rather than their country. Such disagreements rarely extend to criticising the 'squaddies', who are often portrayed, Blackadder-like, as victims/lions led by inadequate politicians/donkeys. The supposed moral basis of western interventions invites disagreement, and in this respect Bosnia, and especially Sarajevo, represented a watershed in the same way Vietnam did for a previous generation of war reporters.

Martin Bell, one of the truly great TV journalists, said of Bosnia, 'For all of us who came from the outside, the Bosnian conflict has been not just another foreign war, but a shocking and defining experience, which has changed our way of doing things and seeing things.'[10] As Martin would himself acknowledge, there have been worse wars, but he is still right that it seemed to change the way things were done. Of most interest in this context was the validation it gave to a more committed, emotional, personalised form of journalism. Of course this had always existed to some degree, but Bosnia seemed to put it into the mainstream.

Martin Bell referred to the '...generally crusading character of the Sarajevo press corps', in support of the Muslims, and some, such as David Rieff, openly defended such commitment, 'If they had gone 'native', as UN officials and some of their colleagues back home liked to sneer, they were unrepentant...That was why, throughout most of the siege, the reporters and television crews were perhaps the only dependable allies the Bosnians had.'[11] Long before Milosevic sought to employ the media as a weapon against NATO the Bosnian Muslims were using it against the Serbs and the international community. Even some in the BBC, the main bastion of traditional objectivity, were affected, with one colleague once telling me, 'We should be bombing the shit out of the bastards (the Bosnian Serbs), and if I have anything to do with it we will.' The trend towards commitment is perhaps accelerated by the rise of personality journalism, where star correspondents and columnists make their name by saying what they think and feel about what they see.

Driven by the imperatives of television, which heavily influences other areas of the media as well, the most successful war journalism (in terms of leading the bulletin or the front page) usually has a powerful emotional punch. It increasingly focuses on the plight of victims, often seeking out individual incidents, and generalising from the particular to symbolise the whole. For the military spokesman this trend is something of a nightmare, because arguments based on statistics look hopelessly inadequate, even heartless, when set alongside a heart-rending picture of an injured child on the wrong end of the statistics. It was Stalin who said, 'Every death is a tragedy, the death of a million a mere statistic', and he knew a thing or two about propaganda, which I guess should make both sides think about how we do our business.

A General may, with good reason, feel he has done well if he carries out a complex and successful operation with only 'light casualties', but if a grieving relative condemns the conflict on the front page of a tabloid, in media terms there is nothing that can be done. The power of victims' relatives, via the media is a modern phenomenon, and not just in war. However the justification for war, and its conduct, is based on a cruel logic; by focussing on the cruelty not the logic emotional journalism soon puts the media and military at loggerheads.

What however is not a modern phenomenon, nor surely even arguable, is the media preference for bad news. Indeed the whole debate became an issue amongst journalists themselves, after the abrupt collapse of the Taleban amidst a barrage of predictions of disaster for the allies. Columnist Polly Toynbee commented, 'There was not even time for the eating of words between the first and last editions of news papers as Kabul fell...That must be why the news passed abruptly from dire warnings of a bloodbath ahead, to dire warnings about the make-up of the Kabul government...So on it goes, seeking out the next possible source of trouble, not stopping for an instant to ponder this deeply embarrassing good news.'[12] In a lighter vein, in 1996 I recall asking General Sir Michael Walker, then running IFOR in Bosnia, how things were going, and he replied, 'We must be doing something right, all the journalists have gone.'

However the consequences for operations underway can be rather more serious. There is no doubt the focus of the media on the weapons that missed in Kosovo and Afghanistan reduced public support for the air campaigns. The constant predictions and reports that NATO would split over Kosovo exacerbated the clear problems there were, but were still much exaggerated, as events proved. It is also arguable that the focus on bad news within NATO extended the conflict because it gave Milosevic more hope that he could hang on, given that relying on NATO splitting was his main strategy. The predilection for bad news also makes the media more vulnerable to being used by totalitarian regimes that can control events in their own countries while feeding material that causes problems for enemies with more open societies. Of course none of the above is to ignore that sometimes the news IS bad, in which case it has to be reported.

If the journalistic love of bad news is old news the galloping pace and impact of new technology has been revolutionising war reporting. As the equipment gets ever more portable the journalist gets ever closer to being able to transmit voice and images in real time in real quality from anywhere at affordable costs. But this seeming journalistic nirvana adds enormously to the pressure on the media, especially broadcasters, by eroding that most precious of all commodities – time. For although the means of sending information has accelerated, the ability to gather it has not. On a hot story the demands to 'feed the beast', as it is called, can be overwhelming, stampeding harried broadcasters into hasty judgements and speculation based on rumour and second hand information. The journalist committed to the endless 'lives', nicknamed by some 'the gob on a stick', can find they have little time to find out any information at all. During the Kosovo crisis, in the 80-odd days that I reported for the BBC from NATO I did almost a thousand broadcasts, broadcasting over 30 a day at some points. I coped – just – but only because after ten years as Defence Correspondent I could usually work out what was going on, and had a long list of good contacts who would take or return my somewhat frantic calls without much delay.

However this constant pressure can induce a kind of frenzy as everyone chases everyone else in a frantic bid to stay ahead of the game, and the inevitable victim is the time for reflection and analysis that produces clarity from the inevitable confusion of half-facts and rumour that surround a crisis. Neither, as the machine roles onward, is there time for the post-mortem to learn the lessons of the day. Day-to-day journalism is not especially reflective at the best of times, but in a crisis the next few minutes is often all that matters. Feeding the beast also produces a restless desire for the new; accentuating the natural impatience of a profession that often has to think in seconds. If a week is a long time in politics, an hour is a lifetime on News24.

Other features of new technology are still working their way through. Live interviews via miniature cameras and transmitters are already with us, so how long before they are sending live images of battle, including perhaps an allied soldier, horribly wounded, screaming for his mother? Explaining that to a shocked public will be a challenge for both the military and the media. The impact of the internet is producing even more information and also a form of democratisation of newsgathering, as it produces a cheap form of DIY broadcasting available to many. This includes the mischievous and malevolent, as well as the honest and concerned. Just as a neatly produced computer-printed document looks more persuasive than something handwritten, regardless of its contents, so a pirated programme enables anyone with a computer to cheaply set up a credible looking site, but the information on it may not meet even the most basic journalistic standards. Unsourced and anonymous it can also be a potent source of disinformation. As a spokesman for NATO in Macedonia in 2001, I had to counter various inaccurate rumours that were propagated via the internet.

Facing the Tide

If the media have become victims of time so have the military – in spades. As stated above the ability to broadcast information quickly now vastly exceeds the ability to acquire it, and of course it is the military that is expected to provide it. Time, or rather the passage of time, was also more the military's friend than it was the media's. Much vital military information, such as preparations for an attack is of only passing sensitivity, and by the time a journalist could report on it, it had already happened and from a military viewpoint was safe to use. This knowledge often enabled the military to take at least some journalists into their confidence, but the reality of real-time reporting strips away such protection. The technical possibility of frequent reporting is also self-fulfilling and creates a demand for it, making it harder for a journalist to sit on information, especially when competitors are also sniffing around.

Neither is the military system set up for the rapid transfer of information. 'The fog of war' often makes it hard enough to find out the facts, but even then the hierarchical structures and chains of command suited to fighting a battle are not appropriate to dealing with a media, which can short-circuit any chain of command by putting the reporter at the scene of the action straight onto air. While the military reports work their way up the system the politician is watching it on BBC World or CNN, and the phone on his desk is already ringing. Initial reports are often sketchy and inaccurate, but already the military are condemned to playing catch-up. No western military operation is launched these days without a media strategy, but the aim of setting the agenda, beloved of all media strategists, mostly founders on the brute fact that the sheer speed of response of the media gives it the initiative as things happen.

This is accentuated by the way small events can have big political consequences. In large scale conflicts the death of one soldier, as indicated in the title of 'All Quiet on the Western Front' could pass un-remarked, but in today's Peace Support Operations one death, or even lesser matters, can be a big story. It puts further pressure on the chain of command, which normally works by filtering out information at each level, so only the really important decisions and information reaches the top. But in media terms, everything can matter, especially if an event is regarded as symbolic of something bigger. Suddenly a Defence Secretary is on the hook, with all the friction that involves. Even this can be a trap, because if minor events can embarrass politicians then the tendency is to be even more cautious at lower levels. Speed of response requires delegating media handling to the person on the spot, but the potential global consequences of even local events mean those at the top want to control everything. Catch-22.

An obvious parallel is with the micro-management of US President Lyndon Johnson, and Defense Secretary Robert McNamara in Vietnam, when individual targets could be decided on in the White House, to the considerable detriment of the overall campaign. The modern glut of media information means there is also a symmetry with the journalists at the frontline, resentfully subject to the 'way we see if from here' judgements of the producer on the home front. Whatever else divides them; common feelings about their respective top brass can still unite the media and military, and are both genuinely felt and artfully used by the skilled operators on both sides.

Time squeezes the military in other ways as well, because while first impressions, updated and very often corrected later, are a journalist's stock in trade, the military is vulnerable to criticism if it changes its story. It is a military truism that first reports are always wrong, but when being first with the story is a journalistic imperative, for the military to say nothing is to hand the initiative to anyone who is prepared to say something. As indicated elsewhere first impressions are vital, often setting the tone for the whole coverage, but if the military report is wrong then the military risks accusations of inconsistency, incompetence, or, worst of all, deceit, with the consequential loss of credibility.

This is what happened over the now infamous Djakovica convoy bombing during the Kosovo air campaign, when mistaken air-strikes on a Kosovar refugee column took six days to account for, after a bewildering series of contradictions and half-explanations. A large section of an increasingly enraged media believed NATO had deliberately lied; the rest believed it was at best incompetent. At the time I believed there was no deliberate attempt to deceive, and when I joined NATO I made it my business to find out what really happened. It was indeed cock-up not conspiracy, but in such circumstances perception is more important than reality. The damage to NATO's credibility was permanent, and to some degree still haunts it now in that if NATO goes to war again the media's memory of such incidents will still be there.

Not only do the military have less time, but more journalists to deal with in that time. Since the Gulf War each succeeding conflict has produced ever more journalists, although the sheer inaccessibility of Afghanistan in Autumn 2001 put something of a brake on the trend. Nevertheless the recent pattern is clear, as is the 'in-out' nature of their presence, with journalists covering stories for shorter periods, and the media circus rapidly moving on. The hundreds of journalists who moved in with KFOR, and often just ahead of it, is legendary, but equally significant is that a week later most had gone. Ironically, as I witnessed, the hastily called-up reinforcements for military PR teams arrived just as the bulk of the media left. When a crisis breaks media teams are often simply swamped, and scores of people could be usefully employed, but often a few days later the storm has passed and few are needed. The British military have attempted to cope with this feast or famine staffing problem by designing a short course to give basic media training to personnel who can be deployed for surge operations. It came into its own with the British-led NATO operation in Macedonia in Autumn 2001, when graduates of this course proved the most useful reinforcements to the media professionals.

The impact of local media is also something that tends to be understated. Traditionally the main focus of PR attention is on its home media or the main international outlets. This is because it buttresses the all-important public support, it is what our politicians are most interested in, and of course it is what we ourselves read and watch. However the nature of modern crisis management means that dealing with the local media is a vital role, when the presence of foreign military forces is more often based on a varying mixture of consent and pressure, with the threat of force a last resort. In that sense working the local media effectively is a distinctly preferable alternative to confrontations with a hostile population. In means dealing with local media is even more of an integral part of modern conflicts and crises. And of course the international media soon leaves, but the military stay, in a situation still fraught with risk and with the local media as their main customer.

In Bosnia, Kosovo and Macedonia hardline media whipping up ethnic hatred has been a very real problem for NATO, KFOR and SFOR. Media standards are variable, and often very low, with many outlets simply propaganda vehicles, routinely printing lies or rumour in a media culture that has not encouraged fair reporting. Even the new breed of young journalists that is struggling to emerge frequently has to struggle against intense pressure from within. In Autumn 2001 in Macedonia it was felt that hard-line media opposition to the government-backed NATO Task Force Harvest was beginning to undermine the operation. It led to a successful revamp of the NATO media operation (in which I was civilian spokesman) in order to confront the media more directly. The exact impact of the media operation is hard to quantify, but it was an essential part of the mix for success, and another reminder that media handling is in many ways on the modern frontline.

The over-focus on 'our' media also ignores the complexity that has been introduced by coalition operations. Not only do you need to keep direct participants 'onside', but often maintain passive support from a variety of other countries. So in the Kosovo campaign, apart from NATO there was the non-NATO EU, the UN Security Council, the countries around Kosovo and former Yugoslavia from whom you needed overflight rights, and so on. In the campaign against terrorism following September 11 the Middle East and Islamic world's media has become central – even superpowers need overflight rights and bases. It is too early to be sure, but in the future the 'Al-Jazheera factor' could well have a similar impact to that of the 'CNN factor' in the last decade. Middle Eastern media does not necessarily follow, or even accept many of the core assumptions of Western journalism, while their relationship to their own governments is also very different.

The challenge this sets for those in charge of media strategy is immense. Even finding out what is being said by such a wide range of media is an immense challenge, and then does anyone have time to read it? The response is no easier. All media, like politics, is local, and the media message of the day that works in one place will fail in another. Even during the Kosovo campaign some NATO members, such as the Dutch, felt NATO's spokesman, Jamie Shea, was too forceful, while others thought he had got it just right. A successful campaign must be simultaneously consistent and highly flexible to adapt to circumstances and different audiences – not easy.

Building Bridges

The commander's conference is a daily ritual on every Western military operation, and every one I have ever attended has had the media not just on the agenda, but also as a key part of proceedings. It would go too far to say the impact of the media dictates events, but its influence is pervasive. Even by focussing in on an area of conflict the media can push a government to act when it would rather not. Does it have to be so?

It is certainly true that a government with a logical policy that it firmly states and clearly explains can lead rather than follow the media. However often what is to be done is far from clear, the public is divided, and governments themselves are uncertain. Under these circumstances what some label the 'something must be done brigade' have maximum impact, accentuated by the randomness of the crises that news organisations choose to cover, which are understandably the product of news values not grand strategy. Against that the media do not stick with issues that strike no chord with the public. Overall it emphasises that if a government does not lead, it may soon find itself forced into following.

Nevertheless even the government that leads on the strategy will still be held to account over the conduct of operations, and as we have seen if the handling of that goes wrong the military are in real trouble. For Western governments the media cannot win wars, but increasingly there is a risk they could cause them to be lost. To some degree the military and their political masters have taken this harsh possibility on board. Media training for the military is now common, media strategies are part of the operational plan, and media doctrines written. But it still has some way to go. Kosovo revealed the problems of getting timely information to those who briefed the press, which not only reflected the 'fog of war' but the systemic difficulty of short-circuiting the command chain. That still applies, and was repeated in the Afghanistan air campaign in 2001 when frustrated politicians and briefers were once again left being asked to respond to allegations of events they knew little or nothing about. The honest spokesman will always be at a disadvantage against the ruthless opponent who makes something up on the spot. Neither can the consequences of this information gap be solved by a message of the day. What is still needed is a high enough priority to be given to shaking timely information out of the system, which would serve both the spokesman and the journalist. The military need here is for delegated authority to the media handlers, which means they must have a sophisticated understanding of issues 'above their pay grade', and the ability to adapt them intelligently and flexibly to the circumstances.

The resources devoted to media handling vary hugely from country to country, but are usually still not enough, either in terms of quality or quantity, against a well-resourced media. Some nations still regard media training as an optional extra. It reflects the fact that for many in the military the media handlers still are not on the top table – until, that is, they go on operations and the trouble starts. This may well be because although its accepted a journalist can leap from talking to a squaddie one minute and a general the next, the system still finds it hard to accept similar short-circuiting from within. It must learn to. Whether at the military or political level it marks the difference between just having a press office and what business calls strategic communications, with the real integration of media issues into strategy, rather than as an add-on. The term Public Diplomacy, which is increasingly used, is some recognition of this factor. For instance, such an attitude may have suggested the US should have taken up more of the many offers of military support for operations in Afghanistan in 2001. A public diplomacy strategy might have indicated the lack of military necessity for this was outweighed by the long-term gains of such visible evidence of a global alliance taking risks together. Later PR attempts to emphasise the size of the allied coalition had to overcome the clearly sense that the US and the Pentagon had earlier spurned offers of help and wanted to go it alone.

Handling the politicisation of conflict also remains an understandable challenge for the military. Traditionally a military spokesman on the frontline stuck to describing the facts about operations, and left the justifications to those further up the line, but if the reporter on the front is setting the global tone of the coverage the spokesman in practice must be able to speak 'above his pay grade'. Justifying as well as explaining controversial operations is why NATO ended up with both a civilian, Jamie Shea, and a military spokesman on the platform during Kosovo, and why I shared a platform with a military spokesman in Macedonia, to handle the highly political but important issues he could not.

Political awareness and handling the media are also becoming necessary parts of the ambitious officer's kit-bag, even at quite junior levels, given that many operations are numerically small but politically sensitive. There are many qualities needed for high command, but given the importance of the media to success there is nothing unfair, all other things being reasonably equal, in a brigadier who can handle the media being favoured over one who cannot. The sensitivity of modern conflict means operational commanders routinely have on their staff a Legad (Legal Adviser) and a civilian Polad (Political Adviser), and I suspect it is time they also had a civilian Medad (Media Adviser), sometimes to protect them from their own civilian masters as much as from the media. It was after all a Commander of NATO's Southern Region, Admiral James Ellis who once said the last people out of Bosnia would be a lawyer and a press officer.

Spinning for Both Sides

It is now time to justify that provocative title. After all it is governments who are supposed to have spin doctors, to massage or even hide the facts in order to present policy, or lack of it, in the best possible way, while journalists read the spin and hit it for a home run (not six – the phrase originated in the US), so revealing the truth. But of course everybody spins, in the same way as the glass is both half full and half empty. On 9 April 2002 the *New York Times* carried a story about US figures showing much improved accuracy for air launched weapons used in Afghanistan, with 75 per cent hitting targets compared to about 50 per cent in the Kosovo campaign. Their headline read, 'Improved US Accuracy Claimed in Afghan Air War', but the next day The Guardian's read 'A quarter of bombs missed in Afghan conflict'. Was the glass three-quarters full or a quarter empty? A spinning spokesman would talk about the 75 per cent and the huge leap in accuracy compared to previous conflicts, while the spinning Guardian reporter would say the 25 per cent still means dead and crippled civilians. Both of course are right, and both of course are spinning.

Spin is lurking everywhere. What would once have been called 'mistakes' now tend to be labelled 'blunders' – one word, but a world of difference. I have no wish to use a steam hammer to crack a too obvious nut, after all people in part choose their newspapers to get daily reinforcement of their world view, but journalists, quick to condemn other's spin, very rarely acknowledge they are spinning in their own way.

In Macedonia, skirting for many months with the very real prospect of civil war in 2001, a major role for international 'briefers' was to counter the constant media hyping of minor incidents and predictions of disaster. The journalists, mostly local, were either motivated by a hardline agenda, or, in the case of the internationals, because they are in a bad news business. Either way, for NATO the consequence we feared was that the raising, and in some cases whipping up, of tension, would become self-fulfilling by strengthening the hands of the already powerful men who wanted conflict.

In such circumstances who is to say who is more right or more moral, the spokesman who selectively uses facts to present an event positively, or the journalist who selectively uses facts to present an event negatively? It could be argued that here the oft criticised press officers were both on the side of the angels, in seeking to forestall a civil war, and factually more accurate, because, contrary to media predictions, there was no civil war in 2001. Of course the counter is that a journalist's job is to observe and report, and the consequences are not his responsibility. There is obvious truth in this, but even leaving aside the times journalists have chosen to seek to influence events, it ignores the fact news is more than a mirror to events. It does not just reflect events it influences them – and as I hope I have already demonstrated, influences them increasingly powerfully.

So, to answer the exam question posed by this book's title about the changing context of war reporting, the balance of power has shifted strongly to the reporter. The media's task now is to think more about the handling of its increasing power with responsibility, firstly by accepting that it is a potentially decisive participant in what it reports.

This means a tough self-examination in a trade which can be more self-regarding than self-analytical; Reith lecturer Onora O'Neil, in a slightly different but still relevant context talked about the 'self-flattering myth of the media, that you are reporting on somebody else's wrongdoing'.[13] Despite noble individual exceptions, the media as a whole does not react well to outside criticism, so I hope he will forgive me if I again quote former BBC war reporter Martin Bell, 'We like to see ourselves as bulwarks or beacons, standing in a principled way against censorship, manipulation and a variety of political pressures to shade the truth. Those are our enemies. But is it not possible that the real enemy lies in the hearts of journalists themselves, in cynicism and unchecked ambition and a willingness to fool with the facts for the sake of a story?'[14]

This is certainly not to say the media is always wrong, far from it, but to point out a group tendency to see itself as victim of the system and on the losing end, when others feel the reverse. Phillip Knightley, author of *The First Casualty*, believes Kosovo marked the final victory of the minders over the media, a judgement that looked frankly odd to the word-shocked survivors of the NATO

PR machine. In Vietnam journalists had remarkable and probably unrepeatable access to the military, but access should not be confused with influence on later conflicts. Particular features also need to be taken into account, such as that air wars are inherently distant from the action on the ground, and single or two-seat fighter-bombers cannot carry passengers. Meanwhile the new mobile media technology increasingly gives the journalist independent access to the frontline, free of 'minders'.

Self-analysis might help prevent the media being exploited by those who would use journalism's own instincts and habits against it.[15] Issues range from the fundamental to the technical; who benefits most from bad news; is balance the same as fairness if it creates a fake moral equivalence; are violent demonstrations laid on for TV cameras representative of wider opinion, and how should they be covered; can we prove that a symbolic event really symbolises something bigger; why are so many predictions of defeat wrong; when does a grave become a mass grave, or a killing a massacre?

None of this is to doubt the fundamental importance of journalism in the war zone. Most BBC correspondents have been privileged to meet those in the conflict area who relied on their information as one of the few reliable things to hold on to amidst the chaos. Well-researched facts, straightforwardly presented are still the journalist's most powerful weapon, and also the hardest thing for others to manipulate.

What also remains true is that an effective journalist and an effective spokesman both fundamentally rely on credibility and trust to make people willing to listen, through finding and providing timely and reliable information. Analysis and interpretation – the spin – may differ, but the differences between the two trades should not disguise the similarities. That's one reason why, in the field, the good spokesman and the good journalist usually get on well. So, having started with Clausewitz, I will end with some advice from this great military thinker, and very occasional spin doctor:

> Great part of the information obtained in War is contradictory, a still greater part is false, and by far the greatest part is of a doubtful character. What is required of an officer (*and war reporter* [emphasis added]) is a certain power of discrimination, which only knowledge of men and things and good judgement can give. ...As a general rule, everyone is more inclined to lend credence to the bad than the good. ...This difficulty of seeing things correctly, which is one of the greatest sources of friction in War makes things appear quite different from what was expected.[16]

NOTES

1. Karl Clausewitz, *On War.* (London, Penguin, 1974), p.382. First published in 1832.
2. Philip Bobbitt, *The Shield of Achilles. War, Peace and the Course of History* (London, Allen Lane, 2002), p. 784. Bobbitt has worked as a national security adviser for both Democratic and Republican presidents, and in the wake of September 11 become required reading for US strategists.
3. Ibid., p.784.

4.   Michael Ignatieff, *Virtual War*, (London, Chatto & Windus, 2000), pp.191-193.
5.   Ibid., p.193.
6.   Bobbitt, op cit., p.325.
7.   General Colin Powell, *A Soldier's Way*, (London, Hutchinson, 1995), pp. 520-521.
8.   Ignatieff, op cit. p.72.
9.   Clausewitz, op cit., p.293.
10. Martin Bell, *In Harm's Way*, (London, Hamish Hamilton, 1995), p.135.
11. Ibid., p. 130; David Rieff, *Slaughterhouse*, (London, Vintage, 1995), p.195 and p.217.
12. *The Guardian*, 14 November 2001.
13. Onora O'Neill, Reith Lecture 5, 'License to Deceive', *Q&A,* BBC Online
14. Martin Bell, BBC R4, 'The Truth Is Our Currency', Pt 4, 23 May 1997.
15. *The Guardian*'s Editor Alan Rusbridger, talking to *Newsweek* (28 August 2000) about general media attitudes, remarked, 'I think the culture of British journalists is such that they don't begin to think about the big issues deeply enough.'
16. Clausewitz, op cit. p. 162.

Afterword

Mark Laity

'Four hostile newspapers are more to be feared than ten thousand bayonets.'
Napoleon Bonaparte[1]

Having finished the preceding chapter in September 2002, I inevitably watched the war unfold in Iraq wondering whether events were about to make me look rather foolish. In the end I am somewhat relieved that I will have to eat my words rather less than so many journalists at the end of March 2003 who were predicting a long war. Indeed Iraq demonstrated in an extreme form many aspects of what I discussed. In doing so it highlighted in a more urgent way some old issues, and also posed a few new ones for both journalists and governments.

The most obvious visible feature of the media's war was the so-called 'embedded' journalists. Of course accredited journalists attached to military units are almost as old as war reporting, but the sheer numbers, allied to new communications technology has had a transformational effect. Certainly the debate within the military as to whether it was a good idea is to a large extent irrelevant, because having allowed such access once to deny it in the future is practically impossible. In any case my initial judgement would be that it was largely positive for both sides.

For the military, facing a media sceptical of anything they do not see with their own eyes, the 'embeds' were a sign of openness and confidence that they had nothing to hide. The main concern had been about breaches in operational security, but journalists overwhelmingly respected the rules about not revealing locations or future plans. In general the reporting was also factual, and by focussing on the ordinary soldier had added credibility, while the public instinctively sympathised with the grunt/squaddie on the ground. In the final stages of the conflict in particular, the extraordinary live coverage also proved the coalition was winning in the face of Iraq's propaganda.

For the media the 'embed' system gave access that was impossible any other way. Sheer practicality makes it very hard for unilateral journalists to keep up with a highly mobile battle, while fluid frontlines also make moving around very dangerous indeed. I was surprised at the suspicion some media 'stars' apparently had about 'embedding' because it was obvious that this war would be different to other recent conflicts, which were more often not only peace support operations but geographically more limited in scope. If you wanted a front seat this had to be the way to go and so far I have heard nothing that suggests they faced censorship beyond the simple rules described above.

Traditionally the problem for embedded journalists has been the inability to easily broadcast or file enough, especially in the era of rolling news. Technology has now solved that problem. Today's kit is not only small, it is quick to set up, fairly reliable, and provided there is power journalists can broadcast continuously even on the move. The era of live battles is here. The full implications are still unclear, because of the coalition's easy victory, and the real test will come when the military take heavy casualties or are losing.

But the sheer flood of information from the frontline did pose a massive problem of explanation and analysis for both sides. The effect was not so much broadcasting, as multiple 'narrow-casting', with a focus on where embeds happened to be rather than an overview. The embed system emphasised the journalistic tendency to generalise from the particular. It meant, for example, the US Marines in the town of Umm Qasr taking their time to clean out a single building containing a small unit of Iraqis became a major battle, and was interpreted as evidence that the town had not been taken by the coalition.

In the same way firefights involving small arms and machine guns and low or no casualties were routinely labelled as 'intense' or 'heavy' and described as 'serious' or 'major' resistance. Having been shot at myself I can testify that being on the receiving end always feels pretty intense, but in the grand scheme of things it is usually fairly minor. The worm's eye view needs to be combined with the bird's eye view. The problem was accentuated by the tendency on TV in particular to ask the reporter at the front to report or comment on issues he could not possibly know.

The real place for an overview should have been further up the chain, but this is where things seemed to break down. The media was clearly unhappy with the Centcom briefings in Doha, and the military is in trouble when a journalist is applauded by colleagues when he asks publicly in a briefing, 'Why should we stay? What's the value to us for what we learn at this million-dollar press centre?'[2] That frustration was compounded by distrust in the briefings, which were seen as heavy on message and light on information. It meant that when the briefer said things were going well, which ultimately proved to be right, he was not believed. If the media failed to put the frontline news in context, then the military share the blame because their higher-level briefings did not persuade a sceptical media. Once again the military's ability to respond quickly to unexpected events left it vulnerable to Iraqi propaganda claims. The British media team in Qatar is regarded as having done rather better, but overall the Doha media operation's failings and perceived lack of credibility were only concealed by rapid success on the battlefield.

The 'fog of war' added to the problem, and was hugely accentuated by the relentless pressure of rolling news. It meant rumours, half-truths, and unverified first reports were hurled onto the air, often indiscriminately. It emphasised the need for both sides to think more before speaking and then speak with precision. Early on for instance, when the coalition talked about 'taking' towns they did not explain that did not preclude pockets of continuing resistance. It meant that every time there was a small firefight in these towns the coalition's credibility dropped a notch. At one stage a 'senior BBC news source' was reported as saying, 'We're getting more truth out of Baghdad than the Pentagon at the moment.'[3] This was frankly absurd, but it indicated the coalition was losing the credibility battle, and with it the information war.

That said the media had a tendency to take an early tentative report, run with it, and then blame the Coalition when their black and white presentation proved greyer as more information came in and the picture became clearer. For instance in the case of the Basra 'uprising' it was obvious the information was patchy, and all that could be said with certainty was that something happened, and this time the British military did caveat their briefing. It was the media that got more carried away, but the Basra 'uprising' was soon quoted as an example of Coalition propaganda, and exploited as such by the Iraqis.

The predilection for bad news, described in the previous chapter, once more seduced the media into embarrassing predictions. *The Times* front page headline of 31 March, 'Generals dig in for long war' was only one of many, and it is perhaps time for the media to assess why its predictions are so often wrong, given its recent track record. Whether a media outlet's readers/viewers/listeners backed the war or not they were not well served by analysis that in general suggested the coalition was in trouble, only to have Baghdad fall within a week. Polly Toynbee's quote about Afghanistan seems equally applicable to Iraq. It is also hard not to have detected almost a note of glee when Rumsfeld's plan was supposedly going awry, and as one pundit wryly noted, 'It is one of the most unpleasant features of punditry that the pundit will secretly exult in disaster if it means that his point of view is vindicated.'[4]

The simmering debate over the reporting from Belgrade during the Kosovo conflict boiled over when it came to Baghdad, and it deserves a more reasoned examination than it has so far received. It certainly deserves better than an intellectually sloppy knee-jerk tendency towards moral equivalence between Centcom in Doha and Baghdad, as if they are competing parliamentary candidates whose statements are reported according to election rules governing balance. The tone of the debate about Baghdad may be affected by the controversy over an article by Eason Jordan, CNN's Chief News Executive, headlined, 'The News We Kept to Ourselves'.[5] In it he described the extent to which CNN had pulled its punches over preceding years, sitting on major stories harmful to Saddam, and all done in order to protect CNN's local staff and avoid expulsion from Baghdad.

In the largely US discussion that followed CNN came in for heavy criticism for its actions, but he was only finally revealing what everyone in the media knew but did not openly talk about – access in Baghdad came at a price, and it could be a heavy one. In the event it did not save CNN from expulsion early in the conflict, and it is unlikely the lesson about being careful to avoid offending the Iraqis went unheeded by others. Recently a *Times* reporter, who had himself been refused a new visa, rummaged around Information Ministry files that revealed the extent to which every visa was vetted. He concluded, 'Those who wrote articles critical of the regime would be banned and risk missing the next big story in Iraq. Those who steered clear of certain subjects, like Saddam's family and human rights abuses could extend their stay.'[6]

The case of 'Comical Ali' is an interesting example. The former Iraqi Information Minister is now a joke figure, but I was struck that until the US tanks were literally to be seen over his shoulder he was reported with a very straight face. Until that point his claims were taken seriously and often used to 'balance' coalition briefings, and went down very well in the Arab world. Even in the as the tanks entered the outskirts of Baghdad and the airport fell his claims that the US was not there were taken seriously by the Baghdad-based media. Indeed even on the day a TV reporter described on air the famous briefing as a 'bravura performance' and calling him a 'very brave man' who had shown 'resilience'. In the crisis points of the war this routine liar was a very effective propagandist, and unchallenged in public. He only became a laughing stock as he fell with his regime and no longer mattered anyway. He had done his job.

It is obviously too easy, and simply unrealistic, to just say no one should have reported from Baghdad unless they had total freedom, but there is a real ethical dilemma about how much of a price should be paid, and how it should be handled. Curiously during the conflict there was often more attention on the Coalition's media handling, and sometimes the most critical were Baghdad-based reporters who were perhaps getting their retaliation in first.[7] Let he who is without sin throw the first stone at CNN.

The impact of the Arab TV stations was even greater than predicted, and for the coalition their handling of them was almost a total failure in terms of trying to influence their output. In more general terms their output consciously fed the hopes, prejudices and opinions of their Arab audience, and if the conflict had truly got bogged down it would have become a major problem for the coalition in sustaining public support. Although it was not really recognised as such, they also represent a partial challenge to western norms of journalistic impartiality. However while the western media had little trouble attacking the blatant bias of Fox News, it was more cautious about commenting on the partiality of Al-Jazeera, perhaps for fear of accusations of cultural imperialism or being anti-Islamic.[8] Whatever the reason, Al-Jazeera is now a semi-global player which challenges the dominance of the western media not just in the Arab world, but also in the growing Islamic community within Europe. Government media public diplomacy departments are so far failing to deal with this new factor. Neither have they yet accepted the sheer scale of the resources and fresh thinking needed to deal with handling world as opposed to domestic opinion.

Overall then, a first assessment of the information battle in Iraq should give both military and media considerable pause for thought, some of it uncomfortable. Certainly the Coalition military and governments seem to be recognising that in general it was only battlefield success that rescued their own information campaigns. Britain's own efforts seem to have been more successful, but ultimately they also sank or swam on the back of the dominant US effort. Part of the aim of the Coalition information campaign was surely to demonstrate the inevitability of winning, and so hasten victory, while persuading the world that the campaign was being fought with accuracy and concern for civilians. History may accept that, but it is hard to say the military persuaded the media while the fight was on.

For the media the 'embeds' were a success, but handling their output and putting it in context was more problematic, and while the public certainly saw a lot did they make sense of it? Amidst the brilliance and bravery of individual reporters the overall impression given by the media made the rapidity of the victory a surprise, while much of the assessment of the Iraqi military response and the Iraqi public mood was wide of the mark. As indicated above, now Saddam is gone, a debate about the price of being in Baghdad during the war and before is surely valid.

This is particularly so, because Iraq emphasised, as I argued in the previous chapter, how media handling is now fundamental to modern conflict. The media, like it or not are a weapon, especially for the weaker side, as even some newspapers argue, 'Saddam has always known he can't win a straight military shoot-out. His only hope has been to delay the outcome as long as possible, while imposing as many casualties both on Americans and in particular on Iraqis. If he could show off enough destruction and carnage long enough for the TV cameras, perhaps he could induce world and especially American opinion to cause President Bush to halt the war.'[9]

Iraq was an example of asymmetric warfare where the West's opponents used tactics such as placing equipment in built-up areas and irregular warfare amidst the civilian population precisely because in our societies there is ever more pressure to reduce civilian casualties and accidental damage. In that sense, to update the old saying about the pen being mightier than the sword, the Iraqi strategy was to hope the television camera would prove mightier than the cruise missile. Saddam failed but others, perhaps in circumstances that favour them more, will try again.

NOTES

1. Napoleon Bonaparte. *Maxims*
2. Reuters report, 30 March 2003
3. *Media-Guardian*, 28 March 2003
4. Boris Johnson, *Daily Telegraph*, 27 March 2003
5. *New York Times*, 11 April 2003
6. Richard Beeston, *Times*, 2 May 2003
7. Eg, 'False Witness', *Guardian*, 4 April 2003; 'Lies, damn lies and military briefings in Doha', *Independent*, 27 March 2003; see for example, 'The ministry of mendacity strikes again', Robert Fisk, *Independent*, 4 April 2003; Andrew Gilligan letter, *Sunday Telegraph*, 20 April 2003
8. See, 'Of all the major global networks. Al-Jazeera has been alone in proceeding from the premise that this war should be viewed as an illegal enterprise.' Faisal Bodi, a senior editor with aljazeera.net, *Guardian* 27 March 2003
9. Editorial, *Wall Street Journal*, 24 March 2003

Contributors

Dr Stephen Badsey is Senior Lecturer in the Department of War Studies at the Royal Military Academy Sandhurst. A specialist on media war, and on the history of military doctrine, he has written, edited or contributed to over thirty publications analysing war and its reporting from the Crimean War to Kosovo, including *The Gulf War Assessed* with John Pimlott, and *Modern Military Operations and the Media.*

Dr Jacqueline Beaumont is a Visiting Research Fellow in the Centre for Humanities Research at Oxford Brookes University. Her interest is in the British National Press from 1880 to 1914 and she has published a number of articles on aspects of Press coverage of the South African War. Currently she is preparing a study of Press treatment of the three sieges, Mafeking, Kimberley and Ladysmith.

Dr Oliviero Bergamini teaches History of Journalism and American History at the University of Bergamo, Italy, and also works as a journalist for RAI, the Italian public television network. He has written extensively in the fields of U.S. military and political history, media history and media studies; as a reporter he has covered events in Iraq, Chechnya, Kosovo and other troubled areas. His research work focuses on the relationship between media representation, public opinion and political power.

Dr Susan Carruthers is Associate Professor in the Department of History at the University of Rutgers, USA. She has published extensively on war and the media and her most recent book, *The Media at War: Communication and Conflict in the Twentieth Century* was published in 2000 by Macmillan/Palgrave.

Dr Mark Connelly is Reader in Modern British History at the University of Kent at Canterbury. His recent publications include: *Reaching for the Stars: A New History of Bomber Command in World War II* (I.B.Tauris, 2001), *The Great War: Memory and Ritual* (Royal Historical Society, 2001) and *We Can Take It! Britain and the Memory of the Second World War* (Longman, 2004).

David Culbert is Professor of History at Louisiana State University, Baton Rouge. His *World War II, Film, and History* (with John Chambers) was published by Oxford University Press in 1996. He is editor of *The Historical Journal of Film, Radio, and Television.* He is also editor (with N. J. Cull and David Welch) of *Propaganda and Mass Persuasion. A Historical Encyclopedia, 1500 to the Present* (ABC-Clio, 2003).

Professor Nicholas J. Cull is Director of the Centre for American Studies at the University of Leicester. His *Selling War: British Propaganda and American Neutrality in World War Two* was published by Oxford University Press in 1995. He has subsequently published widely on issues of propaganda and political use of the media. He is a council member of the International Association for Media and History and is a regular contributor to the *Historical Journal of Film, Radio and Television*. He is currently working on a complete history of the United States Information Agency.

Dr Klaus Dodds is Senior Lecturer in Geography at Royal Holloway, University of London. His research interests include critical geopolitics, foreign policy and the media and the international politics of Antarctica and the South Atlantic. He is author of *Geopolitics in a Changing World* (Longman, 2000) and *Britain and the South Atlantic Empire* (I B Tauris, 2003).

Dr Ilaria Favretto is Senior Research Fellow at Kingston University (London). She is author of *The Long Search for a Third Way: the British Labour Party and the Italian Left since 1945* (London: Palgrave-Macmillan, 2003); *Alle radici della svolta autonomista: Labour Party e PSI, due vicende parallele (1956-1970)* (Roma: Carocci, 2004) and *Storia della Gran Bretagna del ventesimo secolo* (Milano: Unicopli, 2004). She also co-edited with Dejan Jovic a special issue of the *Journal of Southern Europe and the Balkans* (vol 6, no. 2, 2004) on 'Memories of Wars: Italy and the Balkans rethinking the 20th century'.

Dr Jo Fox is Lecturer in Modern History at the University of Durham. She is the author of *Filming Women in the Third Reich* (Berg, Oxford, 2001). She is currently working on a comparative history of film propaganda in Britain and Germany during the Second World War.

Dr Samantha Johnson is lecturer in Modern European History at Cardiff University; currently preparing monograph for publication, entitled 'British Intellectual Society and Europe's "Jewish question", 1890-1939' and working on a long-term project on the Tsarist emigre community of inter-war Czechoslovakia, 1918-1945.

Mark Laity is Special Adviser on Strategic Communications to the Supreme Allied Commander Europe (SACEUR). Before that he was from 2000 to 2003 Special Adviser to the then NATO Secretary General, Lord Robertson, and NATO's Deputy Spokesman. His followed a 22 year career in journalism, including 11 years as BBC Defence Correspondent. He is also a Senior Research Fellow in the Centre of Defence Studies at King's College London, where he is Director of the Centre's Public Diplomacy and Crisis Management Programme.

Dr Siân Nicholas is Lecturer in Modern British History at the University of Wales Aberystwyth. She is the author of *The Echo of War: Home Front Propaganda and the Wartime BBC 1939-45* (Manchester UP, 1996). Her research interests are in the fields of media history and British national culture.

Jeffrey Richards is Professor of Cultural History at the University of Lancaster. His main interests are British popular culture, particularly the influence of cinema, the Victorian theatre and the nature of British national identity. His most recent publications include: *Films and British National Identity (1997)*; *The Unknown 1930s (1998)* and *Diana: the Making of a Media Saint (1999) (co-editor)*. *Imperialism and Music. Britain 1876-1953* (Manchester University Press, 2003).

Dr Roger Smither is Keeper of the Imperial War Museum's Film and Video Archive. He served for six years as Secretary General and is now a Vice President of FIAF, the International Federation of Film Archives. He has written and edited a number of books and articles on the subjects of film history and film archiving, including the *Imperial War Museum Film Catalogue Volume 1: The First World War Archive* (Flick Books, 1994) and *This Film Is Dangerous* an anthology in celebration of nitrate film, published by FIAF in 2003.

Dr Tony Shaw is Senior Lecturer in History at the University of Hertfordshire. He is the author of *British Cinema and the Cold War: The State, Propaganda and Consensus* (I. B. Tauris, 2000) and *Eden, Suez and the Mass Media: Propaganda and Persuasion during the Suez Crisis* (I. B. Tauris, 1996).

Lieutenant Colonel Angus Taverner has served, both as a Regular and Territorial Army officer, for the past 22 years. Commissioned in 1980 into the Royal Artillery, he has worked in Germany, Northern Ireland, Belize, Bosnia, Oman and Zimbabwe. Specifically, he has been involved in working with the media since 1995, when he was appointed to the Media Operations staff in Bosnia. Subsequently, he has commanded the Army's Media Operations Group and, for the last three years, he has been working in the central staff of the Ministry of Defence where he has had responsibility for developing the UK's doctrine and policy in the field of Media Operations. Currently, he is leading a project intended to improve further the military's preparedness and ability to work with the media, both on operations and in crisis.

Philip M. Taylor is Professor of International Communications and Director of the Institute of Communications Studies at the University of Leeds. He is author of numerous works on propaganda, media-military relations and psychological warfare, and a 3rd edition of *Munitions of the Mind* was published by Manchester University Press in 2003.

David Welch is Professor of Modern History and Director of the Centre for the Study of Propaganda at the University of Kent at Canterbury. His recent publications include: *Hitler Profile of a Dictator* (Routledge, 2001); *The Third Reich. Politics and Propaganda* (Routledge, 2nd edn 2002) and, with N.J.Cull and D. Culbert, *Propaganda and Mass Persuasion. A Historical Encyclopedia, 1500 to the Present* (ABC-Clio, 2003)

Christine Whittaker was the BBC film archivist for twenty-five years. She continues her work with her own consulting firm, 'C. Whittaker-Archive Consultants Ltd'. She is currently President of the International Association for Media and History (IAMHIST).

Index